# Theories and Paradigms of Counseling and Psychotherapy

# Theories and Paradigms of Counseling and Psychotherapy

R. ROCCO COTTONE
*University of Missouri—St. Louis*

ALLYN AND BACON
Boston   London   Toronto   Sydney   Tokyo   Singapore

Series Editor: Ray Short
Series Editorial Assistant: Jo Ellen Caffrey
Production Editor: Lisa Feder
Editorial-Production Service: York Production Services
Cover Administrator: Linda Dickinson
Cover Designer: Suzanne Harbison
Manufacturing Buyer: Megan Cochran

Copyright © 1992 by Allyn and Bacon
A Division of Simon & Schuster, Inc.
160 Gould Street
Needham Heights, Massachusetts 02194

**Library of Congress Cataloging-in-Publication Data**

Cottone, R. Rocco.
    Theories and paradigms of counseling and psychotherapy / R. Rocco
Cottone.
       p.    cm.
    Includes bibliographical references and index.
    ISBN 0-205-13444-0
    1. Psychotherapy.   2. Counseling.   3. Psychotherapy—Philosophy.
    4. Counseling—Philosophy.   I. Title.
    RC480.C68   1992
    616.89'14—dc20                                          91–39379
                                                            CIP

Printed in the United States of America

10  9  8  7  6  5  4  3  2         96  95  94  93  92

# DEDICATION

*This book is dedicated to Salvatore and Francesca Cottone, my parents, whose love for me has been unyielding, and whose faith in education and learning has been inspiring.*

# CONTENTS

## 7. Rational-Emotive Therapy: An Internal Psychological Model Therapy Focusing on Thinking

**111**

## 8. Person-Centered Therapy: An Internal Psychological Model Therapy Focusing on Feeling and Emotion

**123**

## 9. Gestalt Therapy: An Internal Psychological Model Therapy Focusing on Thinking, Feeling, and Behavior

**137**

# PREFACE

This book was conceived on a cold winter night in 1984. It was about two in the morning when I finally reconciled myself to sleeplessness and arose to wander around the house. I grabbed a pad of paper and a pencil, and, while sitting at my kitchen table, I had an experience I will never forget. Being trained and experienced in the field of rehabilitation psychology and counseling, and finding a personal and intellectual interest in theory related to marital and family therapy, I was never able to merge what can be viewed as the mutually exclusive philosophical foundations of these two fields. Earlier the evening before, I had finished Lynn Hoffman's (1981) book, *Foundations of Family Therapy,* which was as inspiring to me as it was seminal to the field. With Hoffman's ideas in mind, and stimulated by the cold on that winter morning, I experienced a rush of emotion as everything seemed to fall into place.

Over a period of about two hours that night, I sketched out what has become "a systemic theory of vocational rehabilitation" (Cottone, 1986, 1987; Cottone & Cottone, 1986; Cottone, Grelle, & Wilson, 1988). In fact, it was on that night that I essentially wrote what is today a little-known article, entitled "Toward a Systemic Theoretical Framework for Vocational Rehabilitation" (Cottone, 1986). That article holds a very special place in my heart and mind. For it was during the writing of that article that I realized that counseling had achieved the status of a paradigmatic discipline.

Later that day I re-read Kuhn's (1970) classic, *The Structure of Scientific Revolutions,* a book that defines scientific paradigms. From that day until the writing of this book, I formulated and refined the ideas that have led to a definition of paradigms for the mental health services. This book is about four paradigms of counseling and psychotherapy, thus conceived.

The purpose of this book is threefold. First, it is intended to introduce the idea of paradigms to the counseling and psychotherapy field. As far as I know, to date, such a comprehensive conceptualization of metatheoretical frameworks in counseling and psychotherapy has not been presented. Second, it is meant to provide some examples of theories classified according to the paradigm framework. Under each paradigm, at least one theoretical approach to treatment will be offered as an example, and the most recent paradigms will additionally have an example of a ground-breaking therapy that helped to transition the field to a new way of thinking (a trans-paradigmatic therapy). In this way the book is as much historical as contemporary. The presentation of each therapeutic approach is meant to be both historically and practically relevant. Theories will be classified in one of four ways: (a) paradigm-specific, (b) historically trans-paradigmatic, (c) contemporarily cross-paradigmatic; and (d) within-paradigm variations. Third, this book is intended to introduce new ideas about theoretical developments in the field. The fourth paradigm presented in this book is primarily hypothetical and propositional. It is a best attempt to develop deductively a paradigm based on perception of significant, ground-breaking, and recent theory. It is meant to demonstrate how paradigmatic thinking can lead to new therapeutic approaches, stemming primarily from philosophical rather than empirical grounds. In this way, the fourth paradigm is provided as an example of the importance of philosophy (primarily epistemology) to the field of counseling and psychotherapy. I believe this threefold purpose will be of interest to academics, practitioners, researchers, and students in the field.

It is also important to understand what this book is not. It is not intended to be used individually as an introductory text to counseling and psychotherapy. Although I use this material extensively in a beginning ''Theories of Counseling'' course, I use it as a means of introducing paradigms to students so they may get the big picture before they become theory bound. In that class, I also use a second text, which provides theory-specific summaries by proponents of each approach. The presentation of paradigms appears to have a liberating influence on beginning students, allowing them to study specialized theories of counseling while placing them in a larger professional and practical context. Other books tend to be limited in scope, often ignoring organic-medical or systemic-relational approaches. Therefore, this book was written for academics *for use as one of a set of texts in beginning theories of counseling and psychotherapy courses*. The material fits nicely with material from other texts written as instruments to communicate therapeutic approaches alone. The book also is not intended to be a thorough survey of the field. There are many theories of counseling and psychotherapy that are not presented in this text. The approaches that are presented, however, are examples that should provide readers with enough information to assess other related approaches from a paradigmatic perspective. The therapies that have been chosen, therefore, have been chosen with great care. They are clear-cut examples of paradigm-specific theories, trans-paradigmatic theories (transitional, ground-breaking approaches of historical significance), or contemporary cross-paradigmatic approaches (contemporary attempts to bridge two paradigms).

I have found that this material is well received by students as primary information in advanced theories of counseling and psychotherapy courses, in courses of marital and family therapy, and in seminars on theoretical issues. Beyond assisting beginning students by providing the big picture, the material helps advanced students to analyze theories more deeply within a philosophical and practical framework. It also may facilitate the kind of creative thinking that can lead to meaningful investigation theoretically and empirically.

Practitioners in the field may find this book enlightening as a means of placing their practices within a larger theoretical and professional context. Practitioners are cautioned, however, to understand that, depending on their theoretical orientation, the book may appear to be uneven. For example, psychiatrists or psychologists may find the sections on organic-medical or psychological thinking to be simplistic, whereas the section on systemic-relational or contextual approaches may be alien to them. Likewise, marital/family therapists or social workers may find the systemic-relational ideas to be basic, whereas the organic-medical or contextual ideas may be more challenging. As much as possible, I attempted to be unbiased in the presentation of each paradigm and to give straightforward and simple explanations of each example therapy. But I have anticipated both a neophyte *and* an advanced readership, which is a difficult audience to target without potentially offending or rebuffing. Hopefully, readers will judge this book with its broad intent in mind. Also, my bias for the contextual, I am sure, is evident in the content of this text; I am quite excited about the development of a contextual philosophy in counseling and psychotherapy, which I have been writing about recently in the periodical literature. My excitement comes through toward the end of the book, which I have, over a year's period, debated about toning down. However, my students have relayed that the excitement is communicated in a positive way from their perspective, because it gives them a sense that the field is alive, vibrant, and changing. Therefore, I have left the material in its original form for didactic purposes if not also for self-serving purposes.

There are many people to whom I owe thanks related to the development of these ideas and the writing of the book. First and foremost, my wife, Laura, has been supportive, loving, and patient. She is an inspiration. Beyond her personal support, as an academic herself she has had a major influence on the ideas presented here. Her feedback has been invaluable. Second, my children, Christopher Rocco Cottone and Laura Kristina Cottone, have been wonderfully loving and understanding. On more than one occasion I have had to place their interests aside, and yet they have been unfailing in their love. Third, my colleagues and teachers have been helpful and supportive. To Ray Becvar, my doctoral coursework advisor, I will always be grateful for his foresight related to systemic theory and practice. To Corrine Cope, my master's degree advisor at the University of Missouri—Columbia, I will always be thankful for her emotional and academic support. To my colleagues at the University of Missouri—St. Louis, especially Arthur Smith, my department chair, whose support has been unending, and to Ricky George, who lit the fire in me to write this book, I will always be grateful. To my other colleagues (especially my friends in rehabilitation, psychiatry, and psychology—William Emener, Mitchell Handelsman, Dennis Maki, Vilia Tarvydas, Pete Moran, and Ron Vessell) and my students (especially Robert Greenwell and Geri Redden), who have been both patient and inspiring, my deepest thanks. And finally, I offer a special thanks to the editors of professional journals who have been patient with me and nurturing of my ideas (e.g., Arnold Wolf, Norman Berven, Alan Gurman, Richard Sauber, Charles Clairborn, and Douglas Sprenkle) and to Wayne Spohr and Carol Wada of Prentice-Hall and Ray Short of Allyn and Bacon for helping to bring these ideas to fruition.

Finally, this book is dedicated to my parents, Salvatore and Francesca Cottone, whose faith in education and love for me has been unbounded. They are the foundation upon which this book was written.

At this point, I welcome the reader to engage with me in a dialogue of paradigmatic developments in the counseling and psychotherapy field.

# References

Cottone, R. R. (1986). Toward a systemic theoretical framework for vocational rehabilitation. *Journal of Applied Rehabilitation Counseling, 17*(4), 4–7.

Cottone, R. R. (1987). A systemic theory of vocational rehabilitation. *Rehabilitation Counseling Bulletin, 30,* 167–176.

Cottone, R. R., & Cottone, L. P. (1986). A systemic analysis of vocational evaluation in the state-federal rehabilitation system. *Vocational Evaluation and Work Adjustment Bulletin, 19,* 57–54.

Cottone, R. R., Grelle, M., & Wilson, W. C. (1988). The accuracy of systemic versus psychological evidence in judging vocational evaluator recommendations: A preliminary test of a systemic theory of vocational rehabilitation. *Journal of Rehabilitation, 54*(1), 45–52.

Hoffman, L. (1981). *Foundations of family therapy.* New York: Basic Books.

Kuhn, T. S. (1970). *The structure of scientific revolutions* (2nd ed.). Chicago: University of Chicago Press.

# PART ONE
# Introduction

# 1

# Defining Theories and Paradigms of Counseling and Psychotherapy

AS BEGINNING STUDENTS in the mental health services quickly realize, there are a number of differing theories of counseling and psychotherapy. Often, the theories described in beginning textbooks are presented as discrete, equally valid, and isolated approaches. It is difficult to assess the usefulness of one approach compared to other approaches by nature of the theoretical propositions of the theories themselves. Since counseling and psychotherapy students often lack the exposure to mental health settings necessary to make practice-relevant judgments, they appear to search for a theory that has some intellectual interest for them and which seems to apply to their own personal experiences. Although each theory may be presented as equally valid and useful by textbook authors, in actuality each theory is competitive to some degree, and each theory is useful at the expense of mutually excluding another theory. Therefore, the choice of theory is a serious choice.

It is no secret among experienced professionals that theories of counseling and psychotherapy have proliferated to the point that there is no one dominant way of thinking about how to conceptualize and to treat human problems. But it is also evident that the theories have not been critically analyzed from a larger perspective that crosses professional disciplinary boundaries. Instead of addressing disciplinary issues, most textbook authors organize and present theories according to the chronology of their development, philosophical consistency, or the focus of intervention (e.g., whether the theory is targeted to behavior, emotions, relationships, or thinking).

But from a professional or disciplinary perspective, one finds different views about the nature of problems and the effectiveness of treatment modalities across the traditional mental health professions. The traditional mental health professions include

3

psychiatry, psychology, counseling, social work, psychiatric nursing, and marital and family therapy; each has its own professional identity, practical orientation, and specialized training, which makes for much confusion in agencies and treatment centers where there are a number of professionals serving one client. For example, in many alcohol and drug dependence treatment centers, there is usually a physician overseeing medical treatment, a psychiatric nurse providing auxiliary medical treatments, a psychiatrist or psychologist overseeing diagnostic and treatment services, counselors involved in individualized mental health treatments, and social workers or marital/family therapists overseeing and providing group and family treatment. An astute practitioner must ask, ''Does the client benefit from this multiprofessional treatment?'' And when case management responsibilities are assigned to one practitioner serving as a treatment team leader, the problem may be further compounded. For often, unfortunately, assignment of case coordination responsibility may result more from the traditions underlying the rules of the facility where services are provided than from an assessment of the competence of the case management professional. To this end, it is best that professionals clearly understand the theoretical foundations underlying treatment approaches and professional orientations.

This book is about theories of counseling and psychotherapy. A number of widely accepted theories are presented so that readers will have a good understanding of the mechanics of counseling practice. These theories can be applied by mental health professionals involved in face-to-face communication with clients over issues of client concern. This book also attempts to outline the underlying professional, theoretical, political, and philosophical foundations of traditional and current theories of counseling and psychotherapy. In effect it is not only about theories of counseling and psychotherapy, but it is also about a theory of theories, or a metatheory of counseling and psychotherapy. The term *metatheory* is used here to imply a larger framework—a superordinate theoretical structure distinguishable by operational criteria—which helps to place theories of counseling and psychotherapy into perspective. A metatheoretical perspective provides a means for classifying theories along professional, political, and philosophical grounds. In the supermarket of theories of counseling and psychotherapy, a metatheoretical framework is the equivalent of offering an organizational framework, so that all the types of meat and all the types of potatoes, all the breads and the butters, are placed alongside of each other in an orderly fashion. The metatheoretical framework used in this book is that of *paradigms* of counseling and psychotherapy. The word *paradigm,* although viewed as trendy by many and viewed as confusing by others, is simply a way of saying ''a large, theory-encompassing model.'' The word *paradigm* is borrowed from Kuhn's (1970) classic work describing scientific paradigms, *The Structure of Scientific Revolutions,* and it is modified in this text to apply to mental health services (see Cottone, 1989). Paradigms of counseling and psychotherapy (also called ''counseling paradigms'') are models that, to a large degree, are mutually exclusive and *based on different professional, political, and philosophical positions* related to the nature of the psychotherapeutic enterprise. Because paradigms in the mental health services account for professional and political issues, as well as practical-theoretical issues, the presentation of theories of counseling according to paradigm-relevant issues makes this text unique. Paradigms are larger than theories in counseling and psychotherapy.

Four paradigms will be presented in this text, and each paradigm will have several theories under its wing. The four paradigms are: (a) the organic-medical paradigm; (b) the psychological paradigm; (c) the systemic-relational paradigm; and (d) the contextual paradigm. Each paradigm is defined according to criteria which are outlined and described in chapter 2. The premise of this text is that paradigms are operationally real in the mental health field and, at a high level, they organize professional activities for serving mental health clients. For example, the paradigm operating at a hospital-based treatment center for the severely psychiatrically disabled (probably the organic-medical paradigm), may be quite different from the paradigm operating at a college counseling center (probably the psychological paradigm). Moreover, the paradigm operating at the college counseling center may be quite different from the paradigm operating at a marital or family services agency (probably the systemic-relational paradigm). In each of these settings, paradigms to some degree constrain the activities of the mental health professionals working in those settings. In this sense, beyond being organizational, paradigms are operational frameworks.

Paradigms in counseling or psychotherapy offer new insights into why human service professionals operate as they do. Paradigms, therefore, are frameworks for understanding and frameworks for actions. They define separate realities, each real in its own right, but absolutely distinct and bounded. Understanding paradigms in counseling or psychotherapy is a means to a better understanding of the mental health professions.

The reason a discussion of paradigms to this point has been linked to a discussion of professional roles and responsibilities of the mental health professions is that paradigms, as defined in this book, are directly linked to the politics of mental health

---

## BOX 1-1

### Comparative Definitions

Theories of Counseling and Psychotherapy—specialized therapeutic approaches.

A Metatheory—a scientific, primarily deductive, theoretical framework that provides a "big picture." A metatheory is a theory about theories. The metatheory presented in this book is that of "counseling paradigms."

A Paradigm of Counseling and Psychotherapy (also called a "counseling paradigm")—a means for demonstrating the "big picture" in counseling and psychotherapy. Counseling paradigms are metatheoretical hypothetical operational frameworks that provide a means for classifying and understanding theories of counseling and psychotherapy. What makes the study of counseling paradigms unique is the emphasis on the philosophical, political, and professional (disciplinary) issues underlying paradigms of counseling and psychotherapy.

professions. In fact, one of the six criteria for a paradigm (listed in chapter 2 of this book) is the existence of a group of professionals that adheres to the unique philosophical position underlying the paradigm. It will be argued that in the United States paradigms are often associated with distinct professional groups competing in a political, ethical, and economic context for a limited pool of clients or patients. Each group will have a philosophy that is absolutely distinct among the mental health professions. Yet all groups share the basic philosophy that emotional concerns are amenable to intervention by trained professionals. In this way, the study of paradigms should interest people intrigued by the study of professions as well as those with a penchant for the theoretical and philosophical.

This book is organized into seven parts. Part One defines the historical, philosophical, and professional discipline-related issues that act as a rationale for delineating theories according to paradigms in counseling and psychotherapy. Specific criteria are defined for delimiting counseling paradigms. In Parts Two through Five, the four counseling paradigms are defined: the Organic-Medical, Psychological, Systemic-Relational, and Contextual paradigms. Each paradigm is described according to the criteria defined in Part One, and each paradigm is used to introduce specific theories of counseling and psychotherapy that demonstrate the assumptions and consequential directives of the larger paradigmatic frame of reference. The theories are presented in enough operational detail to provide beginning counselors with a good understanding of what to do when confronted by distressed and confused clients. The theories are also presented in a way that is paradigm relevant, which will appeal to both beginning and advanced readers. Part Six addresses cross-paradigmatic and related issues and provides a detailed discussion about how theories may be categorized according to a paradigm framework. Part Seven addresses the experimental consequences of paradigmatic thinking; a ''contextual'' paradigm-comparative research agenda is proposed.

## Theories, Therapies, and Paradigms

### Theories and Therapies: One and the Same?

There are a number of counseling textbooks that use the word *theory* in their titles. In fact, the terms *theory* and *therapy* are used almost interchangeably in the counseling literature. For example, Ellis's (1962) Rational Emotive Therapy (RET) is presented as a foundation for understanding and predicting behavior, which is exactly what theory is supposed to do. And behavioral therapies derive primarily from the application of theoretical learning principles to the therapeutic situation. Yet the term *theory* deserves closer scrutiny. It is a term that implies a *scientific ideal*—a rational construction representative of some reality. It is both limited by, and limiting of, language. In fact, any good theory should build upon what has come before, while providing a new vocabulary to build upon. Theories, therefore, should provide a language of possibility—a means to predict the future as has never been done before. Theories, at their very best, not only should aid in understanding but should give a new perspective for viewing the body of knowledge of a field. At the very least, theories should provide a new path for experimentation.

There is a relative consensus among scientists, emerging from a philosophy called logical positivism, that scientific theories, if they are to be valued, must be able to be disproved (Popper, 1959). According to positivistic ideals, a good scientific theory allows for operational hypotheses amenable to empirical investigation. In other words, it is important to be able to frame specific questions from a scientific theory and, additionally, there must be a means to answer specific questions. This presupposes the objectification of that which is to be studied. The objectification issue, however, is a difficult one in the study of theories of counseling and psychotherapy, since objectification of the subjective distress of clients is not an easy task.

Related to theories of counseling and psychotherapy, it may not be valid to presuppose the objectification of what is studied across all theoretical lines. Counseling often is related to the subjective distress of clients. Otherwise, a client is usually referred for counseling at the request of a third party who perceives a difficulty. Whether clients are distressed and self-referred or viewed as disturbed and referred by others for professional services, a decision about the success of treatment is as much a professional-political as a personal issue. Accordingly, attempts to assess the effectiveness of one therapeutic approach against another often reduce to: (a) an assessment of the subjective self-assessments of clients; or (b) observations of the behaviors of clients from the perspective of an observer (using instruments or criteria that may reflect primarily the values of the investigator-observer as opposed to a true assessment of what the client values). Because personal and political issues are predominant in defining the nature of what is to be objectified in the study of theories of counseling and psychotherapy, measures of outcome may not be taken for granted. Outcome measures must be viewed as reflecting the priorities of the theoretical framework as much as they are viewed as a reflection of an absolute criterion of mental health. Consequently, it is questionable whether therapies are (or should be treated as) theories in the scientific sense, even though the terms *theory* and *therapy* are used almost synonymously by practitioners, theorists, and textbook authors in the mental health field.

To clarify the confusion about theories in counseling and psychotherapy, in this book the term *theory* will be used in two easily distinguishable ways. First, the term *theory* will mean a therapy-specific framework delimited by the constructs and precepts defined by proponents of a therapeutic approach. When used in this way, it will be referred to as a theory, a theory of counseling or psychotherapy, a counseling theory, or a psychotherapy. Second, the term *theory* will be used to refer to a scientific ideal, as described earlier in this section. Whenever the theory is meant to represent a scientific ideal, the term *scientific theory* will be used. In this way, the two meanings of theory will be easily discernible. Unless the term *scientific* precedes the word *theory,* it can be assumed to mean a counseling theory.

It will be argued in this book that *paradigms of counseling and psychotherapy are amenable to scientific inquiry, and, in fact, are more closely aligned to what is traditionally called scientific theory in the physical sciences or in the more scientific social sciences, such as experimental psychology.* For example, Deese (1972), in *Psychology as Science and Art,* defined scientific theory as follows:

## BOX 1-2

### Comparative Definitions

**Theory of Counseling and Psychotherapy**—a specialized therapeutic approach with one person or group acting as the major proponent. A theory of counseling and psychotherapy is a specialized way to address mental health problems. Techniques, often specific to the therapeutic approach, are associated with each counseling theory. Well-known examples of theories of counseling and psychotherapy associated with the psychological paradigm are: Rogers' "Person-Centered Therapy"; Ellis's "Rational-Emotive Therapy"; and Perls' "Gestalt Therapy."

**Scientific Theory**—a rational ideal constructed to represent reality. Scientific theories are frameworks for experimentation. They presuppose the objectification of that which is studied. Specific operational hypotheses derive from well-grounded theories, allowing such theories to be competitively tested. Two well-known examples of scientific theories are: Einstein's "Theory of Relativity," and Newton's "Dynamics."

*A scientific theory is a set of propositions or statements, some of which are axioms and some of which are assumptions. It is distinguished from pure mathematics or logic by the fact that some propositions can be coordinated with empirical data to produce facts. . . . Theorems are statements that can be regarded as logical consequences of assumptions and axioms. . . . If the empirical facts and theorems agree, the theory is said to be a good one. (p. 29)*

Therefore, scientific theories are sets of propositions based on consensually recognized truths (*axioms*) and/or on theory-specific *assumptions* about the nature of reality. These truths and assumptions are tested in an empirical arena where data from the *real world* is used to test the scientific theoretical propositions. From an extreme positivistic standpoint, when there is a coordination of data and scientific theoretical propositions, absolute reality is defined. However, as the philosophy of science has developed, the idea of studying nature to find *absolute truth* has been replaced by a philosophy that can be described as "postpositivistic." The postpositivistic revolution in science (influenced significantly by Kuhn, 1970) attempts to assess scientific theories as measures of relative truth, rather than measures of absolute truth. Accordingly, the truest test of a scientific theory is a critical test of the scientific theory against a competitive scientific theory. This means that experiments must be devised that compare one scientific theory to another in tests of strength at predicting outcomes. Mindful that "there is almost nothing that remains an eternal verity" (Deese, 1972, p. 31), the "strongest test of a scientific theory is only a comparative one" (Deese, 1972, p. 32). Unfortunately, when discussing counseling theories or psychotherapies, comparative tests have generally found that no one therapeutic approach dominates. This is probably so because theories of counseling and psychotherapy often are founded more upon propositions that are assumptions rather than universally recognized truths (axioms). For instance, Lambert, Shapiro, and Bergin (1986), after reviewing the literature comparing specific therapeutic approaches, concluded:

> *The meta-analytic summary data and the relatively high-quality individual studies reviewed here, in sum, tend toward the conclusion that psychosocial therapies are relatively equal in efficacy. In many respects this is a fair statement. (p. 170)*

However, another general conclusion of well-controlled studies comparing different counseling approaches is that counseling, in and of itself, is better than no counseling at all (Lambert et al., 1986), which is a well-received conclusion, but one that still leaves professionals without guidance regarding the efficacy of differential treatment for differential problems. Counseling paradigms may be a means out of this dilemma.

## Counseling Paradigms

The word *paradigm* was adopted by Kuhn (1970) in what has become a classic exposition on the philosophy of science. Kuhn proposed that change in science occurs not in an orderly process, but through "quantum leaps" or revolutions in thinking that provide gestaltlike theoretical changes in perspective about the nature of reality. Kuhn argued that a "paradigm shift" in science results from: (a) scientific anomaly; (b) an inadequate response to anomaly by the science and theory of the day (what he called "normal science"); (c) a new and competing perspective that better accommodates the anomalous data while incorporating data previously subsumed by the science of the day. Kuhn provided a number of examples, but one that is most salient is Einstein's Theory of Relativity. Einstein's theory essentially accounted for data that was unaccountable within the framework of Newtonian physics. Additionally, Einstein's theory reframed Newtonian ideas in a way that they were placed in context. Einstein's ideas essentially displaced Newtonian ideas from a larger, more universal point of view, while Einstein's formulations were as accurate within a framework previously dominated by the older theory. Today when considering Einstein's ideas, one must think beyond three dimensional space and straight lines. One must think of four-dimensional space-time that is curved by mass.

In counseling and psychotherapy, it is difficult to define a true "paradigm shift," using Kuhn's (1970) conception of a paradigm. One of the reasons for this is the inapplicability of the term *paradigm,* as defined by Kuhn, to the counseling field (Cottone, 1989). Certainly, anomalous data is not enough to challenge a counseling theory, since any alert theorist or practitioner will recognize that therapeutic approaches based on theories of counseling and psychotherapy fail in certain situations and often apply only minimally to others. Clinical and anecdotal data alone provide insights into the limitations of counseling theories. And it can be argued that a therapist subscribing to only one therapeutic model must often fit the client into the theory (as opposed to reassessing the usefulness of the theory of counseling or psychotherapy) when there is not a perfect match between a client's problem and a theoretical approach.

So anomalous data in counseling does not instigate the crisis that otherwise might follow from anomalous data in the physical sciences. Nevertheless, recognition of the presence of anomalous data is a prerequisite criterion to the definition of counseling paradigms, which is a position that will be argued more thoroughly in the next chapter. The reader should understand that anomalous data (anecdotal, observational, *or* empirical) will be defined as a necessary but not a sufficient condition for the delineation of paradigm crisis in the counseling field.

But if anomalous data is not enough, even if accumulated over time and overwhelming in nature, what other conditions must be met to distinguish a paradigm in counseling and psychotherapy? Certainly, one of the clearest ways to define a mental health paradigm is to find adherents—to locate and isolate individual practitioners who subscribe to and practice a therapeutic approach. In the United States, this proves to be an easy task, since the American culture is a certificate-crazed culture where specialties must be identifiable or they risk never being professionally recognized.

When there are adherents to competitor viewpoints, and when adherents of one viewpoint challenge the adherents of another viewpoint both theoretically and within a professional and political context, crisis may be more clearly defined. *Crisis in counseling and psychotherapy appears to be related to a combination of practical-theoretical, professional, and political concerns, which ultimately have the potential to affect the professional survival of paradigm adherents.* For example, in a recent issue of the professional newspaper of the American Association for Counseling and Development (AACD), a large professional organization representing professional counselors, a headline read: "CHAMPUS: Outpatient Care Up; Psychiatrists' 'Market Share' Down" (AACD, 1989). The article summarized the utilization statistics for outpatient care through the Civilian Health and Medical Program of the Uniformed Services (CHAMPUS) program from 1982 to 1987. CHAMPUS is one of the largest medical insurance programs in the world. From 1982 to 1987, although CHAMPUS outpatient visits for mental health services increased by 35 percent, the percentage of visits made to psychiatrists dropped from 36 percent to 21.9 percent. The percentage of visits made to psychologists rose from 28.8 percent to 34 percent in the same period. Other mental health professionals, such as marriage counselors, also benefited. As is evident in these simple statistics, a challenge to psychiatry has arisen from the emergence of professional groups claiming that they are better able to serve the needs of certain client groups than the more established profession of psychiatry. These professional groups were able to convince legislators that their services were worthwhile and competitive with psychiatry, and through political pressure and lobbying, the newer mental health professions gained access to the CHAMPUS client pool.

To a certain degree, what has happened with CHAMPUS is paradigmatic. For example, the American Association for Marriage and Family Therapy (the AAMFT), an organization representing not only a group of mental health professionals but a philosophy about treating "mental disorder," is a true reflection of how philosophy often stands at the forefront of political events. The AAMFT has been very active in lobbying the United States Congress for inclusion of AAMFT's "clinical members"

---

**BOX 1-3**

**The Four Counseling Paradigms**

    THE ORGANIC-MEDICAL PARADIGM
        Primary Professional Adherents: Psychiatrists
        Example Theory: ''Psychiatric Case Management''
    THE PSYCHOLOGICAL PARADIGM
        Primary Professional Adherents: Psychologists
        Example Theories:   ''Rational-Emotive Therapy''
                        ''Person-Centered Therapy''
                        ''Gestalt Therapy''
    THE SYSTEMIC-RELATIONAL PARADIGM
        Primary Professional Adherents: Marital and Family Therapists
        Example Theories:   ''Structural Family Therapy''
                        ''Strategic Family Therapy''
    THE CONTEXTUAL PARADIGM—AN EMERGING PARADIGM
        Proposed Professional Adherents: Professional Counselors
        Proposed Theory: ''Cognitive-Consensual Therapy''

---

as third-party payees and providers of mental health services. The AAMFT is composed, to a large degree, of professionals who adhere to social systems theory as a foundational theory for the mental health services. Accordingly, marriage and family therapists primarily subscribe to the idea that mental disorders are best treated in relational contexts—in *systems of relationships* such as marital relationships or intact family systems. This is antithetical to the philosophical premises of medicine and psychology, where individuals (not relationships) are primarily the focus of treatment. The AAMFT's success at lobbying Congress for its members represents more than a victory for a mental health profession; it represents a victory for a philosophical position about treatment of mental disorders. It is a success reflective of paradigm development and maturation.

## Therapies as Paradigm Subcategories

When one studies to learn a profession, one learns not only about the professional culture specific to the chosen profession, but also about theories specific to the history and development of the field. In some cases the theories may be very specialized, but in fact, the phenomena under study may prove to be understood as well from a completely different, even a mutually exclusive, viewpoint. This is hard for some people to understand, especially if they have not benefited from cross-professional training.

    Counselors primarily learn counseling theories. Marriage and family therapists primarily learn systemic-relational interventions. Psychiatrists primarily learn medical management methods for severe disorders. And psychologists learn primarily how to influence an individual's behavior through non-physical means. All of these professionals learn approaches to serve individuals with emotional disabilities. Obviously there is overlap in these professions, and to say that there is no theoretical crossover is to deny the obvious. However, it is not unusual to find psychiatrists or counselors who are not knowledgeable about systemic-relational theories of family intervention. Likewise, it is not unusual to find family therapists who are not knowledgeable about medical terminology or psychopharmacology. I am reminded of a conversation with a close friend of mine. We were both trained as generalists in the field of rehabilitation psychology. After formal training, I began working with the severely psychiatrically disabled and became interested in the treatment of families, which led me to the study of marital and family therapy. She accepted work as a rehabilitation psychologist working with individuals with head injuries, some who were in comatose states. We were discussing application of systemic-relational principles to work with families of individuals with severe head injuries, but our discussion was constantly sidetracked as we each had to ask each other definitions of terms that were commonly used in our respective subspecialties. I was unacquainted with terms associated with the comatose state, and she was unacquainted with terms associated with dysfunctional relationships. In this instance, my friend and I, both trained in the same field, were experiencing communications difficulties that resulted from specialized training from different paradigms. It was as if we were both entering separate realities.

The case of specialized thinking in professional fields is further compounded when the journals and literature of the fields do not cross-fertilize. Few rehabilitation psychologists read or reference articles in journals of marital and family studies, and few marital and family therapists read or reference articles in rehabilitation journals. The field of vocational rehabilitation, for example, suffers from an inbreeding of ideas (see Elliott, Byrd, & Nichols, 1987; Emener & Cottone, 1989). An inbreeding of ideas appears to stifle creative interdisciplinary thought, and it also produces a highly specialized literature that is not easily understood by outsiders.

Related to therapeutic approaches, the same kind of specialized thinking occurs. Marital and family therapists, for example, should be well acquainted with terms such as *cutoff, equifinality, paradoxical injunction, enmeshment, cybernetics,* etcetera. To a classically trained psychologist, these terms might appear to be quite strange. Yet they reflect terms used in well-known marital and family therapy approaches. Family therapists, for example, learn about strategic (Haley, 1963, 1976) and structural approaches (Minuchin, 1974) to family interventions, whereas a psychologist may learn about Rational-Emotive Therapy (Ellis, 1962), Person-Centered Therapy (cf., Rogers, 1951), or any number of behavioral therapies aimed at the ways individuals think, feel, and act. From the larger perspective, it is perhaps nearly impossible to find individuals who are proficient in several theories across paradigmatic lines. Yet those few individuals who have the ability or inclination to pursue study across paradigms may be in a unique position to influence matters in the directions of both paradigms. In fact, they may prove to be theoretical leaders in their disciplines as they will have the tendency to push theory to its paradigmatic limits.

Regardless, for the purposes of this book, as mentioned earlier, therapeutic approaches clearly associated with a paradigm's basic theoretical propositions will be considered subcategorical. In fact, the paradigm framework allows for a classification of counseling theories in one of four different ways. When a theory is clearly sub-categorical to a paradigm, it will be referred to as a *paradigm-specific* theory. This means that the theory is closely aligned with the basic propositions of the encompassing paradigm. Some theories of historical significance, however, are not easily classified as paradigm-specific. Instead, they are theories that broke new ground and helped transition the field to a new way of thinking—to the development of a newer paradigm. These historical transitional theories will be referred to as *trans-paradigmatic* theories. A third class of theory is a contemporary theory that attempts to cross at least two of the four defined paradigms. These contemporary attempts to integrate the propositions of one paradigm with another are classified as contemporary *cross-paradigmatic* approaches. A final classification of therapies relates to those that integrate diverse approaches within a paradigm. For example, a theory that integrates behavioral and cognitive theories within the psychological paradigm would be one such case. These theories will be called *within-paradigm variations*. Chapter 19 goes into greater detail about these different types of theories of counseling and psychotherapy according to the paradigm framework, especially related to cross-paradigmatic issues.

## Paradigms and Interprofessional Skirmishes

Beyond their ability to provide a framework for understanding theories of counseling and psychotherapy, paradigms provide a way for understanding interprofessional rivalry among the mental health professionals. The issue really comes to the fore when proponents of one paradigm claim that their treatment methods are the most useful for treating clients who have traditionally been treated primarily by proponents of another paradigm. For example, clients diagnosed as psychotic (*psychosis* is defined by the American Psychiatric Association, 1987, as a "gross impairment of reality testing and the creation of a new reality" [p. 404]) have been traditionally treated in medical settings. Although, at face value, a judgment about what type of treatment is appropriate for individuals diagnosed as psychotic may appear to be matter-of-fact, there are serious theoretical skirmishes across paradigmatic lines on this very issue. One well-known skirmish occurred in the marital and family therapy literature in 1989 between a well-known family therapist and social systems theorist, Jay Haley, and a preeminent psychiatrist and professor of psychiatry, Leonard Stein. Haley published an article entitled "The Effect of Long-Term Outcome Studies on the Therapy of Schizophrenia" (Haley, 1989), which was responded to by Stein (1989) in a retort entitled "The Effect of Long-Term Outcome Studies on the Therapy of Schizophrenia: A Critique." Haley essentially argued that many individuals disabled by the psychosis of schizophrenia improve—which contradicts the common stereotype that schizophrenia is a lifelong illness. He cited several longitudinal research studies that indicated that a good number of individuals diagnosed as schizophrenic actually have a good outcome. Haley stated:

> *These are not results of one or two cases, which might be ignored. There were 1,300 subjects studied for longer than 20 years, and one half to two thirds*

*achieved recovery or significant improvement. Not many "psychiatric disorders" have so good an outcome. (p. 129)*

Further, Haley stated, "Such findings cast doubt about the yet-to-be-discovered physiological cause of schizophrenia, and raise the question whether this malady should not be considered a psychological and social problem rather than one in the domain of medicine" (p. 129). Haley went on to criticize the common psychiatric practice of prescribing antipsychotic medication to schizophrenics. He argued that the potentially irreversible harmful effects of such medications outweighed the benefits, especially given the optimistic findings about potential improvement of individuals diagnosed as schizophrenic. Haley cited estimates that 43 percent of individuals who were prescribed antipsychotic medications would suffer tardive dyskinesia, which is often an irreversible brain damage that has serious symptoms of its own. Haley then concluded that since family and other treatment methods have advanced to the point where there is a good likelihood of a positive outcome, they should be primary treatment methods once acute (short-term and severe) psychotic symptoms have resolved. He argued that during acute episodes only protective measures should be used, and that medications should not be used as constraints. Haley stated, "If psychiatrists are to continue to be involved in the treatment of psychosis, they need to give up their focus on social control procedures and to learn to do therapy with disturbed individuals and their families" (p. 131). Haley's arguments clearly reflect his allegiance to the study of relationships as factors involved in the cause and cure of emotional disorder. In fact, he was involved in a classic observational and theoretical study in the early 1950s, the results of which were published as an article entitled "Toward a Theory of Schizophrenia" (Bateson, Jackson, Haley, & Weakland, 1956). In that article, it was hypothesized that one cause of schizophrenia was the "double bind"—a no-win situation in the context of an *interpersonal* relationship. The Bateson et al. work is a milestone work in the development of the systemic-relational paradigm and, early on, Haley was clearly and substantially involved in arguing the applicability of a systemic-relational framework to mental health concerns.

Stein (1989), on the other hand, in his critique of Haley's position, argued a more traditional organic-medical position. Stein, lamenting arguments such as Haley's (1989), stated:

*I have learned to use "whatever works"—and for multiple problems it is most often necessary to use a variety of interventions. With all the problems my patients and I have to cope with, I feel especially burdened when the problem is caused by a fellow professional. There still remain a few who espouse simplistic solutions to complex problems and continue to influence people to think in the same way. (p. 133)*

To make his point, Stein cited studies that indicated that schizophrenia has a multifactorial causation, with an interaction of genetic, psychosocial, and neurobiological factors. Citing findings of twin studies, Stein argued that monozygotic (identical) twins have nearly a 45 percent concordance rate (the probability that if one twin develops the disorder, then the other twin will also). He concluded that "it is clear that biology plays a powerful role in the disorder" (p. 134). But he went on to conclude that "interpersonal environment affects the course of the illness" (p. 134). Stein then argued against Haley's position that antipsychotic medications should not be used; Stein argued that psychosis is a frightening experience to the patient, and to allow such psychotic symptoms to go on while using less effective methods to control them (such as hot tubs, cold packs, and other physical restraints, as recommended by Haley), is a moral injustice. Stein stated:

> *The empirical question is: In the long run, are persons with schizophrenia better off having their psychotic episodes shortened and occurring less frequently by using neuroleptic medication, or are they better off not using medications and experiencing longer periods of psychosis and frequent relapse? (p. 135)*

Stein then argued that until there is a better alternative to antipsychotic medications to shorten the psychotic episodes and to reduce the number of relapses, then medication therapy is the most humane option. But Stein did not stop there; he went on to attack the efficiency of psychotherapeutic methods in the treatment of schizophrenia. He cited a study indicating there are disappointing results related to the treatment of schizophrenia through psychotherapeutic means. He then went on to say that one of the most promising methods for treatment of schizophrenia (the Psychoeducational Family Therapy of Anderson, Reiss, & Hogarty [1986] which is presented in chapter 20 of this text) is based on the assumption that schizophrenics have a biological vulnerability. In effect, Stein makes a credible argument related to the limitations of Haley's position, and Stein makes his case primarily from a philosophy consistent with organic-medical thinking.

As to who is the winner in such debates is a question that is best answered individually by readers of the original works. Most likely, the paradigm from which the reader operates will strongly influence his or her position on the outcome of the debate.

The major point in this discussion is that paradigm proponents often take extreme stands to make the case for their paradigm. These extreme stands help to delimit the boundaries of the paradigm, and also act to aggravate a professional adversarial attitude. The question as to which type of client is best treated by adherents of which paradigm, to date, has not been satisfactorily answered.

To the extreme, proponents of one paradigm may argue that therapists trained in another paradigm are poorly trained to do certain types of treatment, to treat certain types of clients, or to do therapy at all. In fact the issue as to whether "therapy" is being done at all reflects disagreements about what constitutes "treatment" in the medical sense versus intervention into concerns which are primarily defined as problems in living. This distinction in the past was demarcated by the terms *psychotherapy* versus *counseling*.

## Counseling Versus Psychotherapy

Discussions about the distinctions between counseling and psychotherapy are common in respected textbooks describing theories of counseling and psychotherapy. For example, George and Cristiani (1990) stated:

> *One problem facing the counseling practitioner is that of distinguishing between counseling and psychotherapy. Indeed, efforts to distinguish between the two have not met with universal approval. Some practitioners think that such a distinction need not be made and use the two terms synonymously. Others, however, feel that such a distinction must be made. . . . However, once the decision to make a distinction between counseling and psychotherapy has been made, the problems begin; the edges of the distinction may blur and agreement on all the particulars is unlikely. (p. 31)*

Distinctions between counseling and psychotherapy may be made according to such factors as the history of counseling versus psychotherapy, the type of client served (whether the client may be viewed as ill), differences in goals, differences in the settings of practice, or distinctions about the seriousness of the client concern.

These types of distinctions once served a useful purpose before professional counselors began to make headway regarding the role of counselors in traditional medical settings. With the claims of the American Mental Health Counseling Association that mental health counselors can do psychotherapy, the distinction between counseling and psychotherapy has been eroded. Also, the distinctions made regarding counseling settings versus psychotherapy settings are not as clear-cut as in the past. In the past, hospital-based programs used the term *therapy* almost across the board when marketing their programs; but today one hears radio commercials for hospital-based chemical dependency and psychiatric treatment centers calling themselves "counseling" centers. Additionally, more and more individuals trained as counselors are being employed in community mental health settings, psychiatric group practices, hospitals, and other traditional health-service settings. In essence, the distinctions are not serving a useful purpose from the standpoint of the functions of the professionals in their practices or from a differentiation according to professional setting.

Probably the one area where the distinction still has some meaning, however, is in the area of insurance reimbursement. Medical insurance companies, always mindful of how the dollar is spent, have been sticklers about expanding payment beyond the traditional reimbursable mental health service called "psychotherapy." In many states this means that unless a professional is licensed to provide psychotherapeutic services, no matter how similar the service is to psychotherapy operationally, it is not reimbursable. This has caused professional psychologists, social workers, marital and family therapists, and counselors to lobby for laws that clearly allow for reimbursement of their services. These laws are often statutes dealing with either: (a) the definition of practice; or (b) freedom of choice. "Definition of practice" gets to the heart of the issue. If the statute licensing the professional to practice states clearly that a professional is licensed to do psychotherapy, then legally the professional can claim such treatment as part of the domain of professional practice. If the term *counseling* is used, there is room for disagreement, which has especially been a thorn in the side of professional mental health counselors, who would benefit by inclusion of the term *psychotherapy* in counselor regulatory statutes in the definition of practice (in addition to the term *counseling*). Additionally, ''freedom of choice'' laws allow clients the right to choose the professionals that will treat them, and consequently which professionals will receive insurance reimbursement. Professional groups representing psychologists, counselors, social workers, and marital and family therapists have been successful in many states in asserting their rights. However, in some states, some nonmedical mental health professionals must be under the supervision of a medical practitioner (a doctor of medicine or a doctor of osteopathy) in order to receive payment. Politics becomes all the more critical to professional survival when differences influence the pocketbooks of involved parties.

Regardless, in this text, the term *counseling* and *psychotherapy* will be used synonymously. Further, it is predicted that all distinctions between counseling and psychotherapy will become moot, as professional and paradigmatic allegiance will primarily discern the major differences between the activities of professionals, and not the terms *counseling* and *psychotherapy.*

## A Word About Contextualism and the Bias of This Book

Before proceeding, it is important that readers understand that the idea of paradigms of counseling and psychotherapy emerged from a developed philosophy entitled ''contextualism.'' Contextualism is a philosophy that purports that realities are socially constructed. Reality is not simply viewed as objective or subjective. Rather, according to contextualism, there are many potential realities, each bounded and objectified within social contexts (social-consensual domains). The contextual position is both a foundation for the definition of counseling paradigms *and* a philosophy of counseling, which will be expounded upon in Part Five (The Contextual Paradigm) of this book. The four counseling paradigms, as equally legitimate and socially constructed domains, do not exist outside of the contextual philosophy. Therefore, it should be understood from the outset that accepting the concept of paradigms of counseling and psychotherapy is, to a certain degree, an acceptance of the contextual philosophy. Individuals who have difficulty with this sort of thinking are asked to suspend judgment until the text is read and digested, and then to make a decision about the relevance of this line of thinking to current professional practices. This is not to say that the contextual philosophy is the only option; it is to say, however, that it is one option that helps to clarify the nature and foundations of the mental health enterprise. A further discussion on this topic is left for the final chapter of this book, which should help to place the contextual philosophy in an empirical context.

## Chapter Conclusion

This chapter has served to introduce the reader to some of the basic terminology that will be used throughout the book. Terms such as *theory, paradigm, counseling,* and *psychotherapy* have been defined. In addition to philosophical or theoretical issues, professional and political issues have been introduced as relevant to the study of counseling theories. As will be learned in chapter 2, these professional issues play an important role in the definition of a counseling paradigm. Finally, contextualism was defined as the philosophy undergirding the definition of paradigms of counseling and psychotherapy.

## References

American Association for Counseling and Development. (1989, June). CHAMPUS: Outpatient care up: Psychiatrists' 'market share' down. *Guidepost, 31*(18), pp. 1, 19.

American Psychiatric Association. (1987). *Diagnostic and statistical manual of mental disorders* (3rd ed., rev.). Washington, DC: Author.

Anderson, C. M., Reiss, D. J., & Hogarty, G. E. (1986). *Schizophrenia in the family: A practitioner's guide to psychoeducation and management.* New York: Guilford.

Bateson, G., Jackson, D., Haley, J., & Weakland, J. (1956). Toward a theory of schizophrenia. *Behavioral Science, 1,* 251–264.

Cottone, R. R. (1989). Defining the psychomedical and systemic paradigms in marital and family therapy. *Journal of Marital and Family Therapy, 15,* 225–235.

Deese, J. (1972). *Psychology as science and art.* New York: Harcourt Brace Jovanovich.

Elliott, T. R., Byrd, E. K., & Nichols, R. K. (1987). Influential publications and authors in contemporary rehabilitation counseling literature. *Journal of Applied Rehabilitation Counseling, 18*(3), 45–47.

Ellis, A. (1962). *Reason and emotion in psychotherapy.* Secaucus, NJ: Lyle Stuart.

Emener, W. G., & Cottone, R. R. (1989). Professionalization, deprofessionalization, and reprofessionalization of rehabilitation counseling according to criteria of professions. *Journal of Counseling and Development, 67,* 576–581.

George, R. L., & Cristiani, T. S. (1990). *Counseling: Theory and practice.* Englewood Cliffs, NJ: Prentice-Hall.

Haley, J. (1963). *Strategies of psychotherapy.* New York: Grune & Stratton.

Haley, J. (1976). *Problem solving therapy.* New York: W. W. Norton.

Haley, J. (1989). The effect of long-term outcome studies on the therapy of schizophrenia. *Journal of Marital and Family Therapy, 15,* 127–132.

Kuhn, T. S. (1970). *The structure of scientific revolutions, (2nd ed.). Chicago: University of Chicago Press.*

Lambert, M. J., Shapiro, D. A., & Bergin, A. E. (1986). The effectiveness of psychotherapy. In S. L. Garfield & A. E. Bergin (eds.), *Handbook of psychotherapy and behavior change* (pp. 157–211). New York: John Wiley & Sons.

Minuchin, S. (1974). *Families and family therapy.* Cambridge, MA: Harvard University Press.

Popper, K. R. (1959). *The logic of scientific discovery.* New York: Basic Books.

Rogers, C. R. (1951). *Client-Centered Therapy.* Boston, MA: Houghton Mifflin.

Stein, L. (1989). The effect of long-term outcome studies on the therapy of schizophrenia: A critique. *Journal of Marital and Family Therapy, 15,* 133–138.

# 2

# Criteria for Defining Paradigms of Counseling and Psychotherapy*

CHAPTER 1 HAS introduced basic terminology used throughout this text and has acquainted the reader with some basic premises. First, a rationale was given for using paradigms of counseling and psychotherapy as a metatheoretical framework—a large theory-encompassing model for understanding the theories and practices of counseling and psychotherapy. Paradigms of counseling and psychotherapy were also defined as a means for understanding the professional issues that surround the mental health enterprise. In fact, paradigms of counseling and psychotherapy (counseling paradigms) were closely linked to the professional issues associated with the development and maintenance of mental health treatment disciplines.

Second, in chapter 1, theories of counseling and psychotherapy were defined as the traditional therapies or therapeutic approaches taught to practitioners in the mental health disciplines. A counseling theory was differentiated from a scientific theory by definition. A scientific theory was defined as a rational ideal (representative of some aspect of reality) that serves as a framework for understanding and for experimentation. The distinction between counseling theories and scientific theories was not meant to imply that counseling theories are not scientific. Some theories of counseling and psychotherapy do meet the basic definition for a scientific theory. However, not all counseling theories meet the definition of a scientific theory. There must be widespread agreement (by words or actions) in a substantial professional community about ''facts'' related to a counseling theory (i.e., consensually accepted truths) for it to be scientific.

*Special thanks to Rob Anderson, PhD, Professor of Speech Communication at Southern Illinois University—Edwardsville, for his helpful comments on an earlier draft of this chapter.

Otherwise the counseling theory is based more upon assumptions than axioms and it may not be amenable to meaningful empirical investigation. Of the theories of counseling and psychotherapy presented in this text, behavioral theory comes closest to meeting the definition of a scientific theory.

Third, as related to, chapter 1, a paradigm of counseling and psychotherapy was defined based upon Kuhn's (1970) definition of a scientific paradigm. The chapter 1 definition of a counseling paradigm, however, was not operational; it provided only a frame of reference for a more complete definition. This chapter provides a much more complete definition of paradigms of counseling and psychotherapy. Additionally, after the basic criteria for a counseling paradigm are offered and grounded, distinctions between Kuhn's scientific paradigms and counseling paradigms will be made. The distinctions provide a means to a deeper understanding of paradigms in counseling and psychotherapy that will serve students well if they progress to advanced studies or research in the field.

The following six criteria for defining a counseling paradigm are offered as a starting point for critical debate. The criteria for a counseling paradigm are not meant to be absolute. They are offered instead as a set of propositions defined by the actions of professionals in the field. They are meant to be foundations for the development of a consensus across the mental health professions.

Each criterion was chosen for its potential to add (in a cumulative way) to the definition of discrete models or patterns of ideas that constitute theory beyond the therapies of everyday practice. Counseling paradigms, so conceived, represent metatheoretical frameworks for conceptualizing and analyzing the practice of counseling and psychotherapy.

## Criteria for a Counseling Paradigm

What constitutes a paradigm of counseling and psychotherapy? The following criteria, first listed and then discussed in greater detail, are the operational guidelines used in the subsequent chapters to define counseling paradigms. It must be understood that all six criteria must be viewed *in combination* as a definition of counseling paradigms.

**1.** A counseling paradigm must meet a traditional, scientifically based definition of theory;

**2.** A counseling paradigm must have a competitor paradigm against which it can be tested. There must be substantial anomalous anecdotal, observational, or empirical evidence that is not supportive of the competitor paradigm. Additionally, competition must be expressed in the professional and political realm, where issues such as licensure, professional title and practice control, and definitions of practice come to the forefront of issues addressed by practitioners of competitive paradigms.

**3.** A counseling paradigm must be philosophically (epistemologically *and/or* ontologically) distinguishable from its competition.

*Epistemology,* as used here, is defined as theory of knowledge, or the rules for knowing. To say that a paradigm is epistemologically distinguishable is to say that the *focus of study* prescribed by the paradigm is distinct when compared to a competitive paradigm. For example, the study of organic-medical phenomena occurs primarily within the boundaries of the traditional, non-social sciences, such as physics, chemistry, and biology. On the other hand, psychology, generally speaking, prescribes study of observable behaviors within certain well-defined contexts.

To say that a paradigm is *ontologically distinguishable* from its competition is to say that the *assumptions about the nature of reality* are distinct when compared to a competitive paradigm. For example, from a strict social systems theory perspective, *reality* is defined as *relationship;* that is, relationships are assumed to exist as givens (that is why marriage counselors work with the marital ''relationship''). On the other hand, from a strict medical or psychological perspective, people are viewed as *things,* as identifiable entities, which are assumed to exist as distinct from the relations that surround them.

**4.** A counseling paradigm must produce a gestaltlike change in perspective from a competitive viewpoint—a change in perspective that reframes the context of interpretation, and subsequently *reframes the interpretation of cause and effect.* For example, from the organic-medical paradigm perspective, behavior is interpreted on the basis of biology and chemistry. According to the psychological paradigm, behavior derives from an individual entity in a delimited environmental context as affected primarily by nonorganic factors. According to the systemic paradigm, behavior derives from relationship within identified and bounded relationship structures. And according to the contextual paradigm, a definition of cause derives from the socially consensually agreed-upon structures defined as influencing behavior.

**5.** A counseling paradigm must be practiced by an identifiable professional group that, knowingly or unknowingly, adheres to ontological precepts, and that studies problems from the perspective of its dominant epistemology. Marriage and family therapists, for example, adhere to the basic systems theory principle that relationships are identifiable and treatable, and they attempt to define and to study problems in the context of relationship. Additionally, the professional group of adherents must be politically recognizable, and it must have a history of political agitation to gain a set of provincial rights or privileges.

**6.** A counseling paradigm must have, or must have the potential to have, a number of clearly identifiable counseling theories or therapeutic approaches incorporated within its framework. An example that will be discussed in more detail later is the presence of the ''Strategic'' and ''Structural'' theories of family therapy, which both derive from the systemic-relational paradigm. Other examples are Rational Emotive Therapy (Ellis, 1962) and Gestalt Therapy (Perls, 1969), both within the psychological paradigm.

These six criteria, in combination, represent the rules for defining and operationalizing paradigms of counseling and psychotherapy. The remainder of this chapter will present discussions to help validate the reasonableness and utility of each criterion.

Each criterion will be shown to be critical to the definition of paradigms of counseling and psychotherapy.

# Criterion I: Paradigm as a Scientific Theory

A scientific theory is a rational ideal, constructed to represent some aspect of reality. Scientific theories are competitive frameworks for understanding and experimentation. They require objectification of some aspect of reality, so that outcomes are measurable. Hypotheses, basic educated guesses, must be formulated in a way that the propositions of one scientific theory can be tested against the propositions of another competitive scientific theory. Five basic elements common to scientific theories are: (a) propositions, which are either axioms (consensually accepted truths) or assumptions; (b) constructs (which are experience-specific abstractions that derive from propositions); (c) variables (which are constructs that vary in degree and are measurable); (d) theorems (which are connections between constructs); and (e) formats (which are the organizations of theoretical statements) (cf. Deese, 1972; Turner, 1986).

Given this basic definition of a scientific theory, four arguments will be made in this section. First, paradigms of counseling and psychotherapy will be defined as scientific theories. Second, it will be argued that paradigms of counseling and psychotherapy represent a type of scientific theory that encompasses counseling theories or therapies (whether or not the counseling theory is scientific in its own right). Third, counseling paradigms will be defined as consistent with a postpositivism view of science (i.e., dealing with relative rather than absolute truth). Postpositivistic empiricism as presented here will be derived from a *contextual view of knowledge*. Consequently, the contextual paradigm, which is the fourth paradigm presented in this text, serves not only to elucidate a mental health approach, but it also represents a philosophy that helps to put mental health science in perspective. Issues related to the contextual paradigm will be clarified in more detail in Parts Five and Seven of this text. At this juncture, the reader should note that contextualism as a philosophy undergirds the scientific foundation of paradigms. Fourth, counseling paradigms will be defined as testable within the context of *critical paradigmatic experiments* or, in other words, tests of one psychotherapy representing one counseling paradigm against a therapy representing another counseling paradigm within a specified therapeutic context.

## Argument 1: Paradigms as Scientific Theories

In defining paradigms of counseling and psychotherapy as scientific theories, some examples of paradigm-specific propositions, constructs, variables, and theorems may be helpful. The systemic-relational paradigm, which has not been fully explained to this point, can be a useful example, since it is philosophically distinct from the organic-medical and psychological propositions with which readers are probably better acquainted through their undergraduate or preliminary graduate studies. A foundational systemic-relational *proposition* is that reality is composed of relationships rather than things. Relationships are essentially processes between what appear to be things. Given this basic proposition (which is accepted more as an axiom than an assumption in the marital and family therapy field), a basic *construct* deriving from the proposition is that marital relationships exist and can be studied. For instance, marital relationships generally *vary* in nature from very egalitarian (where partners are equals) to very authoritarian (where one partner is the "boss"). A basic *theorem* (connection between constructs) related to the egalitarian or authoritarian nature of a marital relationship is that it reflects the relationships of the marital partners to the larger family systems within which the marriage exists and within a cultural context (where "family systems" and "cultural context" are also "constructs"). Finally, the systemic-relational paradigm is organized (*formatted*) in such a way as to make these definitions (of propositions, constructs, variables, and theorems) clearly discernible.

The organic-medical paradigm also serves as a clear example of how a paradigm meets the definition of a scientific theory. A basic *proposition* of the organic-medical paradigm is that humans should be viewed as biological structures. A basic *construct* deriving from this proposition is that behavioral deviation is based primarily upon a "psychophysiological deficit" (see Anderson, Reiss, & Hogarty, 1986). Symptoms are *variables* that can be assessed; they reflect the degree of psychophysiological deficit. A basic *theorem* is that the psychophysiological deficit is triggered by an external psychophysiological stressor (where the term *stressor* is also a construct). And finally, the organic-medical paradigm is organized (*formatted*) in such a way as to make these definitions clear-cut.

These two examples, although offered prematurely in the sense that the paradigms have not been thoroughly presented, give some basic hints as to the reasonableness of the position that paradigms of counseling and psychotherapy are scientific theories.

## Argument 2: Paradigms as Theory-encompassing Frameworks

Regarding counseling paradigms as scientific theories encompassing several counseling theories or therapies, it is important to reiterate what has been argued already. Counseling paradigms are metatheoretical frameworks of philosophical, professional, and practical significance. Theories of counseling and psychotherapy, on the other hand, are not metatheoretical. Whereas counseling paradigms are part of the big picture—the puzzle itself—counseling theories are smaller, like pieces of a puzzle. Also, in most cases, theories of counseling and psychotherapy are not epistemologically or ontologically distinct. For example, although comparing and contrasting traditional counseling theories within the psychological paradigm will reveal different assumptions about how humans change and learn, the fact remains that *the great majority of psychotherapies in the psychological mold focus on the individual human being as a unit of study* (see Becvar & Becvar, 1988). This is not the case, however, with a systemic-relational paradigm viewpoint, where relationships are the focus of study. Nor is it the case with the contextual paradigm, where fleeting but observable structures are the focus of study. In this regard, counseling theories that have been previously viewed as divergent from a psychological point of view may in fact be viewed as having much in common, whereas counseling paradigms (in this case the psychological, systemic-relational, and contextual paradigms) manifest true differences at a higher level of analysis. Those paradigm-level differences aid in clearly differentiating therapeutic approaches from a larger perspective.

### Argument 3: Postpositivistic Empiricism

Another issue of importance is the deductive nature of paradigms. This is not to say that all counseling paradigms are purely deductively conceived. In fact, there is a foundation of empirical, observational, or anecdotal data at each paradigm's base. Pure deduction or data alone cannot give life to a paradigm, since, as a paradigm is defined in this text, a distinct professional position must be evident. Take as an example the health service field of chiropractic. As controversial as chiropractic may be, as a professional field it may represent a physical health paradigm, as may osteopathy and the traditions of medicine. It can be argued that chiropractic was founded on a wealth of anecdotal evidence supporting the contention that obstruction of the nervous system is primarily causative of disease. Chiropractors argue *as fact* that physical manipulation of the spine to relieve subluxation and pressure on the nervous system can prevent and even cure maladies of body systems linked to the nervous system in specified ways. Chiropractic has been quite successful politically in convincing others of this basic proposition—a proposition that has been vehemently disputed by the medical profession. The issue here is that convincing empirical evidence in support of a position (or in contrast to a position) is not enough to produce or prevent the spread of a paradigm. Politics and the spirit of the day play an important role in the emergence of counseling paradigms. In this sense paradigms are world views, religions of license so to speak, that can be challenged (or challenge) on empirical *or nonempirical* grounds. Because paradigm adherents often claim that their paradigm is untestable on the basis of methods proposed by adherents of a competitor paradigm (see Taggart's, 1989, concerns related to marital and family therapy), questions as to what is right or wrong on critical issues may go unanswered.

However, paradigmatic thinking brings with it an empirical viewpoint that is unique, unbiased, and worthy of special discussion. Paradigmatic thinking rises above the constraints of simply and randomly testing one therapeutic approach against another, and it frees the investigator from the shackles of a strict postivism (in search of absolute truth) to the freedom of a postpositivistic empiricism and a contextual view of knowledge. What this means is that absolute knowledge is not in question. Rather, facts are viewed as resulting as much from the context of the question as from an objective knowable reality. In this sense, theories, hypotheses generation, and empirical findings are all viewed as representing a discovery process (McGuire, 1986). This discovery process is as revealing of the premise that led to hypothesis generation as it is revealing of empirical outcome. For example, for years it has been argued in the family therapy literature that systemic theory and relational epistemology are inconsistent with a positivistic research tradition because relationships are processes that cannot be assessed side by side psychological traits or states as outcomes (e.g., Taggart, 1989). Yet, no alternative research approach of consensual significance has emerged. In fact, there has been no research consensus in the field as to what kinds of findings are definitive in supporting or disputing systemic-relational ideas as applied in mental health settings. However, counseling paradigms offer a framework for *critical paradigmatic experiments,* which brings the issue of empirical investigation to a higher level of analysis. A critical paradigmatic experiment is an empirical framework for testing the assumptions of one paradigm against the assumptions of a competitor paradigm (Cottone, 1989). For example, I argued that family therapies based on clearly defined mental health treatment paradigms could be competitively tested and that such tests would produce findings of significance within the confines of the experimental context (Cottone, 1989). Just as a wheelbarrow and a sled can be compared as means of carrying objects, so too can paradigms be tested as a means of producing certain therapeutic outcomes. However, where sleds may excel (on snowy or ice-covered sloping surfaces) wheelbarrows may fail. Likewise, where wheelbarrows may excel (on level gravel surfaces), sleds may fail. The therapeutic context is definitely a factor, as is the therapeutic approach. It must be remembered that paradigmatic findings demonstrate only for the moment, and within certain contexts, what is true. Absolute truth is not at issue. A finding is given meaning only in the context of consensus in a professional community.

## Argument 4: Critical Paradigmatic Experiments

Finally, the nature of critical paradigmatic experimentation must be addressed. In order for such experimentation to occur, therapies that represent a paradigm in its purest theoretical sense must be defined (e.g., paradigm-specific theories). It may not be enough simply to test one already existing therapy against another already existing therapy, unless it can be demonstrated that each therapeutic approach does not significantly overlap paradigms propositionally. In other words, the counseling theories tested in critical paradigmatic experiments must be purely reflective of a paradigm's propositions. For example, McGuirk, Freidlander, and Blocher (1987) found that psychodynamically oriented psychotherapists make use of relational data. Psycho-analysis, as currently practiced, may not be purely representative of the psychological paradigm, since psychoanalysts are knowingly or unknowingly attending to systemic-relational data. Psycho-analysis as currently practiced, therefore, might not be the best choice as a representative theory of the psychological paradigm, since it involves relational data at the practical level. The propositions of counseling paradigms will be outlined in the succeeding chapters, so defining pure examples of paradigm-specific counseling theories will be more easily accomplished. The need for pure examples of paradigm-specific therapies will not be belabored here. Instead, the issue will be readdressed briefly in chapter 21 (Experimental Issues and Conclusion). However, it is crucial to understand that critical paradigmatic experiments redefine the rules a bit as to what is acceptable as a context of therapy outcome research. Pure examples of paradigm-specific therapies must be used in such experimentation.

## Criterion II: The Presence of a Competition

Paradigms of counseling and psychotherapy do not exist, practically speaking, until there is a competitive paradigm for comparison. In fact, in newly developing professions, it may be that one worldview predominates without awareness of practitioners and researchers. In these cases, it is likely that the term *paradigm* may be misused by theorists who may not be aware of or privy to the kinds of comparative theory and theory-comparative empirical tests that occur in other sciences. What probably occurs is what might be called preparadigm thinking—for example, thinking that different theories of counseling and psychotherapy constitute paradigms.

In the counseling fields, preparadigm thinking has occurred in discussions of behaviorism versus the humanistic or psychodynamic models. Because behaviorism focuses attention on observable behavior, behavioral theories of counseling and psychotherapy may be called distinct compared to non-behavioral counseling theories within the psychological paradigm. But, in fact, when looking at humanism, the psychodynamic model, or behavioral theory, each clearly operates from the assumption that people exist as separate and analyzable entities. Whether actions or words are studied, the fact remains that the focus is the same: the individual. In other words, the similarity among behavioral, humanistic, or psychodynamic approaches is not outstanding until a true competitive paradigm makes its way into the language of the field. When, for example, psychological thinking is compared to a strict contextual viewpoint, true differences emerge. From a contextualistic position, people *do not exist* as separate and analyzable entities; according to a strict contextual viewpoint, people only represent *perceptual phenomena* for the transmission of change and process! The observer and the observed are not distinct. By way of contrast, psychologically, people are viewed as independent entities that are objectively assessable by observers.

It is through a competitive viewpoint that a paradigm's boundaries are best defined. And, as stated earlier, a paradigm does not exist until a competitive viewpoint emerges to challenge it. It is then that people begin to take sides, to argue differing stands on issues of practice, and to more clearly define the limits of a paradigm's applicability. Competition, in this sense, is critical to paradigmatic thinking.

## Criterion III: Epistemological and/or Ontological Significance

In this text, when discussing philosophical differences between paradigms of counseling and psychotherapy, the two branches of philosophy of importance are epistemology and ontology. As earlier defined, *epistemology* refers to a theory of knowledge—a way of knowing. When the word is confronted in this text, the reader should ask, ''What is the focus of study?'' Ontology deals with assumptions about the nature of reality, and when confronted by the word *ontology,* readers should ask, ''What is real and treatable in counseling?'' The box entitled ''Philosophical Differences Across Counseling

BOX 2-1 ━━━━━━━━━━━━━━━━━━━━━━━━━━━━━━━━━━━━━━━━━

## Philosophical Differences Across Counseling Paradigms

| Paradigm | Epistemology (Focus of Study) | Ontology (Nature of Reality) |
|---|---|---|
| Organic-Medical | Biological, chemical and other physical internal influences on behavior | Physical things |
| Psychological | Primarily nonphysical internal and external influences on behavior | Physical and primarily nonphysical things |
| Systemic-Relational | Relationships as they affect behavior | Relationships |
| Contextual | The process of human consensus as an enstructuring process | Change and process |

Paradigms'' should help to outline epistemological and ontological differences across the four paradigms.

## Epistemology and the Behavioral Sciences

Gregory Bateson (1972c), a preeminent systems theorist, has been credited with raising fundamental epistemological issues in the social and behavioral sciences. Although Bateson's epistemological notions may seem confusing because of his multidefinitional application of the word *epistemology* (Dell, 1985), Bateson directly demonstrated how notions of reality, and the theories used to address reality, affect that which is perceived. For example, Bateson (1968/1972a) believed the nature of the individual human being, the nature of culture, and the nature of the human biological and ecological context were all "systemic." Yet he described "the curious twist in the systemic nature of the individual man" as "consciousness . . . almost of necessity, blinded to the systemic nature of the man himself" (p. 434). He stated: "Purposive consciousness pulls out, from the total mind, sequences which do not have the loop structure which is characteristic of the whole systemic structure" (p. 434).

Bateson's reality derived from *difference,* which he defined as an "idea" through interaction. Bateson (1969/1972b) stated: "The world of form and communication invokes no things, forces, or impacts but only differences and ideas. (A difference which makes a difference *is* an idea. It is a "bit," a unit of information)" (pp. 271–272). It is clear that when Bateson began to look to differences *between* things, he began to look to relationships in the observed world. He even began to assess his own relationship to that which he observed.

Bateson's work has been both a source of inspiration and a source of controversy in the human service fields (see discussions in the family therapy literature by Dell, 1982, 1985; Held & Pols, 1985). Regardless, his applications of epistemological thinking to the social and behavioral sciences are milestones in the literature of the mental health services.

## Epistemology, Ontology, and Paradigms

In this book, issues of epistemology and ontology have special importance in defining and understanding counseling paradigms. There are clear-cut epistemological differences across the paradigms of counseling and psychotherapy. For example, whereas an organic-medical therapist would attempt to assess biological influences on behavior (e.g., by taking a family history to assess the prospect of genetic predisposition toward a mental illness), a psychologically oriented therapist in the behavioral mold would assess the history of learning of the individual to assess the external factors affecting a client's behavior. A systemic-relational therapist would do a social history on the client in order to place the client in a social-relational network. And a contextually oriented therapist would analyze the client's language and social contexts to assess operative consensualities. In each of these cases, philosophy directs what the mental health professional does.

Since ontology deals with theories of reality, that is, theories that address the primary "stuff" of the universe, mental health professionals must decide what it is they are going to change through a therapeutic intervention. Mental health professionals, of course, are universally faced with disturbed or distressed clients. From an ontological perspective, mental health professionals must answer the ontological question, "What is real and treatable in counseling?" For example, organic-medical therapists would focus on the human body as a primary target of treatment. Medication would probably be prescribed. Means to prevent triggers that influence physiological reactions would also be a focus of treatment. Psychological paradigm adherents, who focus primarily on nonphysical individual concerns, typically would answer that question by saying the client, as a nonphysical, psychological entity, is real *and* the focus of treatment. However, a systemically oriented marriage counselor would say that what is real as a treatable entity in counseling is the marital *relationship*. For the marriage counselor practicing in a way consistent with a purely systemic-relational approach, individuals cannot and do not exist outside of relationships. In that sense, relationships predominate as a reality in treatment. A contextual paradigm adherent would say that a client is changing anyway, and therapy is used to direct or redirect inevitable change.

The following chapters will provide very clear paradigmatic distinctions on epistemological and ontological issues. Also, the reader will learn that subparadigm *models* emerge on the basis of epistemological and ontological distinctions within paradigms. Subparadigm models will be demarcated in discussions of two of the four paradigms: the psychological and systemic paradigms. In both cases the subparadigm *models* are identified as the internal and external models. On the other hand, the medical and contextual paradigms will not be divided on epistemological or ontological grounds.

# Criterion IV: Distinct Cause-and-Effect Perspective

The issue of cause and effect is critical to differentiating paradigms of counseling and psychotherapy, and it is in this area that true philosophical differences come to the fore among the competitors for paradigm status in counseling and psychotherapy.

The term *cause and effect,* as used here, will relate to assumptions about what determines behavior, and, more specifically, the process that occurs during behavior determination. Traditionally, mental health professionals have assumed that ''things'' cause behavior, whether things are people or objects. If a billiard ball A hits another billiard ball B into a pool-table pocket, it can be said that ball A caused ball B to go into the pocket. According to Newtonian logic, cause and effect represents a linear process, or what can be described as ''A causes B,'' as with the billiard balls. In the human services, when therapists speak of irrational thoughts causing negative emotions, stimuli causing responses, or fixations causing regressions, a basic linear cause and effect perspective is being communicated. In these cases, it is assumed that something has directly caused something else to occur.

But simple linear cause and effect perspectives are being challenged, especially within the advanced social systems theory literature. With the lead offered by Bateson (1972), many contemporary social systems thinkers have incorporated the idea of circular or reciprocal causality into their theorizing (Dell, 1982, 1985; Maturana, 1978, 1980). These theorists are basically saying that viewing cause and effect as a linear process oversimplifies the complex human communication process. Systems theorists have focused on circular causality, stemming from the original works by Bertalanffy (1952, 1968) in the area of biology and general systems theory, and by Wiener (1950) on cybernetics, which is the study of informational and other control mechanisms within living and nonliving systems. The basic assumption underlying the circular causal process is that two ''things'' interact within boundaries that define a relationship or relationships. When these boundaries close off the interaction to outside stimuli, then relational influences (not individual influences) within the boundaries take precedence. For example, when two people interact, each individual will act according to communication from the other individual, which ultimately is influenced by the first individual's presence. In other words, person A is influenced by person B, who was influenced by A in the first place, as each is continually influenced by each other in a circular causal process. The circular causal process means that relationships will develop over time, even if the relationships are relatively isolated from outside influences. In such cases, it is not a matter of one person causing another person to act; instead, both people mutually affect each other's behavior in a reciprocal manner.

As these examples imply, ideas about cause and effect are critical to what counselors and therapists look for during assessment. It also influences what they seek to treat during counseling. Counselors bound to the linear, A-causes-B perspective, will attempt to find what has directly influenced a behavior. Counselors subscribing to a circular idea of cause and effect will attempt to identify the relational process or processes that must be interrupted to create change.

These two views, the linear and circular causal perspectives, represent the broadest distinct categorizations of cause and effect. However, within these two broad categories, subcategorical differences may have paradigmatic significance. For example, within the linear point of view, cause can be identified as resulting from factors internal to the individual or external to the individual. This is a critical difference as applied to the human services, since biological and chemical internal influences may be viewed as different from the sensual influence of environmental stimuli. Likewise, with the circular model, the idea of cause occurring because of factors external to the identified boundaries of the identified system produces a philosophy and approach quite different from the idea of influence occurring only within identified boundaries. And from a contextual perspective, which views the nature of reality as change and process, cause and effect does not emerge as a concern until there is consensus that a structure exists to affect another structure. Cause and effect is a secondary concern to the process of consensus in human interaction. Cause-and-effect perspectives are crucial to the definition of paradigms of counseling and psychotherapy.

## Criterion V: Professional Adherents

The world is a competitive place. Not only do people compete as individuals against others who offer similar salable services or products, people often exist in competitive groups, which can be classified as families, societies, cultures, professions, etcetera. In the mental health treatment field, there are large professional disciplines (such as professional counseling, marital and family therapy, psychology, or medicine) and smaller groups existing according to subdisciplinary interests (such as rehabilitation, sex therapy, chemical dependence treatment, or others).

It seems ironic that credentialing in the mental health field has gone ''crazy.'' Today there is a credential for just about any special interest, including certificates for alcoholism counselors, marital and family therapists, vocational evaluators, rehabilitation counselors, mental health counselors, sex counselors, and more. This emphasis on certification is largely a reflection of a society where little trust is placed in strangers, and evidence must be presented that authorities have acted to verify a professional's knowledge and ethics. Regardless, certificates serve a very useful purpose in identifying individuals who adhere to a body of knowledge and professional ethical standards. In this way, they help to delineate paradigms of counseling and psychotherapy, since distinct theoretical and philosophical assumptions may be at the root of a certificated specialty. And it is those special cases where certificated specialties have a foundation on a distinct body of knowledge that this discussion will focus.

Not all certificated groups are theoretically and philosophically distinct. Some certificated groups, however, clearly have as a foundation a unique framework for viewing human problems. Three human service professional groups appear to exemplify how certificated groups correspond to distinct bodies of knowledge. Those three groups are: (a) *psychiatrists,* certified through the American Board of Psychiatry and Neurology; (b) *psychologists,* certified through the American Board of Professional Psychology; (c) *marital and family therapists,* certified as clinical members of the

American Association for Marriage and Family Therapy. A fourth group, *counselors,* certified by the National Board of Certified Counselors, will be defined as potentially associated with the contextual paradigm. These groups, and the requirements for certification of each profession, help to define the boundaries of paradigms of counseling and psychotherapy,

## Criterion VI: Therapies as Subcategories

As was discussed in chapter 1, theories or counseling and psychotherapy may be considered distinct from paradigms of counseling and psychotherapy. In fact, there may be, and usually are, a number of theories of counseling and psychotherapy that can come under a larger counseling paradigm's aegis. As has been described, certain individually oriented psychotherapies can be classified under the heading of the psychological paradigm. Likewise, the systemic-relational paradigm is associated with specialized relational approaches in marital and family therapy. Both the psychological and systemic-relational paradigms offer many therapeutic options to clinicians. Within the organic-medical paradigm, there appears to be less flexibility for nonmedical practitioners (the target audience for this book); medical dictates prescribe primarily medical actions. Only one organic-medical therapeutic approach, Psychiatric Case Management, will be presented in this text, since it is the mainstay approach used by nonmedical practitioners working in medical contexts. The contextual paradigm, being propositional, is also not associated with a number of therapeutic approaches. Only one propositional therapeutic approach will be offered. All in all, however, paradigms of counseling and psychotherapy translate at the level of practice to a number of possible therapeutic alternatives, and this basic recognition is critical to a definition of a counseling paradigm.

Beyond recognition that paradigms can be associated with a number of theories of counseling and psychotherapy, the relationship between the emergence of therapeutic approaches and the development of paradigms is an issue that needs to be addressed. Historically, the emergence of theories of counseling and psychotherapy has preceded the development of what can be defined as a full-blown paradigm. Freud's (1917/1966) "Psycho-analysis," for example, may well be a milestone therapy in that it diverged from pure biological thinking by recognizing the effect of nonphysical psychological factors on behavior. The revolution in thinking related to emotional disturbance that Freud represents has been unequaled. His work was followed by development of a number of offshoot therapies that maintain the idea that individuals can be helped through face-to-face discussion of: (a) their problems, (b) their histories, and/or (c) their present behaviors. Today, Freudian Psycho-analysis looks more like a psychological theory than a theory deriving from medical practice, even though Freud was a physician.

It may be that certain therapies represent breaks with tradition in a way that they set the stage for further development of a paradigm. Freud's notions broke with pure biological thinking, as he focused on an individual's past and nonphysical constructs such as id, ego, and superego to explain individual behavior. His break with tradition had epistemological consequences (remember, epistemology has to do with what is studied). Freud's focus on the study of the psyche and away from pure study of physiology (or even religion in this case) represented an epistemological break with tradition. Emotional disturbance could now be studied through what a person thinks and feels, at both the conscious and unconscious levels, and this is distinct from believing that emotional disturbance is a biological disease. Freud's Psycho-analysis, therefore, is a foundational therapy in the development of the psychological paradigm.

Therapeutic breaks with tradition preceded the development of the systemic-relational paradigm also. Looking back, one publication stands out as a milestone in the development of the systemic-relational paradigm: Bateson, Jackson, Haley, and Weakland's (1956) article, "Toward a Theory of Schizophrenia." In it the authors defined a *double bind,* a no-win situation in the context of an interpersonal relationship. The authors proposed basic criteria for double binds that they felt put one person in what can be considered a psychological trap. The double bind is significant because it defined a cause of schizophrenia as a relationship—not a defect in the person's biology or psychology. It was a milestone publication, because the authors effectively communicated their hypothesis that "mental" disturbance was basically interpersonal, not literally "mental" in origin. In fact, they defined exactly what they felt was necessary for one person to drive another person crazy!

After the double-bind hypothesis, a number of therapeutic approaches emerged that derived from the thinking of the original group of theoreticians who defined the double bind. For example, Haley (e.g., Haley, 1976) developed his "Strategic" approach to therapy, which makes full use of relational factors in the assessment, conceptualization, and remediation of a problem. Likewise, Jackson and Weakland (1961) extended the double-bind theory to the idea of a therapeutic double bind—a double bind that does not drive one crazy, but instead puts one in a trap so that acceptable behavior is the only option. These are only two of many potential examples of how the double-bind theory translated to revolutionary thinking about therapeutic approaches. In fact, the double-bind theory may be one of a number of factors that has led to the development of the field of marital and family therapy, and certainly, it is an historic milestone in the development of the systemic-relational paradigm.

It is also worth noting that although these milestone theoretical works may be significant to the development of a paradigm of counseling and psychotherapy, it does not logically follow that they represent pure examples of therapy consistent with the new paradigm. In fact, these milestone works can be described by the terms *transitional* or *trans-paradigmatic. A transitional or trans-paradigmatic therapy may have theoretical constructs that are holdovers from the therapeutic traditions with which it breaks.* A classic example of this is the early work of Virginia Satir. Satir's (1967) *Conjoint Family Therapy* proposes that emotional concerns should be addressed in a relationship (e.g., in a conjoint fashion where marital partners, for example, are both seen in therapy together). Obviously, Satir's ideas are systemic-relational; however, her book maintains a clear linkage to the psychological concept of self-esteem. Even though Satir attempts to define self-esteem in relational terms, her work still treats it as if it is a thing unto itself, or in other words, a psychological construct. It was not until her later years that Satir began to move away fully from the concept of self-esteem to a more fully systemic-relational conceptualization of emotional problems. Yet there is no question that her work has a systemic flavor and, retrospectively, even her earliest work is best placed under the rubric of systemic-relational theory.

Given milestone works of paradigmatic significance, later works may be more clearly consonant with the propositions and tenets of a counseling paradigm. For example, the Person-Centered Therapy of Carl Rogers (cf. Rogers, 1951), as it was originally conceived, was less biological in its thinking than Freudian Psycho-analysis. Likewise, Minuchin's (1974) "Structural" family therapy is less psychological or medical than milestone works within the systemic-relational paradigm. These works are less transitional and are much more aligned with a purer conception of a counseling paradigm. They are paradigm-specific approaches.

In the end, a number of therapies or theories can be associated with a counseling paradigm. And a true paradigm will have the potential to spawn therapy offspring as its propositions and tenets are dissected, refined, and extended into practical applications.

In summary, these six combined criteria, first stated and then more thoroughly defined in the previous sections, constitute the definition of a counseling paradigm. The next section will discuss differences between counseling paradigms and Kuhn's (1970) conception of "scientific paradigms."

## Comparing Scientific and Counseling Paradigms

There are some noteworthy differences between scientific paradigms as proposed by Kuhn (1970) and paradigms of counseling and psychotherapy as proposed in this chapter.

First, the emergence of a new paradigm of counseling and psychotherapy results less from scientific anomaly than is the case for scientific paradigms. Scientific paradigms revolve around "normal science," a kind of equilibrium that is a sensitive balance of professional scientific activity. And when certain novelties arise in research data that are not logical within the normal science framework, they take the form of anomalies—inexplicable findings that challenge the basic premises of the paradigm. In the mature sciences, anomalies appear to be cold, hard, and unresolvable. They are the instigators of scientific revolution. On the other hand, the emergence of paradigms of counseling and psychotherapy is much more a political issue. Although there may be anomalous empirical data, such data alone is not enough to set the stage for paradigm shift. Instead, such data must have professional and political consequences for the mental health enterprise. In fact, the data need not be empirical at all (although empirical data may be more influential); the data may be observational or anecdotal. Some classic examples of this are: (a) the emergence of the psychological paradigm out of the psychoanalytic intuitions of Freud; (b) the emergence of the systemic-relational paradigm out of observations of the effect of relationships on mental health; and (c) the emergence of the contextual paradigm out of the feminist critique of social systems theory. Although scientific, empirical anomaly is an influential factor in the emergence of counseling paradigms, *it is not a necessary factor,* as is the case with scientific paradigms. The dissociation of a group of mental health professionals from an existing paradigm is primarily a political act, and such a dissociation is foundational to the emergence of a counseling paradigm.

Second, where scientific anomaly leads scientists to the laboratory, anomaly in the mental health field leads practitioners to political agitation. The political agitation first occurs within existing professions, as new ideas are developed to account for the anomalous data. Later, political agitation occurs outside the professions, as the consequences of a new way of thinking have implications for the development or maturation of a new or existing professional discipline in mental health services.

Third, scientific paradigms, unlike counseling paradigms, rarely coexist side by side as valid positions. With paradigms of counseling and psychotherapy, one can find viable groups of adherents proporting paradigm-relevant issues that seem at times to be ascending to predominance, at other times to be descending and in retreat, but nonetheless viable. It is this waxing and waning of interests in paradigmatic proposi-tions that is characteristic of paradigms in counseling and psychotherapy but unusual from a scientific paradigm standpoint. From a scientific paradigm standpoint, para-digms are displaced through "revolutions," according to Kuhn (1970). Regarding scientific revolutions, Kuhn (1970) stated:

> *Each of them necessitated the community's rejection of one time-honored scientific theory in favor of another incompatible with it. Each produced a consequent shift in the problems available for scientific scrutiny and in the standards by which the profession determined what should count as an admissible problem or as a legitimate problem-solution. And each transformed the scientific imagination in ways that we shall ultimately need to describe as a transformation of the world within which scientific work was done. Such changes, together with the controversies that almost always accompany them, are the defining charac-teristics of scientific revolutions. (p. 6)*

Where scientific paradigms may be viewed as resulting from revolutions, paradigms of counseling and psychotherapy may be viewed as resulting from *dissociations*—that is—one paradigm is spawned from another, but without sounding the death knell of the established paradigm. Counseling paradigms coexist and continue to compete.

Fourth, where scientific paradigms compete and are tested against each other, they are also tested against an objective world. As Kuhn (1970) put it, a scientific paradigm is simultaneously tested against another paradigm and against "nature" (p. 77). Since paradigms in counseling and psychotherapy derive from a contextualist position of reality (nonabsolute at the level of practice), it is context that is relevant in competitive tests of counseling paradigms, not nature as an objective reality. In a study of one paradigm against another, researchers cannot claim they have found *the truth;* rather, they can only claim that they have found *a truth.* Whereas scientific paradigms are relative to each other and to "nature," counseling paradigms are relative to each other and to experimental context.

## Chapter Conclusion

This chapter has served to present the criteria for the definition of a paradigm of counseling and psychotherapy. Six criteria were listed. Each criterion was expanded upon to help validate its use in differentiating mental health services. The six criteria, in combination, represent the operational guidelines for determining counseling paradigms. Further, the concept of paradigm in counseling and psychotherapy was distinguished from the concept of scientific paradigm, so as to allow critical readers a framework for further study and comparison. At this juncture, the discussion will proceed to a discussion of the first paradigm of counseling and psychotherapy—the organic-medical paradigm.

# References

Anderson, C. M. , Reiss, D. J. , & Hogarty, G. E. (1986). *Schizophrenia in the family: A practitioner's guide to psychoeducation and management*. New York: Guilford.

Bateson, G. (1972a). Conscious purpose versus nature. In G. Bateson (Ed.), *Steps to an ecology of mind* (pp. 426–439). New York: Ballantine. (Original work published in 1968).

Bateson, G. (1972b). Double bind, 1969. In G. Bateson (Ed.), *Steps to an ecology of mind* (pp. 271–278). New York: Ballantine. (Original work published in 1969).

Bateson, G. (1972c). *Steps to an ecology of mind*. New York: Ballantine.

Bateson, G., Jackson, D. D., Haley, J., & Weakland, J. (1956). Toward a theory of schizophrenia. *Behavioral Science, 1*, 251–264.

Becvar, D. S., & Becvar, R. J. (1988). *Family therapy: A systemic integration*. Boston: Allyn & Bacon.

Bertalanffy, L. von. (1952). *Problems in life*. London: C. A. Watts.

Bertalanffy, L. von. (1968). *General systems theory*. New York: George Braziller.

Cottone, R. R. (1989). Defining the psychomedical and systemic paradigms in marital and family therapy. *Journal of Marital and Family Therapy, 15*, 225–235.

Dell, P. F. (1982). Beyond homeostasis: Toward a concept of coherence. *Family Process, 21*, 21–41.

Dell, P. F. (1985). Understanding Bateson and Maturana: Toward a biological foundation for the social sciences. *Journal of Marital and Family Therapy, 11*, 1–20.

Ellis, A. (1962). *Reason and emotion in psychotherapy*. Secaucus, NJ: Lyle Stuart.

Freud, S. (1966). *Introductory lectures on Psycho-analysis*. New York: W. W. Norton. (Original work published in 1917).

Haley, J. (1976). *Problem-solving therapy*. New York: Harper & Row.

Held, B. S., & Pols, E. (1985). The confusion about epistemology and 'epistemology'—and what to do about it. *Family Process, 24*, 509–521.

Jackson, D. D., & Weakland, J. H. (1961). Conjoint family therapy: Some considerations on theory, technique, and results. *Psychiatry, 24* (Suppl. No. 2), 30–45.

Kuhn, T. S. (1970). *The structure of scientific revolutions*, (2nd Ed.). Chicago: University of Chicago Press.

Maturana, H. R. (1978). Biology of language: The epistemology of reality. In G. A. Miller & E. Lenneberg (Eds.), *Psychology and biology of language and thought* (pp. 27–63). New York: Academic Press.

Maturana, H. R. (1980). Biology of cognition. In H. R. Maturana & F. J. Varela (Eds. ), *Autopoiesis and cognition: The realization of the living* (pp. 1–58). Boston: D. Reidel. (Original work published in 1970)

McGuire, W. J. (1986). A perspectivist looks at contextualism and the future of behavioral science. In R. Rosnow & M. Georgoudi (Eds.), *Contextualism and understanding in behavioral science* (pp. 271–301). New York: Praeger.

McGuirk, J. G., Friedlander, M. L., & Blocher, D. H. (1987). Systemic and nonsystemic diagnostic processes: An empirical comparison. *Journal of Marital and Family Therapy, 13,* 69–76.

Minuchin, S. (1974). *Families and family therapy.* Cambridge, MA: Harvard University Press.

Perls, F. (1969). *Gestalt therapy verbatim.* Moab, UT: Real People Press.

Rogers, C. R. (1951). *Client-centered therapy.* Boston: Houghton Mifflin.

Satir, V. (1967). *Conjoint family therapy.* Palo Alto, CA: Science and Behavior Books.

Taggart, M. (1989). Paradigmatic play-offs and the search for market share. *Journal of Marital and Family Therapy, 15,* 237–242.

Turner, J. H. (1986). *The structure of sociological theory* (4th ed.). Chicago: Dorsey Press.

Wiener, N. (1950). *The human use of human beings: Cybernetics and society.* Boston: Houghton Mifflin.

# PART TWO
# The Organic-Medical Paradigm

# 3

# The Organic-Medical Paradigm

This chapter will present the first of four paradigms of counseling and psychotherapy. As will be observed, the organic-medical paradigm, as the first paradigm discussed in this book, reflects the type of practice that historically has emerged as one of the first types of treatment for mental disorders. Before the time of Freud, maladaptive behavior was viewed as something evil, devilish, or associated with witchcraft or black magic. As medicine progressed to the extent that medical autopsy and medical pathology became accepted practices, physical studies began to reveal that in some cases of severe behavioral disturbance, biological/organic cause was at the root. For example, "lesions on" or "tumors in" the brain were discovered as associated with severe psychopathological behavior. The link to organic etiology, which was established as the earliest scientific explanation for severe emotional disturbance, is today alive and well in the practice of medicine. In fact, it may be experiencing a renaissance of sorts, as medical research has become more sophisticated and able to produce significant findings supporting organic hypotheses of mental disorder. Physicians, especially psychiatrists, rightfully claim that they are best educated to diagnose and to treat disorders linked to organic cause, and psychiatrists have been quite vocal and even aggressive in expressing this claim, especially when challenged by the psychology profession, which recently has been encroaching psychiatry's turf. In a sense, the challenge of psychology has brought psychiatry back to its medical roots. Due to its historical significance, the organic-medical paradigm will be the first presented paradigm of counseling and psychotherapy in this text.

It should be understood, however, that although the organic-medical paradigm is closely linked to the medical profession, such linkage is not equivalent to equating the organic-medical paradigm with the medical specialty of psychiatry. In fact, there may be many psychologists, mental health counselors, marital and family therapists, psychiatric nurses, or social workers who closely subscribe to organic-medical thinking. These nonmedical practitioners may work closely with medical professionals; the nonmedical practitioners may assist in the medical enterprise, especially diagnostically and through management of treatments adjunctive to medical treatment. Conversely there are many psychiatrists who have abandoned a purist organic-medical perspective, choosing instead to move toward a nonorganic explanation of emotional disturbance, and consequently, a more psychological, systemic-relational, or contextual perspective of treatment. The important point to remember, in this regard, is that the organic-medical paradigm is closely, historically aligned with the medical profession, but, in practice, that alignment may not hold true. The organic-medical paradigm, as defined in the following pages, may be practiced, to some degree, by any qualified mental health professional.

## Historical Overview

### General Discussion of the "Medical Model"

Nathan and Harris (1980) in their text, *Psychopathology and Society,* defined the "organic-medical model of psychopathology." They stated: "The medical model of mental illness implies (1) an organic cause, (2) certain assumptions about diagnostic methods, and (3) a certain approach to treatment" (p. 9). The authors went on to say that an underlying pathological condition is assumed to be at the root of mental disorders. They discussed disorders that have been linked to genetics or metabolic theories, including schizophrenia and manic-depressive illness (bipolar disorder). To date, no clear-cut organic etiological condition has been directly defined as causative of these disorders (although genetic researchers are hinting that they are close to identifying chromosomal correlates to schizophrenia). Regardless, the organic-medical model described by Nathan and Harris has diagnostic and treatment concomitants. For example, diagnostically speaking, looking for signs and symptoms of a disorder, and analyzing their frequency, intensity, and duration, are major means of assessing the presence of a problem of diagnostic significance. In fact, one of the main implications of the medical model is that emotional problems are best understood by classifying them into syndromes (Blaney, 1975). Blaney, (1975) speaking of the medical model in psychiatry, stated, "The best way to understand psychiatric symptoms is by ordering them into syndromes. In this case, the analogy says that the classificatory strategies proven effective with physical disorders will also constitute the most heuristic way to devise a lexicon to describe mental conditions" (p. 911). In this sense, what maladaptive behaviors a mental health professional sees can be viewed as manifestations of an underlying biological or biochemical problem.

Related to treatment, medical practice predominates also. Nathan and Harris (1980) stated, "The medical model for psychological *treatment* follow treatment patterns in physical medicine, where the doctor aims to destroy the underlying pathological agent" (p. 10). Medically oriented practitioners may prescribe or seek medication, electroconvulsive therapy (ECT), vitamin or mineral treatments, or even surgery for their patients in order to ameliorate a patient's maladaptive behaviors or the underlying physical correlates to the disorder. In most cases, these treatments must be prescribed by medical practitioners (doctors of medicine or osteopathy). But in all cases, medically oriented mental health practitioners give credence to the idea that physical causes are at the root of mental disorder.

Of course there are positive and negative consequences associated with such a strict organic model of mental disorder. One of the consequences in favor of the patient is the issue of behavioral responsibility. By a strict organic perspective, cause is out of the hands of the patient, unless the person has actively acted to affect his physiological response (e.g., through drug abuse). Blaney (1975) stated while discussing the medical model related to personal responsibility, "Just as an epileptic is not to blame for having knocked over a vase during a seizure, a 'mentally ill' person is not responsible for his aberrant thoughts, feelings, or behaviors; they should be viewed as exogenous to his free will" (p. 911). On the negative side, the labels consistent with medical taxonomy may be more damaging than the disorders themselves for some individuals. Labels have a way of affecting other people's responses to individuals carrying such labels. There is no question that a person would respond quite differently to an unkempt person labeled a "genius" versus an unkempt person labeled a "schizophrenic." Labels affect a person's expectations about behaviors, and subsequently, they can have an effect on the behaviors of the person with the expectancy (Rosenthal, 1968). More ominously, it is possible that a label may derive more from the context of labeling than from any factor internal to the labeled individual. Rosenhan (1973) carried out a classic experiment involving confederates (experimental volunteers acting a role) who went to psychiatric institutions complaining only of hearing a voice (a common experience), and almost across the board these "normal" individuals were admitted with a diagnosis of psychosis and kept in the hospital for extended observation. The evidence shows that many factors play into the role of diagnosis, and some of these factors are not necessarily consistent with organic-medical ideals.

## The Emergence of Psychiatry as a Medical Specialty

Before Freud, any problems observed in a patient were understood either as manifestations of the unobservable physical realm or from the unexplainable religious or mystical realm (Conrad & Schneider, 1985). Freud, as the father of psychiatry, bridged the gap, attempting to demonstrate the biological linkage of a concept he developed—the "psyche," or mind. Although his position wavered in written correspondence to his associates, in the end Freud came down hard on the side of defining psychiatry as a science, and he was intent on defining disorders of the mind as "diseases." As Szasz (1974) stated: "I maintain . . . that Freud did not *discover* that hysteria was a mental illness. He merely asserted and advocated that so-called hysterics be *declared* ill" (p. 37). Ironically, at the same time Freud moved medicine out of the realm of the purely physical (and into the realm of the psychological), his ideas were foundational to the *medical* specialty of psychiatry, which today has at least one branch, biological psychiatry, maintaining the position that biological factors are the root causes of mental disturbances. Although Freud's (1917/1966) "Psycho-analysis," by today's standards is more closely aligned with the psychological paradigm as defined in this text, Freud can also be viewed as the father of a professional discipline with some practitioners taking an extreme physical and nonpsychological view of mental disturbance.

However, the actual roots of modern-day biological psychiatry can be traced to several decades before Freud's works in the nineteenth-century works of Emil Kraepelin and Eugen Bleuler. Conrad and Schneider (1985) stated:

> With the publication of Psychiatrie, *which went through several revisions between 1883 and 1913, Kraepelin changed the classification system of mental illness. His descriptions of the symptom complexes of dementia praecox and manic-depressive psychosis, the two major categories of mental disorder, are still used today. He believed that dementia praecox (literally, early senility) was characterized by progressive deterioration and that manic depression (severe uncontrollable mood swings) tended to improve and recur spontaneously. Kraepelin, fully committed to the medical model, proposed only organic etiologies for mental disorders and viewed them as physical diseases. Eugen Bleuler noted that all dementia patients do not inevitably degenerate, and in 1911 he created a modified and expanded category he called* schizophrenia. *The great concern for classification of mental illness characterizes the development of psychiatry. (p. 53)*

Other organicists followed. Even with the psychologization of mental illness through the works of Freud, an underlying movement in psychiatry maintained an organic/biogenic position. For example, in 1938, Kallman published *The Genetics of Schizophrenia,* which was a study of families of individuals with schizophrenia. Kallman showed that closeness of kinship was related to the likelihood of developing schizophrenia. He supported his original ideas with additional studies (Kallman, 1946), which showed higher concordance rates among identical than fraternal twins, even when reared apart. He developed a genetic theory of schizophrenia based on his findings. Although his research has been criticized on methodological grounds, independent research has tended to support his original general conclusions. Today, it is widely accepted that the more severe mental disorders, such as schizophrenia or bipolar disorder (manic-depressive illness), are biologically and genetically predisposed. Today, the biological psychiatry movement is flourishing, especially with advances in genetic research.

The extreme physical or biological view of mental disorder is embodied in the propositions of the organic-medical paradigm of counseling and psychotherapy, which follow.

## Propositions

The propositions of the organic-medical paradigm of counseling and psychotherapy are as follows:

1. The focus is always on the individual.

2. Individuals can be, and must be, assessed. It is assumed that an individual's behavior is biologically and physically linked. It is also assumed that people have inherited traits or conditions that endure and represent predispositions to act.

3. Personality predispositions (traits or conditions), when extreme, may be classified or diagnosed based on symptoms (disorder-consistent behaviors) that vary in frequency, intensity, and duration.

4. Symptoms manifested historically, or during a diagnostic interview, are of diagnostic significance.

5. Causes can be directly defined. If a cause is not known, it is assumed that science has not determined the cause but will determine the cause in the future.

6. Symptoms and/or conditions can be isolated for treatment, with an expert authority acting to affect the status of the individual. The therapeutic act is primarily targeted toward biology, biochemistry, or physiology.

7. Professional expertise can be gained only within the framework of training based upon the scientific method. Science defines what is right or wrong, acceptable or unacceptable. Experts must be thoroughly screened for knowledge and acceptable training in their science. Experts are given legal authority to diagnose and to treat individual psychopathology. Professionals are defined as: (a) expert authorities; and (b) authorities in professional relationships with patients.

8. Individuals are responsible only to the degree that they possess rationality, which derives from their physical makeup. If not responsible, professional expert authorities take responsibility for decisions related to the well-being of patients according to applicable laws and statutes.

9. If responsible, then patients are culpable, not only for their acts, but also for following therapeutic directives, and ultimately, for the success of their treatments.

10. Treatment naturally follows diagnosis. Failure, therefore, results from misdiagnosis, mistreatment, or failure of responsible patients to follow therapeutic directives.

## Tenets of Practice

The tenets of the organic-medical paradigm of counseling and psychotherapy are as follows:

1. Diagnosis is founded on the assumption that a patient's problem is internally based. It is assumed that the internal factors associated with a disorder can be made to manifest themselves in behavior in a controlled diagnostic setting (with the diagnostician using a standard interview format).

2. The individual and his or her diagnosed disorder are the targets of treatment.

3. Treatment is focused on affecting the individual, primarily internally, through medical means (e.g., medication). Treatment may also involve interventions to control extraneous factors (internal or external) that may trigger unwanted physiological responses.

4. Counseling tends to be *educational*. The patient must be educated about his or her disorder and the functional limits that derive from the disorder. Counseling may

also focus on *problem solving,* in order to resolve difficulties that arise in the patient's personal adjustment. Problem solving may control stressors and triggers of unwanted responses that otherwise might sabotage treatment. Finally, counseling is used to assist in the *monitoring of behavior,* especially the symptoms and signs of disorder.

**5.** Lessening or removal of a client's symptoms may be considered a "success" treatment-wise, especially for the more severe mental disorders. The effectiveness of a treatment is often measured by comparative relapse rates across different types of organic-medical treatments. The ideal outcome of organic-medical treatment, however, is reintegration of the disabled person into a meaningful and fulfilling societal role.

**6.** The physician and the counselor (sometimes the same person) are viewed as professional authorities on matters that concern patients. However, case managing professionals are bound by professional ethical standards that place the interests of the patient above all else.

## Epistemological and Ontological Definitions

The organic-medical paradigm directs researchers to study the biological-physical nature of human beings as related to aberrant behavior. The focus, or course, is on the individual, but it is inside of the individual that is the locus of pathology. External factors can only perturb the basic physical structure that is genetically created. External stimulation or deprivation then acts only physically to alter the structure that is present through the biological developmental process. In the end, it is the structure and makeup of the organism that causes behavior.

Consequently, scientists who study behavioral problems from an organic-medical perspective will ask questions that relate to genetics (both at the level of human reproduction and at the level of microgenetic issues, such as DNA analysis), neurological makeup (including nervous cell structure), biochemical factors in neuropsychiatric function (such as the study of neurotransmitters), and developmental issues (such as actuarial data of those affected with disorders and the demographics of affected individuals) all of which can add to a literature that helps to explain how physical factors affect human behavior. The issue is: What is *inside* individuals that makes them manifest specified symptoms in certain situations?

Ontologically, the organic-medical model stems from the basic belief that physical structures, tangible and reducible, exist as entities that represent what is real. This means that humans as reducible but independent entities, can be dissected (literally) and reduced to the level of organic analysis, and that in the final analysis, some factor or thing (such as a lesion, a chemical imbalance, a defective gene) will prove to be definitive of behavioral syndromes.

## Cause and Effect

Cause and effect is primarily *linear* from an organic-medical perspective. This means that once a medical cause is defined, it will logically follow that there will be a direct result in behavior. To a large degree, the behavioral effect may be viewed as predictable based on the defect/difference in physical structure of the misbehaving individual. For instance, it has been hypothesized that there will be a chromosomal aberration found to account for the syndrome of behavior described by the term *schizophrenia,* and that once the genetic defect is located, it will be predictive of the manifestation of the disease in individuals perturbed in such a way as to facilitate a psychotic breakdown. Although some may say that the environment has an interacting effect on the emergence of disorder, a pure organic-medical theorist would redefine the interaction effect as nothing but a trigger to set off what is programmed to occur. From a pure organic-medical perspective, the focus is clearly on what happens inside the individual, as opposed to what occurs outside the individual.

## Professional Adherents

The one group that most exemplifies the medical model in mental health service is the profession of psychiatry. The credential most valued by psychiatrists is the diplomate in psychiatry and neurology from the American Board of Psychiatry and Neurology, Inc. (ABPN). The ABPN is a freestanding nonprofit organization founded in 1934 by committees from several professional medical organizations, including the American Psychiatric Association, the American Neurological Association, and the Section on Nervous and Mental Diseases of the American Medical Association. Among the goals of the ABPN listed in its mission statement in its brochure is the following one: ''[To] describe, in terms of knowledge and skills, a physician-specialist with expertise in evaluation, diagnosis and treatment of patients with psychiatric and/or neurological disorders, or who require psychiatric and/or neurological assessment.''

The 1988 requirements of the ABPN for certification (diplomate status) are as follows. Applicants must first hold a valid license to practice medicine or osteopathy. They must also complete the ABPN's specialized training in psychiatry, neurology, or neurology with special qualification in child neurology. Essentially, this specialized training encompasses a year's postgraduate training usually in general medicine (an internship) plus at least three years in residency training approved as a psychiatric residency by the ABPN. Candidates for certification must also pass an examination.

The examination in psychiatry has a neurology component, just as the neurology examination has a psychiatry component. As with the organization of the ABPN, this dual specialty examination reflects the perceived overlap in the specialties.

The ABPN uses the *Diagnostic and Statistical Manual of Mental Disorders, Third Edition, Revised* (American Psychiatric Association, 1987) as its primary authority in psychiatric diagnostic nomenclature. Candidates must pass a written examination. Upon passing the written exam, candidates must sit for an oral examination. Passing both examinations is required to be awarded a certificate (a diplomate in psychiatry).

As is obvious, becoming a psychiatrist is not an easy task. One must become a physician (an eight-year post-high-school commitment). Then one year of internship is required. Then a three-year residency is required. This minimum allows for the specialty practice of psychiatry. But to be recognized as a board-certified specialist, a psychiatrist must go through the examinations required by the ABPN. Since many candidates for diplomate status fail the examinations, it may take a psychiatrist upwards of seven or eight years to become certified after having completed formal training.

Of course, the medical training of the psychiatrist distinguishes him or her from professionals in other mental health professions. Medical training is necessary for medical diagnostics or biologically/chemically based treatments. Such diagnostic and treatment methods are clearly founded in the sciences, which are required as training at the premedical coursework level (premedical students must take courses in biology, chemistry, and physics). The professional training of psychiatrists, therefore, is best suited for the provision of the full range of diagnostic and treatment methods consistent with the organic-medical paradigm.

## Therapies as Subcategories

As was described in chapter 2, paradigms have the potential to have several subcategories of treatments that exemplify paradigm propositions. In this case, an example therapy will be offered in the chapter that follows: Psychiatric Case Management. Psychiatric Case Management is an application of organic-medical propositions to the treatment of individuals with diagnosed mental disorders. It is one of many approaches to treatment consistent with organic-medical propositions; however, it is one of the few organic-medical approaches that can be accomplished by nonmedical therapists. Other approaches, such as a combination of electroconvulsive therapy and medication, will not be presented in this text due their principally medical means of intervention. Since the primary target audience of this text is composed of nonmedical practitioners, Psychiatric Case Management will be the only purely organic medical approach presented. However, readers are referred to a later section of this text on Cross-paradigm issues where they will find (in chapter 20) Carol Anderson's ''Psychoeducational Treatment of Patients with Schizophrenia,'' which is a cross between organic-medical and systemic-relational propositions and tenets.

## Chapter Conclusion

This chapter has served to introduce the first paradigm of counseling and psychotherapy. The propositions and tenets of the organic-medical paradigm were listed. Organic-medical epistemological, ontological, and causative issues were discussed. The profession of psychiatry, a medical specialty, was defined as best suited by training to use organic-medical means of diagnosis and treatment. A subcategory of treatment was described. The following chapter will present a therapeutic approach consistent with organic-medical propositions.

# References

American Psychiatric Association. (1987). *Diagnostic and statistical manual of mental disorders (3rd ed. rev.)* Washington, DC: American Psychiatric Association.

Blaney, P. H. (1975). Implications of the medical model and its alternatives. *American Journal of Psychiatry, 132*(9), 911–914.

Conrad, P., & Schneider, J. W. (1985). *Deviance and medicalization.* Columbus, OH: Merrill.

Freud, S. (1966). *Introductory lectures in psycho-analysis.* New York: W. W. Norton. (Original work published in 1917)

Kallman, F. J. (1938). *The genetics of schizophrenia.* New York: Augustine.

Kallman, F. J. (1946). The genetic theory of schizophrenia: An analysis of 691 schizophrenic twin index families. *American Journal of Psychiatry, 103,* 309–322.

Nathan, P. E., & Harris, S. L. (1980). *Psychopathology and society* (2nd ed.). New York: McGraw-Hill.

Reid, W. H. (1983). *Treatment of the DSM-III psychiatric disorders.* New York: Brunner/Mazel.

Rosenhan, D. L. (1973). On being sane in insane places. *Science, 179,* 250–258.

Rosenthal, R. (1968). Self-fulfilling prophecy. *Psychology Today, 2,* 44–51.

Szasz, T. S. (1974). *The myth of mental illness.* New York: Harper & Row.

# 4

# Psychiatric Case Management:
## An Organic-Medical Therapy Focusing on Individuals

AS MENTIONED IN chapter 3, psychiatrists are primarily suited to working within the boundaries of organic-medical propositions and tenets, but other professionals can be involved in therapeutic approaches aligned with the organic-medical paradigm of counseling and psychotherapy. Psychiatric Case Management, as a counseling approach and as described in this chapter, can be used by psychiatrists. However, it can also be used by psychologists, mental health counselors, marital and family therapists, and other mental health professionals when there is involvement of a physician overseeing medical treatments. However, nonmedical practitioners are limited when serving patients receiving organic-medical treatments. Nonmedical practitioners are limited to noninvasive, nonradioactive, or other nonphysically involved diagnostic techniques. Also, they cannot perform treatments involving medications, electroconvulsive therapy (ECT or electroshock therapy), or other physically or legally restricted treatments. For the most part, however, nonmedical mental health professionals can be actively involved in the diagnostic and treatment processes. The science of psychiatry is not finely developed; by medical standards, psychiatric diagnostic processes are inexact (Woodruff, Goodwin & Guze, 1974). Consequently, once global physical causes can be discounted ("ruled out"), the diagnostic process for any mental health professional is very much the same. Behaviors will be observed in a diagnostic interview situation. The patient's history, family background, medical and psychological record, and other pertinent information will be used. And the diagnosing professional will derive an impression as to the nature of the disorder. The diagnostic classificatory scheme most used in the United States is that of the American Psychiatric Association's (APA, 1987) *Diagnostic and Statistical Manual of Mental Disorders, Third Edition, Revised* (the DSM-IIIR). The DSM-IIIR defines a mental disorder as:

> *A clinically significant behavioral or psychological syndrome or pattern that occurs in a person and that is associated with present distress (a painful symptom) or disability (impairment in one or more important areas of functioning) or with a significantly increased risk of suffering death, pain, disability, or an important loss of freedom. In addition, this syndrome or pattern must not be merely an expectable response to a particular event, e.g., the death of a loved one. Whatever its original cause, it must currently be considered a manifestation of a behavioral, psychological, or biological dysfunction in the person. Neither deviant behavior, e.g., political, religious, or sexual, nor conflicts that are primarily between the individual and society are mental disorders unless the deviance or conflict is a symptom of a dysfunction in the person, as described above. (p. xxii)*

Obviously, an internal perspective of cause is purported. A disorder is viewed as "dysfunction *in* the person" [emphasis added]. Actually, however, the DSM-IIIR is more liberal about defining cause than has been presented in the organic-medical propositions previously listed in chapter 3 (primarily due to the political lobby of psychology which has influenced DSM-IIIR definitions). The DSM-IIIR does allow for "behavioral" or "psychological" factors in the definition of disorder. Comparatively, the organic-medical paradigm and Psychiatric Case Management represent extreme positions, primarily founded on a strict *biological psychiatry* (see Shagass et al., 1986, for an example of empirical studies in this area). Regardless, even assuming a strict biological psychiatry, a thoroughly trained mental health professional should be able to make the important distinctions related to differential diagnosis in a majority of the cases seen in everyday practice, with physicians being consulted when there are signs of organicity, problematic functional diagnoses, or medical treatments needed. Some conditions, such as organic mental disorder (brain dysfunction), will have clear-cut organic etiology. Other mental disorders may not have such clear-cut etiology; however, as discussed in the propositions of the organic-medical paradigm, there is the expectation that science will define the biological/organic causes of a disorder if given enough time and adequate resources.

Probably the most comprehensive and accessible resource on current practices in psychiatry is Kaplan and Sadock's (1989) *Comprehensive Textbook of Psychiatry/V*. This fifth-edition text provides a broad view of psychiatric practice, and it describes many organic-medical diagnostic and treatment approaches. Readers are referred to the Kaplan and Sadock work for in-depth discussions on topics such as medical assessment, psychiatric interviewing, mental status assessment, psychiatric diagnosis, psychiatric report writing, and medication management, many of which will be discussed briefly in this chapter. The Kaplan and Sadock text also describes many commonly used psychosocial treatments, which are more clearly aligned with the other paradigms in this text; they will not be discussed in any systematic way in this chapter.

Because no outstanding contemporary proponent of the organic-medical paradigm has emerged, there is no one proponent of Psychiatric Case Management listed in this chapter. Consequently, no biographical sketch will be included in this chapter, unlike other therapy-specific chapters in this text. Many individuals through the history of psychiatry have contributed to what can be classified as organic-medical Psychiatric Case Management. Most notably, the American physician Benjamin Rush has been defined as a significant figure in the history of psychiatry. This chapter, rather than reflecting one person's theory of counseling, however, is an integration of ideas from theorists, practitioners, and from observations of current psychiatric practices. It is a best attempt to present a contemporary counseling theory consistent with current, individually focused, organic-medical propositions and tenets.

## The Foundational Theory

### The Target of Counseling

The target of psychiatric case management is the individual patient and his or her mental condition. A mental condition is assumed to have a physiological correlate, although the etiologies (clear-cut causative factors) of mental conditions are unknown. Mental health professionals must identify symptoms (expressed by patients) and signs (observed by the diagnostician) consistent with diagnoses of mental disorders. A diagnosis, from a strict organic-medical stance, is identification of a disease. As Woodruff, Goodwin, and Guze (1974) stated:

> When the term "disease" is used, this is what is meant: a disease is a cluster of symptoms and/or signs with a more or less predictable course. Symptoms are what patients tell you; signs are what you see. The cluster may be associated with physical abnormality or may not. The essential point is that it results in consultation with a physician who specializes in recognizing, preventing, and, sometimes, curing diseases.
>
> It is hard for many people to think of psychiatric problems as diseases. For one thing, psychiatric problems usually consist of symptoms—complaints about thoughts and feelings—or behavior disturbing to others. Rarely are there signs—a fever, a rash. Almost never are there laboratory tests to confirm the diagnosis. What people say changes from time to time, as does behavior. It is usually harder to agree about symptoms than about signs. But whatever the psychiatric problems are, they have this in common with "real" diseases—they result in consultation with a physician and are associated with pain, suffering, disability, and death. (pp. x–xi)

Woodruff et al., went on to describe diagnoses as "conventions," useful categorizations, which have explicit definitions and predictable courses. Woodruff and his associates were very empirical in providing a classification schema, including such categories as schizophrenia and affective (mood) disorders within the psychiatric diagnostic realm, but avoiding such classifications as certain personality disorders, which they claimed were studied too little to provide conclusive guidance as to their diagnostic usefulness.

From an organic-medical standpoint, then, an individual's disease is diagnosed according to an accepted psychiatric nosology (classification), and then it is targeted for treatment.

---

**BOX 4-1** ━━━━━━━━━━━━━━━━━━━━━━━━━━━━━━━━━━━━━━━━

## Some Brief Definitions of Psychiatric Terms

**Abstract thinking:** Ability to think in a high-level associative way. To say that an apple and an orange are both fruits is an example of a high-level abstraction. To say that they both can be eaten is an operational similarity and is more concrete than abstract.

**Affect:** Emotional expression associated with environmental stimuli, usually as observed by another person. For instance, smiling when smiled at in an interview is appropriate affect. Showing no emotion when told a funny joke or a sad story is ''flat'' affect. Limited emotional expression is ''blunted'' affect. Demonstrating an unanticipated emotional response is called ''inappropriate'' affect. ''Labile'' affect is quickly changing.

**Axis:** A diagnostic arrangement used to communicate to other professionals the conditions of the patient. Functional and organic mental disorders are listed on Axis I. Developmental and personality disorders are listed on Axis II.

**Blocking:** Referring to halted thought processes; for instance, when one stops a thought in mid-sentence.

**Circumstantial thought:** Speaking in circles, irrelevantly, and coming to a point upon questioning only after much irrelevant speech.

**Clang associations:** Rhyming thoughts or speech.

**Compulsion:** A distressful predisposition to act a certain way. For example, a hand-washing compulsion, where the patient washes his or her hands excessively.

**Content of Thought:** The patient initiated topics of conversation, usually during a diagnostic interview. Delusional, hallucinatory, and obsessional material is considered significant to content of thought.

**Deja vu:** A feeling one has been someplace where one hasn't been.

**Delusion:** A false conclusion. Common delusions are persecutory (''They are trying to hurt me''), paranoid (''They are out to get me''), somatic (''There's something inside of me eating my organs''), of influence (''They are trying to affect my thinking''), of reference (''They are talking about me on TV''), and systematized delusions (which are well-developed and held together by a logical thread).

**Depersonalization:** Losing one's sense of self.

**BOX 4-1**    *Continued*

**Depression:** A low mood.

**Dysthymia:** A pattern of depressions, generally not extreme.

**Echolalia:** Mimicking sounds.

**Echopraxia:** Mimicking motions or postures.

**Elation:** A high emotional feeling, the opposite of depression.

**Euphoria:** Extreme elation.

**Euthymia:** Normal mood.

**Feelings of unreality:** A sense of loss of touch with one's world.

**Flights of ideas:** Pressured speech combined with loose associations.

**Flow of thought:** Whether the person speaks in a way that is spontaneous, smooth, logical, and coherent, without internally produced interruptions, blocking, looseness of associations, circumstantiality, or tangentiality.

**Functional Disorder:** Having to do with one's operation in an environment, as opposed to organic disorders, which relate to one's bodily structure.

**Grandiosity:** A false sense of importance.

**Hallucinations:** False perceptions involving any one or more of the five senses—auditory (hearing), visual (seeing), tactile/kinesthetic (feeling), gustatory (tasting), or olfactory (smelling).

**Histrionic:** Extremely dramatic.

**Hypomanic:** A pattern of elevated mood, bordering on mania.

**Illusion:** A distorted perception.

**Insight:** One's understanding of one's situation.

**Jamais vu:** Feeling one has not been someplace where one has been.

**Judgment:** One's ability to make basic social decisions.

**Loose associations:** A thought sequence where there is little logical thread, which is manifested to the extreme in a word salad (expression of unrelated words in a sequence).

**Mania:** An extreme psychotic euphoria.

**Memory:** Retention of information. Immediate memory involves retention of materials for seconds, short-term memory involves retention for minutes or hours, and long-term memory involves retention for a day or longer.

**Mood:** Emotional state as described by a patient. Usually down (dysthymic), up (euphoric), or normal (euthymic).

**Mute:** Lack of speech.

**Neologisms:** A new word, usually totally newly constructed or a combination of other words. For example, ''nulicious'' combines nutritious and delicious.

*Continued*

**BOX 4-1**    *Continued*

**Neuroleptic drugs:** Powerful antipsychotic medications.

**Neurosis:** A disorder usually causing significant distress to oneself but not to others. It is typically characterized by excess anxiety and other symptoms, such as depression.

**Obsession:** A distressful predisposition to think about something.

**Organic/Organicity:** Having to do with the physical makeup of the body, as opposed to functional concerns, which relate to one's operation in an environment. Organicity is often used to refer to brain damage.

**Orientation:** Being knowledgeable about one's surroundings, specifically related to one's person, place, time, and situation. Oriented times three means oriented to person, place, and time. Oriented times four means oriented to person, place, time, and situation.

**Paranoia:** Extreme suspiciousness or a feeling that someone is out to cause one harm.

**Perseveration:** A recurring thought or action that appears out of the conscious control of the patient and is usually associated with brain damage or organicity.

**Pressured speech:** When one speaks forcefully, as if a thought must be pushed out.

**Prodromal symptoms:** Symptoms that precede a full-blown active phase of a disorder.

**Prognosis:** An educated medical prediction.

**Psychosis:** An invented reality, often manifested by hallucinations, delusions, or operational incoherence.

**Residual symptoms:** Symptoms that follow a full-blown active phase of a disorder.

**Scanning:** Visually hyperactive. Looking around quickly.

**Sign:** An observed behavior or finding that supports a diagnosis.

**Somatization:** Undue focus on body functioning or disorders, often without evidence of organicity.

**Suicidal potential:** The presence of suicidal ideas, plans (how it will occur), and intentions (when it will occur).

**Symptom:** A complaint by a patient of diagnostic significance.

**Tangential thought:** Going off the topic and never answering questions.

**Tardive dyskinesia:** A relatively permanent neurological disorder (brain damage) that results from the use of powerful antipsychotic medications.

**Vigilance:** Overalertness regarding environmental stimuli.

## The Process of Counseling

Psychiatric Case Management often begins once there has been at least a provisional diagnosis and when severe unmanageable symptoms, if present, have been stabilized. Psychiatric Case Management counseling has four purposes: (a) *to ameliorate or reduce any factors (internal or external to the individual) that may stress the individual,* thereby preventing the triggering of maladaptive physiological responses and exacerbation of symptoms; (b) *to educate the patient and/or his or her family about the disorder* and how best to adjust to the disorder; (c) *to monitor the effects of medications* (both main effects and unwanted side-effects); and (d) *to assess the mental status of the individual* to detect and to record the presence of symptoms and signs, which is necessary to analyze the overall effect of treatment and to adjust treatments accordingly.

---

**BOX 4-2** ━━━━━━━━━━━━━━━━━━━━━━━━━━━━━━━━━━━━━━━

### Abbreviated DSM-IIIR Criteria for a Diagnosis of Schizophrenia

The following criteria have been abbreviated from the *Diagnostic and Statistical Manual of Mental Disorder (3rd ed. rev),* published by the American Psychiatric Association (1987).

**Criteria:**
A. The presence of characteristic psychotic symptoms in the active phase of the disorder. One of the following three items must be met:
   1. bizarre delusions;
   2. prominent hallucinations, involving a voice perceived throughout the day for several days, or providing running commentary of actions, or of two or more voices conversing;
   3. two or more of the following;
      (a) delusions;
      (b) prominent and persistent hallucinations;
      (c) incoherence or marked loosening of associations;
      (d) catatonic behavior;
      (e) flat or grossly inappropriate affect.
B. Evidence of deterioration of functioning from a previous level of functioning.
C. Mood disorders must be ruled out. Mood symptoms should be brief compared to other symptoms of schizophrenia.
D. Continuous signs of disturbance for at least six months, with an active phase of disturbance. Prodromal (preceding the active phase) or residual (following the active phase) syndromes are included in the assessment of six months of disturbance.
E. Direct organic factors, such as drugs, cannot be established as factors initiating and maintaining the disturbance.

---

The process of Psychiatric Case Management is an ongoing process of individual counseling and assessment, where the patient meets with a counselor to discuss his or her concerns and present status. Assessment occurs continually through the process of counseling, but it is useful and recommended that formal mental status assessments should be accomplished and recorded at least on a monthly basis during outpatient (nonhospital) treatments. Educational interventions with the patient and with other involved individuals should occur soon after diagnosis. For hospitalized patients, educational interventions should occur before discharge.

## Counselor Role

The counselor role in Psychiatric Case Management is threefold: a counselor must be a monitor, educator, and problem solver. *As a monitor,* the counselor must be expert at identifying symptoms and signs consistent with a mental disorder. He or she must also be able to recognize signs that are *prodromal* (typically preceding) or *residual* (typically following) acute exacerbations of a mental disorder. An *acute exacerbation* is a short-term worsening of symptoms, and it is during exacerbations that symptoms and signs more clearly meet diagnostic criteria. The counselor must also be knowledgeable about medications and medication interactions in order to identify main (wanted) effects and unwanted side-effects of the medications and to understand the signs of appropriate or inappropriate medication.

*As an educator,* the counselor must be able to teach clients and other significant individuals in the patient's life about the disorder and its clinical course. Manifestations of the disease must be communicated in a way that is helpful, and not frightening, to patients and their families. The latest research findings on the disorder should be communicated, and the prognosis (a prediction of the probable course and outcome of the disease) must be presented in an understandable way. The counselor must educate the patient and others about the importance of medical treatment compliance, and about the likelihood of future exacerbations.

*As a problem solver,* the counselor must be prepared to direct the patient when problems arise, to assist the patient in the everyday management of stressors. Internal and external stressors must be managed. For example, the tendency of depressive patients to catastrophize must be monitored, and the counselor must be directive about solving problems associated with a tendency to interpret concerns out of proportion. External factors, such as employment concerns, the drug culture, family stressors, etcetera, must be understood and addressed appropriately in counseling. The counselor must be willing and able to assist patients to develop reasonable solutions to the everyday problems associated with life with a mental disorder.

## Goals of Counseling and Ideal Outcomes

The primary goal of counseling is the amelioration or control of symptoms and/or signs of disorder. A secondary goal is to assist patients to make realistic decisions related to life-styles and goals, in order for them to accommodate their conditions. It is understood that many mental disorders will have lifetime consequences, and it is imperative that patients understand and adjust to their disorders. Just as a diabetic must make adjustments in his or her life according to the dictates of diabetic treatment, so too, must the individual with a mental disorder make adjustments to his or her disability. Ideally, symptoms and signs will remit through treatment, and, through prudent follow-up care and life-style adjustments, there will be no recurrence of acute symptoms.

## General Procedures

### Assessment

Although seemingly simplistic, the diagnostic process in psychiatry is a much more complicated matter than matching a patient's symptoms to a diagnostic category. The *DSM-IIIR* (APA, 1987) has "decision trees for differential diagnosis" that provide the recommended sequence for determining the specific disorder under study. These decision trees for the major mental disorders are useful in defining the process of diagnosis according to psychiatric dictates. The process is quite complex and involves an analysis of the person's family background (which may have genetic as well as social/economic implications), levels of education and intelligence, environment factors (present and past, so that environmental triggers may be identified), and other factors.

The psychiatric examination is characterized by a thorough interview with a specialized examination of the person's mental status and symptomatology. The diagnostic interview will provide in-depth questioning about such matters as the claimant's medical and psychiatric history, family history (medically and otherwise), educational background, vocational history, symptom history (including the frequency, intensity, and duration of symptoms or complaints), social history, military experience, drug or alcohol abuse history, and other relevant historical matters. Once a thorough background has been accomplished, a physician may physically examine the patient, most usually performing a thorough neurological examination, to rule out (discount) neurological disorder. Then a complete mental status examination will be accomplished in the physician's office. The mental status examination will explore, in an objectified way, the patient's general behavior (e.g., dress, grooming, psychomotor activity), content of thought, flow of thought, affect (the evaluator's assessment of mood within the interview context), mood (the patient's assessment of his or her recent mood), neuroadaptive functioning and daily activities (such as sleep, sex, self-care, etc.), memory, concentration, ability to abstract, the patient's insight into his or her problems, basic social judgment, and orientation to person, place, time, and situation. It is the manifestation of symptoms or signs during the mental status examination that is the most trustworthy interview-related diagnostic indicator. For example, if a patient of average intelligence is unable to subtract 3's sequentially starting from 20, then this may be viewed as a sign of poor concentration. Additionally, if the claimant describes a dysphoric mood, appears to have a depressed or flattened affect to the evaluator, shows signs of sleep and appetite disturbance, shows retarded psychomotor activity, and continually complains about not being able to get motivated, then these factors should lead to consideration of a mood disturbance (e.g., depression). On the other hand, if the patient complains of dysphoric mood, but does not demonstrate consistent behaviors during the mental status examination, then the evaluator must question either the nature and severity of the concern *or* the credibility of the complainant. There may be no severe mental impairment or distress, or there may be other signs or symptoms that will take the diagnostic process another direction decisionally. Regardless, the mental status examination is an important tool in the medical diagnostic process.

Once an assessment has been made, the evaluator must weigh the data and form some impression about the nature of the disorder. The *DSM-IIIR* (APA, 1987) provides guidance for how this takes place, and beyond decisional rules, it provides a format for reporting the impression. The *DSM-IIIR* has a five-axis system of diagnosis. An axis is a diagnostic structural arrangement, which is a means of standardizing how diagnoses are communicated. There are two basic axes that can be used by *all* qualified mental health professionals licensed to diagnose mental disorders: Axis I for clinical syndromes, and Axis II for developmental disorders and personality disorders. (The three other axes will not be discussed further in this text. Interested individuals should seek guidance from the *DSM-IIIR* for a complete discussion of the five-axis system.) Conditions such as schizophrenia, bipolar disorder, major depression, etcetera, are aligned on Axis I. Conditions such as antisocial personality disorder, pervasive developmental disorder, etcetera, are arranged on Axis II. An example of the format for recording such impressions is given in the *DSM-IIIR* as follows:

> *Axis I:*   *296.23*   *Major Depression, Single Episode, Severe without Psychotic Features.*
> *303.90*   *Alcohol Dependence.*
> *Axis II:*   *301.60*   *Dependent Personality Disorder (Provisional, rule out Borderline Personality Disorder).*

The numbers assigned to each diagnosis constitute the *DSM-IIIR* ''codes'' for classification; they are a shorthand summation of disorders. In many cases when, for instance, a client should not know a diagnosis for fear of misunderstanding it, and when that patient may have access to insurance forms or other sources of such information, a code alone may be used.

From an organic-medical perspective, the major purpose of differential diagnosis is differential treatment.

## Treatment/Remediation

Once diagnosed, it is the responsibility of the treating professional to provide or to obtain appropriate medical treatment for the patient, which should include psychotherapy or supportive counseling, and follow-up. *Differential treatment follows differential diagnoses,* so in many instances, different types of treatment will be used across standard diagnostic categories. However, in most cases, organic-medical treatment will involve some form of medication. In addition, psychotherapy or supportive counseling

**BOX 4-3** ━━━━━━━━━━━━━━━━━━━━━━━━━━━━━━━━━━━━━━━━━━

## Mental Status Examination

Ask the client: "What symptoms have you experienced in the last 48 hours?"
Record response: _____

Ask the client: "What symptoms have you experienced in the past?"
Record response: _____

*Orientation to:*    Person (   ); Place (   ); Time (   );
                          Situation (   ).

*General behavior:*
Eye contact: present (   ); absent (   ).
Normal motor activity (   ); increased motor (   ); decreased motor (   ); agitation (   );
tremor (   ); tics (   ); peculiar posturing (   ); unusual gait (   ); repetitive acts (   );
seductive posturing (   ); angry outburst (   ); impulsive (   ); hostile (   );
withdrawn (   ); evasive (   ); passive (   ); aggressive (   ); naive (   ); dramatic (   );
manipulative (   ); dependent (   ); uncooperative (   ); demanding (   );
negativistic (   ); vigilance (   ); scanning (   ); other (   )—describe: _____

*Content of thought:*
Check if present and describe frequency, intensity, duration:
_____ Delusions (paranoid, influence, somatic, grandeur, of reference, systema-
              tized, or other):
_____ Hallucinations (auditory, visual, olfactory, gustatory, kinesthetic):
_____ Obsessions:
_____ Compulsions:
_____ Phobias:
_____ Suicidal thoughts or plans:
_____ Assaultive or homicidal thoughts:
_____ Antisocial attitudes:
_____ Suspicious:
_____ Feelings of unreality:
_____ Thoughts of running away:
_____ Somatic (bodily) complaints:
_____ Guilt ideas:
_____ Ideas of hopelessness/worthlessness:
_____ Excessive religiosity:
_____ Sexual preoccupation:
_____ Blames others:
_____ Other:

*Continued*

**BOX 4-3**    *Continued*

*Speech and flow of thought:*
Goal directed ( ) OR   loose ( );
                                    circumstantial ( );
                                    tangential ( ).
Spontaneous ( ) OR blocked ( ).
Deliberate ( ) OR pressured ( ).
Check if present: neologisms ( ); clang associations ( ); flight of ideas (loose +
pressured) ( ); perseveration ( ); echolalia ( ); echopraxia ( ); excessive ( );
reduced ( ); slow ( ); loud ( ); soft ( ); mute ( ); slurred ( ); stuttering ( ).

*Affect* (emotional tone observed and defined through observation by the interviewer):
Appropriate ( ); Inappropriate ( ). If inappropriate, check—
    flat ( ); blunted ( ); elated ( ); labile ( ); angry ( );
    histrionic ( ); anxious ( ); silly ( ); depressed ( ).

*Mood* (emotional state as subjectively described by client):
Euthymic (normal) ( );
Dysthymic (depressed) ( );
Euphoric (elated) ( ).

## Cognitive Mental Status Assessment
*Immediate memory and concentration:*
Ask client to subtract 7's backward from 100 in a serial fashion. Record responses:
_____   _____   _____   _____   _____   _____

Ask client to subtract 3's backward from 20 in a serial fashion. Record responses:
_____   _____   _____   _____   _____

Ask the client to repeat the following sequences of numbers and check if correct:
2-5 ( ); 3-8-4 ( ); 7-4-8-3 ( ); 8-2-0-1-4 ( ); 8-2-1-9-0-4 ( ); 3-9-7-2-8-4-1 ( ).
Ask the client to reverse the following sequences—check if correct: 5-8 ( ); 4-9-1 ( );
2-7-3-6 ( ); 6-1-0-5-8 ( ); 5-2-8-9-1-4 ( ).
*Short-term memory:* Ask the client to tell you what he or she had for breakfast;
record response _____
*Long-term memory:*
Ask client to name five recent U.S. presidents and record:
_____

*Current knowledge:* Ask client to name one major recent news event; record response
_____

Ask client to name the state's governor: _____
Ask client to name a local city's mayor: _____

*Abstract thinking:*
Ask client to explain the saying: 1. A rolling stone gathers no moss: _____
_____

2. The grass is always greener on the other side: _____
_____

**BOX 4-3**  *Continued*

*Insight and judgment:* Poor insight (   ); Poor judgment (   ).

*Other symptoms of neurological significance:*
Headaches: no (   ); yes (   ), frequency, intensity, duration: _____
_____

Dizzy spells? describe:

Any recent changes in the following? walking (   ); talking (   ); vision (   );
hearing (   ); memory (   ); balance (   ); thirst (   ); sense of direction (   );
sleep (   ); handwriting (   ); sexual responsiveness (   ). Explain:

Have any of the following phenomena occurred? Dropping things out of hands (   );
reaching for something and missing while looking (   ); deja vu (   ); jamais vu (   );
forgetting what was said in mid-sentence (   ); forgetting names of common things (such
as a pencil, cup, lamp, etc.) (   ); uncontrollable hand trembling (   ). Describe:

Do any of the following illnesses run in the family?
epilepsy (   ); Parkinson's disease (   ); Alzheimer's disease (   ); schizophrenia (   );
depression or manic depression (   ); alcoholism (   ); Down's syndrome (   );
neurological disease (   ).
Describe:

Has the client ever experienced: ringing in the ears (   ); pain when moving the
head (   ); contact with poisonous chemicals (   ); recent loss of control of bow-
els or bladder (   ); pain or numbness in any part of the body (   ); head injury (   ).
Describe.

**************************************************************

*Diagnostic Impression (Use DSM Axis I & Axis II):*

    Axis I:
    Axis II:
_____

is common. The ultimate responsibility for medication management rests on the
shoulders of the physician, although in practice, other mental health professionals may
provide information to the physician so that the process may be interactive among
involved professionals on the case.

    The American Psychiatric Association, at the time of this writing, is in the
process of developing a companion manual to the *DSM-IIIR*. The new manual is to be
a treatment manual, listing commonly prescribed treatments for specific disorders. The
American Psychiatric Association (1984) already has a text that lists common psychi-

atric treatments, but it is not organized around *DSM-IIIR* diagnoses. Others have published treatment manuals according to diagnostic classification (e.g., Reid, 1983). They usually categorically follow the diagnoses of the *DSM* in current usage and offer recommended specific treatments for specific disorders, sometimes including recommended medication and dosages, types of psychotherapy, and other treatments of preference. These books are useful references for medical as well as nonmedical professionals subscribing to the organic-medical paradigm of counseling and psychotherapy.

### Case Management

The case management of an individual receiving organic-medical psychiatric treatment involves skillful interprofessional communication. Aside from the assignment of medical responsibilities to an attending physician, all involved professionals are responsible to ensure effective, ethical, and appropriate treatment.

Nonmedical counselors or psychotherapists coordinating nonmedical treatments on cases receiving medical attention must be able to regularly observe the patient and to report the patient's status in oral or in written forms to other involved professionals. The treating counselor must be prepared to do crisis intervention and to coordinate emergency services when necessary. He or she should be well versed in medical treatments, especially related to side-effects (unusual or unwanted effects) as opposed to main or wanted treatment effects. There must be a continual monitoring of symptomotology. Physical and social environmental stressors must be identified and controlled or ameliorated, when possible. The treating counselor must be alert to community resources and should be knowledgeable about the availability of services and the means for obtaining services for patients.

Case notes should be detailed, precise, and thorough. One of the clearest signs of the incompetency of a Psychiatric Case Management professional is the failure to record in ongoing case notes the frequency, intensity, and duration of symptoms and signs of a disorder. Progress from a Psychiatric Case Management perspective cannot be assessed unless attention is focused on the presence, absence, or degree of symptomatic behaviors. Regular and thorough mental status examinations should be performed. Monitoring of medication and other treatment compliance is critical, and medication blood-level assessments may need to be made to ensure that medications have been taken as prescribed (with physician approval).

Counseling sessions should be regularly scheduled in order to prevent or to lessen any internal or external factors that may negatively affect progress toward goals.

The Psychiatric Case Management professional must be educated, competently trained, and medically sophisticated. He or she must be an able communicator and an astute observer as well as a skilled counselor.

## Specialized Techniques

Probably the most comprehensive list of techniques associated with the organic-medical paradigm is provided by the American Psychiatric Association (1984) in its book

## BOX 4-4

### Example Psychiatric Report

The following psychiatric report is based on a real report of a seriously ill patient. However the material has been extensively modified to protect the rights of the patient.

#### Psychiatric Evaluation of an Active Schizophrenic

*Identification:*    The patient is a 29-year-old single white male, referred for a psychiatric examination by a mental health agency.

*Expressed complaint:*    "My father wants me to see you."

*Patient description of current status:*    The patient states he was never in "analysis." His doctor falsely said that he had a neurological disorder. His whole problem was "temporal mandibular joint syndrome." This condition made his brain concentrate on his jaws. He feels like he has two mouths. The jaw condition caused "an input into my brain." Others may think of a wife but he thinks of his brain itself. He says he was never given a diagnosis but he made his own diagnosis of his jaw condition. Nervous conditions come from the jaw and send signals of pain up his spinal cord to his brain stem. Abraham Lincoln had the same disease, according to what television told him. He also needs glasses. He requested glasses from the welfare agency. He diagnosed his own eye condition as "congenital familial cataracts." This condition causes him to put more effort into his vision than others. When asked about medications, he states he took Haldol [an antipsychotic drug] a year ago. He's been off of Haldol one year. It had no effect whatsoever. It was a major tranquilizer. It took his thought about society away from him. He had the correct idea about society which is that education in society is for training animals not people. He calls himself a "philosophical scientist." He went on to say that his hearing is bad as well as his vision.

     Obtained medical records indicate he has been hospitalized at the state institution on four occasions. He was seen there in a psychotic state each time with features of paranoia, grandiosity, bizarre behavior, threats to murder the U.S. president, attempts to become a refugee to Russia or Cuba, delusions that the government had placed "control boxes in my brain," that the government owes him large sums of money, and that news people are after him. Diagnoses varied from atypical psychosis to paranoid schizophrenia. There was repeated documentation for pernicious cannabis abuse. He had been smoking marijuana since he was age 13. It brought about his quitting high school. He had been treated with oral neuroleptics as well as intramuscular injections of Haldol. He was, at one point, thought to have tardive dyskinesia, but this was never proven. Although there was no acting-out behavior reported, he was known to sleep with a gun. He had responded to neuroleptics but proved to be noncompliant and had recurrences. Delusions of influence by microwave radar, radio, and television were also reported in other admissions to the state hospital. Paranoid preoccupations with television brainwashing to control him were reported. Medical and neurological studies

*Continued*

**BOX 4-4**   *Continued*

were found to be unremarkable. Other neuroleptics treatments than Haldol included treatment with Navane. Psychological testing revealed a full scale IQ of 100.

*Medical history:*   He reports he broke his leg four or five years ago. He was hit on the head with a bottle at a bar. No history of skull fractures, subdural hematoma, or concussion.

*Contributing social, developmental and family factors:*   The claimant was born and raised in a midwestern urban area. He has one brother and one sister. He stated: "My family, between you and me, has signs of mental instability. My sister and mother are irrational. My brother is retarded and epileptic. My father believes whatever the government tells him." He stated that his father has "no intelligence." Of his childhood, he states, "I was mentally deprived as a child of correct sensory input. My mind was conditioned and brainwashed. I woke up to intelligence when I was 24. I am improving since then in mental nonpsychotic thinking." He mysteriously reports that he had "put on makeup as a psychotic. I have a human life in the micro-cosmos." His language tends to be grandiose as well as extremely tangential. He repeats that, "I am single in psychosis. Two people mingle their souls together in marriage contracts." He stated that he has never married in order to avoid becoming single and then psychotic. He completed two years of high school and dropped out. He quit because he "abhorred the word *education*." He stated that he is "a doctor and a scholar. I deal with people who are psychotic." He could not give a clear account of his occupational history. "I worked on lawns as a child. I mean flowers." He stated he went to a technical school, worked in some filling stations, worked for a department store, and worked in a car manufacturing plant for two years. He was a vendor at the city stadium for three months one year ago. He's done no regular job for more than a year. He doesn't remember how long ago. He now lives in an apartment by himself. His father paid for two month's rent. He had been living with his parents. His parents will be cutting him off if he doesn't get a job or some sort of benefits. He denies any police record. He could give no description of social attachments or interactions. His habits include a pack of cigarettes a day. He denies ever using illicit drugs or alcohol, entirely contradictory to the medical records.

*Mental status assessment:*
   *Observed general behavior:* A 29-year-old while male, appearing about his stated age. He's 5 feet, 8 inches tall, weighs 140 pounds. Blood pressure—120/80; pulse—80; respirations—16. There was no eye contact. He was clean with adequate personal hygiene. No unusual mannerisms. Psychomotor activity was within normal limits. He was markedly digressive in speech. He was suspicious and became angry from time to time as he discussed paranoid preoccupations with the government, society, and education. He tends to be histrionic.

**BOX 4-4**    *Continued*

*Flow of thought:* Extremely tangential to a point of being almost unintelligible. Neologisms and complex, disorganized phraseology is noted. He is illogical and irrelevant. He definitely shows loosening of associations.

*Content of thought:* Multiple delusional systems. Extremely poor reality testing. His body is controlled by brain boxes installed by the government. The government wants to slow down his thinking so that he will not reveal their plots against him and others. A door has been placed in his brain. "The circuitry of my intelligence has been cross-fired." He's forced to get false brain signals. He has to protect himself in order to evade persecutors from the government. Television warns him and threatens him. His intelligence is too powerful to be eliminated by the government, however. Grandiosity pervades the entire interview. No suicidal ideas were elicited. No homicidal ideas were elicited.

*Mood and affect:* Mood is dysthymic, with blunted affect. He's indignant and angry about his father's requests of him. At times he appears histrionic.

*Orientation and cognition:* He is oriented times three, but not to the purpose of the examination. Judgment and comprehension are extremely poor. If he found a stamped addressed letter on the sidewalk, he'd open it. He could interpret simple proverbs, such as "the grass is always greener." Memory: digit span was 6 of 7 forward, and 4 of 6 backward; he recalled 3 of 3 items in 1 and 5 minutes; he had cereal for breakfast. He could name five presidents—Washington, Lincoln, Kennedy, Nixon, Reagan. Concentration: serial seven subtractions from 100 were accurate to 79. He could name three major cities and one current news event. Insight is extremely limited—when asked about his condition, he stated, "I believe I am in excited isocratic suffrage."

*Functional limitations:*

*Social:* He is severely socially constricted and isolated. Related to his relations to others, he stated: "I am very opinionated, according to others. I sense hostility to me due to people wanting to degrade American life. My brain is overwhelmed to see and hear the sights. I have pain from my back due to electrical discharges from my jaws going to my left occipital lobe."

*Daily activities:* He spends his day in his apartment and walking the streets. He says he spends most of his sixteen waking hours every day killing the bugs in his apartment and studying "diseases and pathogens." He said he is too busy "teaching myself what I am deprived of." He doesn't eat much, and he depends upon his family for meals and shopping. He doesn't manage money. He says he has "no expenses."

*Ability to concentrate on simple tasks:* Extremely limited, distracted, extremely delusional, hallucinating at times.

*Diagnosis:*

    Axis I:    Schizophrenia, paranoid type, active.
    Axis II:   No diagnosis.

*Continued*

**BOX 4-4**    *Continued*

*Prognosis:*

This man is actively psychotic. He's delusional, hallucinatory with marked tangentiality, loss of reality testing, grandiosity, delusions of influence and persecution. He's totally without insight. He has shown no sustained remission despite four hospitalizations at the state hospital. He is noncompliant with medications. He is unpredictable, unable to make useful contact, unable to communicate socially. He is bizarre in attitude. Flow of thought is illogical. He is socially withdrawn. Prognosis is extremely poor. He would ideally be treated with long-term institutionalization. Repeat hospitalizations are predictable. He is not capable of self-sufficiency, self-support, or of adequate nutrition. Hygiene contrarily appears relatively appropriate. He is unable to relate with peers, family, or figures of authority. He is not competent to manage any benefits provided him.

Thank you for this interesting referral.

Sincerely yours,
T. Smith, MD
ABPN Diplomate in Psychiatry

---

entitled, *The Psychiatric Therapies.* In that book, five classifications of organically-based therapies are defined: (a) pharmacotherapies; (b) nutritional therapies; (c) electroconvulsive therapies; (d) psychosurgery; and (e) other somatic therapies, which include disulfiram (antabuse) treatment for alcoholics, the use of stimulants for children with attention deficit disorder, hormone therapy, sleep-deprivation therapy for treatment of depression, etcetera. Other treatment types are also addressed in the text; they are classified as psychosocial therapies, which include psychotherapy, group therapy, family therapy, biofeedback, and other approaches that are more closely aligned with the other paradigms in this text.

The most commonly used of these organic-medical techniques is pharmacotherapy, also commonly referred to as "medication therapy," "psychiatric chemotherapy," or "drug therapy." Pharmacotherapy is the most comprehensive and widely used medical treatment method in psychiatry. Medications are used to control anxiety symptoms, mood disorders (such as bipolar disorder and major depression), psychoses (such as schizophrenia) or other disorders where certain chemicals have been found to control or ameliorate symptoms. Treatments by medications is probably the most effective way quickly to lessen symptomotology and to modify behavior. However, it is not without controversy (see Haley, 1989; Szasz, 1974).

Electroconvulsive Therapy (ECT), also called electroshock therapy (EST), is another commonly used treatment that is almost exclusively used today with severe mood disorders such as depression or bipolar disorder (manic-depressive illness). ECT involves systematized and exact electrical stimulation of portions of the brain. With disorders such as severe unmanageable depression, ECT has been found to be highly effective (American Psychiatric Association, 1984). Controlled studies have demonstrated that it is quick and effective in reducing severe depressive symptoms, thereby preventing suicide and other self-inflicted harm in severely depressed patients. With regular follow-up maintenance treatments, it can also prevent relapse. Regardless, it is a controversial technique that arouses much public criticism, debate, and scrutiny.

Nutritional therapy is less controversial than its counterparts at face value. When used prudently, it is a more natural biological approach to mental disorder (albeit a less effective or inappropriate approach with many disorders). Nutritional therapy is used when there are nutritional deficiencies (e.g., soluble vitamin deficiencies in alcoholics) by increasing the amount of needed nutrients in the body. There are also several nutrients or food contents that have been implicated in certain disorders by their presence, for example, allergens. In these cases, nutritional therapy requires deletion of certain foods from the diet. Some nutritional substances may also be toxic if overingested, and nutritional therapy helps to ensure that dietary intake is controlled.

Psychosurgery is the severing, removal, or invasive stimulation of brain tissue or connective fibers. One of the most well known psychosurgical procedures is *prefrontal lobotomy,* which involves severing connections between the prefrontal lobes of the cerebrum and the remainder of the brain. It was used primarily with aggressive and assaultive patients. Today, lobotomies are infrequently performed, although, with medical advances more specialized, surgical procedures have been developed to sever, remove, or stimulate certain portions of the brain implicated in certain disorders. At present, especially with mood disorders, it is viewed ''as a treatment of last resort,'' and then only under special considerations (American Psychiatric Association, 1984). Time will be the truest test of developments in psychosurgery.

Overall, these common medical approaches are implemented by trained medical practitioners with the intent of modifying behavior at the biological level. There are serious side and main effects to these treatments, and counselors involved in Psychiatric Case Management must be thoroughly knowledgeable about such effects.

## Recent Developments or Criticisms

To a large degree the fate of Psychiatric Case Management depends on the fate of the organic-medical philosophy in psychiatry. The organic-medical approach to psychiatry has been attacked in many ways from many sources. For example, psychologists more aligned with the psychological paradigm (which will be discussed in chapter 6) criticize organic-medical adherents on the grounds that the organic-medical perspective denies what they believe is the predominance of psychological and social factors at the root of human behaviors. For example, behaviorists have challenged the organic-medical approach by demonstrating that by affecting the environment of the individual with a severe disorder (such as childhood autism) they can have a significant positive affect on the behavior (Lovaas, 1987). Additionally, some psychologists argue that psychological factors, such as poor self-concepts or environmental psychological deprivations, are at the root of what the psychiatric profession has labeled as mental disorder. In fact, psychologists define such problems not as diseases, but as ''maladjustments,'' and they usually use normative behavioral frameworks as standards for assessment.

Probably the most credible challenge to organic-medical ideas has come from the psychiatrist Thomas Szasz (1970, 1974, 1978). For example, Szasz (1974) described the idea of ''mental illness'' as a ''myth.'' He claimed that misbehavior should be seen just as that—a behavioral deviation—and it should be treated as such. He has argued convincingly that the medicalization of human social and psychological problems is an injustice to the treated person and to society. He argued that the actual role of the psychiatrist is akin to that of a ''judge,'' and he felt, unless there was clear-cut organic etiology, that the treatment of social and behavioral problems was outside of the realm of medicine. He argued instead for a social, psychological, and linguistic understanding of behavioral disturbances.

Another source of criticism from within the profession of psychiatry has come from the community psychiatry movement. The community psychiatry movement has taken psychiatry out of the hospital and into the community in order to redefine the boundaries of psychiatry to include the social and psychological spheres. The community psychiatry movement downplays the medical aspects of its work and emphasizes the social and psychological aspects of mental disorder. It has expanded the province of psychiatry to include nonmedical social and cultural factors.

Regardless, strict organic-medical practitioners argue that just because etiology is unknown does not mean something is not a disease (Woodruff et al., 1974). They argue that practitioners must be empirical in their approach to human problems, and if the evidence solidly supports the contention of biological or chemical causation, even if such a contention has not been proven, then they assert that it is imprudent to treat such concerns as anything but medical. In fact, there have been many studies that support the idea of genetic linkage to some of the most severe ''mental disorders,'' such as schizophrenia, bipolar disorder (manic-depressive illness), alcoholism, and others (see the summaries according to disorders in Woodruff et al., 1974). Further, some research is demonstrating a predominance of genetic factors in defining personality predisposition, separate from actual mental disorder (Tellegen et al., 1988). The results of empirical studies of twin concordance rates (the rates at which both individuals in twin pairs manifest a personality trait or a disorder), for example, convincingly support the idea that genetics is a primary factor in the development of some mental disorders. With the most severe disorders, there is a higher concordance rate among identical twins than fraternal twins, and an even greater difference between identical twins and nontwin siblings, even if the individuals in a twin pair or siblings are reared in separate environments.

There has been a remedicalization effort going on in psychiatry, primarily apparently for political reasons. Psychiatrists, by aligning with the organic-medical position, appear to be attempting to differentiate themselves clearly from other nonmedical mental health professions, such as psychology. For example, in 1989, the

Association for the Advancement of Psychology circulated a document entitled ''Psychiatry Declares War on Psychology,'' written by Rogers Wright and Charles Spielberger, both past presidents of a division of the American Psychological Association. In that document, Wright and Spielberger stated:

> *Another aspect of psychiatry's war on psychology is reflected in its efforts over the past decade to ''medicalize'' itself, i.e., to identify with organized medicine. This has, at times, gone to ridiculous extremes in asserting an organic basis for every type of problem or misbehavior that troubles humankind. Though many ''explanations'' are given to justify these efforts, the predominant driving force seems to be economic, reflecting ''skyrocketing'' medical costs which have contributed to the declining role of psychiatry as the intervention of choice in the treatment of troubled human beings. The ''medicalization'' strategy not only blatantly attempts to carve an exclusive turf for psychiatry, but it is also designed to enhance the probability of reimbursement for ''medical/psychiatric'' services, while limiting the consumer's freedom of choice and disenfranchising psychologists from many health care delivery plans. (p. 2)*

It appears that battle lines have been drawn over the provincial rights of the mental health professions, and psychiatry is defending itself by means of its medical roots. Any remedicalization by psychiatry will likely drive it further from its competitors and toward a purely organic-medical approach to treatment, which will have consequences for mental health professionals practicing Psychiatric Case Management.

## Paradigm Fit

### Focus of Study

The focus of study of counseling practitioners using Psychiatric Case Management is the individual patient and his or her ''disorder,'' as primarily interpreted as internally and physically caused. Behavior is interpreted as a reflection of what goes on inside an individual. Severe behavioral deviation is viewed as an indicator that there is something wrong inside the individual that is likely biologically or biochemically based. Counselors subscribing to the Psychiatric Case Management approach will be alert to any signs or symptoms that are defined as diagnostically significant. They observe the individual, and they infer the internal.

### View of Nature of Reality

Reality is composed of things. People are viewed as largely isolated entities, bounded primarily by the limits of their physical systems. Diseases or disorders are characterized as syndromes—things to be cured. Once a disorder has been diagnosed, it is viewed out of its social context and treated within a controlled medical setting.

Organic science is a world of chemistry, biology, and physics. It is strictly empirical. Causes and effects are assumed to be identifiable. The organic-medical researcher continually attempts to identify the organic link to specified types of behavior. Advanced genetic research is an area of research that is receiving focused attention by organic-medical researchers attempting to uncover the biological roots of psychiatric disorders.

Both at the level of research and practice, organic-medical mental health professionals view reality in concrete, individualized terms.

### Consonance with Paradigm Propositions and Tenets

The focus of Psychiatric Case Management is the individual patient. Patients are assessed, and severe symptomotology is assumed to be biologically based or predisposed. The Psychiatric Case Management professional is an expert as evaluating a symptom's frequency, intensity, and duration.

Causes are directly and linearly defined, as the Psychiatric Case Management counselor attempts to identify factors internal or external to the individual that may perturb the physical symptom and trigger biologically predisposed reactions. The external environmental factors associated with symptoms or disorders are viewed as "triggers" rather than direct causes. Cause is internal to the individual.

There is a strict scientific foundation of training for professional counselors wishing to work within organic-medical dictates. Psychiatric Case Management is based on empirical science, and professional counselors must be well educated on scientific findings relevant to specific disorders and the treatments that directly and linearly affect the course of disease. Professionals using Psychiatric Case Management methods will, in most settings, be required to demonstrate credentials and experience consistent with clinical training in the field.

There is clear-cut consistency between the propositions and tenets of the organic-medical paradigm and Psychiatric Case Management.

## Chapter Conclusion

This chapter has introduced a type of counseling theory that is closely associated with the organic-medical paradigm. The presentation in this chapter is purposefully purist and extreme in its interpretation of Psychiatric Case Management; it is hoped that readers will get a precise picture of how paradigm-specific developments translate to the practice of counseling and psychotherapy. It is a contention of this presentation that Psychiatric Case Management is widely practiced in the mental health field, although, historically, it has not been strictly defined or recognized as a counseling theory. With the medicalization of the psychiatric profession, and with the clinical emphases predominating in other mental health professions (e.g., clinical psychology, clinical mental health counseling, clinical marital and family therapy, and psychiatric social work) it is assumed that Psychiatric Case Management will proliferate and develop into a widely acknowledged and applied counseling approach.

# References

American Psychiatric Association. (1984). *The psychiatric therapies*. Washington, DC: American Psychiatric Association.

American Psychiatric Association. (1987). *Diagnostic and statistical manual of mental disorders (3rd ed., rev.)*. Washington, DC: American Psychiatric Association.

Haley, J. (1989). The effect of long-term outcome studies on the therapy of schizophrenia. *Journal of Marital and Family Therapy, 15,* 127–132.

Kaplan, H. I., & Sadock, B. J. (1989). *Comprehensive textbook of psychiatry/V* (5th ed.). Baltimore, MD: Williams & Wilkins.

Lovaas, O. I. (1987). Behavioral treatment and normal educational and intellectual functioning in young autistic children. *Journal of Consulting and Clinical Psychology, 55,* 3–9.

Reid, W. H. (1983). *Treatment of the DSM-III psychiatric disorders*. New York: Brunner/Mazel.

Shagass, C., Josiassen, R. C., Bridger, W. H., Weiss, K. J., Stoff, D., & Simpson, G. M. (1986). *Biological Psychiatry, 1985*. New York: Elsevier.

Szasz, T. S. (1970). *The manufacture of madness*. New York: Harper & Row.

Szasz, T. S. (1974). *The myth of mental illness* (rev. ed.). New York: Harper & Row.

Szasz, T. S. (1978). *The myth of psychotherapy*. Garden City, NY: Anchor Press/Doubleday.

Tellegen, A., Lykken, D. T., Bouchard, T. J., Wilcox, K. J., Segal, N. L., & Rich, S. (1988). Personality similarity in twins reared apart and together. *Journal of Personality and Social Psychology, 54,* 1031–1039.

Woodruff, R. A., Goodwin, D. W., & Guze, S. B. (1974). *Psychiatric diagnosis*. New York: Oxford University Press.

# PART THREE

# The Psychological Paradigm

# 5

# The Psychological Paradigm:
## *Internal and External Models*

THE PSYCHOLOGICAL PARADIGM is one of two paradigms where specific "models" of causation will be distinguished. (The other paradigm with models is the systemic-relational paradigm.) The reason models are defined within the psychological paradigm is the clear-cut causative differences between two subgroups in the larger psychology field. The two subgroups within psychology define the cause of human behavior from two different viewpoints—internal to the individual and external to the individual. Because defining cause directs a focus of study, the models are also epistemologically different. The two models will be called the internal psychological and external psychological models. Essentially, individuals subscribing to the internal model (often identified under the rubric of "subjectivism" or "humanism") have an orientation or preference for "individual understanding and subjective reality" (cf. Barclay, 1968, p. xx). Individuals subscribing to the external model (often identified under the rubric of "objectivism" or "behaviorism") have an orientation or preference for "cultural norms and scientific reality" (cf. Barclay, 1968, p. xx). These two diverse orientations are of epistemological significance, because the focus of study differs from psychological factors inside the individual to psychological factors outside the individual. However, the psychology field, as a larger disciplinary force, has been able to keep these two subgroups (the internalists and externalists) from dividing the field into separate professional groups of political and professional significance. In effect, one may find professional psychologists who subscribe primarily to the internal/subjectivist viewpoint, while it is just as easy to find other psychologists who subscribe to the external/objectivist viewpoint. Both of these types of professionals, nonetheless, define and identify themselves as psychologists, and they maintain credentials consistent with their affiliation to psychology as a larger political lobby. It is the affiliation of these diverse groups to the larger psychology field at the professional and political levels that helps to classify them as cohorts and adherents to the psychological paradigm. Therefore, the internal and external psychological models will be viewed as distinct epistemological and causal positions within the larger psychological paradigm. Where the psychological paradigm clearly meets all six of the criteria for paradigms defined in chapter 2, the internal and external psychological models are distinguished primarily on epistemological and causal grounds. The two models do not meet all six criteria for a counseling paradigm.

## Historical Overview

### Foundations

Defining the history of psychology as related to the psychological paradigm in mental health services is no easy task. In fact, whole courses are taught on the history and systems-of-thought representing the psychological field. Regardless, there are two major theoretical lines of thinking that have developed into full-blown psychotherapeutic orientations: the internal psychological and external psychological positions. This section will briefly identify significant developmental markers of these two models as applied to mental health problems.

From the internalist perspective, the works of Freud (e.g., Freud, 1917/1966) are significant milestones. Although Freud was trained as a medical doctor, he broke from the traditions of medicine and explored the realm of psychological and mental processes. He found that psychological and mental processes were intimately associated with physical health. Yet, as a physician, he remained true to a way of thinking that placed biological and physical causation at the root of mental processes. For example, his theoretical ideas, when examined closely, are consistent with Darwin's ideas. The "id," the selfish, prurient, and aggressive part of the human psyche, is viewed as linked to biological drives at the deepest level of human nature. Through the id, the sexual and aggressive instincts (survival instincts) are realized at a psychological level.

Regardless of theoretical linkage to biology, Freud was a believer in analysis of the psyche by means of the spoken word. He focused on internal experiences to guide him in his exploration of *mind as an entity*. In the final analysis, it was the labeling of internal experiences that led to his most significant discovery—the unconscious. He led patients in the examination of their most personal experiences, and he delved into his own experiences, which he viewed as representative of the psyche of all humankind. His views are not optimistic, since the human being must continually struggle with a conflict between the biological and the social aspects of self. Yet, his ideas help in the understanding of the most asocial and selfish of human behaviors. Today, Freud's ideas are applied by professionals who call themselves "psychoanalysts," a group composed primarily of psychiatrists and psychologists with allegiance to the basic theoretical ideas of Freud and his theoretical descendants. Nevertheless, Freud's ideas are viewed with scorn by others who hold a more optimistic ideal of human mentality.

It is through the works of the humanists that the more optimistic internalist point of view is presented. Significantly, Maslow (1954, 1971) presented a positive view of human nature, breaking from the predominance of psychoanalytic thinking in mental health services of his time. He proposed that humans are motivated by higher ideals, and he developed a hierarchical model of need attainment and psychological development. According to Maslow, the human appetite for growth in the mental realm is whetted by success, that is, by movement up the ladder of human psychological needs. At the most basic level are the physiological needs. When satisfied, then safety needs predominate. When safety needs are met, love and belongingness needs become critical. And with love and belongingness, individuals can develop positive self-concepts and self-esteem. The highest level of human psychological functioning was defined by Maslow as ''self-actualization.''

Being self-actualized means that one has met his or her highest psychological need—fulfilling one's potential. It is a *state of being* characterized by the highest of human values, which are brought to life by those few individuals who have ''arrived.'' Some examples of individuals who might be considered self-actualized

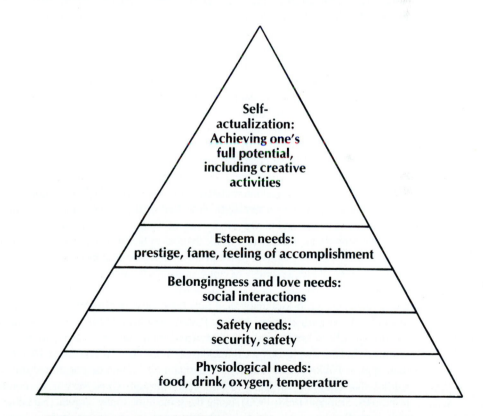

*Maslow's hierarchy of needs. © 1986 Wadsworth, Inc.*

are: Albert Einstein, Eleanor Roosevelt, Gandhi, Walt Whitman, and Abraham Lincoln. Some traits (see Maslow, 1971, and the list in Maslow, 1968, p. 26) common among self-actualized individuals include: (a) devotion to some unselfish cause; (b) concentrated effort; (c) recognition and use of one's abilities; (d) having experienced what can be defined as "peak experiences," which are noncontrived moments of mental ecstasy when an individual feels attuned to his or her universe; (e) spontaneity and creativity; and (f) an increased acceptance of self, others, and nature. As is obvious in these descriptions, Maslow valued extraordinary human accomplishment. But his theory is only retrospective—it probably is more of a reflection of what is valued in an existing culture than a predictable and measurable course of human development. Regardless, from a counseling standpoint, the works of Carl Rogers (1951) embody and extend the ideals of the humanists in the tradition of Maslow. Rogers (e.g., Rogers, 1951) developed a therapeutic approach that is fully appreciative of the human capacity for self-direction. His approach, once called "non-directive," is now labeled "Client-Centered" or, most recently, "Person-Centered." Through his person-centered approach, humanistic values are enacted in therapeutic interaction.

The external psychological model developed separately from internal psychological theories. The external psychological model is best represented in the works of the behaviorists. Behaviorism (Skinner, 1938, 1953; Watson, 1913, 1919; Watson & Rayner, 1920) challenged the view of internal control or self-control of behavior by addressing the effect of environmental influences on behavior. Theoretically and empirically, behaviorists demonstrated that humans are controlled to some degree by environmental contingencies (operationally defined relationships between behaviors and external events). And a logical and direct offshoot of behavior theory is behavioral therapy (e.g., Kazdin, 1977; Wolpe, 1958, 1973), which stems from a philosophy that the human is controlled externally, by environmental stimuli. The behavioral therapeutic relationship is such that one person has "control" over resources or the needs of another. And with guidance of an expert authority, contingencies of behavior are changed until maladaptive behaviors are ameliorated.

The behavioral point of view has been quite controversial, especially from the perspective of the optimistic internalists, who view "free will" as predominating over behavior. The optimistic internalists view free will as representative of the human condition. The behavioral viewpoint, by way of contrast, is externally deterministic and basically conveys an attitude that is antithetical to the idea of a person having internal control over his or her destiny. From a strictly behavioristic stance, a person is controlled by environmental factors, and behavior is quite predictable based on an analysis of past behavioral contingencies. In effect, the behavioral stance explains human behavior in a way that is closer to explanations of how other (less intelligent) animals behave. For example, the empirical works of Ivan Pavlov demonstrated that animals can respond physiologically to nonphysiological environmental cues *associated with* factors that ordinarily produce a physiological response (Pavlov, 1957). Watson and Rayner (1920) then applied Pavlov's basic findings to human beings, and demonstrated through case studies that children can learn to have fears through some very basic conditioning principles. Skinner (1938; 1953), using the same philosophy, argued that behaviors are also controlled by events occurring after responses (e.g., the rewards or punishments that follow behaviors). Skinner adopted an extreme position, first delimited by Watson (1924/1930), which challenged all internal structural psychological processes. Skinner's position was characterized as fully external or a "radical" behaviorism; he believed that human thinking was the result of the external environmental factors that condition humans to act as if they think. Therefore, according to behavioral principles, just as the likelihood of a animal's behavior can be increased by reward, so, too, a human being's behavior can be affected.

Regardless of the perspective that is taken (the internalist or externalist psychological viewpoint), there is similarity in both of these viewpoints when analyzed from a larger analytic framework. Both focus on the individual. In both cases, psychological factors are predominant over biological factors in determining behavior. Both are based on linear causality, that is, something affects something else in a straightforward, nonreciprocal manner. And both are consistent with interventions aimed at the individual or the direct environment of the individual. This similarity is clearly manifest in the basic propositions of the psychological paradigm, which are presented later in this chapter.

Before proceeding with basic psychological propositions, however, a critique is presented of the organic-medical viewpoint. Criticisms of organic-medical ideals are associated with the growth and credibility of the psychological paradigm.

## A Critique of Organic-Medical Propositions

As was described in chapters 1 and 2, paradigms of counseling and psychotherapy do not emerge in isolation. They are competitive, and new paradigms emerge during times when there is anomalous anecdotal and empirical data that challenges a predominant theory or framework. This is true of the psychological paradigm against the backdrop of organic-medical thinking.

In a special way, Freud's ideas are foundational to psychological thinking and also foundational to the organic-medical propositions. Freud, for example, is considered the "father of psychiatry." But, as stated earlier, from a paradigm perspective, Freud's ideas are considered transitional (trans-paradigmatic), having concepts that are holdovers from the therapeutic traditions from which they break. At the same time that Freud broke with the traditions of medicine in developing the psychological concept of "psyche" (mind), he also maintained allegiance to medical dictates by his linkage of the psyche to biological instincts. Freud also maintained the idea of "illness" when he referred to what, by today's standards, can be clearly discerned as nonorganic psychological concerns. In this way, Freud medicalized his discoveries. Today, by organic-medical dictates, professionals treat disorders or illnesses, and treatments are called *therapies*. There is a strong, underlying medical message in such language.

Thomas Szasz (1970, 1974, 1978) has been an outspoken critic of organic-medical ideas as applied to mental health issues. He led a credible challenge against psychiatry and the organic-medical perspective of treatment, thereby lending credence to the psychological paradigm. Szasz, a psychiatrist, in a book that has become a classic in the mental health field, entitled *The Myth of Mental Illness* (Szasz, 1974), essentially

*Thomas Szasz*

attacked his own profession and the organic-medical methods of solving mental health problems. Szasz (1974) stated:

> *It is customary to define psychiatry as a medical specialty concerned with the study, diagnosis, and treatment of mental illnesses. This is a worthless and misleading definition. Mental illness is a myth. Psychiatrists are not concerned with mental illnesses and their treatments. In actual practice they deal with personal, social, and ethical problems in living. (p. 262)*

Szasz disputed the psychiatric contention that emotional concerns constitute diseases or illnesses. He said that use of medical terms to describe problems in living was "metaphoric," that is, a comparison that is not literally true. In fact, he viewed the use of the term *mental illness* as a very misleading and even destructive metaphor. Instead, he preferred to view human concerns in their social and linguistic contexts, thereby espousing a psychosocial framework for understanding and influencing human behavior. In fact, Szasz has taken the position that if an emotional concern cannot be found in a corpse, it should not be considered mental *illness,* literally meaning that a "real" disease leaves evidence of physical pathology. Therefore, if there is a lesion on the brain found in the corpse of a person who demonstrated unusual behavior, then such behavior can be assumed to have been biologically based. Likewise, if organic factors can be identified by medical means and correlated to behavioral concerns, then the concerns enter the domain of medicine. Szasz made the case that medicine should be strictly biological, physical, and chemical, and it should not traverse the psychological and social realms. Szasz stated:

> *So-called psychiatric problems continue to be cast in the traditional framework of medicine. The conceptual scaffolding of medicine, however, rests on the*

*principles of physics and chemistry, as indeed it should, for it has been, and continues to be, the task of medicine to study, and if necessary to alter, the physicochemical structure and function of the human body. Yet the fact remains that human sign-using behavior does not lend itself to exploration and understanding in these terms. We thus remain shackled to the wrong conceptual framework and terminology. (p. 4)*

Further, Szasz stated: "And the language of psychiatry (and psychoanalysis) is fundamentally unfaithful to its own subject: in it, imitating medicine comes before telling the truth" (pp. 4–5). Szasz argued vehemently against the medical metaphor. He felt psychiatrists were pretending to cure disease, while actually they were social control agents (akin to judges) making decisions related to individual behavioral deviance. He argued that morality should not be the domain of medicine.

Although Szasz's solution to the mental illness myth cannot be considered purely psychological (see Szasz, 1974, for a detailed discussion), the fact remains that his challenge to the organic-medical paradigm lends credence to any position that focuses less on the biological aspects of human behavior. The fact that he was a psychiatrist made his attack on psychiatry all the more credible. Szasz's work is a good example of how theory can be challenged on philosophical grounds.

But organic medical thinking has not only been challenged philosophically. Behaviorists, for example, have empirically demonstrated that severe psychiatric concerns can be affected by behavioral learning principles. One of the best examples of behavioral evidence supporting the contention that nonorganic factors can influence what was previously considered "illness" is the case of autism in children. Lovaas (see Lovaas, 1987, for a recent discussion on this issue) has shown that autistic children can be made to act normally using behavior modification techniques. The kind of evidence that behaviorists have garnered in support of their position is substantial. Such evidence is anomalous to purely organic-medical thinking. It demonstrates that even those individuals who seem severely biologically disturbed can be modified through psychological means. The psychological position, then, is that nonorganic factors play a major role in controlling human behavior.

## The Psychological Solution

In practice, the psychological solution to the limitations of pure organic-medical thinking is to focus on nonorganic factors affecting behavior (just as Szasz, 1974, and Lovaas, 1987, have done). The psychologically oriented therapist, although mindful of biology, downplays its importance on behavior. Mind, language, thinking, feeling, and/or measurable behaviors become the focus of study. Biology, chemistry, and physics are viewed as playing a very small role in determining everyday behavior. This frees the therapist from the constraints of organic-medical means of assessment and treatment. Accordingly, propositions of the psychological paradigm are nonorganically based, although there is still a clear focus on the individual.

# Propositions

The basic propositions of the psychological paradigm are as follows:

**1.** The focus is always on the individual.

**2.** Individuals can be and must be assessed. It is assumed that individuals possess characteristics, traits, or behavior patterns, primarily developed over time through internal or external psychological processes, that endure and represent predispositions to act. Individuals are assumed to possess self-concepts, skills, abilities, personality traits, interests, attitudes, values, maladaptations, etcetera, that can be evaluated and categorized, depending on the prevalence, appropriateness, or acceptability of behaviors, thoughts, feelings, or skills.

**3.** Causes can be directly and linearly defined, and the outcome of a causative factor can be isolated for study and modified through directive intervention. If a cause is not known, it is assumed that science has not determined the cause, but will determine the cause in the future.

**4.** Change always occurs by someone doing something to someone else. The therapeutic act is aimed at mentality, emotionality, or behavioral contingency, where an expert authority acts to create change in an individual's internal psychological process or to change what an individual has learned through the control of direct external factors.

**5.** Professional expertise is gained within the framework of training based on quantitative and/or qualitative scientific methods. In the end, science defines what is right or wrong, acceptable or unacceptable. Experts must be thoroughly screened for intelligence, knowledge, and acceptable training in the psychological sciences.

**6.** Psychologists are legally/professionally sanctioned to assess and to intervene in concerns of a personal nature as expert authorities in relationships with their clients, and limits of psychological practice are clearly defined in professional regulatory statutes.

**7.** Individuals are responsible to the degree that they possess rationality, which derives from their psychological makeup as viewed within a normative framework. If not responsible, professional expert authorities may be asked to assess and to influence those factors that contribute to the person's maladaptations so that such maladaptations may be lessened and/or ameliorated.

**8.** If responsible, then clients are culpable, not only for their acts, but also for following therapeutic directives, and ultimately for the success of their treatments.

**9.** One person can influence a second person only to the degree that the first person affects the characteristics, skills, or psychological conditions (internal and external) of the second person. A person can influence another person by accident (inadvertently) or through knowledge of the other person's characteristics, skills, or the internal/external psychological factors that affect behavior.

**10.** Failure results from poor or inaccurate evaluation of internal or external psychological factors that influence behavior, from poor or inaccurate application of corrective technique, or from failure of responsible clients to follow therapeutic directives.

## Tenets of Practice

**1.** The therapeutic act is aimed at the individual client, usually in a setting where communication and/or behavior can be isolated from extraneous influences, in order to distinguish those thoughts, feelings, or behaviors that are the targets of treatment. The target of treatment may vary according to the therapeutic approach, but always with the understanding that internal or external psychological factors are at work and must be identified and changed in order to change behavior.

**2.** A psychologically oriented therapist most often begins therapy with an assessment of the individual client's basic functioning. A client's basic thoughts, feelings, or behaviors are analyzed and evaluated according to criteria of mental health consistent with the therapeutic approach. Even at the base of those therapeutic approaches that deemphasize diagnostic evaluation (e.g., Person-Centered Therapy, Gestalt Therapy), there is at least *an assumption* made about the capability of the client. For example, according to Person-Centered Therapy, *all clients* are viewed as basically capable of full functioning, growth, and change through therapeutic interaction. The fact that some therapeutic approaches assess all clients the same way does not negate assessment as basic to psychological tenets of practice.

**3.** Treatment involves the development of those conditions necessary to create change of the client's behaviors, thoughts, or emotions. The conditions relevant to change may be viewed as inherent in the therapeutic relationship or as reflective of factors that affect a client externally in identified settings. Regardless, the therapist attempts to design a therapeutic situation where certain conditions are present that theoretically are associated with change and human psychological development. Several examples, which will become clearer in the chapters presenting psychologically oriented therapies that follow, are: (a) the psychodynamic (psychoanalytic) psychotherapist facilitates ''transference''—which is a projection of a past relationship onto the therapist; (b) the Person-Centered Therapist facilitates several interpersonal conditions that are viewed as necessary and sufficient to produce change; (c) the Rational-Emotive Therapist produces an atmosphere where irrational thoughts can be brought forth and disputed; (d) the Gestalt Therapist creates a therapeutic relationship that facilitates self-awareness; and (e) the Behavior Therapist develops a relationship with the client that allows for the analysis and manipulation of external factors that may be affecting a client's behavior.

**4.** Resolution of a client's concerns involves acknowledgment or demonstration by the client that certain feelings, thoughts, and/or behaviors have changed in a way that is consistent with a theoretically based definition of mental health, adjustment, or adaptation.

**5.** Therapy is undertaken with the client's best interests in mind. Therapy is principally a mutually agreed-upon activity, where the client consents to therapy. In this regard, many psychologically oriented therapies involve formal, or at least tacit, agreements about what is to occur in therapy. Some approaches (e.g., behavioral approaches) may even involve the development of a formal therapeutic contract, which explicitly defines what is expected of the client and the therapist during therapy. For those clients where an external authority (a third party) has defined the intent and extent of the therapeutic endeavor, therapists are still viewed ethically as primarily responsible to their clients (and not the third parties responsible for initiation or even payment of treatment).

## Epistemological and Ontological Considerations

The psychological paradigm directs practitioners and researchers to study primarily the nonbiological internal or external processes that are associated with behavior. As with the organic-medical paradigm, the focus of study is the individual. According to the internal psychological model, it is what occurs inside the individual cognitively or emotionally that best explains behavior. According to the external model, it is what occurs outside the individual (the external environmental or social stimuli) that directly influences an individual's behavior. The internal and external models of the psychological paradigm are epistemologically distinct. According to the internal viewpoint, the locus of study is within the boundaries of the body, in that conceptually illusive but logically sensible construct called "mind." According to the external viewpoint, the locus of study is outside the boundaries of the body, in the stimuli that trigger human responses. From the externalist position, mind is not a result of internal structure or dynamics; rather, "thinking" is a learned response of a physical organism reacting to its environment. As Skinner (1953) concluded in a chapter entitled "Thinking" in his monumental work *Science and Human Behavior:* "If our account of thinking is essentially correct, there is no reason why we cannot teach a man how to think" (p. 256).

Aside from the clear epistemological differences between the internalists and externalists within the psychological paradigm, at the practical, therapy-relevant level, researchers and therapists must always attempt to analyze the individual, primarily through one-to-one interview data, in order to assess what psychological factors, internal or external, may predominate in relation to an expressed concern. Of course, those professionals adhering strictly to either the internal or external psychological models will, in all likelihood, assess and conceptualize problems from the model of choice. For instance, where a behaviorist would look to external factors and a process of learning as the cause for a phobic response (Wolpe, 1958, 1973), an internal model Rational-Emotive Therapist would look for irrational thinking (Ellis, 1962). Likewise, those professionals adhering to one or another specialized therapeutic approach within either the internal or external models might also do the same. From an internalist perspective, for example, a psychoanalyst might look at unconscious conflicts as a source of distress, whereas a practitioner subscribing to the Person-Centered approach of Rogers (cf. Rogers, 1951) might focus on the client's self-concept. Regardless, it is one premise of this chapter that these epistemological differences do not overshadow the similarities of therapeutic approaches within the paradigm. When all is said and done, the basic presuppositions about what is known about a client are held in common among all therapeutic specialties within the psychological paradigm. Knowledge is gained through a rational analysis of problems primarily in a one-to-one relationship.

BOX 5-1

### Example Psychological Report

The following psychological report is based on a real report of a diagnostic evaluation of an alcoholic client. The material has been extensively modified to protect the rights of the client.

#### Psychological Evaluation of an Alcoholic

John Jones is a 28-year-old male referred for a psychological evaluation by a state agency. The purpose of the evaluation was to assess the client before therapeutic and vocational planning. An assessment of cognitive and emotional functioning was requested.

Mr. Jones arrived nearly two hours late for his evaluation. He explained he confused the street name with another similar street. He was neatly attired, but he had a body odor.

When asked what problems led to his referral, he said, "my nerves." Also he explained that one time he had a kidney problem which resulted in a lifting restriction, but this does not present a problem presently. Later into the evaluation, he revealed he is a recovering alcoholic; he was recently released from a treatment program. His length of sobriety is "ninety days." He was hospitalized voluntarily for thirty-two days beginning October 14th. He attends Alcoholics Anonymous (AA) meetings, and he says he can contact his sponsor if he has problems.

Educationally, Mr. Jones completed twelve years of formal education, graduating from high school. He has never had other training.

His work history is mainly composed of farm work. He recently lost his 180-acre farm, which he purchased with a government loan. He worked as a farm laborer on two jobs previous to venturing on his own. His only other major work was as a dairy laborer. He worked in the dairy nine years and had "supervisory duties." He was fired from his job and said the termination was "probably related to alcohol." His occupational goal is to become a computer programmer, but he knows little of the field.

His social history is significant. His wife left him six months ago and refuses to see him. She lives in an apartment with his three children, ages 6, 5, and 2. He wants to blame his wife for his problems, but recognizes alcohol was probably the main problem. At present he is living with a male friend who also just recently was treated for alcoholism. They live on what money they make at odd jobs.

For recreation he goes to the movies. He is actively looking for employment. He smokes about two packs of cigarettes a day (down from four packs), and he drinks forty cups of coffee a day. He had seven cups of coffee before coming to this evaluation. He has never been in the military. He possesses a valid driver's license, but he may lose it, due to a "Driving While Intoxicated" (DWI) charge. He may be going to court soon on the DWI charge.

#### Test Results

In addition to the diagnostic interview, six instruments were used for this evaluation. They were: the Wide Range Achievement Test (WRAT); the Wechsler Adult Intelli-

*Continued*

**BOX 5-1**    *Continued*

gence Scale—Revised (WAIS-R); the Memory-for-Designs test (MFD); the Diagnostic Assessment of Reading Errors (DARE); the Minnesota Multiphasic Personality Inventory (MMPI); and the Thematic Apperception Test (TAT). The results are as follows:

*Achievement:*    Mr. Jones's WRAT scores on the three achievement measures are as follows:

| Scale | Grade Level | Standard Score | Percentile |
|-------|-------------|----------------|------------|
| Reading II | 7.8 | 92 | 30 |
| Spelling II | 8.9 | 103 | 58 |
| Arithmetic II | 6.2 | 94 | 34 |

The standard scores should be compared to an average of 100. For his norm group (600 subjects ages 25 to 34), he scored in the *average* range on all scores. He showed relative strength in spelling over reading and arithmetic.

*Intelligence:*    The following are Mr. Jones's scaled scores on the eleven subtests of the WAIS-R. His scores can be compared to the average scaled score for each subtest, which is 10. A score must deviate more than 3 points from the average to be considered significantly different from the norm.

| Verbal Subtests | | Performance Subests | |
|-----------------|---|---------------------|---|
| Information | 8 | Picture Completion | 9 |
| Digit Span | 9 | Picture Arrangement | 6 |
| Vocabulary | 7 | Block Design | 14 |
| Arithmetic | 6 | Object Assembly | 9 |
| Comprehension | 9 | Digit Symbol | 8 |

Given these scaled scores, his Intelligence Quotients (IQs) are as follows:

Verbal IQ = 85
Performance IQ = 94
Full Scale IQ = 87

Mr. Jones is presently functioning in the *low average* range of measured intelligence, with a Full Scale IQ of 87. There was no significant difference between his verbal and performance IQs, which indicates relative consistency in these two major subcategories of intelligence. An analysis of the subtests revealed low average to defective performance on all scales, except the Block Design Scale. The Block Design Scale was

**BOX 5-1**   *Continued*

significantly above all other scales; it measures visual perception, motor coordination, and visual-motor transcoding. His lowest scales were in the defective range. They were: Arithmetic (a measure of concentration, attention, and mathematical reasoning); and Picture Arrangement (a measure of interpretation of social situations, sequencing, and visual alertness). There was a mild degree of intrascale scatter on the Information and Vocabulary scales that might be indicative of educational deprivation.

*Visual Motor Functioning:*   On the Memory-for-Designs test, he scored a raw score of 1, a score in the normal range and not indicative of visual motor difficulties.

*Assessment of Reading Problems:*   The DARE test was administered to check for possible reading difficulties. The DARE is a multiple-choice spelling test that identifies error patterns typically associated with learning disabilities in reading and written expression. Mr. Jones scored 37 correct responses which was consistent with low average performance when compared to 12th grade male norms (percentile rank—27). His error pattern was well within a pattern expected by chance. This profile is *not* consistent with a diagnosis of a reading or written learning disability.

*Personality:*   Mr. Jones' highest MMPI clinical scales and the corresponding T-scores (with a mean of 50 and a standard deviation of 10) are presented below (male norms). The validity scales, however, indicate that this profile should be interpreted with caution. He admitted to a large number of unusual experiences, feelings, or symptoms. There is also the possibility of a very poor self-concept. The three validity scales in combination indicate that he is probably crying out for help.

| Scale | T-Score |
|---|---|
| 8-Schizophrenia | 96 |
| 6-Paranoia | 91 |
| 9-Mania | 83 |
| 7-Psychasthenia | 79 |
| 4-Psychopathic deviation | 76 |
| 2-Depression | 72 |
| 5-Masculinity-feminity | 71 |

The two highest scales in combination can be interpreted as indicating marginal psychological adjustment. There are probably intense feelings of inferiority. Relationships with others are probably unstable and characterized by resentment. This pattern has been found to be common among individuals with thought disorders. Individual scales show confused thinking, resentfulness and suspiciousness, and restless impulsiveness. His thinking is probably rigid and meticulous. He is dissatisfied with his social relationships. He tends to be moralistic. There is evidence that he is probably

*Continued*

**BOX 5-1**    *Continued*

somewhat rebellious or nonconformist. There is moderate depression, pessimism, and worry. He will tend to be a sensitive individual.

Responses to the TAT stimulus cards were not elaborate and showed concrete as opposed to creative imagination. Overriding themes included the ideas of wrongdoing and retribution, with predominant moralistic overtones. He exhibited a tendency to blame, to search for blame, and to aggressively view the wrongdoer. There was also evidence of a realistic well-ordered attitude toward work duties, with identification of ''hard work'' as something to be rewarded. There was no evidence of bizarre content or maladaptive thought processes.

## Mental Status

Mr. Jones was oriented to person, place, time, and situation. There was no evidence of delusions, hallucinations, incoherence, compulsions, obsessions, or phobias. Speech was goal-directed. Affect was appropriate. Eye contact was good but with slight visual scanning. There was no smell of alcohol.

## Conclusion

On the basis of the above findings, the following DSM-III diagnoses are offered for your consideration:

    Axis I:     303.93 Alcohol Dependence, in early remission
                305.90 Caffeinism
    Axis II:    V71.09 No diagnosis on Axis II

Mr. Jones can be described as a 28-year-old recovering alcoholic. It seems he has substituted caffeine for alcohol, and during the diagnostic interview he expressed symptoms consistent with caffeinism (including restlessness, nervousness, diuresis, gastro-intestinal complaints, and periodic heart palpitations). Given his recent dependence on these two drugs, it is difficult to define any maladaptive personality predispositions, although it appears obvious he has an addictive personality. Indeed, a second evaluation may be warranted after both the alcohol and caffeine problems are under control to examine the nature of other personality concerns.

There is strong evidence of confusion and emotional adjustment difficulty, but this is common in recovering alcoholics; Mr. Jones ''hit bottom,'' losing his farm, home, and wife and children. To be anything but confused in this circumstance would be unnatural. However, he shows the classic alcoholic personality: a poor self-concept, moralistic attitudes, interpersonal difficulties, and poor planning ability. Additionally, his desire to go into computer work may be indicative of lack of insight. For example, when he was told his math skills were poor, he was surprised; he said he thought he was good in math.

This man desperately needs vocational success, and this may require vocational rehabilitation counseling. He is confused as to his occupational possibilities. Counsel-

**BOX 5-1**   *Continued*

ing should be directive, and activities should be targeted to areas where there is a strong likelihood of success. Additional failure may facilitate a quick return to alcohol.

Training in the trades seems more appropriate than technical training in a field requiring superior intellectual functioning.

His continued sobriety and attendance at AA meetings should be monitored closely. He also needs counseling and, perhaps, if his personality concerns do not resolve with continued sobriety, in-depth psychotherapy.

Thank you for referring Mr. Jones.

Sincerely,


M. Thompson, PhD
Diplomate, ABPP

---

It is assumed that problems can be reduced (as in reductionism), and that there are direct and linear causes (as in linear determinism). Further, it is assumed that people and their problems exist unto themselves in an absolute (as opposed to a relative) sense. Individuals are treated primarily as independent entities, having identities all their own and problems bounded to a large degree by their individual identities. Individuals are viewed as having skills, abilities, personality traits, self-concepts, maladaptations, and so forth. Counseling goals are viewed as primarily "self"-oriented.

Therapeutic approaches within the psychological paradigm from trait-factorism (Williamson, 1939) to humanism (e.g., Rogers, 1951) to behaviorism (Wolpe, 1958) focus primarily on the individual. Such counseling theories derive from a philosophy that things exist, have their own natures, and can be directed and, since people "possess" intelligence, they have the ability to direct themselves. The individual is viewed as educable, yet change is viewed as an individual process.

## Cause and Effect

Cause and effect is linear from a psychological perspective. This means that once an internal or external factor is identified as affecting the individual, it logically follows that there will be a direct, identifiable result in behavior associated with the factor. To a large degree, outcome (within the cognitive, behavioral, or affective domain) may be viewed as predictable based on the environmental factors directly influencing the individual.

But as with the epistemological differences between the internal and external psychological models, there is a clear difference related to cause and effect between these two models.

From an internalist perspective, what causes behavior is internal to the individual. Effectively, humans are viewed as self-directed. Literally, this means that humans cause what they do by way of internal psychological processes—humans can plan, anticipate, and execute what needs to be done without reliance on others and without basing decisions solely on external data. Since humans can think, anticipate, and direct themselves in their daily activities, they are quite distinct by nature and degree of difference from other animal species.

From an externalist position, what causes behavior is external to the individual. Effectively, humans are viewed as directed by outside influences. This means that humans have no ability to direct themselves, unless, of course, self-directive behavior has been programmed and learned primarily through external factors. What occurs is always a result of outside stimulation and programming. Self-direction appears to be a reality only because a person's learned history is not evident in present behavior. Present behavior is a direct result of past learning, not a reproduction of past learning. Accordingly, behaviorists focus on present behavior, and they do not surmise as to what occurred in the past, *except* to assume environmental influences led to present behavior. Accordingly, behavioral therapies are present-oriented and future-oriented.

## Professional Adherents

The primary professional adherents to the psychological paradigm, of course, are psychologists. Psychology, as a professional service field, has blossomed since the 1940s when the first licensure efforts were made (Dorken, 1976). In fact, psychologists today, in many states, have benefited from aggressive legislative activity that has resulted in clear definitions of psychology practice, control of the titles "psychology" and "psychological," control of the practice of psychology, client freedom to choose psychological services instead of the services of psychiatrists (for clients with medical insurance), and even hospital privileges. Psychologists actively and successfully have challenged the medical profession's "corner on the market" of mental health service provision. Their success is partially based on their linkage to the traditional university research community and to their ability to produce research evidence of the effectiveness (both cost-wise and outcome-wise) of their treatment methods. Cost and outcome comparisons have specifically been made against the medical/psychiatric profession.

Today, to become a practicing psychologists is not an easy task. It requires graduate education to the doctoral degree, one or more years of supervised practice (most usually in a health care setting), and an acceptable score on a very competitive objective licensure exam, where the national average score is usually the cutoff for passing. Some states additionally require an oral or specialty examination.

Psychologists have actively embraced the medical approach to professional education, and the American Psychological Association (APA) has strongly encouraged preprofessional bachelor's degree training in psychology, admission to four-year academic training programs in professional psychology, and a formal internship. The APA's recommendation on professional education has quickly become the preferable route of educational preparation, and credentialing bodies have followed by modifying their standards to mirror APA recommendations.

Once trained and licensed, psychologists may obtain specialty certification through the American Board of Professional Psychology (ABPP). The ABPP was originally founded as the American Board of Examiners in Professional Psychology in 1947, well before psychology regulatory statutes (e.g., licensure laws) proliferated. Its role then was to identify professionals who met basic education and training in psychology, in the absence of legal regulatory mechanisms. Today, as a certification body, the ABPP acts to identify already licensed professional psychologists as specialists in specified subdisciplines of the field. ABPP certification is not "competitive to" or "duplicative of" licensure, although it is valued as a credential, and some licensure boards will recognize it as adequate for licensure on the basis of reciprocity (cooperative licensure between states without a requirement for reexamination of knowledge or credentials).

The ABPP, at the time of this writing, certified specialists in the following six areas: clinical, counseling, clinical neuropsychology, forensic, industrial/organizational, and school psychology. The basic requirements for certification included "a doctoral degree in psychology," preferably from a program accredited by the APA. It is in the analysis of the degree program that the uniqueness of the psychological paradigm is exemplified. Basic, nonspecialty coursework must include training in: (a) research design and methodology; (b) ethics and standards; (c) statistics; (d) psychometrics; (e) biological bases of behavior; (f) cognitive-affective bases of behavior; (g) social bases of behavior; and (h) individual differences. In addition, there must be evidence of relevant specialty coursework and supervision in the specialty. This curriculum, in other words, must be broadly based. Yet the curriculum is clearly focused on psychological research data related to physical, linguistic, and social influences on behavior, where deviance is primarily normatively defined by means of statistics and psychometrics.

Given this foundation, when the actual practice of psychology is analyzed some clear distinctions from the medical profession appear. Lahman (1980) has provided a summary of psychology licensure statutes in the United States and Canada, and it is easy to see that psychologists have carved a niche of practice that is competitive, yet not duplicative of psychiatry. The major distinctions in the definition of practice, of course, are limitations related to the practice of medicine. Although psychologists are able to "diagnose" psychopathology, they must do so without recourse, at their direction, to biological data. For instance, psychologists cannot order invasive diagnostic procedures. And in treatment of psychopathology, psychologists cannot prescribe medication or administer medical/biological treatment. Therefore, such treatments as medication, electroconvulsive or electroshock therapy (ECT or EST), surgery, etcetera, are absolutely forbidden. The psychologist is left, primarily, with nonphysical treatment approaches, most commonly described as "psychotherapy."

Although psychologists diagnose and treat mental disorder, they primarily base their diagnoses on normative information and test data (for instance, scores on the Minnesota Multiphasic Personality Inventory, MMPI, or the Millon Clinical Multiaxial Inventory, MCMI), and they treat such disorder on the assumption that people can learn and change their pathological conditions within a psychotherapeutic (usually one therapist, one client) context.

In fact, the term *learning,* as a scientific study and treatment approach, is probably the most concise descriptor of the psychological treatment philosophy. There-fore, since people ''learn'' to be psychopathological, they can unlearn their pathology. And the psychologist's job is precisely educational within a therapeutic (remedial) context.

## Therapies as Subcategories

There are many theories of counseling and psychotherapy that derive from psychological thinking. Many therapies, therefore, can be associated with the psychological paradigm. In the chapters that follow, several therapeutic approaches will be described.

In chapter 6, Freud's (1917/1966) Psycho-analysis will be presented as a transitional (trans-paradigmatic) therapy, since his theory is a good example of how theory may diverge from the hegemonic thinking of the day, providing a new direction for future practitioners. Following the chapter on Psycho-analysis, two chapters will present internal psychological paradigm therapies, each representing an example of an approach focusing on a different aspect of human functioning—thinking and feeling. Chapter 7 presents Ellis's (1962) Rational-Emotive Therapy. Chapter 8 presents Rogers's Person-Centered Therapy (cf., Rogers, 1951). A third internal model therapy, Perls's (1969) Gestalt Therapy, is described in chapter 9. Gestalt Therapy focuses on thinking, feeling, and behaving. Finally, an external psychological model therapy is presented in chapter 10—Behavior Therapy. In the chapter on behavior therapy, details of the external psychological model are presented, including thorough discussions of theories of classical and operant conditioning, which are at the foundation of behavioral techniques. Two behavior therapy techniques are then described in detail: Systematic Desensitization (Wolpe, 1958, 1973) and Token Economy (Kazdin, 1977).

The psychological paradigm is rich with therapeutic approaches that represent subcategories of the larger psychological orientation. Through the following chapters, readers should get a broad understanding of how a paradigm and its subcategorical therapies interrelate.

## Chapter Conclusion

This chapter has provided an operational list of propositions and tenets of the psychological paradigm. The histories of two separate models within the psychological paradigm were briefly presented. Philosophical and causative issues were explored. Psychologists were identified as the primary professional adherents to psychological paradigm propositions and practical tenets. Several therapeutic approaches were listed as paradigm-consistent. The five following chapters will detail specific therapeutic approaches associated with the psychological paradigm.

# References

Barclay, J. R. (1969). *Counseling and philosophy: A theoretical exposition.* New York: Houghton Mifflin.

Dorken, H. (1976). *The professional psychologist today.* San Francisco: Jossey-Bass.

Ellis, A. (1962). *Reason and emotion in psychotherapy.* Secaucus, NJ: Lyle Stuart.

Freud, S. (1966). *Introductory lectures in psycho-analysis.* New York: W. W. Norton. (Original work published in 1917.)

Kazdin, A. E. (1977). *The token economy: A review and evaluation.* New York: Plenum.

Lahman, F. G. (1980). *Licensure requirements for psychologists: USA and Canada* (2nd ed.). Evansville, IN: University of Evansville Press.

Lovaas, O. I. (1987). Behavioral treatment and normal educational and intellectual functioning in young autistic children. *Journal of Consulting and Clinical Psychology, 55,* 3–9.

Maslow, A. H. (1954). *Motivation and personality.* New York: Harper & Bros.

Maslow, A. H. (1968). *Toward a psychology of being* (2nd ed.). New York: D. Van Nostrand.

Maslow, A. H. (1971). *The farther reaches of human nature.* New York: The Viking Press.

Pavlov, I. P. (1957). *Experimental psychology and other essays.* New York: Philosophical Library.

Perls, F. (1969). *Gestalt therapy verbatim.* Menlo Park, CA: Real People Press.

Rogers, C. R. (1951). *Client-centered therapy.* Boston: Houghton Mifflin.

Skinner, B. F. (1938). *The behavior of organisms: An experimental analysis.* New York: Appleton-Century-Crofts.

Skinner, B. F. (1953). *Science and human behavior.* New York: The Free Press.

Szasz, T. S. (1970). *The manufacture of madness.* New York: Harper & Row.

Szasz, T. S. (1974). *The myth of mental illness.* New York: Harper & Row.

Szasz, T. S. (1978). *The myth of psychotherapy.* Garden City, NY: Anchor Books/Doubleday.

Watson, J. B. (1913). Psychology as the behaviorist views it. *Psychological Review, 20,* 158–177.

Watson, J. B. (1919). *Psychology from the standpoint of a behaviorist.* Philadelphia: Lippincott.

Watson, J. B. (1930). *Behaviorism* (Rev. ed.). Chicago: University of Chicago Press. (Originally published in 1924.)

Watson, J. B., & Rayner, P. (1920). Conditioned emotional reactions. *Journal of Experimental Psychology, 3,* 1–16.

Williamson, E. G. (1939). *How to counsel students.* New York: McGraw-Hill.

Wolpe, J. (1958). *Psychotherapy by reciprocal inhibition.* Stanford, CA: Stanford University Press.

Wolpe, J. (1973). *The practice of behavior therapy.* New York: Pergamon Press.

# 6

# Psycho-analysis:

## A Trans-paradigmatic Theory Bridging the Organic-Medical and Psychological Paradigms*

PSYCHO-ANALYSIS WAS DEVELOPED by Sigmund Freud, MD. The first time the term *psycho-analysis* appeared in print was in 1886. With publication of two of Freud's major works, *The Interpretation of Dreams* in 1900 and *The Psychopathology of Everyday Life* (published in journal form in 1901 and in book form in 1904), psychoanalytic ideas were publicized. Freud's works represent a break with the traditions that preceded them in a way that facilitated a reframing of the cause and cure of emotional maladjustments. Before Freud's time, emotional concerns were viewed as caused either by demons and possession or, to the other extreme, by physical causes (such as lesions on the brain). Although Freud was a physician, his refining of the concept of ''psyche'' as a nonphysical personal phenomenon was a milestone in the development of the psychological paradigm. Freud, although clearly a *transitional theorist* who broke new ground theoretically, maintained close linkage to biological thinking. Therefore, his theory is less purely psychological than many of the theories that followed. Clearly, however, his works act as a bridge between organic-medical and psychological thinking. Psycho-analysis, therefore, is a *trans-paradigmatic* theory.

*Special thanks to Steven Weiner, Ph.D., Clinical Psychologist with Care and Counseling, Inc., of St. Louis, Missouri, for his helpful comments on an earlier draft of this chapter.

95

## Sigmund Freud, MD: A Biographical Sketch

A complete chronology of Sigmund Freud's life and a brief narrative biography were published by Gay (1966, 1989). These two publications were used in the writing of this section as primary sources for describing Freud's life.

Sigismund (Sigmund) Schlomo Freud was born in 1856 in what is now Pribor, Czechoslovakia. His family later settled in Vienna, Austria, where Freud spent his youth. In 1873 Freud enrolled at the University of Vienna, where he studied medicine. He earned his medical degree in 1881. Between entering the University and finishing his degree, Freud developed a passion for research. Actually, his degree was slow to come because of his involvement in research at the University.

In 1882, Freud met his future wife, Martha Bernays. Although Freud and Martha Bernays were secretly engaged in 1882, they delayed wedding plans because Freud lacked a stable income. Subsequently, he accepted a position at the Vienna General Hospital and later set up a private medical practice in 1886. During this time he continued to do research and, in fact, wrote a paper about the then unexplored properties of cocaine. Later in 1886, Freud and Martha Bernays were married.

Over Freud's early professional years, he met several individuals who would have lasting effects on his theory. One was a French neurologist, Jean-Martin Charcot, who studied hysteria and was a proponent of hypnosis. Freud also came into contact with Josef Breuer, a prominent internist, who would later coauthor a book with Freud, *Studies on Hysteria* (in 1895). In fact, Anna O., a woman with bizarre and hysterical symptoms who was a patient of Breuer's, would be the "founding patient of psychoanalysis" (Gay, 1989, p. xxxii). Gay (1966) stated that Anna O. "demonstrated to Freud's satisfaction that hysteria originates in sexual malfunctioning and that symptoms can be talked away" (p. xii).

It was in the 1890s that Freud's ideas about the "psychical" causes of certain symptomatic behaviors began to mature. Through those years, he wrote several brief works that helped form his ideas. It was in 1900 that his classic work, *The Interpretation of Dreams* was published; it received a "cool" reception and sold only 351 copies in its first edition (Gay, 1966). *The Psychopathology of Everyday Life,* a second major publication, was published in book form in 1904 and received a "wider audience" (Gay, 1966, p. xiv).

In 1902 Freud accepted an appointment as an associate professor at the University of Vienna. In the years that followed, Freud was very productive. He worked with difficult patients and often wrote case studies or articles on the problems he encountered. His ideas began to have more influence, especially in Vienna. Later, contacts were made with two individuals who would hold important places in the psychoanalytic and psychotherapy movements. First was Carl Jung, from Zurich, Switzerland, who was supported by Freud to become a leader in the psychoanalytic movement. Jung later disagreed with Freud in an acrimonious split over issues of the role of the sexual drive, libido, in the formation of a class of emotional disturbances called "neurosis." Secondly there was Alfred Adler of Vienna, an early adherent of Freud's, who also later differed with Freud over the issue of primary drives at the root of emotional disturbance. These two individuals went on to develop theories that competed with Psycho-analysis but also paralleled Freud's ideas by maintaining a strong allegiance to ideas of the unconscious.

Although World War I stalled the spread of psychoanalytic ideas, Freud was prolific even under the tension of seeing his sons go to war. (All of his sons survived the war). In 1915, for instance, Freud began to deliver a series of lectures on his theories, published in 1917 as *Introductory Lectures on Psycho-Analysis* (Freud, 1917/1966). That work clearly described his ideas and helped to secure him a wide audience (Gay, 1966). However, the growth of Nazi Germany and the successful German invasion and occupation of Austria in 1938 had a serious personal effect on Freud. He was forced under the influence of anti-Semitism to leave Vienna near the end of his life. He left Vienna after his daughter, Anna, "was summoned to Gestapo headquarters." She suffered distress over the incident, but was physically unharmed (Gay, 1966, p. xxii). Freud and his family moved to London in 1938.

Freud was extremely prolific, leaving many well-articulated written positions related to Psycho-analysis. His influence on what is now the psychotherapeutic field cannot be overemphasized. Freud recognized the gap in theory relevant to human functioning (between biology and religion), and he filled the gap in a way that created a new perspective. Although his theory has been critiqued by many, its place in history is well secured.

Freud died in 1939.

## The Foundational Theory

### The Target of Counseling

Freud's conception of the self is very structural. He views the internal workings of the mind, the *psyche,* as organized but dynamic. Essentially, the psyche is composed of three major sections: the conscious, the preconscious, and the unconscious. The conscious was compared to the unconscious by Freud (1940/1949) as follows:

> *[The conscious] is the same as the consciousness of philosophers and of everyday opinion. Everything else psychical is in our view 'the unconscious.' We are soon led to make an important division in this unconscious. Some processes become conscious easily; they may then cease to be conscious, but can become conscious once more without any trouble: as people say, they can be reproduced or remembered. This reminds us that consciousness is in general a highly fugitive state. What is conscious is conscious only for a moment. (p. 16)*

The unconscious, on the other hand, is a deep-seated symbolic reservoir. It is manifest only at times when individuals are in a somnolent state, for example, through the process of dreaming or hypnosis. Otherwise, what is unconscious is unknown. However, there is a psychical process termed the "preconscious," which is a part of the psyche between the two extremes of the conscious and the unconscious. The material in the preconscious is retrievable; it is "capable of becoming conscious" (Freud, 1940/1949, p. 17). Describing the relative nature of conscious, preconscious, and unconscious material, Freud (1940/1949) stated:

> *The division between the three classes of material which possess these qualities is neither absolute nor permanent. What is preconscious becomes conscious, as we have seen, without any assistance from us; what is unconscious can through our efforts be made conscious, and in the process we may have a feeling that we are often overcoming very strong resistances. (p. 17)*

It was precisely his understanding and definition of the unconscious that led Freud to develop his Psycho-analysis. Because the human being could be psychologically held captive by his or her own unconscious, a means to free up the material stored there was necessary. That is precisely what Psycho-analysis is all about.

However, Freud's conception of a structured psyche divided into three parts was not adequate for understanding the interplay of conscious and unconscious material that he observed in everyday life. He needed a dynamic—a means of movement between the unconscious, preconscious, and the conscious. At the same time, he needed a way to conceptualize the idea of "self" in a way that incorporated biological and cultural factors. The means to this end was the development of three dynamic aspects of self: the id, the ego, and the superego.

The *id* is the aspect of self most linked to biology and heredity. It is, consistent with Darwin's (1859/1984; 1874) theory of natural selection, sexually and aggressively motivated. Rather than logic, it is driven primarily by *libido,* the life force. In a sense, the id represents the prurient, selfish, hedonistic aspects of humaness. It is motivated primarily by two instincts: the sexual instinct and the aggressive instinct (what Freud first called the "destructive" instinct). The id lives deep in the unconscious.

The *superego,* on the other hand, is an aspect of self that is developed primarily through cultural rather than biological means. Although the superego is present from birth (as a far-evolved extension of the id), it is malleable, especially in the first six years of life. It lives primarily in the conscious part of the psyche. It is influenced mainly by the individual's relationships to his or her parents, and consequently, it represents parental injunctions. In this way, it is the cultural conscience (moral code) of the personality—the civilized aspect of the personality. However, where civilization prevents the expression of unreigned sexual and aggressive activity, the superego becomes the antithesis of the id. In this way, the superego and the id are antagonistic in the personality. If the superego and the id are in unremediated conflict, then disintegration of the personality can occur (where integration of the personality reflects the constructive, adaptive sense of human functioning). The superego is actually a close extension of the ego, and it is thereby vulnerable to weakness in the ego.

The *ego* is the rational mediator of biological and cultural influences on the personality. Freud (1940/1949) said that the ego "acts as an intermediary between the id and the external world" (p. 2). It has the "task of self-preservation" (p. 2), and, if

**The Psyche**

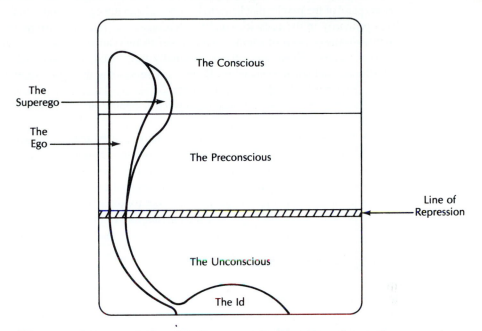

Diagrammatic representation of the human psyche. The id lives deep in the unconscious. The ego and superego are extensions of the id. The superego lives primarily in the conscious and preconscious. The ego lives primarily in the conscious and preconscious, but it may enter the unconscious in somnolent states, repressing unwanted psychic material as it retreats to the conscious when threatened. The line of repression represents the border between the unconscious and conscious states.

it is strong, it maintains control over oppositional forces in the personality. Freud (1940/1949) stated:

> *The ego strives after pleasure and seeks to avoid unpleasure. An increase in unpleasure that is expected and foreseen is met by a* signal *of anxiety; the occasion of such an increase, whether it threatens from without or within, is known as a* danger. *(p. 3)*

Therefore, when the ego is conscious and alert to potential difficulties arising from cultural versus biological conflicts, it experiences anxiety, a chief characteristic of *neurosis*. Neurosis is mental distress in which the ego is still organized and moderating opposing forces, but the ego is still vulnerable. If, on the other hand, the ego were to give over to the id-superego conflict, a *psychosis* might emerge. In psychosis, unrelenting sexual and aggressive instincts from the unconscious predominate, and contact with the external world is lost.

The ego is a close relative of the id. It evolved from the id and reflects the social requirement for human survival. Without the ego, the human would be purely animalistic. Luckily, there is a line of repression between the unconscious and the preconscious parts of the psyche that helps to keep the id and the ego separate. In fact, the ego lives primarily in the conscious and the preconscious, retreating to the unconscious mainly during periods of somnolence in order to reorganize without the influence of external factors. When internally or externally threatened, however, the ego's main defense mechanism is *repression*. Repression represents the ego's retreat from the unconscious while abandoning in the unconscious any threatening psychological material. Repression is a way of pushing down threatening or dangerous psychological material.

What Freud proposed was a picture of the self represented by a psyche divided into three parts (the conscious, preconscious, and the unconscious) and affected by three dynamic mechanisms—the id, ego, and superego. The interplay of conscious and unconscious material is reconciled by the biological and cultural demands on the organism that are moderated by the ego. In order for there to be psychological health, there must be a strong, healthy ego. (See the diagram of the psyche.)

## The Process of Counseling

The process of Psycho-analysis is the process of uncovering the psychological history of the individual and removal of symptomatology through a "talking cure." Psychoanalysis began when Freud's colleague, Josef Breuer, described to Freud his treatment of Anna O., a woman who showed severe physical symptomatology without physical correlates. In his account of his treatment of Anna, Breuer (Breuer & Freud, 1885/1889) described how her symptoms (which included paralysis of certain body parts) were affected by discussion of their origins. Her symptoms were especially affected when Anna was in a hypnotic state. In fact, as part of her disorder, Anna entered into a hypnotic state regularly in the evenings. Breuer stated:

> *That in the case of this patient the hysterical phenomena disappeared as soon as the event which had given rise to them was reproduced in her hypnosis—made it possible to arrive at a therapeutic technical procedure which left nothing to be desired in its logical consistency and systematic application. Each individual symptom in this complicated case was taken separately in hand; all the occasions on which it had appeared where described in reverse order, starting before the time when the patient became bed-ridden and going back to the event which had led to its first appearance. When this had been described the symptom was permanently removed.*
>
> *In this way her paralytic contractures and anaesthesias, disorders of vision and hearing of every sort, neuralgias, coughing, tremors, etc., and finally her disturbances of speech were 'talked away'. (p. 72)*

Psycho-analysis was born. Although Breuer is credited with the first "talking cure," it was Freud who recognized the implications of his work and who developed the procedures described by Breuer into a comprehensive theory of treatment of mental disorder. *Catharsis* was used by Freud as the technical term for "talking cure." ("Talking cure" was coined by Anna O. in her description of her own treatment). Catharsis is a "purging of the mind, a sort of unburdening of the mind," according to Brill (1921, p. 8).

The process of Psycho-analysis, then, is a process of providing an atmosphere in which the patient can explore his or her history without constraint, revealing his or her most intimate memories, especially those memories surrounding the emergence of symptomatic behavior.

To understand Freud's process of therapy, it is important to understand his theory of personality. For Freud, the sexual instinct predominated in the emergence of neurosis. He even felt that Breuer, in his presentation of Anna O.'s case study, underplayed the role sexuality held in the emergence of her symptoms. Of course, others disagreed with Freud on the role of the sexual instinct in the development of mental disorder (such as Adler and Jung), and one has to wonder why Freud so steadfastly held to his position. The answer may be threefold: (a) in the privacy of the therapeutic relationship, patients probably spoke openly about sexual issues, since they were probably sexually frustrated by a restrictive cultural and societal attitude, which probably prevented people from acknowledging, much less discussing openly, their sexual urges; and (b) the findings of Freud's self-explorations, including his interpretations of his own dreams, were highly sexual, and these subjective experiences were viewed as representative of biological processes common to all humans; and (c) Freud's views on the sexual instinct were consistent with Darwin's theories. Moreover, Freud's ideas, being seminal, were largely initially ineffectively challenged by alternative viewpoints. Freud viewed the sexual drive (manifested quantitatively by libido) as resulting from processes in the darkest but most basic reaches of human nature.

What this all means is that humans, according to Freud (1940/1949), must be viewed as highly sexual beings. Even from birth humans primarily seek pleasurable sensations and sexual stimulation. Freud postulated several stages in childhood psychosexual development: the oral, anal, phallic, and genital phases. These stages are critical to psychical functioning, because libido can become *fixated* (disproportionally distributed) to objects associated with the stages of development. Freud (1940/1949) stated:

> *During the study of sexual functions we have been able to gain a first, preliminary conviction, or rather a suspicion, of two discoveries which will later be found to be important over the whole of our field. Firstly, the normal and abnormal manifestations observed by us (that is, the phenomenology of the subject) need to be described from the point of view of their dynamics and economics (in our case, from the point of view of the quantitative distribution of the libido). And secondly, the aetiology of the disorders which we study is to be looked for in the individual's developmental history—that is to say, in his early life. (p. 13)*

A fixation may occur at a particular stage of development and the individual may be *cathected* (charged with libidinal energy) to particular objects associated with the fixation at that stage of development. Such fixations will have a dramatic effect on ''adult erotic life'' (p. 10), since, under external stress, the individual may psychologically *regress* (return) to that level of functioning. Freud stated:

> People fall ill of a neurosis if they are deprived of the possibility of satisfying their libido—that they fall ill owing to 'frustration', as I put it—and that their symptoms are precisely a substitute for their frustrated satisfaction. (p. 428)

Libidinal frustration, then, leads to regression of psychological functioning associated with a childhood stage of psychosexual development, and symptomatically, the individual will demonstrate behaviors consistent with fixations at that stage. In this way, childhood development, frustrations during psychosexual development and subsequent fixations, and later libidinal frustration and regression are closely associated with neurosis and symptomatic behavior.

The process of self-exploration through Psycho-analysis, then, must take a person back to those points where symptomatic behaviors first emerged, which likely are linked to early childhood developments.

## Counselor Role

The primary role of the therapist, beyond providing an atmosphere for full exploration of the client's history, is to help to strengthen the client's ego. Freud (1940/1949) stated: ''The ego is weakened by the internal conflict and we must go to its help'' (p. 30). The importance of the ego in mental health is clearly communicated by Freud in the following passage:

> According to our hypothesis it is the ego's task to meet the demands raised by its three dependent relations—to reality, to the id and to the super-ego—and nevertheless at the same time to preserve its own organization and maintain its own autonomy. The necessary precondition of the pathological states under discussion can only be a relative or absolute weakening of the ego which makes the fulfilment of its tasks impossible. The severest demand on the ego is probably the keeping down of the instinctual claims of the id, to accomplish which it is obliged to maintain large expenditures of energy on anticathexes. But the demands made by the super-ego too may become so powerful and so relentless that the ego may be paralysed, as it were, in the face of its other tasks. We may suspect that, in the economic conflicts which arise at this point, the id and the super-ego often make common cause against the hard-pressed ego which tries to cling to reality in order to retain its normal state. If the other two become too strong, they succeed in loosening and altering the ego's organization, so that its proper relation to reality is disturbed or even brought to an end. We have seen it happen in dreaming: when the ego is detached from the reality of the external world, it slips down, under the influence of the internal world, into psychosis. (pp. 29-30)

Essentially, the psychoanalyst must assist the ego by making it aware of the conflicts and the challenges from both biological and cultural sources, so that the ego can mediate these forces and make decisions for adaptive living. The psychoanalyst expects "complete candour" on the part of the ego (Freud, 1940/1949), and in return there is discretion on the part of the therapist. The fundamental rule for the client is:

> *He is to tell us not only what he can say intentionally and willingly, what will give him relief like a confession, but everything else as well that his self-observation yields him, everything that comes into his head, even if it is* disagreeable *for him to say it, even if it seems to him* unimportant *or actually* nonsensical.
> *. . thus [he will] put us in a position to conjecture his repressed unconscious material and to extend, by the information we give him, his ego's knowledge of his unconscious. (p. 31)*

This knowledge is critical to reconciliation of the internal forces that heretofore have led to desintegration of the personality. The therapist's *interpretation* is critical to going beyond the stage of recognition on the part of the client. The therapist's tasks can be summarized as follows: (a) the therapist should produce ego self-knowledge in the client; and (b) the therapist must accurately interpret material from the client's unconscious. If done effectively, it is assumed that symptoms will diminish or disappear.

There are many traps in the process of psychoanalysis that make the therapist's task difficult, but there is one ally that proves to be of special importance. That ally is *transference*. According to Freud (1940/1949), transference is the phenomenon by which the client actually sees in the therapist a "reincarnation of some important figure out of his childhood or past, and consequently transfers on to him feelings and reactions which undoubtedly applied to this prototype" (p. 31). Often, the image of a client's parents are transferred onto the therapist. Transference can be positive or negative, just as feelings toward parents can be positive or negative. Regardless, *transference allows for the restructuring of the superego,* since it takes the individual back to an earlier time when relations had a significant impact on the formation of the personality. In this sense, transference gives the client a second chance. The newly educated super-ego (educated under the watchful eye of a trained therapist) can undo the mistakes of earlier learning—literally undermining fixations and cathected libido. By respecting the patient's individuality, the therapist can help to reconstruct the personality so that libidinal drives are more fully reconciled with the injunctions of a newer, more accepting super-ego. Consequently, the patient, through transference, relives a part of his or her past in the relationship with the therapist. Subsequently, the client is given a new opportunity. But the role of the therapist through the transference process is a tricky one, since the therapist might be trapped by his or her own transferences in relation to the client (countertransference). In this case, a therapist might be unable to extricate him or herself from his or her own personality, thereby becoming a victim of his or her own unreconciled libidinal impulses. For example, a male therapist confronted by a female client who views the therapist through transference as a strong father figure, might succumb to his own sexual feelings, just as a disturbed father might when confronted seductively by a loving daughter. (Remember Freud's theory was very sexual, and he even defined the child-parent relationship as highly incestuous at the unconscious level). So, the therapist must constantly battle with countertransference, which could lead to actions that would be counterproductive to the psychoanalytic task.

### Goals of Counseling and Ideal Outcomes

The main goals of Psycho-analysis are ego self-knowledge and ego strength. Freud (1940/1949) stated: ''What we desire . . . is that the ego, emboldened by the certainty of our help, shall dare to take the offensive in order to reconquer what has been lost'' (p. 35). Further, Freud stated:

> *We serve the patient in various functions, as an authority and a substitute for his parents, as a teacher and educator; and we have done the best for him if, as analysts, we raise the mental processes in his ego to a normal level, transform what has become unconscious and repressed into preconscious material and thus return it once more to the possession of his ego. (p. 38)*

Obviously, the ego takes precedence in the healthy personality, and it is the therapist's goal to put the ego in its rightful place as a rational voice and moderator of divergent forces in the personality.

## General Procedures

### Assessment

Assessment in Psycho-analysis is first a medical process, as originally conceived. The individual patient is examined (if not physically then through a complete history), regarding the symptoms from which he or she wants relief. Symptoms are viewed in a classic medical sense as indicators that something is wrong internally. Although there is no analogy to ''germs'' in the physical sense, psychoanalysts proceed from the assumption that something is wrong with the inner workings of the patient. Some basic hypotheses can be made based on psychoanalytic assumptions (such as an overcontrolling super-ego or an unremitting libidinal drive), but these hypotheses are held in abeyance until a clear exploration of the patient's unconscious processes is undertaken.

### Treatment/Remediation

Treatment is taken to remediate the ego, to strengthen it, and to reveal conflicting forces in the personality. Treatment may involve analyzing dreams, hypnosis (although Freud used hypnosis less and less in his later years), free association (the process of allowing the client to respond spontaneously and in an unrestricted way to either the analyst's cues or to self-concentration on symptoms), and other means of releasing repressed material. The intent is to clarify the events associated with symptomatic behavior, with the aim of reconstructing those events psychologically.

## Case Management

Case management is an ongoing process of analysis, interpretation, and reanalysis. The patient and the analyst may meet several times a week, sometimes for several years. Because the client's history (especially the symptomatic history) must be fully understood and brought to conscious light, it takes a concerted effort and a long-term commitment to successfully undergo Psycho-analysis. This commitment must be understood from the beginning of therapy, and it is incumbent upon the therapist to communicate clearly about the potential benefits and dangers of undergoing Psycho-analysis. Because of the potential cost and commitment in time, it is also wise for the therapist to describe alternative treatment methods. In that way, the client is fully informed before consenting to psychoanalytic psychotherapy.

Psycho-analysis usually takes place in a comfortable office. The client is allowed to be comfortable and may recline on a couch or sit in a nearby chair. The analyst usually sits in a way that he or she can observe the patient, although it is ideal if the patient cannot observe the analyst. Note taking during sessions is important, since these notes will help the analyst to uncover unconscious processes. Sessions ordinarily last from thirty to fifty minutes.

# Specialized Techniques

There are several techniques associated with Psycho-analysis which will be briefly described. It should be remembered that learning Psycho-analysis is not an easy task. It takes many years of training, supervised experience, and personal analysis under the direction of a trained analyst. In this light, the following techniques are offered as a didactic means to help represent Freud's theory of counseling and psychotherapy. The list is not meant to be a comprehensive accounting of psychoanalytic techniques; nor is it meant to be an adequate means to direct beginning therapists. Students interested in becoming psychoanalysts should seek direction from trained analysts at approved psychoanalytic training centers.

Some of the techniques consistent with Psycho-analysis are:

**1.** *The cathartic method.* As mentioned earlier, *catharsis* is the technical term for the talking cure. A major task of the therapist is to allow for a free flow of information from the client's ego to the therapist. The intent is to free the client through open discussion. As Brill (1921) stated:

> *Every hysterical symptom represents some mental or emotional disturbance that has taken place in the person's life in the past; there were occurrences of a disagreeable and painful nature which every individual likes to forget. Their*

> *[psychoanalysts'] idea was that if a patient can recall the unpleasant situation which gave origin to the symptom and live it over, so to say, he loses the symptom; that words are almost equivalent to the action, and that in going over some painful experience in the past there is what they called an* abreaction . . . *in which the painful emotions associated with the experience were liberated and thus ceased to create physical disturbances. (p. 8)*

By means of the cathartic method, symptoms are overcome.

**2.** *Free association.* Arlow (1989) stated that Freud developed free association as a technique as follows:

> *Because many of his patients could not be hypnotized, he dropped hypnosis in favor of forced suggestion, a technique of recollection fostered by the insistent demanding pressure of the therapist. Among other things, this technique produced artifacts in the form of sexual fantasies about childhood, which the patient offered the therapist as if they were recollections of actual events. Taking advantage of his new operational concepts of the dynamic unconscious and the principle of strict psychic determinism, Freud reduced the element of suggestion to a minimum by a new technical procedure in which he asked his patients to report freely and without criticism whatever came into their minds. (p. 34)*

By simply allowing a client to tell everything that comes to his or her mind, the therapist can "trace all the forces that were responsible for the symptoms" (Brill, 1921, p. 15). Patients are simply asked to maintain attention on the task at hand, as they let their minds roam freely among the images and thoughts associated with problematic behaviors. Once revealed, the therapist constructs interpretations of these recollections that can help the client to understand his or her own internal workings. Thus, the client's internal processes can be brought under conscious ego control.

**3.** *Facilitating and interpreting transference.* The analysis of transference is a classic psychoanalytic technique. It assumes, according to Arlow (1989) that:

> *At a certain stage in the treatment, when it appears the patient is just about ready to relate his current difficulties to unconscious conflicts from childhood concerning wishes over some important person or persons in his life, a new and interesting phenomenon emerges. Emotionally, the analyst assumes major significance in the life of the patient. The patient's perceptions of and demands upon the analyst become inappropriate, out of keeping with reality. The professional relationship becomes distorted as he tries to introduce personal instead of professional considerations into their interaction. Understanding transference was one of Freud's major discoveries. He perceived that in the transference, the patient was unconsciously reenacting a latter-day version of forgotten childhood memories and repressed unconscious fantasies. (p. 39)*

Through the development of transferences, resistance and defenses come forward as a means to protect the ego from unconscious material. Yet it is the ''working through'' (Arlow, 1989, p. 39) of such resistances and defenses that is important to a resolution of conflicts within the personality. Through the process of analysis, the therapist attempts to make the transferences understood so the client can experience in the present what occurred in the past. The intent is awareness, and, at the same time, a rebuilding of the superego with fuller acceptance of the client's biological needs. Freud (1940/1949) stated:

> If we succeed, as we usually can, in enlightening the patient on the true nature of the phenomena of transference, we shall have struck a powerful weapon out of the hand of his resistance and shall have converted dangers into gains. For a patient never forgets again what he has experienced in the form of transference; it carries a greater force of conviction than anything he can acquire in other ways. (p. 34)

The analysis of transference, therefore, plays a major role in the psychoanalytic process.

**4.** *Dream interpretation.* While discussing dream interpretation, Freud (1940/1949) stated:

> But what makes dreams so invaluable in giving us insight is the circumstances that, when the unconscious material makes its way into the ego, it [the unconscious] brings its own modes of working along with it. . . . It is only in this way that we learn the laws which govern the passage of events in the unconscious and the respects in which they differ from the rules that are familiar to us in waking thought. (p. 24)

Freud felt that symptoms and dreams were similar since they involved unconscious material amenable only under circumstances in which the ego was reclining. Essentially, dreams reflect conflicts between the forces in the personality. The therapist requests that the patient recall his or her dreams in depth. In that way, the analyst can take notes and attempt to piece together aspects of the dream that may clarify repressed wishes and impulses. The interpretation of dreams is founded on the idea that what is unconscious can be known and understood if one understands the basic biological drives of the human being. Dreams are interpreted in light of the biological instincts of sex and aggression.

These four techniques can be considered foundational to Freud's Psycho-analysis.

## Recent Developments or Criticisms

To a degree, what has been presented here represents Freud's theory up until the day he died, but it is not in any sense a complete accounting of his ideas and their later implementation. There are a number of issues that cannot be covered in such a short summary that should not be overlooked. Readers, for instance, are directed to the work of Anna Freud (Sigmund's daughter); her book *The Ego and Mechanisms of Defense* (A. Freud, 1936) is a classic psychoanalytic text that describes ego defense mechanisms, such as repression, introjection, and projection. Freud's later emphasis on *insight* (a spontaneous clear-cut moment of understanding) as a means to awareness should not be overlooked, either. As Fine (1973) stated: ''Freud's early emphasis on catharsis has been almost entirely superseded by his later emphasis on insight and the subsequent stress on the reorganization of the character structure'' (p. 21). In this sense, one of the valued outcomes of therapy is a patient's *insight* into his or her functioning (which translates to a deep-felt awareness that is unlikely to be forgotten). Readers are directed to Freud's own works for further exploration of these issues and to those works of his contemporary and subsequent adherents for a more complete and recent explication of his theory.

Freud's ideas have been lauded and criticized. Critics argue that his ideas, although at the time viewed as scientific, are actually reflections of Freud's own subjective experiences. Thus, his theory is viewed as nonobjective. Behaviorists, for example, argue that Freud's concepts are not objectively measurable, and therefore, they are not viewed as useful according to behavioral or positivistic criteria.

Freud's emphasis on sexuality is also a point of contention. Although it can be argued convincingly that sexuality plays an important part in the survival of the species and in human (especially young adult) motivation, the fact that Freud subjugated all aspects of human psychological growth, development, and functioning to the sexual drive seems to deny the other nonsexual aspects of humanness.

Feminist theorists have also launched a credible attack on Freud's ideas, especially the role Freud gave to the concept of ''penis envy.'' This concept openly espouses male superiority and implies the subordination of female personality development to that of the male. Freud's position, by today's standards, is extraordinarily sexist.

Regardless of criticism, his ideas broke new ground. Psycho-analysis thus represents a milestone, especially as viewed from the perspective of the psychological paradigm of mental health services.

## Paradigm Fit

### Focus of Study

Freud's focus of study is dualistic. At the same time he views the human psyche as a thing unto itself, he fully connects the psyche to human biology by linking the id to the human body. Therefore, the mind and the body are viewed as distinct but connected entities. In that sense, Freud's epistemology is an offshoot of Newtonian logic, where force, energy use, and growth are all linear cause-and-effect processes.

Freud viewed the human psyche in a structural sense. He conceived of the psyche in a physical way. When analyzing his theory, one gets the impression that he saw the psyche, with all its components, as a real and structural "thing." His writings reflect his continued efforts to demarcate and to understand inner mechanisms.

## View of Nature of Reality

Freud's view of human nature is quite pessimistic. His theory fully recognizes that human cruelty and abuse are realities. Freud viewed human beings as sexually and aggressively driven and, especially when confronted by patients who have committed unconscionable crimes, Freud's perspective offers a logical framework for assessment and understanding.

It is clear-cut from his works that Freud viewed people as entities that exist to a large degree separately and independently. In fact, his emphasis on the need for individuals to be autonomous is revealing of his view of the human as a separable unit. Society, too, has a thinglike quality, as the human is continually confronted by conflicts between biological and cultural pressures (as if culture exists as a discrete phenomenon). Freud's view of nature and reality, then, is very structural and concrete. It separates biology, psychology, and culture, yet it is dynamic in its descriptions of how these factors interrelate. The term *psychodynamic* to describe Freud's Psycho-analysis, therefore, is quite appropriately reflective of biological, psychological, and cultural "things" in motion.

## Consonance with Paradigm Propositions and Tenets

As a transitional theory, Freud's ideas are a mix of what has been defined in this book as organic-medical and psychological thinking. The focus is clearly on the individual and on assessment of the individual, consistent with both paradigms. However, Freud believed that he was assessing biological and instinctual drives when delving into the unconscious. From a strictly psychological perspective, such an interpretation of the unconscious would be downplayed in favor of a more purely psychical explanation (e.g., that dreams represent an unwinding of conscious events).

Causation is viewed as linear, which is again consistent with both paradigms. However, although symptoms and conditions can be isolated for treatment, the means of treatment has a very medical as opposed to psychological flavor. In a way, Freud's Psycho-analysis can be considered a type of surgery on the mind. It is a means to get right in the middle of things and to excise anything that blocks the flow of natural processes. Psychopathology is primarily viewed as biologically based, especially when psychosis is viewed as the result of dominating sexual and aggressive *instincts*. In this way, Psycho-analysis is closely aligned with organic-medical thinking.

Ideally, the training of a therapist is both medical and psychological. However, psychologists have only recently, and as the result of legal suits, been allowed admission to institutes providing *full* psychoanalytic training (American Psychological Association, 1988). Until 1988, only physicians could be admitted to full psychoanalytic training.

As a trans-paradigmatic theory of counseling and psychotherapy, then, Psycho-analysis shows theoretical and practical linkage to both the organic-medical and psychological paradigms.

## Chapter Conclusion

This chapter has served as an introduction to counseling theories associated with the psychological paradigm. The development of Psycho-analysis was a milestone in the development of the mental health service field. It was revolutionary for its time and has been unequaled in its influence on the way human nature is viewed. As a trans-paradigmatic psychotherapy, it provides a good example of how ground-breaking ideas can lead to development of comprehensive, competitive viewpoints in the field of counseling and psychotherapy.

## References

American Psychological Association. (1988). Lawsuit settlement opens psychoanalytic training to psychologists. *American Psychological Association Practitioner, 2*(3), 1.

Arlow, J. A. (1989). Psychoanalysis. In R. Corsini & D. Wedding (Eds.), *Current psychotherapies* (4th ed., pp. 19–62). Itasca, IL: F. E. Peacock.

Brill, A. A. (1921). *Basic principles of psycho-analysis.* New York: Washington Square Press.

Breuer, J., & Freud, S. (1989). Studies on hysteria: Case I: Fraulein Anna O. In P. Gay (Ed.), *The Freud reader* (pp. 61–86). New York: W. W. Norton. (Original work published in 1895.)

Darwin, C. (1874). *The descent of man and selection in relation to sex* (2nd ed.) Chicago: Rand McNally.

Darwin, C. (1984). On the origin of species by means of natural selection. In R. Jastrow & K. Korey (Ed. & Commentator, respectively). *The essential Darwin,* (pp. 57–228). Boston: Little, Brown & Co. (Original work published in 1859.)

Fine, R. (1973). Psychoanalysis. In R. Corsini (Ed.), *Current psychotherapies* (pp. 1–33). Itasca, IL: F. E. Peacock.

Freud, A. (1936). *The ego and the mechanisms of defense.* New York: International University Press.

Freud, S. (1900). *The interpretation of dreams.* Standard ed. Vol. 4. New York: W. W. Norton.

Freud, S. (1901). *The psychopathology of everyday life.* Standard ed. Vol. 6. New York: W. W. Norton.

Freud, S. (1949). *An outline of psycho-analysis.* New York: W. W. Norton. (Original work published in 1940.)

Freud, S. (1966). Introductory lectures on psycho-analysis. New York: W. W. Norton. (Original work published in 1917.)

Gay, P. (1966). Freud: A brief life. In J. Strachey (Ed. and translator). *Introductory lectures on psycho-analysis.* New York: W. W. Norton.

Gay, P. (1989). Sigmund Freud: A chronology. In P. Gay (Ed.), *The Freud reader.* New York: W. W. Norton.

# _7

# Rational-Emotive Therapy:
## *An Internal Psychological Model Therapy Focusing on Thinking*

RATIONAL-EMOTIVE THERAPY (RET) was developed by Albert Ellis, PhD, in 1955 (Ellis, 1989a). One of his major publications presenting his approach was a book entitled, *Reason and Emotion in Psychotherapy* (Ellis, 1962). In that book, Ellis defined his basic therapeutic approach. Since that time, Ellis and his associates have been prolific in defining and communicating the basic tenets of RET. Many publications have appeared in print, and RET is a highly researched therapeutic approach. RET, as the name implies, is a highly cognitive approach for understanding personality and for doing therapy.

## Albert Ellis, PhD: A Biographical Sketch

Albert Ellis was born in Pittsburgh, Pennsylvania, in 1913. At an early age Ellis suffered from an illness, nephritis, and he almost died from complications following an infected tonsil (Dryden, 1989). Between the ages of 4 and 9, he was hospitalized nine times, which affected his schooling and curtailed his involvement in physical activities. In fact, throughout his life, Ellis has been affected by illnesses. In middle age he was diagnosed as diabetic, a lifelong condition that has required significant life-style adjustment. Beyond facing his illnesses, Ellis learned early in life to be helpful

**111**

*Albert Ellis*

to others. He viewed his mother as "a neglectful woman in her own nice way," and, he took an active role in his family, especially helping with his younger siblings. Consequently, he adopted a helping attitude early in life. In fact, Ellis said in an interview in 1989:

> *I always seemed to have been the kind of person who, when unhappy, made an effort to think about and figure out ways to make myself less unhappy. In a way I was a born therapist for myself. It certainly came naturally to me. Later on, I used this problem-solving tendency to help my friends with their problems, but first I used it with myself (see the interview of Ellis conducted by Dryden, 1989, p. 540).*

Although he had much to be sad about, he apparently learned that he could make himself less unhappy through effort, and he applied this basic philosophy to his own life and later in his relationships with others.

Ellis grew up and was college educated in New York City. He earned a business degree at the City College of New York. In 1943 he earned an MA from Columbia University in clinical psychology and started a private practice in counseling about the same time. He later (1947) earned a PhD degree in clinical psychology from Columbia University. He was trained in classic Psycho-analysis, but he felt uncomfortable using psychoanalytic techniques. His disenchantment with Psycho-analysis later led to the development of Rational-Emotive Therapy.

Ellis frequently tells stories at his workshops about how he overcame his fear of women—a story that not only reflects a personal philosophy but also reflects upon the development of RET. At age 19, to overcome his fear, he forced himself "to talk to a hundred girls in a row in the Bronx Botanical Gardens during the period of one month" (see Dryden's 1989, interview). He later married and divorced twice, and presently lives with a woman who has been his partner since 1964. He is a model of his own theory, in that he believes that thinking and acting or, in other words, cognition and action, rule over the emotions. Ellis's view derived from his readings of the philosopher Epictetus, who carried forth ideas from earlier philosophers about disturbance deriving from *one's view* of things.

Ellis has held several clinical and teaching positions, but for most of his career he has been in private practice while directing his institutes in New York (e.g., the Institute for Rational Living, Inc.). He taught at Rutgers University and New York University. He worked for a while as the Chief Psychologist of the New Jersey State Diagnostic Center, and also as a Chief Psychologist at the New Jersey Department of Institutions and Agencies. He has been a consultant to the Veterans Administration.

Dr. Ellis received the award for Distinguished Professional Contributions from the American Psychological Association in 1985. He is a fellow of several prestigious professional organizations. Ellis has been a prolific writer, and his bibliography filled sixteen pages of the *American Psychologist* in a 1986 issue of the journal (Ellis, 1986). He has been one of the most influential theorists in the field of counseling and psychotherapy.

## The Foundational Theory

### The Target of Counseling

Ellis (1989a) has simplified his theory into an A-B-C-(D) model of thinking and feeling, which to a large degree presents his therapeutic approach and the target of therapy. The model is as follows:

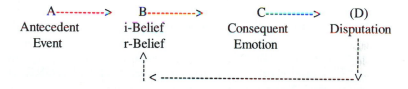

According to this model, people are born with the potential to think rationally or irrationally, that is, to hold rational beliefs (rB) or irrational beliefs (iB). People, being cognitive beings, tend to perceive and think more or less concurrently with their feelings and behaviors. In fact, Ellis believes that when a human is confronted by an antecedent event (A), it is the cognitive event or belief (B) associated with the event which results in emotional consequences (C). Essentially, the way one thinks affects the way one feels and behaves. When, however, the emotional consequences are self-defeating, then they are most likely the result of irrational beliefs, which can be actively disputed (D) in therapy by trained professionals or by the client himself or herself, once taught how to identify and to dispute irrational thoughts (cf., Ellis & Harper, 1975).

Ellis (1962, 1989c) emphasized how people interpret what happens to them; this is true as the basis of his theory of personality and as the foundation of his theory of psychotherapy. Accordingly, when a person exhibits severe emotional maladjustment, it is assumed that it has stemmed from some "magical, empirically unvalidated thinking" (p. 199). According to Ellis, it is disputation of irrational beliefs by way of ideas firmly grounded in the logico-empirical tradition that can help to minimize or even ameliorate emotional maladjustment. The therapist, and subsequently the client himself or herself, must actively attack those thoughts and images that result in emotional malfunctioning. According to Ellis (1989c), since people have a tendency to think irrationally, it takes "hard work and practice" to straighten out such "crooked" thinking (p. 200).

## The Process of Counseling

Ellis (1989c) stated that people have a "tendency to irrational thinking, self-damaging habituations, wishful thinking, and intolerance" (p. 197), which can be exacerbated by the social environment. Ellis holds that about 80 percent of the personality is determined by heredity. Nevertheless, he feels people can learn to change their thinking so that the outcomes of their thinking can be positive and nondistressing. A therapist, then, must essentially target a person's beliefs, point "B" as presented in the A-B-C-(D) diagram, in order to change the client's "most basic values," if, in fact, those values keep the client "disturbance prone" (Ellis, 1989c, p. 198).

Ellis (1989a) claimed that almost all irrational ideas seen in therapy can be summarized by three "basic" irrational beliefs: (a) "I must be liked by all people"; (b) "You other people must treat me nobly and think the way I do"; and (c) "You must give me exactly what I want when I want it." Notice the word "must" is present in each basic irrational belief. Ellis believed that "shoulds" and "musts" are at the foundation of dogmatic and irrational thinking. Accordingly, they *must* be disputed in therapy. Ellis (1989a) also stated that if a client can actively dispute his or her own irrational beliefs so that he or she begins to think rationally in a spontaneous way, then an "E" can be added to the A-B-C-(D) model. That "E" stands for an "*effective new philosophy*," based on rational beliefs.

## Counselor Role

Ellis essentially sees therapy as educational. His approach is active. He believes, in fact, that in the early stages of counseling the therapist may do more talking than the client. Although not ignoring what clients have to say, Ellis (1989c) makes it clear that the therapist should be stern, focused, and convincing in efforts to demonstrate irrational ideas that are at the foundation of a client's distress. Ellis (1989c) argued that therapists should not be "thrown" by distress; rather, they should use distress and emotion to prove to clients that they (the clients) are bound to irrational thinking, thereby distressing themselves. All the while, the therapist must continually check to see if the client is understanding what is being taught. Clients must learn the three basic insights

(Ellis, 1989a) of RET: (a) we basically upset ourselves through our beliefs; (b) no matter when or where our crooked thinking began, previous distress does not cause subsequent distress; and (c) if we change our irrational beliefs continually through work and practice (behaviorally) we will think rationally.

### Goals of Counseling and Ideal Outcomes

Although symptom removal is a goal of RET, it is not the final goal. Ellis (1989c) stated: "The usual goal of RET, therefore, is not merely to eliminate clients' presenting symptoms but to help rid them of other symptoms as well and, more importantly, to modify their underlying symptom-creating propensities" (p. 199). Since the way one thinks is at the root of the symptom-creating propensities, one's thinking must be modified.

# General Procedures

### Assessment

From the very early sessions of Rational-Emotive Therapy, the therapist makes a concerted effort to understand the *ideas* behind the emotions manifested and described by the client. Although traditional means of assessment may be used, they are less important from an RET perspective than face-to-face dialogue. The therapist does a great deal of questioning, talking, and educating in the early sessions. Ellis (1989c) stated, about the early actions of therapists:

> In most instances, they quickly pin the client down to a few basic irrational ideas. They challenge the client to validate these ideas, show that they contain ex-tralogical premises that cannot be validated; logically analyze these ideas and make mincemeat of them; vigorously show why they cannot work and why they will almost inevitably lead to renewed disturbed symptomatology; reduce these ideas to absurdity, sometimes in a highly humorous manner; explain how they can be replaced with more rational theses; and teach clients how to think scientifically, so they can observe, logically parse, and minimize any subsequent irrational ideas and illogical deductions that lead to self-defeating feelings and behaviors. (pp. 215--216)

The therapist, then, as early as the assessment process, takes an active directive role. Assessment is thereby directly tied to therapy, targeted to the definition of irrational beliefs, and quickly followed by an educational attitude and approach to the client.

### Treatment/Remediation

Treatment is action-oriented. As will be discussed in the section on recent developments, Ellis (1989a) has become much more behavioral in his approach, although he makes it clear that thinking, and not behavior, must be changed for there to be lasting results.

Treatment is highly educational. Yet the therapist can challenge the client to act and think in different, more productive ways. The idea is to remediate, to provide learning experiences to assist in the undoing of self-defeating thinking. Whatever is effective in bringing about a change in attitude and thinking is considered reasonable as a technique from the RET perspective. Therefore, implosive techniques (where a client is asked to submerge him or herself in situations that create uncomfortable feelings, in order to implode—explode inwardly—the overwhelming thoughts and emotions associated with the situation), classically behavior-oriented techniques, skill training, role playing, etcetera, are viewed as useful options as techniques directed by the therapist. But these techniques are always viewed as secondary to disputation of irrational beliefs, which is the mainstay remediator according to RET.

### Case Management

The setting for Rational-Emotive Therapy is the therapist's office, usually informally arranged, so that the therapist and client can sit without barriers between them. The therapist is encouraged to be down-to-earth, using language the client can understand. Tape recording of sessions is highly encouraged and, in fact, clients are encouraged to bring their own tape recorders so they may record sessions and thereby have an audio tape to listen to subsequent to the session. In this way, clients may study the teachings and directives of the therapist, benefiting additionally from what occurred in the therapist's office (Ellis, 1989c). Although a warm relationship is valued in therapy, it is not viewed as necessary (Ellis, 1962). Therefore, therapists are encouraged to be rational and in control throughout treatment. They can be "feeling" in therapy, but not at the expense of rationality. If a client cries, for instance in the therapy session, the therapist would not necessarily attempt to be empathic; instead, the therapist would remain rational and in control, maintaining the focus on the ideas that led to the crying. Case notes should be used to record hypotheses about how the client thinks, to record the client's irrational beliefs the therapist believes he or she has uncovered, and to record the actions taken by the therapist in the form of directives, homework assignments, arguments, etcetera.

## Specialized Techniques

Related to specific techniques, Ellis (1989a) listed a number of techniques, some of which are direct offshoots of RET, and others that were developed by other theorist/therapists. Some of those techniques are:

**1.** Positive visualization, imaging, and thinking. Clients are asked to think, imagine, or to get a mental picture of a positive outcome as a result of rational thinking.
**2.** Reframing. The therapist redefines a bad situation into a good one.

**3.** Referenting. The therapist helps the client to see the whole picture rather than just a part of the picture.

**4.** Thought stopping. The therapist acts to stop or block a thought as a means of temporary relief.

**5.** Semantics. The therapist helps the client to change his or her basic language, that is, to make it more positive.

**6.** Proselytizing. To proselytize is to attempt to convert someone. In RET, the therapist attempts to convert the client to a more rational way of thinking.

**7.** Problem solving. The therapist defines options for solving problems based on rational rather than irrational thinking.

**8.** Cognitive distraction techniques. The therapist attempts to distract the client into such activities as sports, art, or politics. The distraction is a means of temporary relief.

**9.** Emotive techniques. The therapist assists the client in being self-provocative, dramatic, or even evocative. For example, a client may be asked to give a forceful disputational speech during therapy.

**10.** Rational-Emotive imagery. The client is asked to imagine, in an irrational way, the worst thing that can possibly happen and then to change the feeling in an implosive way through a change from irrational to rational thinking.

**11.** Shame attacking exercises. The therapist actively disputes thoughts preceding shame feelings, and the therapist may even ask the client to go into public and to do something shameful while disputing shameful irrationalities in order to prevent shameful feelings.

**12.** Relationship establishment. The therapist attempts to demonstrate positive regard for the client, while teaching the client to like himself or herself. This is a valuable technique, but it is not necessary for producing lasting personality change.

**13.** Humor. The therapist attempts to reduce irrationality to absurdity.

**14.** Role playing. The client is asked to role play certain behaviors and ways of thinking or interacting.

**15.** Stories, fables, and analogies. Rational ideas are dramatized through therapist storytelling or use of analogies.

**16.** Group therapy. In group situations, clients can see the benefits of rational thinking and the disadvantages of irrational thinking while learning how to dispute their own and other individuals' irrationalities.

**17.** Behavioral techniques. Techniques such as in vivo desensitization or the use of reinforcers or punishments can be used to affect immediate behavioral change, which should be followed by the development of an effective new philosophy.

**18.** Skill training. Active training of skills in the following areas can be used as adjuncts to RET: assertiveness, sexual functioning, communication, and social relations.

Essentially, Ellis wants people to make a profound philosophical change as well as to change behavior. The preceding techniques are examples of concrete ways therapists can achieve behavioral, emotional, or philosophical change in clients.

## Recent Developments or Criticisms

Ellis (1989c) described Rational-Emotive Therapy as "a comprehensive cognitive-affective behavioral theory and practice of psychotherapy" (p. 197). It is interesting that Ellis uses both the terms "affective" and "behavioral" in his descriptions of his approach. Actually, he has become more behavioral in his most recent years, and his earlier works focused more on the impact of cognition on how people feel and act. His approach is becoming similar to the methods of theoreticians who are developing integrative approaches (cf. Meichenbaum's, 1990, "Cognitive-Behavior Modification"). In fact, looking over the list of techniques used by the Rational-Emotive therapist, one must ask, "How does this differ from purely behavioral therapy?" Ellis answers such questions by stating that the major difference is the focus on thinking as the factor underlying behavior. Change in behavior alone does not solve problems. The problems will reemerge unless a deeper change in philosophy and thinking has occurred. This is consistent with his early stated holistic philosophy about human nature, but paradoxically, it is also a reflection of reduction of human nature primarily to thinking rather than feeling or acting. Nevertheless, Ellis (1989c, 1990) has recently argued that his therapy should not be viewed as simply rationalistic—he has come to view thinking, feeling, and behaving as *interactive*—and therefore, RET trainees are taught to focus on all aspects of humanness as they attempt to produce changes. Regardless, Ellis's critics (e.g., Schwartz, 1982, 1984) have convincingly argued that Ellis, in his writings, clearly gives primacy to cognition.

It is the issue of holism versus reductionism that brings to light an observation that can be commonly viewed when studying well-known counseling theories. It seems that major theorists, to a large degree, isolate some aspect of human functioning, focus upon it, and target it as an intervention while, at the same time, ironically, downplaying its "thingness." This is clearly the case with Ellis's RET related to the primacy of cognition, and even more specifically related to the issue of rationality. It is implicit in his approach that rationality and irrationality are treated as logically distinct—at least as extremes on a continuum—if not as things unto themselves. In fact, Ellis (1989c) has defined irrational thinking as "absolutistic," whereas he has defined rational thinking as "non-absolutistic" (p. 213). Yet Ellis in his theoretical writing also links rationality and irrationality to their consequences in a way that one's thinking and the consequences of one's thinking are almost indistinguishable. If a way of thinking becomes self-defeating, it is considered irrational. In this sense, rationality and irrationality are relativistic, behavioral concepts. As a criticism, then, it appears that Ellis has hedged his own definition, and the concepts of rationality versus irrationality can be viewed as either distinct, absolute, and personality-relevant, or as relative behavioral concepts. In either case, the theory is vulnerable; if irrationality is relative to behavior, then it is always secondary or at least conditional to behavior, and, therefore, behavior should be the focus of study and not thinking. On the other hand, if rationality and irrationality are viewed as personality-relevant, absolute concepts, then his theory is seriously flawed in not providing a complete theory of personality (see Ziegler, 1989). In effect, one must construct a theory of personality around Ellis's writing, since he does not clearly and concisely lay out such a theory, as other theorists have done (such as Freud, Rogers, and others). Ellis (1989c) agrees with similar criticisms, as he has stated: "RET is not a 'fully developed, comprehensive personological system.' It is mainly a theory of personality change, and even in that respect it could be, and I hope that eventually will be, more fully developed and comprehensive" (p. 203–204).

Another criticism of Ellis's RET is its assumption that all disorders derive from similar irrational thinking. Therapists subscribing to Beck's (1976) "Cognitive Therapy" criticize Ellis's position by offering an alternative position. While discussing differences and similarities between RET and Cognitive Therapy, Beck and Weishaar (1989) stated:

> *A profound difference between these two approaches is that cognitive therapy maintains that each disorder has its own typical cognitive content. The* cognitive profiles *of depression, anxiety, and panic disorder are significantly different and require substantially different approaches. RET, on the other hand, assumes that all psychopathology has a similar set of underlying irrational beliefs. (p. 288)*

Cognitive Therapists view cognition as a much more complex process than do RET adherents.

Essentially, critics of Ellis have forced him to revise, or at least restate, his thinking. To a degree, Ellis's restatements or revisions have shed light on RET's strengths, but also on its weaknesses. Nevertheless, RET is a useful and effective means for changing the way clients think and behave, and as such, it is a valuable counseling theory.

## Paradigm Fit

### Focus of Study

RET is very focused on the individual. Theoretically, attention is primarily on the way the individual thinks (cognitive primacy), with secondary but localized attention on how the individual feels and acts (Schwartz, 1982, 1984). Ellis's model, then, is consistent with the psychological paradigm. Although individuals can be significantly affected within the A-B-C-(D) model of therapy, Ellis views irrationality as constitutionally rooted in human nature (Ziegler, 1989). Cause of maladjustment appears to be linear, although his recent works are pointing to an interactive framework (e.g., Ellis, 1990). Although Ellis (1989b) has argued for the concomitancy (simultaneity) of thoughts, behaviors, and emotions, according to his foundational theory cognition supersedes behavior and emotion as a linear, causative factor of emotional maladjustment.

### View of Nature of Reality

Consistent with RET tenets, a person (client) is viewed as an individual entity, influenced interpersonally but secondarily to one's constitution. There is a clear conception of mental health versus mental maladjustment. Ellis (1962) stated:

> *Sustained negative emotions (other than those caused by continuing physical pain or discomfort) are invariably the result of stupidity, ignorance, or disturbance; and for the most part they may be, and should be, eliminated by the application of knowledge and straight thinking. For if perpetuated states of emotion generally follow from the individual's conscious or unconscious thinking; and if his thinking is, in turn, mainly a concomitant of his self-verbalizations, then it would follow that he is rarely affected (made sad or glad) by outside things and events; rather: he is affected by his perceptions, attitudes, or internalized sentences about outside things and events. (pp. 53–54)*

Maladjustment is associated with "crooked thinking." Adjustment is associated with "straight thinking."

### Consonance with Paradigm Propositions and Tenets

There is clear consistency between Ellis's RET and the propositions of the psychological paradigm. Individuals are viewed as bounded entities, to a large degree affected by internal psychological processes. Individuals possess predisposed traits, which predispose behaviors and emotions largely in a linear fashion. Change occurs by an individual disputing irrational beliefs—with a preference toward approaches dealing with mentation. All clients are assessed as to their potential for rational thinking. Change occurs by way of knowledge that is empirically grounded. Failures are associated with what can be classified as difficult client types, for example, the "chronic avoiders or shirkers who keep looking for magical solutions," the "inhibited or defensive," and the "resistant" (Ellis, 1989c, pp. 229–230). In this way, Ellis's RET is a good example of a cognitively-oriented counseling theory classified within the psychological paradigm.

## Chapter Conclusion

Ellis's Rational-Emotive Therapy is a classic example of a therapeutic approach consistent with the psychological paradigm. RET emphasizes what a client is thinking as related to problems (as opposed to feeling or behaving). RET is also consistent with the internal model of the psychological paradigm, since it focuses on the internal workings of the individual, as is evident in such concepts as "rational and irrational beliefs." The next chapter presents another internal psychological model counseling theory—Carl Rogers's Person-Centered Therapy. The focus of Person-Centered Therapy is on feeling.

# References

Beck, A. T. (1976). *Cognitive therapy and the emotional disorders*. New York: International Universities Press.

Beck, A. T., & Weishaar, M. E. (1989). Cognitive therapy. In R. J. Corsini & D. Wedding (Eds.), *Current Psychotherapies* (pp. 285–320). Itasca, IL: F. E. Peacock.

Dryden, W. (1989). Albert Ellis: An efficient and passionate life. (An interview with Albert Ellis). *Journal of Counseling and Development, 67,* 539–546.

Ellis, A. (1962). *Reason and emotion in psychotherapy*. Secaucus, NJ: Lyle Stuart.

Ellis, A. (1986). Bibliography. *American Psychologist, 41,* 380–397.

Ellis, A. (1989a). *A one-day workshop on rational-emotive therapy*. Presented at the Saint Anthony's Medical Center–Hyland Center, May 19, 1989, in St. Louis, Missouri.

Ellis, A. (1989b). Comments on my critics. In M. E. Bernard & R. DiGiuseppe (Eds.), *Inside rational-emotive therapy: A critical appraisal of the theory and therapy of Albert Ellis* (pp. 199–233). San Diego: Academic Press.

Ellis, A. (1989c). Rational-emotive therapy. In R. J. Corsini & D. Wedding (Eds.), *Current psychotherapies* (pp. 197–238). Itasca, IL: F. E. Peacock.

Ellis, A. (1990). *The revised ABCs of rational-emotive therapy (RET)*. Paper presented at the second ''Evolution of Psychotherapy'' conference, Anaheim, California, December 14, 1990.

Ellis, A., & Harper, R. A. (1975). *A new guide to rational living*. North Hollywood, CA: Wilshire Book Company.

Meichenbaum, D. (1990). *Cognitive-behavior modification: An integrative approach in the field of psychotherapy*. Paper presented at the second ''Evolution of Psychotherapy'' conference, Anaheim, California, December 13, 1990.

Schwartz, R. M. (1982). Cognitive-behavior modification: A conceptual review. *Clinical Psychology Review, 2,* 267–293.

Schwartz, R. M. (1984). Is rational-emotive therapy a truly unified interactive approach?: A reply to Ellis. *Clinical Psychology Review, 4,* 219–226.

Ziegler, D. J. (1989). A critique of rational-emotive theory of personality. In M. E. Bernard & R. DiGiuseppe (Eds.), *Inside rational-emotive therapy: A critical appraisal of the theory and therapy of Albert Ellis* (pp. 27–45). San Diego: Academic Press.

# 8

# Person-Centered Therapy:

## *An Internal Psychological Model Therapy Focusing on Feeling and Emotion**

PERSON-CENTERED THERAPY was developed originally as a "nondirective" or "client-centered approach" by Carl Rogers, PhD, in the early 1940s. As a therapeutic approach it has had a pervasive impact on the field of psychology. It is one of the purest examples of a therapy focused on feeling and emotion as a means of change and personal development. As a therapy, it is very process oriented, emerging from "the necessary and sufficient conditions for therapeutic personality change" (Rogers, 1957), which will be elaborated later in this chapter. As a philosophy, it is founded on a positive perspective of mental health, deriving from the view that humans have a tendency toward full functioning. As it has evolved, the original "Client-Centered Therapy" has become a "person-centered" approach, reflecting Rogers's unyielding faith in human growth through human interaction and downplaying the clinical context in which "therapy" usually occurs. In this text, for historical purposes and to reflect the changes in the approach itself, whenever a reference is made to foundational ideas originally closely aligned with Rogers's early theoretical conceptions, the title "Client-Centered Therapy" will be used. On the other hand, when relating to later theoretical developments or the evolution of Rogers's approach, the title "Person-Centered Therapy" will

* Special thanks to Rob Anderson, PhD, Professor of Speech Communication at Southern Illinois University at Edwardsville, for his helpful comments and editorial assistance on an earlier draft of this chapter.

be used. Readers should not be confused by this dual method of referring to Rogers's therapy; rather, the dual approach reflects significant developments in Rogers's thinking over the years. It should help to clarify the ambiguities of evolved meanings for individuals wishing to understand better his theory.

## Carl R. Rogers, PhD, A Biographical Sketch

Carl Ransom Rogers was born in 1902 in Oak Park, Illinois. His father was trained as an engineer at the University of Wisconsin. His mother was a homemaker. His earliest years were spent in an upper-middle-class neighborhood in Oak Park (Kirschenbaum, 1979). His family later moved to a farm in nearby Glen Ellyn, Illinois, where Carl spent his later childhood and adolescent years. His family was very religious.

Carl was a very bright young boy and skipped one year in school. He was an excellent student in grade school and in high school (Kirschenbaum, 1979). He later attended the University of Wisconsin at Madison and majored in agricultural studies. Before leaving Wisconsin, he married a childhood playmate, Helen Elliott. He subsequently enrolled at Union Theological Seminary in New York, where he attended on scholarships. While in the seminary, Rogers enrolled in education and psychology courses at nearby Columbia University, which significantly influenced him. He later left the seminary, preferring to study at Columbia University's Teachers' College (in 1926), where he would take coursework in educational psychology. He received his MA degree in 1928 and his PhD degree in 1931, both from Columbia University. His doctoral dissertation was entitled, *Measuring Personality Adjustment in Children Nine to Thirteen Years of Age*.

After attaining the PhD, Rogers remained in New York working as a psychologist until 1940; he then accepted a position at the Ohio State University to be a Professor of Clinical Psychology. At Ohio State he became thoroughly engrossed in the academic life, while maintaining a schedule that allowed him to counsel students and supervise counselor trainees. Under the pressure of teaching, he felt obligated to develop his own position on counseling, and in late 1940, he presented a paper at the invitation of the University of Minnesota that he described as significant to the development of Client-Centered Therapy. The reaction to his paper inspired his first major work, *Counseling and Psychotherapy: Newer Concepts in Practice* (Rogers, 1942), which today is viewed as a classic. In 1945 he moved to the University of Chicago, lured by an opportunity to develop a counseling center. It was while he was teaching and counseling at the University of Chicago that Rogers published his book, *Client-Centered Therapy* (Rogers, 1951), which is foundational to his position on human growth, understanding, and change. His years at Chicago were very productive, and it was there that he became widely recognized. However, as if driven by a "pioneering spirit," Rogers accepted a position developed for him at the University of Wisconsin (see the discussion of his move in Kirschenbaum, 1979). At Wisconsin, Rogers applied his theory to severely disturbed psychotics. His time and work at Wisconsin, which produced outcome studies with mixed findings, proved to be a very personally stressful, primarily due to serious disagreements among his colleagues (see Kirschenbaum, 1979; Gendlin,

1988). He later left the University for La Jolla, California, where he remained until his death in 1987. In La Jolla, he was a fellow with the Western Behavioral Sciences Institute.

Rogers received many distinguished awards in his lifetime. He was awarded the American Psychological Association's "Distinguished Scientific Contribution" award in 1956. Because of the application of his theories to the study of peace, he was nominated for a Nobel Peace Prize. He was truly an outstanding theoretician and counselor, and his impact upon the field of counseling and psychotherapy will be long-lasting.

## The Foundational Theory

### The Object of Counseling

In describing the foundational theory, the focus will be on Roger's earliest expositions of his theory. Rogers's Client-Centered Therapy, as originally conceived, was a therapy focusing on the individual and upon the self. The "self" and the "self-concept" are foundational constructs that reflect Rogers's early ontology—the self as an identifiable aspect of individuality. (Although in his later years, Rogers moved away from viewing the individual in structural terms, his thinking never completely reconciled a structural concept of self with a process orientation in therapy.) Rogers (1951) defined the self-structure as follows:

> *The self-structure is an organized configuration of perceptions of the self which are admissible to awareness. It is composed of such elements as the perceptions of one's characteristics and abilities; the percepts and concepts of the self in relation to others and to the environment; the value qualities which are perceived as associated with experiences and objects; and the goals and ideals which are perceived as having positive or negative valence. It is, then, the organized picture, existing in awareness either as figure or ground, of the self and the self-in-relationship, together with the positive or negative values which are associated with those qualities and relationships, as they are perceived as existing in the past, present, and future. (p. 501)*

Further, in describing the development of the self from childhood, Rogers stated: "The child . . . begins to perceive himself as a psychological object, and one of the most basic elements in the perceptions of himself as a person who is loved" (p. 502). It is noteworthy in these quotations that the self is predominant as a personality construct. It is an organizing principle in Rogers's theory of personality. It is a means of understanding his philosophy. The self is viewed as an organized pattern of perceptions, yet Rogers stated that the self is also "fluid" to a degree. In this way, the self is not immune to experience. It is not so structured that it is unalterable. Yet, the self is more constant than perception. It provides continuity to the personality. As such, the personality becomes amenable to counseling.

## The Process of Counseling

Rogers's exposition of the "necessary and sufficient conditions for therapeutic personality change" in 1957 is perhaps the best summary of his foundational theory of change. Those six conditions, paraphrased in the following, are useful for understanding both his theory of personality and his ideas about therapy. In effect, the six conditions define how the self is positively affected in an interpersonal context. The six conditions are:

**1.** Two persons are in psychological contact.

**2.** The first, who shall be termed the client, is in a state of incongruence, being vulnerable or anxious.

**3.** The second person, who shall be termed the therapist, is congruent or integrated in the relationship.

**4.** The therapist experiences unconditional positive regard for the client.

**5.** The therapist experiences an empathic understanding of the client's internal frame of reference and endeavors to communicate this experience to the client.

**6.** The communication to the client of the therapist's emphatic understanding and unconditional positive regard is to a minimal degree achieved.

According to Rogers (1957), if all of these six conditions are met over a period of time, they are *sufficient* to be associated with healthy personality change.

The terms *empathy* and *unconditional positive regard,* introduced in the six conditions, will be more fully defined in a section which follows, entitled "Counselor Role." The terms *psychological contact, congruence,* and *incongruence* require further immediate elaboration.

*Psychological contact,* as defined by Rogers (1957) means that when two people interact, "each makes some perceived differences in the experiential field of the other" (p. 96). According to Rogers, the difference that one person makes in interaction with another person does not necessarily have to be consciously recognized—it can be "subceived" (sensed at a nonconscious or even an organic-physical level). But at some level, there must be some effect due to the interpersonal relationship.

*Incongruence* is a term that Rogers used to describe psychological maladjustment. Rogers (1951) felt that psychological maladjustment exists "when the organism denies to awareness significant sensory and visceral experiences, which consequently are not symbolized and organized into the gestalt of the self structure. When this situation exists, there is a basic or potential psychological tension" (p. 510). When a person essentially denies to conscious awareness his or her own sensory or visceral experiences, he or she is denying important information to the self. Such experiences must be fully recognized for psychological health. Rogers believed that all such "sensory and visceral experiences" should be symbolically and consistently incorporated into "the concept of self" (p. 513). When experiences are in a "consistent relationship with the self,'' there is psychological *congruence*. As an example, assume for a moment that a young man accidentally brushes up against another young man in skin-to-skin contact. Skin-to-skin contact is arousing to humans, and unless perceived through other sense organs, humans cannot identify the sex of the individual with whom they have made contact. In the case of the young man, if he felt aroused by the skin contact with the other man, he could: (a) accept the arousal, and depending on his sexual preference, incorporate the experience into the self-structure. (If heterosexual, the arousal could be viewed as simply a natural response to physical stimulation.); (b) deny the experience to awareness, thereby pushing aside sensory data, which potentially could cause distress when confronted with similar data in the future; or (c) accept the arousal, and misinterpret it as an absolute sign of unitary sexual preference, which could produce panic in a person who has viewed himself as heterosexual. (Response ''c'' effectively requires denial of past arousal when in contact with females.) Response A is a congruent response. Responses B and C are incongruent responses.

In effect, Rogers developed a picture of the human being which includes a real self (involving sensory and visceral experience, and ultimately, what one *feels*) and a perceived self (which may be consistent or inconsistent with experience). When there is awareness of the real self, and there is consistency between the real and perceived self, there is congruence.

It is also true that the individual has a ''self ideal'' (Rogers, 1951, pp. 140–142). The self ideal is a concept of self related to what one hopes or dreams of being. Ideally, an individual's real, perceived, and ideal selves should all be consistent; when they are not consistent, a person may manifest psychological distress in some form.

## Counselor Role

Related to the role of the counselor, Raskin and Rogers (1989) stated:

> *The basic theory of person-centered therapy is that if the therapist is successful in conveying genuineness, unconditional positive regard, and empathy, then the client will respond with constructive changes in personality organization. Research has demonstrated that these qualities can be made real in a relationship and can be conveyed and appreciated in a short time. (p. 170)*

One of the primary tasks of the counselor is to demonstrate the necessary and sufficient conditions for therapeutic personality change.

*Empathy* basically is defined as the therapist's ability to attend to and to live the feelings and attitudes of the client. Essentially, the therapist should attempt to ''feel'' from the client's perspective, and although it can never be known whether this has been accomplished, the fact that the therapist expresses interest in such understanding is viewed as adequate for facilitating change.

*Unconditional positive regard* relates to a positive, nonjudgmental, and accepting attitude conveyed by the therapist. In effect, no matter how the client acts at the moment of therapy, the therapist must convey that the client is respected as a human being, and, even if the therapist cannot agree with something a client says or does, the therapist can accept him or her fully, as a person, without judgment.

*Genuineness* and *congruence* are practically equivalent concepts related to the therapist's role in the therapeutic relationship. Congruence, as stated earlier, relates to consistency between the real and perceived selves. The therapist must have the ability to understand and to express his or her own feelings in an open and unfettered way. The therapist must be aware of, and must not deny, his or her real self during the therapeutic encounter. For example, Raskin and Rogers (1989) addressed the issue of therapist fatigue as follows:

> *An effective way of dealing with the common occurrence of therapist fatigue is to express it. This strengthens the relationship because the therapist is not trying to cover up a real feeling. It may act to reduce or eliminate the fatigue and restore the therapist to a fully attending and empathic state. (p. 172)*

Accordingly, the therapist must be fully human in therapy, just as he or she expects the client to be fully human. Ultimately, the therapist must be a model of "congruence" and open communication.

## Goals of Counseling and Ideal Outcomes

Probably the clearest explanation by Rogers of the ideal outcome of therapy is contained in his book, *On Becoming a Person: A Therapist's View of Psychotherapy* (Rogers, 1961). In that book, Rogers describes how a fully functioning person can emerge from therapy:

> *For the client, this optimal therapy would mean an exploration of increasingly strange and unknown and dangerous feelings in himself, the exploration proving possible only because he is gradually realizing that he is accepted uncondition-ally. Thus he becomes acquainted with elements of his experience which have in the past been denied to awareness as too threatening, too damaging to the structure of the self. He finds himself experiencing these feelings fully, com-pletely, in the relationship, so that for the moment he is his fear, or his anger, or his tenderness, or his strength. And as he lives these widely varied feelings, in all their degrees of intensity, he discovers that he has experienced himself, that he is all these feelings. He finds his behavior changing in constructive fashion in accordance with his newly experienced self. He approaches the realization that he no longer needs to fear what experience may hold, but can welcome it freely as part of his changing and developing self. (p. 185)*

A fully functioning person is a fully feeling and experiencing person.

At first glance, Rogers's conception of full functioning appears very similar to Abraham Maslow's concept of "self-actualization" (Maslow, 1954, 1968, 1971). About the same time Rogers was developing his ideas related to personality change and therapy, Maslow was developing his ideas related to personality development and motivation, and Maslow was refining the concept of self-actualization. Both ideas appear to have been founded on an earlier work by Goldstein (1934/1959) who first adequately defined the term *self-actualization*. But there are differences between Rogers's and Maslow's concepts, which were made clear by Rogers (1961, 1963). These differences help to bring to light what Rogers viewed as the ideal outcome of therapy.

Self-actualization is a concept that describes what Maslow (1954) believed was a state of being: the ultimate in human mental and emotional maturation. Self-actualization results from the natural tendency for humans to grow and develop psychologically as their basic or foundational needs are met. Self-actualization represents a description of the epitome of mental health—a level of "being," not "becoming." Self-actualized individuals can be viewed as having "arrived." Rogers's (1961) conception of "the fully functioning person," on the other hand, is less fixed. He stated: "It seems to me that the good life is not any fixed state. . . . It is not a condition in which the individual is adjusted, or fulfilled, or actualized" (pp. 185–186). Although Rogers's and Maslow's conceptions of mental health are similarly founded on the idea that if basic conditions are met, individuals will naturally tend toward optimal psychological adjustment, there is a glaring difference in their final views of optimum functioning. In contrast to ideas such as Maslow's, Rogers defined full functioning as "a process, not a state of being. . . . It is a direction, not a destination" (p. 186). In summarizing his position, Rogers stated:

> The good life, from the point of view of my experience, is the process of movement in a direction which the human organism selects when it is inwardly free to move in any direction, and the general qualities of this selected direction appear to have a certain universality. (p. 187)

In this sense, the fully functioning person is free to become whatever he or she can. From Maslow's view, the outcome of growth is viewed as more clearly predestined.

Accordingly, the Client-Centered Therapist is basically viewed as a facilitator of growth and movement toward *the process* of full functioning. This is a position that was unchanged by Rogers even as he moved toward a more person-centered approach (Rogers, 1987).

## General Procedures

### Assessment

Diagnosis, in the classic organic-medical sense, is completely avoided in Client-Centered Therapy. In fact, Rogers (1951) made an explicit case against diagnosis, indicating in some ways that it can be deleterious to the therapeutic relationship. Rogers felt that diagnosis placed the locus of evaluation on the therapist, instead of the client; he felt the client should be self-evaluative. Also, Rogers believed that the traditional process of diagnosis has social implications; for instance, one implication is that the client should be controlled by a professional who should accept the role of manager of the client's life. Rogers felt both of these implications of classic diagnosis warranted its avoidance. On the other hand, he viewed the *process* of therapy and diagnosis as one—as an evolving process. Rogers (1951) stated:

> *In a very meaningful and accurate sense, therapy is diagnosis, and this diagnosis is a process which goes on in the experience of the client, rather than in the intellect of the clinician. (p. 223).*

Rogers stated that only the client can diagnose, since "the client is the only one who had the potentiality of knowing fully the dynamics of his perceptions and his behavior" (p. 221). Accordingly, the process of diagnosis is an ongoing process accomplished primarily by the client.

### Treatment/Remediation

The focus of treatment is the individual. Treatment occurs in a therapeutic relationship. Although the therapeutic relationship can be extended to include other individuals in groups or families, the primary focus of attention in therapy is upon an individual's experiences in the here and now, reflecting the match between the experienced, perceived, and ideal selves. When the six necessary and sufficient conditions for therapeutic personality change are met, a positive outcome is expected (Rogers, 1957). These conditions may be met in settings other than one-to-one counseling, such as group counseling (Raskin & Rogers, 1989).

### Case Management

The Client-Centered Therapist makes every effort to make the client comfortable. Sessions are held at mutually agreed-upon times, and the therapist makes every effort to accommodate the client's needs and desires. This is not to say that the client dictates the mechanics of therapy, but rather, the client's position is respected.

The audio or videotaping of sessions is encouraged with permission of clients. Counselors, especially beginning counselors, will find recordings of sessions of special usefulness in understanding the client's values and experiences. Case notes should reflect what occurs in counseling, using language consistent with the basic theories of personality and change. Care is taken to be nonjudgmental, and case notes and tape recordings are used to facilitate the process of subsequent therapy sessions. Therapy is scheduled in a way that is compatible with expressed client needs and the organizational constraints of the therapist.

## Specialized Techniques

Client-Centered Therapy is a therapy founded on both belief and trust. As Rogers (1951) stated, there is belief "that the individual has a sufficient capacity to deal constructively

with all those aspects of his life which can potentially come into conscious awareness"
(p. 24). There is trust that the therapeutic relationship will bring forth the tendency
toward full functioning in each individual. It is a therapy founded on a positive view
of human nature. This translates at the level of practice to communication that allows
the client and therapist to be fully human, expressive of feelings, and nonjudgmental.
The therapist does not give advice or interpretations. Instead, he or she reflects
personally what the client has said, or, through techniques such as paraphrasing, the
therapist facilitates, reflects, and/or mirrors the client's own interpretations. In this
way, the client is more self-directive within the therapeutic relationship, and since the
client is fully accepted by the therapist, the client can be fully self-revealing, without
fear of being judged or devalued. Through the client-centered approach, a therapist
helps a client to come face-to-face with the client's real self.

Beyond the more global methods used in therapy, such as empathy and unconditional positive regard, specific techniques consistent with Client-Centered Therapy and
exhibited by Rogers in his therapy sessions are:

**1.** Paraphrasing verbalizations—restating what a client has said in different
words. This is done often as both a means of checking what has been communicated
for accuracy and as a means of cueing further responses. Example: "I understood what
you said to mean. . . ."

**2.** Paraphrasing nonverbal messages as feelings—stating in words, which are
reflective of feelings, what the therapist observes in a client's behavior. Example: "I
see the pain that comes through in your tears. . . ."

**3.** Acknowledging through nonverbal behaviors—responding to the client
through actions. Rogers appears to use head nods and movements to signify that he is
listening and attending to the client. The use of nonverbal behavior is also a means of
recognizing the statements and actions of the client. Example: After a client states, "I
feel more accepting of my aggressive feelings," the therapist might nod and respond
"umm-hmm."

**4.** Self-disclosure—revealing something about oneself as a therapist as a means
of making psychological contact and as a means of being congruent. Example: "I
sometimes have trouble expressing my feelings, too."

**5.** Expressing emotions—stating in the here and now what the therapist is
feeling. Example, "I am feeling a little concerned about what you just said, and I'm
not sure what it means."

## Recent Developments or Criticisms

The therapeutic process of Client-Centered Therapy, as it was originally conceived,
was best summarized by the term *nondirective.* In fact, the term *nondirective* preceded
the use of the term *client-centered,* and for a period immediately following 1951 both
terms were used synonymously (e.g., Rogers 1951). Rogers (1951) stated, while
talking about the philosophical orientation of the counselor: "He can be only as
'nondirective' as he has achieved respect for others in his own personality

organization'' (p. 21). However, the term *person-centered* was used by Rogers in his latest works, reflecting his faith in the individual and the need to view individuals from a positive, nonclinical standpoint. His ideas in his later years became much more egalitarian, much less concerned with maladjustment, and much more reflective of his deep faith in humanity. Sanford (1987), speaking of the evolution of the ''client-centered'' approach to the ''person-centered'' perspective, described the therapeutic process as follows:

> *The organismic growth in the concept of the therapeutic experience brought with it not only a wider field of functioning for the client, but a broadening of the concept of the therapist, functioning in the climate of the person-centered approach, and compatible with the metaphor of companion on a journey—a more experienced and mature companion, but quite different from an expert or a doctor who prescribes a remedy, or a wise person who knows the ''solution'' and will bring the patient around to it in due time, or at least will reveal in the process the causes of the illness or dilemma. (p. 191)*

Rogers was an optimist, and his ideas were a manifestation of a deep-seated belief in the process of human growth through human interaction (Sanford, 1987). In fact, his work is well respected by some in the field of speech communication, as it positively contributed to a philosophy about dialogue as a mode of communication (see the excellent discussion by Cissna & Anderson, 1990, on this topic). As Cissna and Anderson (1990) stated:

> *Carl Rogers was raised an American psychologist. As an American, he was taught that the individual is inherently important and that the pursuit of that which enhances the individual is the greatest value. As a psychologist, he was trained not only in a scientific method founded on prediction and control and on operationalism, but also in the belief that the real stuff of human life and of therapy is psychological. Against that training, Rogers struggled all his life to find a vocabulary in which he could express the reality of relationship as he experienced it. Though a psychologist, his focus was beyond the psyche, and on dialogue. (p. 139)*

In one sense, Rogers can be viewed as an interactionist (or as a contextualist as defined later in this text), although he lived at a time when the language of psychology and psychotherapy was focused almost exclusively upon the individual. In this way, Rogers appears to be a theoretician locked into an emphasis on the individual, although, paradoxically, his work recognized fully the use of relationship as a process unto itself. This is meant both as a compliment to Rogers and as a criticism of his work. He broke new ground by emphasizing the therapeutic relationship, yet he was bound to a theory that appeared selfish in its focus on the ''self'' as a final arbiter of truth.

Probably a more compelling reason that Rogers moved away from the term *non-directive therapy* as applied to his theory was his encounters with behaviorists. Rogers was best known at a time when behaviorism was on the rise in American psychology. In fact, it seemed that the behaviorists (e.g., Skinner) and the humanists (e.g., Rogers) were often viewed as opposing camps, or schools of psychology. In the heat of debate, Rogers was confronted by the fact that humans could be behaviorally conditioned to respond in ways reflective of self-expression—that is, reinforced by the behaviors of the therapist. Greenspoon and Brownstein (1967), speaking of non-behaviorally oriented psychotherapists as cognitive theorists, stated:

> Though the behaviorist has not accepted the construct of awareness, he has attended to the variables that affect the verbal responses from which the cognitive theorist has inferred awareness, as well as to the function of the verbal response itself. The behaviorist has tended to accept the verbal response per se and to investigate the antecedent conditions that produced it. At the same time he has also been willing to consider any unique functions of the verbal response that may apply to the behavior under consideration. The cognitive theorist, on the other hand, has not accepted the verbal response per se but rather has used it to infer awareness, which he then attempts to relate to the behavior under observation. (p. 305)

The behaviorists argued that therapists should simply focus on behavior, its antecedents, and consequences, while refraining from inferring other causes (see Greenspoon & Simkins, 1968). In fact, Rogers was involved in a debate with B. F. Skinner, the preeminent behaviorist (recorded during the 1956 American Psychological Association convention), which subsequently appears to have affected his position about the *directive* nature of his therapy. Rogers, confronted with arguments that client-centered therapists condition responses in clients, responded as follows, according to Kirschenbaum (1979):

> Rogers, in the symposium with Skinner and on other occasions, acknowledged that the client-centered therapist is engaged in the reinforcement and control of the client's behavior. To a group of graduate students at the University of Rochester, he said, ". . . if you think of therapy as operant conditioning and certainly there is enough evidence in that field to make us think very seriously about the meaning of that—then I've come to feel that perhaps my hypothesis would be that effective therapy consists in the reinforcing of all experienced feelings. So then when you have reinforced all the feelings of the individual, then he can be all of those and he can be himself." To Skinner at the APA he said, "As therapists, we institute certain attitudinal conditions, and the client has relatively little voice in the establishment of these conditions. We predict that if these conditions are instituted, certain behavior consequences will ensue in the client. Up to this point this is largely external control, no different from what Skinner has described. . . . But here any similarity ceases." (p. 273)

In effect, the behaviorists mounted a credible challenge to Rogers's conception of nondirective therapy. And it appears that Rogers modified his theory to acknowledge the directive aspects of his work.

Another criticism of Rogers's Client-Centered Therapy related to diagnosis. Rogers's position is that diagnosis and treatment are one, and that everyone has the capacity to grow toward full functioning. To a large degree, Rogers's (1951) position on diagnosis and assessment ignores the obvious. First, for therapy to occur, there must be some degree of incongruence. Otherwise, what would mask as therapy would actually be two congruent persons in dialogue (which would be quite acceptable from a speech communication standpoint, but fails in the real sense of treatment). Two congruent persons in dialogue can hardly be conceptualized as therapy, which almost always occurs in an authoritative context. Assessment, in the sense that there must be a measure of client incongruence, is a prerequisite to therapy, and, although formal diagnosis and assessment are not operationalized in the process and techniques of Client-Centered Therapy, they are implicit in the therapeutic context. Additionally, although a Client-Centered Therapist might view himself or herself as nonjudgmental, the fact that he or she has faith in the client's own resources, and communicates such, is a judgment that cannot be escaped. The Client-Centered Therapist's assessment of individuals seeking treatment is always the same—that is, each person is viewed as having the capacity for growth and self-enhancement. *All* clients are assessed as having growth potential, which should not be misunderstood to mean that assessment has not occurred. This position appears naive from an organic-medical perspective, where severely disturbed behavior has been associated with genetic predisposition. Ultimately, a truly nonassessing therapy would have to be grounded upon a theory of personality that did not make distinctions about mental health versus mental maladjustment; Client-Centered Therapy is not such a therapy.

Rogers was also criticized by Albert Ellis, who vehemently disputed Rogers's six necessary and sufficient conditions for therapeutic personality change as neither individually necessary nor cumulatively sufficient to produce change in clients (Ellis, 1958). Ellis argued that each one of the conditions, or all of the conditions, can be absent, and individuals still can improve from a psychological standpoint.

Regardless of criticisms, Rogers' Client-Centered Therapy is one of the most significant contributions to the psychotherapy literature. He made a major impact both at the theoretical and philosophical levels. In one sense, he has been a moral conscience of the field of counseling and psychotherapy, always reminding theoreticians that people need to feel valuable and wanted, which comes through clearly in the evolution of his theory to a more person-centered approach.

## Paradigm Fit

### Focus of Study

There is clear consistency between Rogers's Client-Centered Therapy and the epistemological underpinnings of the psychological paradigm. Clearly, the focus of treatment in Client-Centered Therapy is the individual. Clearly, the "self" is a psychological construct, developed through internal and external psychological processes, that endures and represents a predisposition to act. Rogers's focus on the individual "self," his unyielding faith in human nature, and his continuous study of the process of individual change through psychotherapy reveals his emphasis on the individual as a primary locus of study.

### View of Nature of Reality

In regard to the nature of reality, Rogers's view is mixed in his written works. At times he appears to be viewing individuals as bounded psychological entities. At other times, he appears to emphasize the nature of relationship as the ''reality'' of therapy. However, in his early work it is clear that the individual self-concept constitutes a sort of object of intervention. The actions of the therapist are designed to produce a directional change, from incongruence to congruence. There is a clear conception of mental health—full functioning. Although the therapy is viewed as process, and there is a process-oriented undertone to his writings, ultimately, Rogers's early theory relied heavily on the definitions of structures—the real, perceived, and ideal selves.

### Consonance with Paradigm Propositions and Tenets

There is clear consistency between Rogers's ideas and the great majority of the nine propositions of the psychological paradigm. The cause of psychological maladjustment is directly and linearly defined—that is, distress results from incongruence that occurs when experiences are denied or not organized into the self-structure. Change occurs by someone affecting internal psychological processes and facilitating self-growth. Professional expertise as a Client-Centered Therapist is best gained through training in the qualitative and quantitative scientific methods (Rogers, 1951, 1987, is quite explicit about his faith in and reliance on the scientific method), even though Rogers recognized that paraprofessionals could apply Client-Centered Therapy concepts without extensive training. Related to assessment, all clients are viewed as inherently rational, incongruent, and changeable. Positive outcomes occur when necessary and sufficient therapeutic conditions for personality change are met within an interpersonal context. And failure is often viewed as: (a) a failure of the counselor to build a therapeutic relationship; (b) reflecting the fact that a certain type of client cannot be helped (i.e., failure associated with, as Rogers [1951] stated, a ''certain classification of personality diagnosis''); and (c) reflecting the inability of the counselor to accept fully certain types of clients (Rogers, 1951, p. 189). Given the consistency between psychological paradigm propositions and Rogers's theoretical position, Client-Centered Therapy is a good example of a therapy that can be associated with the internal model of the psychological paradigm.

## Chapter Conclusion

Rogers's Client-Centered Therapy is a classic example of a therapeutic approach consistent with the psychological paradigm that emphasizes what the client feels (as opposed to thinking or behavior). It is also consistent with the internal model of the psychological paradigm, since it focuses on the internal workings of the individual, as is evident in such concepts as "self" and "self-concept." However, in Roger's later years he began to move away from the idea of treating disturbance of the self-concept and toward the idea of growth through interpersonal dialogue. He began to view dialogue itself as growth-enhancing when certain conditions were present, and he began to see that his ideas had applications beyond clinical settings to a truly person-centered way of social interaction. As Sanford (1987) stated, his ideas evolved from a means for facilitating a "fully functioning self" to enhancement of a "fully functioning self within the society," which involves "social awareness/involvement" (p. 191).

# References

Cissna, K. N., & Anderson, R. (1990). The contributions of Carl R. Rogers to a philosophical praxis of dialogue. *Western Journal of Speech Communication, 54*, 125–147.

Ellis, A. (1958). *Critique of requisite conditions for basic personality change.* Paper presented at the meeting of the American Academy of Psychotherapists, August 9, 1958, in Madison, Wisconsin.

Gendlin, E. T. (1988). Carl Rogers (1902–1987). *American Psychologist, 43*, 127–128.

Goldstein, K. (1959). *The organism: A holistic approach to biology derived from psychological data in man.* New York: American Book. (Original was published in 1934)

Greenspoon, J., & Brownstein, A. (1967). Awareness in verbal conditioning. *Journal of Experimental Research in Personality, 2*, 295–308.

Greenspoon, J., & Simkins, L. (1968). A measurement approach to psychotherapy. *The Psychological Record, 18*, 409–423.

Kirschenbaum, H. (1979). *On becoming Carl Rogers.* New York: Delta.

Maslow, A. H. (1954). *Motivation and personality.* New York: Harper & Bros.

Maslow, A. H. (1968). *Toward a psychology of being.* New York: D. Van Nostrand.

Maslow, A. H. (1971). *The furthest reaches of human nature.* New York: The Viking Press.

Raskin, N. J., & Rogers, C. R. (1989). Person-Centered Therapy. In R. J. Corsini & D. Wedding (Eds.), *Current Psychotherapies* (pp. 155–194). Itasca, IL: F. E. Peacock.

Rogers, C. R. (1942). *Counseling and psychotherapy: Newer concepts in practice.* Boston: Houghton Mifflin.

Rogers, C. R. (1951). *Client-Centered Therapy.* Boston: Houghton Mifflin.

Rogers, C. R. (1957). The necessary and sufficient conditions for therapeutic personality change. *Journal of Consulting Psychology, 21*, 95–103.

Rogers, C. R. (1961). *On becoming a person: A therapist's view of psychotherapy.* Boston: Houghton Mifflin.

Rogers, C. R. (1963). The concept of the fully functioning person. *Psychotherapy: Theory, research and practice, 1*, 17–26.

Rogers, C. R. (1987). Rogers, Kohut, and Erickson: A personal perspective on some similarities and differences. In J. Zeig (Ed.), *The evolution of psychotherapy* (pp. 179–187). New York: Brunner/Mazel.

Sanford, R. C. (1987). An inquiry into the evolution of the client-centered approach to psychotherapy. In J. Zeig (Ed.), *The evolution of psychotherapy* (pp. 188–197). New York: Brunner/Mazel.

# 9

# Gestalt Therapy:
## *An Internal Psychological Model Therapy Focusing on Thinking, Feeling, and Behavior*

GESTALT THERAPY WAS developed by Frederich S. Perls, MD. The beginning of Gestalt Therapy is identified best by the writing of Perls's classic work, *Ego, Hunger, and Aggression,* which was originally viewed as a revision of Freud's Psycho-analysis. It was written in 1941 and 1942 and was published in South Africa in 1946. The book was later published in England in 1947 (Perls, 1947/1969). Perls also wrote several other books, including *Gestalt Therapy Verbatim* (Perls, 1969), and with two associates, *Gestalt Therapy* (Perls, Hefferline, & Goodman, 1951). Because the word *Gestalt* implies viewing organisms holistically, Gestalt Therapy focuses not only on what one thinks or feels, but also on behavior—all viewed in the here and now. In this way, Gestalt Therapy is unique as a counseling theory, while also offering a distinct perspective of mental health.

## Frederich (Fritz) Perls, MD, a Biographical Sketch

Frederich (Fritz) Salomon Perls was born in Berlin in 1893. His autobiography, a free-floating integration of his life and this theory, entitled *In and Out of the Garbage Pail* (Perls, 1969b), describes little of his younger years, especially the years in Germany before he earned an MD degree. After earning his MD degree at the Frederich Wilhelm University in Berlin in 1921, he received training in Psycho-analysis in Berlin, Frankfurt, and Vienna. He later (in 1926) worked under Kurt Goldstein at the Institute for Brain Damaged Soldiers. Goldstein is widely known for his holistic view of organisms and his definition of the term *self-actualization* (Goldstein, 1934/1959). At the time, Gestalt psychology was receiving much attention in intellectual circles, and Perls was introduced to the work of Gestalt psychologists while he worked with Goldstein. As part of his psychoanalytic training, he was analyzed by Wilhelm Reich, a leading theoretician and psychoanalyst of his day. In his autobiography, Perls described himself as a "mediocre psychoanalyst" (Perls, 1969, p. 1), and yet he recognized his role as a "possible creator of a 'new' method of treatment" (p. 2).

After leaving Germany due to the rising influence of Hitler, Perls moved to Amsterdam in 1933 and then to South Africa (in 1934), where he established a psychoanalytic institute in Johannesburg. Under the influence of Gestalt psychology, and disenchanted with how unyielding psychoanalysts were, Perls began to develop a different position. In the early 1940s he wrote his classic book, *Ego, Hunger and Aggression* (Perls, 1947/1969), which was partially coauthored by his wife, Laura Perls. With the publication of this book, Gestalt Therapy was born. It is interesting that the title of the book reflects Perls's early holistic thinking—ego reflecting thinking, hunger reflecting feeling, and aggression reflecting behavior.

Perls later left South Africa (in 1946) with the rise of Apartheid (see the discussion of this in Perls, 1969b). He then settled in New York, where he established the New York Institute for Gestalt Therapy (in 1952). The remainder of Perls's life was essentially spent training therapists, writing, giving workshops, and establishing training centers. He set up the Cleveland Institute of Gestalt Therapy in 1954. He moved to California and associated with the Esalen Institute between 1964 and 1969. Shortly before his death, he established an institute in Vancouver, British Columbia.

Perls is best remembered as a lively figure who brought to the mental health field a unique philosophy and perspective about mental health. His work incorporates emergent European philosophy and a deep understanding of human suffering, which probably reflects his years of clinical experience as a physician and as a psychotherapist. His theory is one of the most creative accomplishments in the history of psychotherapy.

Perls died in California in 1970.

## The Foundational Theory

### The Target of Counseling

The target of Gestalt Therapy is the individual perceiver as he or she lives (flows through) life. The individual is continually forming figures (gestalts) out of the background that is composed of the social and physical environment. In this process, it is important for the individual to maintain a sense of self—an awareness of one's boundary with the outside world. Perls, Hefferline, and Goodman (1951) defined the self as follows:

> *Self may be regarded as at the boundary of the organism, but the boundary is not itself isolated from the environment; it contacts the environment; it belongs*

*to both, environment and organism. Contact is touch touching something. The self is not to be thought of as a fixed institution; it exists wherever and whenever there is in fact a boundary interaction. (p. 373)*

It is through awareness at any moment that the individual can fully experience his or her world. Yet this boundary between self and other is not impermeable. There is a constant interplay of the inside and outside world through awareness of boundary contact. As Kempler (1973) stated:

*Healthy coordinated awareness flows ceaselessly between two points and is itself continually being modified. The healthy awaring apparatus moves back and forth between internal knowledge and an object outside the person and then back again to the deepest knowledge within relative to the object. (p. 258)*

Awareness of one's boundary in the present is analogous to mental health. It is a type of mental flexibility that allows one to live continually in the present, fully cognizant of self and other. Perls (1970) stated: "To me, nothing exists except the now. Now = experience = awareness = reality. The past is no more and the future not yet. Only the *now* exists" (p. 14). When the individual is unable to differentiate self from other, or the self splits, or there is an undue focus on the past or the future, there is disturbance. Therapy then is a process of dialogue with the individual to help him or her come to understand the boundaries of the self and to experience life in the present.

### The Process of Counseling

The process of Gestalt Therapy is best exemplified in several general principles, which follow. The process of Gestalt Therapy is essentially a process of maintaining these principles actively in counseling. The principles are:

**1.** Holism. According to Gestalt principles, "the whole is greater than the sum of its parts." This is an underlying principle of Gestalt Therapy as well as Gestalt psychology (Perls et al., 1951). Consequently, during therapy, one of the major tasks is to help the client get a whole sense of the self. Although the personality is viewed holistically, polarities are present. Polarities are parts of the personality that are opposites, yet they complement each other (Yontef & Simkin, 1989). One major aspect of the process of Gestalt Therapy, then, is a process of integration—or *centering*—in order to allow natural polarities to exist, while healing the splits arising from dichotomous forces. Perls (1947/1969) stated:

*There is a famous book which shows the catastrophic results of idealism clearly enough, if you only understand it correctly: the story of Dr. Jekyll and Mr. Hyde. Dr. Jekyll represents an ideal, not a human being. He is an unselfish benefactor of mankind, loyal in spite of frustrations, and chaste in the face of strong instincts. To materialize his ideal he uses the "means whereby" of repression;*

> *he represses his animalistic existence; he hides in Mr. Hyde the jackal (Jekyll). The human being has been differentiated into the opposites ''angel'' and ''devil,'' the one praised and welcome, the other detested and repulsed; but the one can as little exist without the other as can light without its shadow. (pp. 271–272)*

Gestalt therapists essentially attempt to bring polarities into a larger context, that is, within a phenomenological whole.

According to Perls et al. (1951), splits in the personality may be manifested as: (a) retroflections (where a person acts upon herself or himself as a target when, instead, the environment should be acted upon; retroflections essentially split the self into ''doer'' and ''done to''), (b) introjections (something from the outside has been incorporated into the organism, but has not been fully accepted or accommodated by the organism—psychologically the equivalent of undigested food), and (c) projections (there is a part of one's own personality that is externalized but is not seen as part of the organism—for instance, seeing one's own sexual urges in another person's behavior). Dichotomous thinking and splits in the personality go hand in hand, and Gestalt Therapy attempts to allow dichotomies to be viewed as complementary polarities, thereby preventing further disintegration of the personality. For example, a man who is unable to integrate the feminine aspects of his personality is doomed to dichotomous thinking—that is, feeling he is either a man or a woman. Gestalt Therapy would fully encourage integration of this man's femininity into his picture of himself, his gestalt, just as it would encourage integration of the masculine aspect of a woman's personality into a larger picture of a whole personality.

2. Figure and Ground. In the social realm, the idea of figure and ground is easily understood as that of self and environment. To have a sense of gestalt, one must differentiate oneself from one's context, while being able to connect or separate (contact or withdraw) appropriately from the environment. (The environment is often composed of other individuals). In *confluence* (fusion) the distinction between figure and ground (self and other) becomes unclear. An example would be an adult woman living a life to please her mother because, separate from the mother, she has no sense of self. The opposite of confluence is *isolation,* where all connectedness with others is lost. The socially constricted individual is considered ''isolated,'' since there is no real *contact* made with others.

*Contact* is the process of getting through the boundary of another person (Perls, 1969a). It involves sensory stimulation, contiguity, and may involve talking and moving; it involves a ''full engagement with whatever is interesting at that moment'' (Polster & Polster, 1973). It occurs in therapy by means of ''dialogue'' (Yontef & Simkin, 1969). Dialogue is the process of making contact through interpersonal interaction—of sensing ''me'' and ''not-me'' while interacting with another. In order to make contact through dialogue, the therapist must be fully present, reflective of self and the other, committed to the interaction, and focused on actions and feelings as well as words. Making contact with another person is a useful means to a better understanding of one's self. It is in the interpersonal realm that one can truly come to know the self.

**3.** Here and now. The Gestalt therapist continually focuses on the present. There is nothing but the here and now (Perls, 1969a). The Gestalt Therapy process is designed to help the client focus on the present, with the aim of therapy to bring about *awareness*. According to Yontef and Simkin (1989), awareness is a sense of self and environment (figure and ground) in the here and now involving ''full sensorimotor, emotional, cognitive, and energetic support'' (p. 333). For example, if a mother is feeling a split between her protective mother instinct and her anger at her abusive adult child (a retroflection), a therapist might point out the conflict by making the mother aware that when she speaks of her child, she speaks lovingly, but she also clenches her fist in anger. The therapist might then ask the mother to focus on the first, to feel the anger in the here and now, and to let it flow through the rest of her body so that feelings, verbalization, and expressions are consonant with a more holistic picture of self. The goal of such an exercise is to bring therapy into the present, and to help the client gain *insight*. Insight is a special type of awareness that is an immediate sense of the unity of the otherwise split personality. *Awareness is the only goal of Gestalt Therapy.*

**4.** Therapy is horizontal, not vertical. In other words, the therapeutic relationship is an ''I-Thou'' relationship, where two people are equals in dialogue rather than one person being one-up and the other being one-down in the client-therapist relationship (in the classic psychoanalytic sense of the therapist being in control). Therapy, then, is ideally a process of co-experience, in which the therapist has awareness in the here and now, as he or she facilitates the client's experience in the here and now.

**5.** Awareness in the here and now leads to change. The therapist is continually designing experiences for the client that bring both the therapist and the client fully into awareness of the here and now. It is through awareness that clients have the opportunity to take full responsibility for themselves. Once the person has a sense of figure and ground (self and other) and when dichotomies are recognized as polarities within a larger gestalt whole, then the person can move forward and make decisions necessary to solve problems.

These five basic principles guide the process of Gestalt Therapy.

## Counselor Role

The role of the Gestalt therapist is distinct in many ways from other therapies. Proponents of the Gestalt approach view it largely as an art form, and Perls himself eschewed viewing his therapy as technique. Rather Gestalt Therapy purists view the work of the therapist as implicit in the basic principles of Gestalt Therapy, listed in the previous section. They allow for much variability in the way the therapist approaches a client, but always with adherence to the basic principles. In this way there is an ''implicit'' philosophy of intervention. As Naranjo (1970) stated:

> *The Gestalt therapist places more value in action than in words, in experience than in thoughts, in the living process of therapeutic interaction and the inner change resulting thereby than in influencing beliefs. Action engenders substance*

*or touches substances. Ideas can easily float by, cover up, or even substitute for reality. So nothing could be more remote from the style of Gestalt therapy than preaching. Yet it involves a kind of preaching without injunctions or statements of belief, just as an artist preaches his world-view and orientation to existence through his style. (p. 48)*

The therapist's style of presentation, what he or she does, is as much Gestalt Therapy as is what the therapist says. The therapist essentially attempts to engage the client in dialogue—to make contact with the client to bring the client into the present, while maintaining a philosophical allegiance to the basic principles of holism and centeredness. Perls et al. (1951) stated:

*Our view of the therapist is that he is similar to what the chemist calls a catalyst, an ingredient which precipitates a reaction which might not otherwise occur. It does not prescribe the form of the reaction, which depends upon the intrinsic reactive properties of the materials present, nor does it enter as a part into whatever compound it helps to form. What it does is to start a process and there are some processes which, when once started are self-maintaining or autocatalytic. This we hold to be the case in therapy. What the doctor sets in motion, the patient continues on his own. (p. 15)*

In this sense, the therapist enters into a process called "therapy," with the intent of making contact with the client. As long as the basic Gestalt Therapy principles are adhered to, therapy is viewed as productive.

## Goals of Counseling and Ideal Outcomes

Gestalt Therapy is not a problem-solving therapy (Yontef & Simkin, 1989). It is a therapy that is best used with individuals who seek self-growth and understanding. Clients faced with the need to solve a problem immediately would be ill-served by Gestalt Therapy. On the other hand, a basic premise of Gestalt Therapy is that individuals who are in touch with themselves, who are aware in the present, who have a good clear sense of self and environment, when confronted by decision making are able to make decisions that are congruent with their needs and self-concepts. In this sense, awareness and self-understanding are prerequisites to effective living. According to Yontef and Simkin (1989), "in Gestalt therapy, the only goal is awareness" (p. 337).

Related to outcomes, Perls et al. (1951) stated:

*The criteria of therapeutic progress cease to be a matter of debate. It is not a question of increased "social acceptability" or improved "interpersonal relationships," as viewed through the eyes of some extraneous, self-constituted authority, but the patient's own awareness of heightened vitality and more effective functioning. (p. 15)*

Awareness is viewed as both content and process. It is a deep understanding, while at the same time it is a means of understanding. It is a process by which attention and awareness become one, while as an outcome it is a definition of selfhood. As Laura Perls (1970) stated:

> Gestalt therapy, with its emphasis on immediate awareness and involvement, offers a method for developing the necessary support for a self-continuing creative adjustment—which is the only way of coping with the experience of dying and, therefore, of living. (pp. 128–129)

Where awareness may appear to be overstated as an outcome of therapy, it is reflective of Perls's faith in the self and in full experience in the present. He was an optimist, and his position can be viewed as humanistic, especially when contrasted with Freud's negative view of human nature (from which Perls's ideas were an outgrowth). Where Freud viewed life as a struggle, Perls viewed life as an opportunity.

## General Procedures

### Assessment

Because Gestalt Therapy is present-focused, the therapist is not directed to do history taking. From the very beginning of therapy, the therapist, rather than diagnosing the patient in the classic sense, seeks to guide the client in exploration of himself or herself in the present. Yontef and Simkin (1989) stated:

> Rather than maintaining distance and interpreting, the Gestalt therapist meets patients and guides active awareness work. The therapist's active presence is alive and excited (hence warm), honest, and direct. Patients can see, hear, and be told how they are experienced, what is seen, how the therapist feels, what the therapist is like as a person. Growth occurs from real contact between real people. Patients learn how they are seen and how their awareness process is limited, not primarily from talking about their problems, but from how they and the therapist engage each other. (pp. 338–339)

Diagnostically, then, it is assumed that the client is not fully integrated at some level. Several therapeutic hypotheses may be formed. It may be that the client's self is split in some sense—through a retrogression, introjection, or projection. This is similar to the idea that some aspect of self is being denied (consciously, or, more likely, unconsciously), and the split in the personality will need to be healed. Or it may be hypothesized that the patient is living in the past or the future, while denying primary experience in the here and now. Or it is possible that the client's experience is dichotomized in some way, where the self and other are viewed as not one at the contact boundary, but separate and distinct—not complementary, but contradictory. In this way, wholeness is lost, and the individual needs to be centered at the point and moment of interpersonal contact in therapy. These are hypotheses the Gestalt therapist uses in working with clients. But using these hypotheses is not synonymous with classic diagnosis. In Gestalt Therapy, there is no final determination or interpretation. Diagnosis *is* the process of therapy. It is not separable. The therapist never is bound to one view of the client. The therapist enters into dialogue to facilitate growth in his or her own personality and the client's personality—to take the client and himself or herself to full experiencing and awareness in interpersonal interaction. Where Carl Rogers is loving, Perls is making love. Where Albert Ellis is defining the irrational, Perls is living irrationality with the client. All concerns are ''brought to'' and ''lived in'' the present.

## Treatment/Remediation

According to Enright (1970), the basic task of the therapist in remediation is ''to help the patient overcome the barriers . . . that block awareness, and to let nature take its course . . . so he can function with all his abilities'' (p. 108). Further, Enright described how the therapist must have a watchful eye, focusing on ''splits'' in the patient's attention—for example, where organismically the individual is acting (even unconsciously) in a way that is incongruent with his or her words and actions. Voice tone, motoric actions, gestures, and all nonverbal cues are hints as to organismic functioning, to which the client may not be consciously attending. Enright stated:

> My task begins when these other ''unconscious'' activities begin to stand out in the total gestalt and vie with the verbal content. I then encourage the patient(s) to devote some attention to these other activities, asking him to describe what he is doing, seeing, feeling. I make no interpretations but simply draw awareness to these phenomena, and let him make of them what he will. (pp. 108–109)

It is noteworthy that ideally, but not necessarily, interventions, such as the one just described, are noninterpretive. Whenever possible, the patient should make interpretations of his or her own behavior.

## Case Management

Case management is the process of maintaining contact with the client while facilitating the interpersonal relationship consistent with Gestalt Therapy principles. The therapist is not viewed as the one in control per se. The principle of the ''I-Thou'' relationship holds at the level of case management. The therapist mutually works through the business aspects of counseling with a client. The therapist recognizes the client's responsibility for himself or herself. This is not to say that the therapist is inactive and nondirective. In fact, the Gestalt therapist can be very active in therapy by teasing, cajoling, frustrating a client, and reflecting back to the client the client's response. In this sense, the therapist acts not only as a catalyst (as stated earlier), but also acts as a mirror, reflecting the client back upon himself or herself. It is valued when the client is aware, but it is also valued for the therapist to make observations as to whether the client is aware. These observations of a trained therapist are considered valid and reflective of what the client feels, thinks, and does. In this sense, a one-upness of the therapeutic relationship is not escaped, although it is downplayed in ongoing case management activity by means of the "I-Thou" principle.

Gestalt Therapy can be accomplished also in group settings, as long as the group facilitator fosters the basic Gestalt Therapy principles described earlier.

Audio or video taping of sessions is encouraged. Audio and video tapes may be helpful to the therapist in assessing inconsistencies in the patient's thoughts, feelings, and actions. Such recordings, however, do not substitute for therapy in the here and now, which is a primary focus of therapeutic activity. Notes are not taken during sessions, since such activity may interfere with contact between client and counselor. However, notes should be recorded after the session reflecting what happened in therapy to cue the therapist's memory before future meetings.

## Specialized Techniques

Perls did not like to view his work as technique. He felt the use of the term *technique* sounded manipulative and controlling. However, if one observes Perls, there is no question that he uses several methods to engage and to influence the client. Some of the methods that follow were described by Levitsky and Perls (1970), and others have been observed in Perls's videotaped works:

**1.** *Paraphrasing client nonverbal behaviors.* A Gestalt therapist does this in two ways. First, a Gestalt therapist might simply describe a behavior operationally, which then cues a client's own interpretation; for example: "Your foot is moving." Second, a therapist might interpret a person's nonverbal activity: "You are pouting like a little girl." In both of these cases, the paraphrase is meant to reflect back behaviors of which the client might be unaware.

**2.** *Misparaphrasing client nonverbal behaviors.* This appears to be manipulative at face value, and it is used usually in an effort to engage resistant clients. By interpreting a client behavior in a way that the client is likely to disagree, the client is engaged in interaction, and dialogue usually ensues. For example, to a resistant and disengaging ex-convict, the therapist might say, "I interpret your silence as deep-seated feelings of concern for me." Since the resistant client may dispute the interpretation, it is hoped that interpersonal contact with the client can be initiated.

**3.** *Focusing questions.* Focusing questions are questions designed to get the client to attend to certain experiences. The classic Gestalt Therapy focusing question, described in Yontef and Simkin (1989, p. 341) is: "What are you aware of (experiencing) now?" Any question that brings the client into contact with his or her own experience in the present is considered a focusing question, such as "How are you feeling now?" or "What are you thinking now?"

**4.** *The empty chair technique.* This is a method in which the therapist asks the client to view an empty chair and to pretend that another person is in the chair, or that some aspect of the client's own personality is in the chair, and then the client is asked to have a dialogue with the empty chair. This is essentially an integrating technique, used to help the client deal with retroflections, introjections, or projections at the root of splits in the personality. A classic example of how this technique could be used in therapy is that of "top-dog," and "underdog" (Levitsky & Perls, 1970), which is considered a classic dichotomized split in the personality. The concept of top-dog roughly translates to the psychoanalytic concepts of superego, the "shoulds" and "oughts" in the personality. According to Levitsky and Perls (1970), the underdog is "passively resistant, makes excuses, and finds reasons to delay" (p. 145). Levitsky and Perls stated that: "When a division is encountered, the patient is asked to have an actual dialogue between these two components of himself" (p. 145). The patient simply imagines the response, and replies in a continuing dialogue until there is some insight or awareness gained.

**5.** *Enactment.* Yontef and Simkin (1989) described enactment as having the patient "put feelings or thoughts into action" (p. 342). "Playing the projection" is a classic enactment described by Levitsky and Perls (1970). Playing the projection is an enactment of an attitude that the client perceives as reflective of another person's personality (when in fact it may be a projection of the client's own personality), and, once enacted, the client is asked "whether this is possibly a trait he himself possesses" (p. 146). Exaggeration and reversal are other types of enactment. Exaggeration is where the person is asked to exaggerate some feeling, thought, or movement. Reversal is where the person is asked to act the part of some aspect of the personality that is not usually manifested—for example, playing the exhibitionist if one is timid (Levitsky & Perls, 1970).

**6.** *"Stay with it" commands.* These are commands made by the therapist for the client to continue to feel, experience, and act in a way that is integrative of the personality. Yontef and Simkin (1989) describe this as allowing the patient to build and to deepen his or her awareness. "Stay with it" commands follow expressions by the client that appear to be insights or which can lead to awareness.

These are just several techniques that are consistent with Gestalt Therapy.

## Recent Developments or Criticisms

One of the obvious criticisms of Gestalt Therapy is that it borders on game playing with the client (see Patterson, 1973). In fact, in the hands of an unethical or improperly trained practitioner, it could easily be viewed as cruel or teasing, instead of constructive and fruitful. Also, the idea of full interpersonal contact with another person can easily be used as a rationale for having sexual relations with clients, which is *absolutely unethical* according to codes of conduct for the mental health professions. In addition, because there is no objectified measure of outcome ("awareness" is a subjective phenomenon), it is difficult to dispute its effectiveness or even to document its potential harm. Regardless, Gestalt Therapy is a process-oriented therapy, and as such, it offers the ethical practitioner a means to make meaningful interpersonal contact with a client.

The interpersonal contact issue is an important one. Gestalt Therapy makes full use of the therapeutic relationship, as it is recognized that one lives in a very social world, where *figure and ground* reasonably translates to *self and other.* The interpersonal nature of Gestalt Therapy is a strength, from a practical, therapeutic standpoint, but it is also a theoretical weakness. Gestalt Therapy, while it fully recognizes the interpersonal relationship therapeutically, is constrained by its emphasis on the individual as a perceiving *entity.* Theoretically, the perceiver is reified, and relationships only act to help define the perceiver. Perls (1969a) described the nature of a living perceiving organism in the following quotation: "What is an organism? We call an organism any living being, any living being that has organs, has an organization, that is self-regulating within itself. . . . The organism always works as a whole" (p. 5). Without the perceiver, there can be no construction of figure against ground. So the individual *always* works from an internal frame of reference. Perls described the relationship of the organism to the environment as follows:

> *Now let's talk a bit more about the relationship of the organism to its environment, and here we introduce the notion of the ego boundary. A boundary defines a thing. Now a thing has its boundaries, is defined by its boundaries in relation to the environment. In itself a thing occupies a certain amount of space. Maybe not much. Maybe it wants to be bigger, or wants to be smaller—maybe it's not satisfied with its size. We introduce now a new concept again, the wish to change based upon the phenomenon of dissatisfaction. Every time you want to change yourself, or you want to change the environment, the basis always is dissatisfaction. (p. 7)*

Although the ego boundary is not described by Perls as a *fixed thing,* the thingness of his definition cannot be denied. In fact, there is much similarity between Perls's definition of "ego" and Freud's definition of ego, which Perls himself addressed (Perls, 1947/1969). Perls (1947/1969), speaking of the human being, stated: "He achieves this subjective integration by the process of identification—the feeling that something is part of him or that he is part of something else. . . . Thus I agree with Freud that the Ego is closely related to identification" (p. 140). Consequently, the perceiver, as an internally "identified" organism, cannot be completely affected by external relationships, which is a position that requires one to believe that both relationships and individuals are distinct and dichotomous to a degree, which is inconsistent with the holistic philosophy of Gestalt Therapy. In this way, Gestalt Therapy has not fully integrated the concept of the individual "organism" into a more pure interpersonal dynamic. Or in other words, if individuals are so easily influenced within the Gestalt Therapy interpersonal context, why are they not viewed as maleable processes instead of internally directed organisms? From a contextual standpoint, this kind of inconsistency is unacceptable and is more readily reconciled by a more complete process-oriented, interpersonal construction of self, where self is viewed as relationships. Gestalt therapists appear to be unaware or at least unclear about this philosophical inconsistency, which makes the theoretical foundation vulnerable. Readers will more fully understand this criticism when introduced to the contextual paradigm.

Another criticism of Gestalt Therapy is its emphasis on "awareness." It can be argued that distressed individuals are already overaware, and that facilitating more awareness is counterproductive in such cases. Polster and Polster (1973) addressed this concern, and essentially rebutted the concern by differentiating self-consciousness with awareness, where self-consciousness is defensive and awareness is integrative.

Regardless, Gestalt Therapy proponents have been active and effective in clarifying the Gestalt position related to techniques and processes. Perls appeared to have had a difficult time communicating his ideas in a simple, straightforward manner, and the burden for clear conceptualizations of his position has fallen upon others. His adherents have, to a large degree, ferreted out the basic principles and techniques consistent with Perls's underlying philosophy (see M. Polster, 1987, for a clear and concise summary).

Currently, attempts have been made to "humanize" the technique of Gestalt Therapy. Perls was often viewed as inhumane in application of his technique, even though he can be classified as a humanist according to his optimistic view of human nature. To remedy this contradiction, E. Polster (1990) has developed a style of therapy that incorporates a humanistic interpersonal spirit with the sometimes confrontive techniques of Gestalt Therapy. He, in effect, has attempted to facilitate the goals of Gestalt Therapy by emphasizing the "power of simple human exchange." As a highly skilled practitioner, E. Polster has demonstrated how one can be loving and confrontive at the same time.

To the credit of the latest generation of leaders of the Gestalt Therapy movement, the approach is becoming more clearly delineated and refined.

## Paradigm Fit

### Focus of Study

The focus of study is the individual perceiver. Describing the Gestalt psychology movement, Polster and Polster (1973) stated:

> *The gestalt psychologists investigated the dynamics of the act of perceiving. They theorized that the perceiver was not merely a passive target for the sensory bombardment coming from his environment; rather, he structured and imposed order on his own perceptions. Basically, he organized perceptions of the incoming sensory stream into the primary experience of a* figure *as seen or perceived against a background, or* ground. *(p. 29)*

Although there is a constant interplay between figure and ground in the definition of self (Kempler, 1973, Perls et al., 1951), the individual *organism* is the organizer of experience. The human being is viewed as an active organism experiencing life at a contact boundary with an everchanging environment. Even though the organism is in contact with an everchanging world, without a *structured* sensing organism, there can be no perception. Therefore, the individual organism and his or her perceptions in *interaction* with the environment are the focus of study.

## View of Nature of Reality

Gestalt Therapy's position on reality can be defined by describing reality as interactive, where things are essentially constructed as perceptions or figures against a background. The thingness of reality is a reflection of the perceiving organism's gestalt. It is a phenomenological position. Although it is phenomenological, it is a position that does not deny an external reality. It is fully consonant with an assumption that *the background exists, just as the perceiving organism exists, and that there is contact between the organism as a thing and the external world as a continually flowing process.* In this sense, it is a position that assumes the presence of an objective everchanging external world and a bounded psychological entity (e.g., the ego).

## Consonance with Paradigm Propositions and Tenets

Clearly the focus of Gestalt Therapy is on the individual. Individuals, although not assessed in a classic organic-medical diagnostic sense, are evaluated through a process of therapy, where there is a constant interplay between the client and the therapist. During the ongoing interplay between the client and the therapist, the therapist attempts to assess splits in the personality, looking for inconsistencies between (a) the client's verbal and nonverbal behaviors; and (b) the client's actions, expressed feelings, and thoughts. Cause of disturbance is viewed as a lack of awareness, primarily deriving from disturbance between the individual perceiving organism at the environmental contact boundary. Change occurs within the individual through an interpersonal process, where essentially the therapist catalyzes the inherent potential for growth in the client. Therapists must be trained in the philosophy of Gestalt Therapy so they may adhere to the basic principles and techniques consistent with Gestalt Therapy philosophy. Failure in therapy results from the client's resistance, or from a therapist's failed efforts to create the opportunities for growth within the therapeutic context.

Gestalt Therapy is a clear-cut example of a theory of counseling and psychotherapy consistent with the internal model of the psychological paradigm.

# Chapter Conclusion

Gestalt Therapy is an approach that helps to produce an integration of a client's feelings, thoughts, and actions into his or her perception of self. It is extremely useful in helping clients to grow and change while being aware of their behaviors and feelings. It helps clients to live fully in the present. It is a counseling theory that clearly fits with the propositions of the psychological paradigm, and, specifically, the internal model of the psychological paradigm. Its focus on feeling, thinking, and behaving is unique among therapies aligned with the psychological paradigm.

# References

Enright, J. B. (1970). An introduction to gestalt techniques. In J. Fagan & I. L. Shepherd (Eds.), *Gestalt therapy now* (pp. 107–124). New York: Harper & Row.

Goldstein, K. (1959). *The organism: A holistic approach to biology derived from psychological data in man.* New York: American Book. (Original was published in 1934.)

Kempler, W. (1973). Gestalt therapy. In R. Corsini (Ed.), *Current psychotherapies,* (pp. 251–286). Itasca, IL: F. E. Peacock.

Levitsky, A., & Perls, F. (1970). The rules and games of gestalt therapy. In J. Fagan & I. L. Shepherd (Eds.), *Gestalt therapy now* (pp. 140–149). New York: Harper & Row.

Naranjo, C. (1970). Present-centeredness: Technique, prescription, and ideal. In J. Fagan & I. L. Shepherd (Eds.), *Gestalt therapy now* (pp. 47–69). New York: Harper & Row.

Patterson, C. H. (1973). *Theories of counseling and psychotherapy* (2nd ed.). New York: Harper & Row.

Perls, F. (1969). *Ego, hunger, and aggression.* New York: Vintage/Random House. (Originally published in 1947.)

Perls, F. (1969a). *Gestalt therapy verbatim.* Menlo Park, CA: Real People Press.

Perls, F. (1969b). *In and out of the garbage pail.* Lafayette, CA: Real People Press.

Perls, F. (1970). Four lectures. In J. Fagan & I. L. Shepherd (Eds.), *Gestalt therapy now* (pp. 14–38). New York: Harper & Row.

Perls, F., Hefferline, R. E., & Goodman, P. (1951). *Gestalt therapy: Excitement and growth in the human personality.* New York: Dell.

Perls, L. (1970). One Gestalt therapist's approach. In J. Fagan & I. L. Shepherd (Eds.), *Gestalt therapy now* (pp. 125–129). New York: Harper & Row.

Polster, E. (1990). *Gestalt therapy: Humanization of technique.* Paper and demonstration presented at the second "Evolution of Psychotherapy" conference in Anaheim, California, December 15, 1990.

Polster, E., & Polster, M. (1973). *Gestalt therapy integrated.* New York: Random House.

Polster, M. (1987). Gestalt therapy: Evolution and application. In J. Zeig (Ed.), *The evolution of psychotherapy* (pp. 312–322). New York: Brunner/Mazel.

Yontef, G. M., & Simkin, J. S. (1989). Gestalt therapy. In R. Corsini & D. Wedding (Eds.), *Current psychotherapy* (4th ed., pp. 323–361). Itasca, IL: F. E. Peacock.

# 10

# Behavior Therapy:
## External Psychological Model
## Theories and Techniques
## Focusing on Behavior

THIS CHAPTER WILL be organized slightly differently than the other chapters in this part of the text. The reason stems primarily from the fact that behavior therapy is not easily associated with one outstanding proponent, although there are several theoreticians and researchers who are most often associated with behavioral approaches in counseling and psychotherapy. Therefore, the focus of the beginning of the chapter will be on the empirical works of two major researchers, Ivan Pavlov and B. F. Skinner, who developed learning theories that have serious implications for the treatment of emotional concerns. These learning theories will be summarized at some length, since it is imperative that counselors have a good understanding of them before attempting to do Behavior Therapy.

It is also noteworthy that the term *Behavior Therapy,* does not represent one consensually agreed-upon position in the mental health services. There is no predominant unifying "Behavioral Therapy" as the chapter title implies. In fact, there are a number of different schools of behavior therapy, each distinct in its own way, yet each subscribing to an externalistic view of human influence. Therefore, to some degree, this chapter will appear to be less coherently organized than other chapters. The other chapters are held together logically by works of one predominant theorist; this is not the case with Behavior Therapy.

After the basic learning theories—classical conditioning and operant conditioning—are decribed, two specialized counseling methods will be presented in the "Specialized Techniques" section of the chapter. They are: Wolpe's (1973) "Systematic Desensitization'' and Kazdin's (1977) ''Token Economy.'' There are a number of reasons why these two approaches have been chosen. First, each represents a counseling technique associated with one of the two different learning theories—that is, Systematic Desensitization is closely aligned with classical conditioning, and Token Economy is an approach closely aligned with operant conditioning. Second, both have been found to be reasonably effective and well-researched methods, which is consistent with the operational philosophy of behaviorism (Watson, 1924/1930). And third, they are applied in diverse settings. Systematic Desensitization is used in office settings predominantly. Token Economies are often applied in institutional settings.

Related to the use of Token Economies in institutional settings, it can be argued that such an approach does not constitute counseling or psychotherapy in the usual sense. However, it has been my experience that counselors should have some preparation in this area, so that they have a clear vocabulary and understanding of how operant techniques are applied to human beings, even if they are not directly involved in day-to-day management of a Token Economy program. This is especially important for beginning practitioners working at psychiatric rehabilitation facilities or in programs for the severely intellectually deficient.

This chapter, then, provides a discussion of two learning theories and two specialized techniques (deriving directly and respectively from the learning theories) that can be applied in mental health settings.

## Biographical Sketches of Ivan Pavlov and B. F. Skinner

### Ivan Pavlov

Ivan Petrovich Pavlov was born in 1849 in the town of Ryazan in Russia. His father was a priest, and Pavlov attended a local seminary, where he felt he had excellent teachers. In 1870 he entered Petersburg University and studied natural history, with a major in physiology and a minor in chemistry. He later studied medicine with the intent of becoming a professor, rather than practicing medicine. By the age of 41, he was appointed to a position as a professor in a medical academy and also worked as a researcher and department head at an institute for experimental medicine. There he carried out his physiological research. However, he became interested in psychological processes and how nervous system activity was affected by sensory stimuli. Through his experiments, he learned that otherwise noninfluential objects could be made to influence physiological processes by means of association with activating stimuli. Although he considered himself a physiologist, he spent a good number of his years studying such mental processes.

According to Marx and Hillix (1973), in 1904, Pavlov was awarded the Nobel prize for his ''investigations of glandular and neural factors in digestion'' (p. 97).

Pavlov died in 1936.

### B. F. Skinner

Burrhus Frederic Skinner was born on March 20, 1904, in Pennsylvania. His father was a lawyer, and his mother was a homemaker. At an early age he was known to be inquisitive, having a fascination with mechanical things (Kirschenbaum & Henderson, 1989). He also loved to read and write.

Skinner majored in literature at Hamilton College in Clinton, New York, with the intent of being a fiction writer. But after receiving awards and graduating Phi Beta Kappa, he spent a year writing fiction and "discovered the unhappy fact that I had nothing to say" (as cited in Kirschenbaum & Henderson, 1989, p. 79). He became intrigued with the writings of Bertrand Russell and John Watson, which changed his career course. He pursued and received his PhD degree in psychology form Harvard University in 1931. He received several postdoctoral fellowships there, and later taught psychology (from 1936 to 1945) at the University of Minnesota, and from 1945 to 1947 at Indiana University where he was chairman of the Department of Psychology. In 1947 he took a professorship at Harvard University, where he actively taught until 1974 and where he remained as Professor Emeritus of Psychology until his death in August, 1990, at the age of 86.

Skinner was a man who believed and acted his own theory. He strongly felt that humans could condition themselves to achieve certain behaviors, and he was known for keeping charts of his own behavior and presenting himself with rewards for achievements. He strongly believed that humans are externally controlled, and that freedom, as an internal psychological phenomenon, is a result of external conditioning. He was prolific throughout his life; one of his most recent publications, *Recent Issues in the Analysis of Behavior* (Skinner, 1989), is a contemporaneous and readable summary of his ideas. Skinner received the American Psychological Association's Distinguished Scientific Contribution Award in 1958. In 1968 he received the National Medal of Science, and in 1971 the Gold Medal of the American Psychological Association. He was a member and fellow of several scholarly and learned societies.

Skinner is widely known to have taken up the banner of "behaviorism," and his work will have a lasting effect on experimental psychology and the field of counseling and psychotherapy.

## The Foundational Theories

### Classical (Respondent) Conditioning

Ivan Pavlov has been credited with developing classical conditioning theory. Classical conditioning is best understood as *learning through association*—one object becomes psychologically linked with a second object through a process of repeated and simultaneous pairings of the two objects.

As a physiologist, Pavlov was interested in the physiological reactions of animals under experimental conditions (e.g., the salivation responses of canines). However, he also was intrigued by the psychological phenomena which he uncovered in his work. Pavlov (1916/1957) described how certain objects can be psychologically associated with food to excite a salivation response in an animal:

> *It has been proved that any agent of the external world can be made a stimulus of the salivary gland. Any sound, odour, etc., may become a stimulus that will excite the salivary gland exactly in the same way as it is excited by food at a distance. As to the precision of the fact, there is no difference whatever; it is only necessary to take into account the conditions in which the fact exists. What, then, are the conditions which can become stimuli of the salivary gland? The chief condition is coincidence in time. The experiment is performed as follows. We take, for example, a certain sound which has no relation to the salivary gland. This sound acts on the dog. Then we feed the dog or introduce acid into its mouth. After several repetitions of this the sound itself, without the addition of food or acid, begins to excite the salivary gland. There are altogether four or five, at most six conditions under which any stimulant, any agent of the external world, becomes a stimulus of the salivary gland in the dog. Once this is so, once it has become a stimulus under a definite series of conditions, it will always act with the same precision as food or as any rejected substance introduced into the mouth. . . . Actually this is a law-governed reaction of the organism to an external agent effected through the medium of a definite part of the nervous system. (pp. 397–398)*

In the preceding passage, Pavlov was essentially describing classical conditioning—the association of a stimulus (sound) with an object (food in this case), so that the stimulus produces the same reaction as the original object. Several basic classical conditioning principles are as follows.

There are certain animal responses which are physiologically based (respondents). For instance, a hungry dog will salivate when presented food. Human infants, for instance, respond with fear when they hear a loud noise. When a response is physiologically based, it is considered an unconditioned response. No conditioning of any sort is necessary for the response to occur. It occurs quite naturally when certain stimuli are present. (A stimulus is a condition that affects the organism through any of five senses—visual, auditory, olfactory [smell], gustatory [taste], and tactile/kinesthetic [touch].) In effect, when an organism is sensorily confronted by certain stimuli, certain unconditional responses can be predicted. Specific stimuli that produce unconditioned responses (UCR) are called unconditioned stimuli (UCS).

time

Unconditioned Stimulus ---------------------------------> Unconditioned Response
      (UCS)                                           (UCR)

Examples:

    Food Powder (UCS)  --------------------------------> Salivation in Dog (UCR)

    Loud Noise (UCS)  --------------------------------> Human Fear (UCR)

    Skin Pinprick (UCS) --------------------------------> Withdrawal Reflex (UCR)

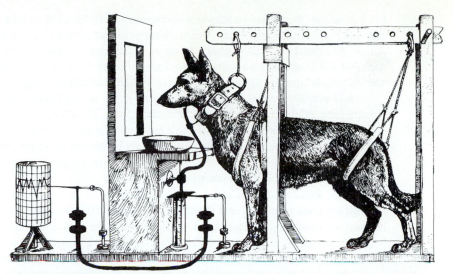

A dog strapped into a harness for an experiment on classical conditioning of salivation. The experimenter can ring a bell (CS), present food (UCS), and measure the response (CR and UCR) without direct contact with the animal.

In all cases, there is a direct correspondence between the presentation of an unconditioned stimulus and an unconditioned response.

What Pavlov found was that when a stimulus that otherwise produced no noticeable effect (a neutral stimulus, NS) was associated with an unconditioned stimulus (which always produced an unconditioned response), the neutral stimulus could be made to produce a very similar response. For instance, when a bell is repeatedly and simultaneously rung at separate presentations of food powder to a hungry dog, the bell becomes associated with the food powder and alone will produce a salivation response much like the salivation response of the dog when food is present. In effect, the neutral stimulus (the bell), which otherwise would not produce a salivation response in a dog, can be made to produce salivation. Diagramatically, this type of learning through association looks as follows:

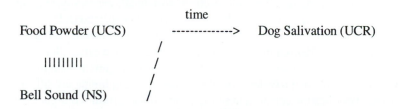

The lines (||||||||) above the words ''Bell Sound (NS)'' represent the *repeated* sounding of the bell (the neutral stimulus) when food powder is placed in sensory perception of the dog. *Also, the bell sound is made at the same time that the food powder is presented.*

In other words, there must be temporal contiguity—both the UCS and the NS must be presented at about the same time. This is a basic principle of classical conditioning—as Pavlov described it—"coincidence in time." Therefore, *repetition* of the neutral stimulus and *temporal contiguity* (coincidence in time) between the neutral stimulus and the unconditioned stimulus are two basic classical conditioning principles.

It is noteworthy that if the bell is rung *after* the food powder is presented, the conditioning effect is not as strong. Presenting the NS after the UCS (backward conditioning), therefore, is not as effective as presenting the NS at the same time as the UCS. Also, the NS can be presented immediately before the presentation of the UCS (forward conditioning) and the NS will have near or as good an effect as with simultaneous NS and UCS presentation.

Once the neutral stimulus has been associated with the unconditioned stimulus through temporal contiguity and repetition, the neutral stimulus takes on properties of its own for producing a response in the organism. The neutral stimulus, therefore, becomes a conditioned stimulus (CS), which produces a conditioned response (CR) that is very similar to the unconditioned response (UCR). In the previous example, the sounding of the bell alone (without food powder presentation) would produce salivation almost to the degree that the food powder produced salivation in dogs. Diagramatically, classical conditioning looks as follows:

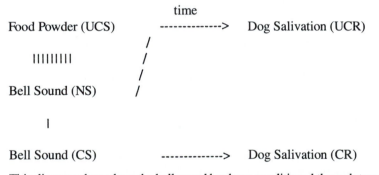

This diagram shows how the bell sound has been conditioned through temporal contiguity and repetition to produce a response of salivation. In this way, the bell sound (a neutral stimulus that has become a conditioned stimulus), on its own, produces a salivation response (conditioned response). Pavlov showed that dogs could be made to salivate upon presentation of conditioned stimuli. In effect, an animal's nervous system can be taught to react to otherwise neutral stimuli through a process of associational learning.

A more meaningful and personal example is that of thunder and lightning and the fear response evidenced in young children. As mentioned earlier, loud noises produce fear responses in humans. Thunder, of course, can be quite frightening, even when a human is physically protected from the elements. But lightning is really not dangerous to a human when the human is in safe quarters. In fact, flashes of light as a general rule do not produce fear responses in humans. People are frequently confronted with light flashes in everyday life, and although a flash of light may orient a person, it will not usually produce fear. But it is well understood that lightning can cause a fear response in children. Actually, it is not the flash of lightning that causes the fear—it is the association of the lightning with thunder which produces fear in children, even in the safety of their homes. Diagramatically, the association of lightning and the fear response to thunder look as follows:

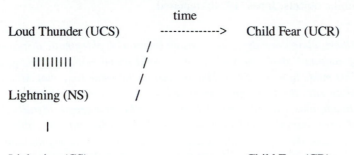

As is presented in this example, lightning flashes can produce a fear response in children that is very similar to the fear response resulting when there is a loud thunderclap. Classical conditioning has occurred. Almost every time there is thunder, lightning precedes it (forward conditioning). There is repetition and temporal contiguity between thunder and lightning. After such conditioning occurs, lightning will produce fear even in the absence of the sound of thunder.

As was mentioned earlier, there must be simultaneity or at least forward conditioning—the lightning and thunder must occur about the same time. If the lightning, however, were to occur after the thunder (backward conditioning) it would not have the same effect. The ease of conditioning, in the lightning and thunder example, reflects the power of forward conditioning.

The importance of this kind of learning through association was not fully explored as applied to humans by Pavlov. It was John B. Watson, credited with being the "Father of Behaviorism" (Watson, 1924/1930; Watson & Rayner, 1920), who recognized the consequences of Pavlov's ideas for human behavior. Watson, in a classic experiment, attempted to condition a fear response in a young child, Little Albert. Using classical conditioning principles, Watson and Rayner (1920) associated the presentation of a white rat (as a neutral stimulus) to the presentation of a loud, frightening noise (remember human children react to loud noises in an unconditioned manner). See the following diagram:

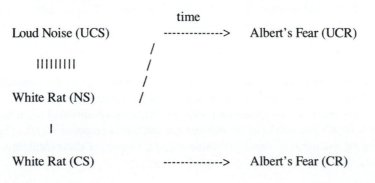

Over time, the child came to associate the presentation of the white rat with the loud noise to the degree that the white rat, alone, produced a fear response. Not only did the child fear the white rat, but his fear *generalized* (spread) to become associated with other similar objects. Jones (1924b) reported:

> *Albert, eleven months of age, was an infant with phlegmatic disposition, afraid of nothing "under the sun" except a loud sound made by striking a steel bar. This made him cry. By striking the bar at the same time that Albert touched a white rat, the fear was transferred to the white rat. After seven combined stimulations, rat and sound, Albert not only became greatly disturbed at the sight of a rat, but this fear had spread to include a white rabbit, cotton wool, a fur coat, and the experimenter's hair. It did not transfer to his wooden blocks and other objects very dissimilar to the rat. (pp. 308–309)*

Watson's intent, however, was to go beyond the actual conditioning of fear in a child. He wished to show that fear could be unlearned, just as it could be learned. Unfortunately, Little Albert was "adopted by an out-of-town family" shortly after he was conditioned to fear white rats (Watson, 1924/1930); deconditioning of the fear never was accomplished! It was left to one of Watson's students, Mary Cover Jones (1924a; 1924b), to demonstrate how fear could be unlearned through classical conditioning principles. Jones (1924a) described how deconditioning of a child's fear could be accomplished by using food as a stimulus to produce a response incompatible to fear:

> *During a period of craving for food, the child is placed in a high chair and given something to eat. The feared object is brought in, starting a negative response. It is then moved away gradually until it is at a sufficient distance not to interfere with the child's eating. The relative strength of the fear impulse and the hunger impulse may be gauged by the distance to which it is necessary to remove the feared object. While the child is eating, the object is slowly brought nearer to the table, then placed upon the table and, finally, as the tolerance increases, it is brought close enough to be touched. Since we could not interfere with the regular schedule of meals, we chose the time of the mid-morning lunch for the experiment. This usually assured some degree of interest in the food and corresponding success in our treatment. (pp. 388–389)*

Essentially Jones extended classical conditioning principles to the deconditioning of fear. She associated an unconditionied stimulus (food) that produced a pleasant unconditioned response (satiation) with the formerly conditioned stimulus (a white furry animal) that produced an unwanted conditioned response (fear). The diagram shows the extension of classical conditioning for reasons of deconditioning:

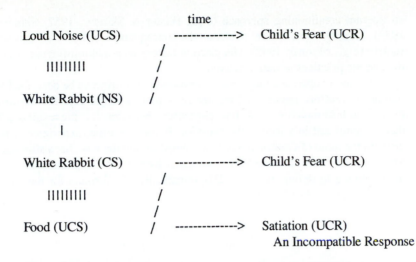

The child's satiation and pleasant responses to food proved to be, to some degree, *incompatible* with the fear response. And through contiguity and repetition (represented by the lines under the CS [| | | | | | | | | |]) the child was *deconditioned* to the previously conditioned fear response.

Through Watson's work (Watson & Rayner, 1920) and the works of Mary Cover Jones (1924a, 1924b), Pavlov's classical conditioning was applied to humans, not only to condition certain responses, but to decondition unwanted responses. The therapeutic application of classical conditioning principles was realized.

## Operant Conditioning

B. F. Skinner's work has been immensely influential in the field of counseling and psychotherapy. He was a prolific writer and, in his works, he applied his experimental findings to personal, therapeutic, educational, social, and cultural situations. For example, in a recent work, Skinner (1989), discussing the "operant side of behavior therapy," stated:

> The conditions of which behavior is a function are sometimes under control, in homes, for example, and in schools, workplaces, hospitals, and prisons. Therapists may change these conditions for their own purposes if they are part of a family or if they teach, employ workers, or administer hospitals or prisons. Professionally, they advise those who do so. They help parents with their children or spouses with their spouses; they advise teachers; they recommend new practices in hospitals and prisons. They can do so because some of the conditions under which people live can be controlled. (p. 79)

Skinner believed that his findings apply beyond the animal laboratory, where some of his ground-breaking technical work was done. In addition to describing his experimental operant conditioning approach (e.g., Ferster & Skinner, 1957; Skinner, 1938, 1953), Skinner wrote several books on the consequences of his work for culture and society (e.g., Skinner, 1948). His place in history as a major influence over psychotherapeutic practices is well preserved.

Skinner's operant conditioning approach very simply can be described as conditioning by reinforcements. In fact, one of Skinner's major contribution to learning theory was his emphasis on what happens after a behavior. It is the result of a behavior that is significant in affecting the behavior. Before his time, experimental psychologists, in the mold of Guthrie or Hull, attempted to find the way that a stimulus (S) and a response (R) were connected. They primarily focused on what went before a behavior in attempting to define its cause. Diagramatically, the formula for human behavior before Skinner looked like this:

$$S \text{ -----------> } R$$
$$\text{Stimulus} \qquad \text{Response}$$

But Skinner, following the lead of Thorndike (1905), began to look at what happens after a behavior to determine its contingencies. Skinner recognized it was the relationship of the response to a *stimulus following the response* that was primarily a predictor of the likelihood of a behavior occurring again. For Skinner, the formula of behavior looked like this:

$$S \text{ -----------> } R \text{ -----------> } Sr$$
$$\text{Stimulus} \qquad \text{Response} \qquad \text{Reinforcing Stimulus}$$

The emphasis in this formula is on the reinforcing stimulus, that is, what happens after a response. If a man said "sit" to a dog, and the dog randomly or accidentally sat, the likelihood of the dog sitting upon future commands is increased if the man gave the dog a reward after his first command. In this example, the behavior or response is considered an "operant." Operants are simply emitted behaviors. The dog was rewarded for sitting; therefore, it is more likely it will sit upon command in the future. The operant behavior was reinforced. In effect, Skinner's major accomplishment was to take the emphasis off the behavior preceding a response. In fact, experimentalists before him seemed to be wearing blinders that prevented them from seeing anything related to a behavior except what came before it. Skinner's position required them to go beyond the S--->R framework. Skinner focused on operants and the outcomes of the operant behavior.

It is no secret that animals and people are influenced by rewards. Individuals are frequently rewarded or punished for their behaviors. The rewards and punishments, obviously, come after the behaviors. Rewards and punishments have a major controlling effect on what is subsequently done. But it is not as simple as understanding that rewards and punishments influence behavior. Skinner went into great detail about how behavior is affected, primarily in his book *Schedules of Reinforcement* (Ferster & Skinner, 1957). Readers should also know there are several excellent primers on Skinner's work, which are useful in providing quick summaries of Skinner's ideas (e.g., Reynolds, 1968). It is important to begin with an understanding that there are different possible outcomes to an action. Four basic outcomes were defined by Skinner:

**1.** An operant can be positively reinforced. *Positive reinforcement is the process by which the likelihood of a response increases upon the presentation of a stimulus.* A positive reinforcer is defined by its result. Giving a child candy when the child is behaving well, if good behavior follows, is an act of positive reinforcement. The candy, being a stimulus following well-behaved actions, is considered a positive reinforcer. Other examples of positive reinforcers are pay bonuses for exceptional employees, sales commissions for salespersons, medals for star athletes, etcetera. Very simply, if something is rewarding, it is usually a positive reinforcer.

**2.** An operant can be negatively reinforced.. *Negative reinforcement is the process by which the likelihood of a response increases upon the removal of a stimulus.* Assume for a moment that there is a rat in a cage with a painful electrical current running through the floor of the cage; the only way the rat can stop the painful electrical current is to press a lever. If the rat presses the lever, and the current ceases, then the rat's behavior has been negatively reinforced. It is more likely the rat will press the lever when again confronted by an electrical charge in the floor. Negative reinforcement occurs only when there is an aversive or painful situation. When an organism acts to stop the painful or aversive situation, and succeeds, then the behavior of stopping the painful situation is negatively reinforced. But actually, there are three different types of negative reinforcement: (a) acts that stop an aversive stimulus; (b) acts of escape from an aversive stimulus; and (c) acts that prevent an aversive condition (see Kazdin, 1977). Any of these three behaviors can be considered negative reinforcement, since the behavior is more likely to occur in similar subsequent situations.

Note that both positive and negative reinforcement increase the likelihood of behavior. Negative reinforcement should not be confused with punishment, which decreases the likelihood of a behavior.

**3.** An operant can be punished. *Punishment is the process by which the likelihood of a response decreases upon the presentation of a stimulus.* Punishment usually involves the presentation of an aversive stimulus. A son who is slapped by his mother upon reaching for dessert before finishing dinner, who then avoids prematurely reaching for desert in the future, has been punished. The likelihood of the child prematurely reaching for the dessert is decreased by the presentation of an aversive stimulus—the slap. An athlete who is fined for misbehavior on a playing field, who then refrains from future misbehavior, has been punished. In both these examples, a stimulus was presented that was aversive to the individual, thereby decreasing the likelihood of future behavior.

**4.** An operant can be extinguished. *Extinction is the process by which the likelihood of a response decreases upon the removal of a stimulus.* Extinction usually involves removal of a rewarding stimulus. For example, a teenager who volunteers to cut a neighbor's lawn, who has been paid in the past for doing the work, but who never receives subsequent payment, is less likely to volunteer in the future. A child reaching into what was previously an always full cookie jar, only to find upon repeated attempts that there are no cookies in the jar, is less likely to continue looking in the jar for cookies. In both these examples, the likelihood of a behavior has decreased, because a stimulus (reward) has been removed.

Both punishment and extinction decrease the likelihood of a behavior.

Punishment is the most effective means for quickly preventing a behavior. But punishment has some very serious drawbacks. First, it must be consistently and continuously applied. If one instance in a sequence of behavior is overlooked (not punished) then there is a chance that it will be negatively reinforced (increased in likelihood because the punishment has been removed). Second, punishment does not instruct the subject (an individual or animal) about the appropriate behavior. The subject may appear confused. In this sense, it does not educate about the wanted or expected behavior. Third, punishment is often followed by aggressive responses by the punished organism. Aggression is often an unwanted side-effect of punishment. Skinner, accordingly, has convincingly argued against the use of punishment, and in favor of positive reinforcement and extinction as modifiers of behavior (Skinner, 1948).

To be a behavior therapist using operant conditioning, it it absolutely imperative to understand these four types of influence on behavior.

But beyond understanding the nature of what happens after a behavior and its subsequent influence on later events, Skinner also recognized that there are different schedules (ways) of maintaining a behavior, especially through positive reinforcement. There are five different schedules of reinforcement that can be used to maintain a behavior. They are (numbered parenthetically):

A. A continuous reinforcement schedule. (1)
B. Intermittent reinforcement schedules.
   1. Ratio Schedules
      a. Fixed ratio (2)
      b. Variable ratio (3)
   2. Interval Schedules
      a. Fixed interval (4)
      b. Variable interval (5)

A continuous reinforcement schedule is the easiest to understand. Simply, each wanted behavior is rewarded. No matter how fast or how slow, or in what time frame, each emission of a wanted behavior is reinforced. For example, every time a pet dog sits on command, it receives a treat.

Intermittent reinforcement schedules, on the other hand, require reinforcement of a partial number of responses. There are four intermittent schedules (fixed ratio, variable ratio, fixed interval, and variable interval).

### Ratio Schedules

A ratio schedule reinforces one of every so many responses. For example, if the ratio of rewards-to-behaviors is one reward for every five emissions of behaviors (a ratio equal to 1/5), then one-fifth of the behaviors are reinforced. If it is the fifth response in the sequence that is always rewarded, then the reward is on a fixed-ratio schedule— every fifth response is reinforced in a fixed pattern. A fixed-ratio schedule of reinforcement is demonstrated by the following sequence of letters, where each X is an emitted response, and each R is an emitted response that is rewarded:

```
------------------------> time  > -------------------------->
   0XXXXR XX XX R XXX X R XX X X RXXXXR
      |          |         |          |         |
```

The fifth responses in each sequence are indicated by lines underneath the letters. Note that the time between the fifth responses may differ, but every fifth response received a reward. In this case each rewarded response was the fifth response. This is a fixed-ratio schedule.

A variable-ratio schedule still maintains a set ratio, say 1/5 (one reward in every five responses) but the response that receives the reward within the five emissions may vary. See the following sequence of letters, where, again, each X represents an emitted response, and each R is an emitted response that is rewarded:

```
------------------------> time  > -------------------------->
   XXRXX RX XX X XXX R X XX X X RXRXXX
      |          |         |          |         |
```

The fifth responses in each sequence are indicated by lines underneath the letters. Note that the time between the fifth responses may differ, but one in every group of five responses received a reward. In the first group of five responses, the third response received a reward; in the second group of five responses, the first response received the reward; in the third group of five responses, the fourth behavior received the reward; in the fourth group of five responses, the fifth response received a reward; etcetera. In each case, the ratio of one reward for every five responses was maintained, even though the event that was rewarded varied in each group of five responses. This is a variable-ratio schedule.

### Interval Schedules

Unlike ratio schedules, interval schedules do not involve counting responses. Rather, time is the issue. If an interval of time is set at ten seconds, for example, then, one reward occurs in every ten-second interval. The response that receives the reward within the time period is *fixed* at the response that is closest to the end of the time interval. This is a fixed-interval schedule of reinforcement. See the following sequence of letters, where, again, each X represents an emitted response, and each R is an emitted response that is rewarded:

```
----------------|-----------------| time ----------|-----------------|----------------|-->
  X X XXX XR X X  X X  R  XXX X XRXXXX X X R XXX X X R
```

The ten-second intervals are noted on the time-line above the response letters, divided by the straight vertical lines. Note that the behaviors that are rewarded are in all cases the behaviors occurring at exactly the end of the ten-second intervals, *or* the behaviors immediately following the end of the ten-second intervals. In this way, time is the factor setting the reinforcement pattern. About every ten seconds, a response is rewarded, no matter how many or how few responses occur in the ten-second interval. This is a fixed-interval schedule.

A variable-interval schedule, like the fixed-interval schedule, does not involve counting responses. Time is the issue. Again, assuming that an interval of time for reinforcement is set at ten seconds, then, one reward occurs in every ten-second interval. The response that receives the reward, however, varies within the time period. It *is not* fixed at the response that is closest to the end of the time interval. It can occur any time within each ten-second interval. See the following sequence of letters, where, each X represents an emitted response, and each R is an emitted response that is rewarded.

```
----------------|-----------------| time ---------|-----------------|----------------|-->
X X XXX XR X R  X X  X  XXX R XXRXXX X X X XXR X X X
```

The ten-second intervals are noted on the time-line above the response letters, divided by the straight vertical lines. Note that the behaviors that are rewarded always occur sometime in the ten-second intervals, but the time of reinforcement in the intervals varies in each ten-second interval. In the first ten seconds, the reward comes exactly at the end of the period; in the second ten seconds, the reward comes near the beginning of the period; in the third ten seconds, the reward comes near the end; and in the fourth ten-second period, the reward comes at the beginning of the period; etcetera. Time is the factor setting the reinforcement pattern. Within every ten seconds, one response is rewarded, no matter how many or how few responses occur in the ten-second interval. But the time in each ten seconds where the reward occurs, varies for each ten-second interval. This is a variable-interval schedule.

Understanding these types of reinforcement schedules is very important, especially in clinical settings where continuous reinforcement of wanted behaviors becomes very expensive in time, effort, and resources. In fact, the continuous reinforcement schedule (where every response is rewarded) is very vulnerable to extinction (a decrease in the likelihood of a behavior due to the removal of a reinforcing stimulus). It is the easiest schedule of reward for the subject to *un*learn upon removal of rewards. On the other hand, the variable ratio and variable interval schedules of reinforcement are the least vulnerable and most immune to extinction. In effect, the intermittent schedules have rewarded the subject for not being rewarded some of the time (interval schedules) or for not being rewarded every response (ratio schedules). The variable ratio and variable interval schedule even make the rewards less predictable. The subject then learns to be patient about rewards! Intermittent reinforcement schedules make the behaviors more enduring in the face of removal of positive reinforcers.

### Shaping

So far, a great many details have been presented about how behaviors are affected by events that follow them, and how certain wanted behaviors can be maintained. Little has been said about how wanted behaviors are first emitted. In fact, the behaviors that are wanted by the behaviorist may not occur naturally. They may not exist in the subject's behavioral repertoire. In such cases, it is the responsibility of the behaviorist to encourage the wanted behavior. The behavioral method for encouraging new behaviors is called ''shaping.'' Shaping is the process by which a wanted behavior is successively approximated—semblances of the wanted behavior are systematically rewarded, increasing the likelihood of the wanted behavior's occurrence. In this way, the subject is rewarded for any behavior that comes close to the behavior that is wanted, and, through a process of waiting for and rewarding appropriate operants, the behaviorist slowly assists the subject in building the wanted behavior. Kazdin (1977) stated: ''In shaping, the terminal behavior is achieved by reinforcing small steps or approximations toward the final response rather than reinforcing the final response itself'' (p. 12). Skinner demonstrated this clearly with rats in what he devised as a reinforcement chamber (what is now known as a Skinner box). To get a hungry rat to push a lever to get food pellets, it is first necessary to reward any behavior of the rat that is close to the lever. As the rat gets closer to the lever, the rat is rewarded with a food pellet. Each subsequent approach to the lever is rewarded, until, finally, perhaps by accident, the lever is engaged by the rat, which produces an immediate reward. Shaping is a means of ensuring that wanted behaviors will be manifested.

### Primary and Secondary Reinforcers

There are certain types of stimuli that act as reinforcers quite naturally. For example, a hungry rat will respond to food, a thirsty animal will respond to water, and so on. According to Reynolds (1968), when stimuli are ''able to reinforce behavior without the organism's having any particular previous experience with them'' (p. 11), they can be considered *primary reinforcers*. In humans, deprivation-related primary reinforcers include food, water, sleep, and sex (broadly defined as skin-to-skin contact). Humans, for example, appear especially naturally attracted to foods with sugar, salt, and fat content. Moreover, other stimuli can become reinforcers. Reynolds (1968) stated that conditioned, or *secondary reinforcers,* ''acquire the power to reinforce operants through a procedure which is similar to that of respondent [classical] conditioning'' (p. 11). When an otherwise neutral stimulus has been associated with a primary reinforcer consistent with the principles of classical conditioning, it can acquire reinforcing properties. The classic example of a secondary reinforcer is money. Money cannot be eaten or used as drink but it can be associated with (used to purchase) food or drink. Secondary reinforcers, as with money, are very powerful reinforcers.

Given these basic operant behavioral principles, behavior therapists can modify human behavior in mental health settings, as will be described later in this chapter by means of Kazdin's (1977) Token Economy.

## The Object of Counseling

The object of counseling consistent with Behavior Therapy is a specified, identifiable, and measurable behavior. There is no assumption of psychological process beyond what can be observed. This basic principle was defined by Watson (1924/1930). Watson stated:

> *We believed then, as we do now, that man is an animal different from other animals only in the types of behavior he displays. . . . The raw fact that you, as a psychologist, if you are to remain scientific, must describe the behavior of man in no other terms than those you would use in describing the behavior of the ox you slaughter, drove and still drives many timid souls away from behaviorism. (p. v)*

Behaviorally oriented therapists, therefore, focus on observable behaviors, and they describe behaviors in operational terms. An operational term is a definition according to actions—nothing is implied. A behaviorist would say, ''The man raised his finger to his eyebrow and scratched it three times in a downward fashion.'' A nonbehaviorist might say, ''The man appeared to be thinking.'' Nonbehavioral hypothesizing is not consistent with the focus of Behavior Therapy.

## The Process of Counseling

The process of counseling is a process of defining maladaptive or distressful behaviors and then establishing procedures to ameliorate them. The counselor meets with the client to define behavioral objectives, and then the counselor acts in an ongoing process of behavioral assessment and environmental modification to change the external factors affecting an unwanted behavior. The process of counseling may differ according to the specialized technique used, and the reader is directed to the ''Specialized Techniques'' section of this chapter to gain a clearer understanding of the process of counseling according to specific techniques.

## Counselor Role

The counselor role is that of technician and educator. The Behavior Therapist acts to coordinate a program designed to change behavior, primarily by implementing operant or classical conditioning principles. It is also important for the counselor to establish a behavioral contract with the client, which essentially defines a consensus that the client's problem is anticipated to be modifiable by means of external influence on the client's behavior. The counselor clearly defines the goals and objectives of counseling and the methods for achieving goals.

## Goals of Counseling and Ideal Outcomes

The goal of Behavior Therapy is a change in behavior. Since the behaviors undertaken for modification through behavioral means are measurable, the outcomes of therapy are measurable. Ideally, the client will leave therapy without symptomatic behavior, or at least with a diminution of unwanted behaviors. It is the behavioral therapist's responsibility to assess whether the targeted behaviors have been diminished consistent with the patient's expressed interests at the beginning of therapy.

## Specialized Techniques

### Joseph Wolpe's Systematic Desensitization

Joseph Wolpe's (1958, 1973, 1990) "Systematic Desensitization" technique is probably one of the best and most widely practiced examples of behavioral therapy. Wolpe, an MD psychiatrist, owing much to the works of B. F. Skinner (1953), Watson (Watson, 1913; Watson & Rayner, 1920) and H. J. Eysenck (1960), took behavioral theory and adeptly applied it to mental health services. In fact, Systematic Desensitization builds upon the works of Watson, and specifically one of Watson's students, Mary Cover Jones (Jones, 1924a, 1924b) who extended the classical conditioning model to the realm of deconditioning fear, as was discussed earlier in this chapter.

Wolpe, in his attempts to decondition anxiety in patients, tried several means to ameliorate the anxiety response without using food as the deconditioning stimulus, as Jones (1924a) had done. Food, as it will be learned later, is not the best stimulus to produce a response incompatible to anxiety. Wolpe was thwarted in his efforts until he learned of Jacobson's (1938) "Progressive Relaxation" technique. Progressive Relaxation is a technique by which a deep-muscle relaxation is accomplished through a series of exercises. Progressive Relaxation brings about a response in the client that is antithetical to the anxiety response. Also, progressive relaxation is a technique that is easy to do, can be taught to clients, and produces a response with practice that is strong enough to counteract an unwanted anxiety response. It also has the additional benefit

*Joseph Wolpe*

of not requiring motor activity on the part of the patient in relation to the anxiety-pro-ducing stimulus. The patient, once relaxed, just has to relax and use his or her imagination. In effect, Wolpe combined the theoretical and practical work of Jones with Jacobson's "Progressive Relaxation" technique to produce "Systematic Desensitization." Systematic Desensitization is a technique used primarily to decondition fear responses by pairing the stimulus that produces the unwanted anxiety response with a command to relax (which with practice can produce a deep-muscle relaxation).

Theoretically, Systematic Desensitization is based on a principle of learning, "reciprocal inhibition," which Wolpe (1958) discussed in detail in his classic work, *Psychotherapy by Reciprocal Inhibition*. The principle of reciprocal inhibition is defined as follows:

> *If a response antagonistic to anxiety can be made to occur in the presence of anxiety-evoking stimuli so that it is accompanied by a complete or partial suppression of the anxiety responses, the bond between these stimuli and the anxiety responses will be weakened. (p. 71)*

Essentially, classical conditioning theory is extended through the principle of reciprocal inhibition to the realm of removing certain unwanted responses. Wolpe (1958) went on to describe several methods of applying the principle of reciprocal inhibition to human concerns, all without the use of food as a stimulus producing the response incompatible to the unwanted responses. The reason food is avoided is that the actual mechanism by which a response antagonistic to anxiety is produced by eating is unclear. Wolpe opted for more clear-cut anxiety-antagonistic responses, through direct relaxation, the sexual response, or even the assertive response.

Beyond introducing Systematic Desensitization and describing details of the approach in his 1958 work, Wolpe (1973) further refined and described the procedure in his book *The Practice of Behavior Therapy*. Four "separate sets of operations" are required in Systematic Desensitization:

1. Training in deep-muscle relaxation.
2. The establishment of the use of a scale of subjective anxiety.
3. The construction of anxiety hierarchies.
4. Counterposing relaxation and anxiety-evoking stimuli from the hierarchies. (p. 104).

These four operations will be expanded upon briefly in the following pages under three general headings, consistent with Wolpe's description in his text. For brevity's sake, what follows is modified and summarized from his 1973 text. The reader is referred to Wolpe (1958, 1973, 1990) as original sources for detailed descriptions of the technique.

**1.** *Training in deep-muscle relaxation.* Essentially, Wolpe (1973) recommended following Jacobson's (1938) approach with some modification. Wolpe shortened the length of time required to learn the technique to about six sessions. He also instructs his patients to practice at home.

Progressive Relaxation involves directives by t
groups of muscles on command, followed by a cor
procedure helps to produce a fatigued feeling in the
patient the difference between tension and relaxatio
dure is summarized in the following paragraph, but a
according to the experience of the author.

The patient is asked to get into a comfortable p
chair or a therapy couch. The procedure is straight
and the intent is simply described as educational,
relax and to experience a relaxation feeling thro
procedure is "progressive" because the therapist starts with one area of the body,
usually the hands, and works systematically and logically through tangential muscle
groups. For example, after the patient's hands have been tensed and relaxed upon
command of the therapist (sometimes with several repetitions of the same muscle group
to ensure patient recognition of relaxation), then the therapist asks the patient to tense
and relax the forearms, then the upper arm, then the shoulders, and subsequently, in
sequence, the back of the neck, the face, the mouth and tongue, the front of the neck,
the chest, the stomach, the groin, the front of the upper legs, etcetera, around the body.
In this way, all major muscle groups are systematically (sometimes repetitively) tensed
and then relaxed. Finally, after all major muscle groups have been relaxed, the therapist
instructs the patient to produce a total body tensing and relaxing with deeper and deeper
feelings of relaxation (almost in a hypnotically suggestive way). With practice this
technique can produce deep relaxation that is resistant to the effect of anxiety-producing
stimuli.

Although Wolpe (1973) described a six-session process for teaching the patient
Progressive Relaxation, whereby certain muscle groups are focused upon each session,
the preceding approach may facilitate an even quicker accomplishment of deep relaxation, and the approach can be easily learned by patients.

**2.** *The establishment of the use of a scale of subjective anxiety and the construction of an anxiety hierarchy.* Operations 2 and 3 listed previously are combined in this
section and modified, since they are related activities.

Because Systematic Desensitization is a procedure that is targeted to reduce
anxiety consistent with classical conditioning principles, it is necessary to have clearly
defined anxiety-producing stimuli delineated to associate with relaxation. The fact that
Systematic Desensitization does not require the presentation of the actual anxiety-producing stimuli is in its favor from a practical standpoint. Actual in vivo (real-situation)
desensitization is often not possible within the confines of a mental health practitioner's
office, and to go outside the office could involve a great expense both time-wise and
financially. Accordingly, Wolpe (1973) developed his technique so that the stimuli that
trigger the unwanted response could be imagined—mentally conjured, so to speak—in
order that the individual can be deconditioned to images of the stressful situations.
Wolpe argued that deconditioning to imagery was effective at producing reduced
anxiety in real-life situations. However, the images must be adequate, and it is
noteworthy that some patients have difficulty conjuring adequate images, which would

...ke them poor candidates for this technique. Regardless, the patient is asked to imagine the least anxiety-producing situation and the most anxiety-producing situation related to the experienced distress.

The therapist must act to clearly discern what it is the patient fears. A fear of dogs, for example, may actually be a fear of the germs that dogs carry and spread through licking. A very different set of images would need to be developed (i.e., not of dogs, but of images of the spread of germs) if, in fact, germs were the stimuli producing the anxiety. Once the actual fear-producing situation is defined, the therapist asks the patient to assign a point value of 100 to the most fear-producing image, and 0 points to the least fear-producing image. This effectively constitutes a continuum of distress, from 0 to 100. A hierarchy of fear-producing stimuli is then developed with the patient defining images of situations somewhere between the two extremes on the continuum of distress. Most usually, patients are able to develop a hierarchy with about ten or more images. The major task of the therapist is twofold: (a) to help the patient to develop a meaningful hierarchy of images from the least disturbing image to the most distressing image; and (b) to ensure that the distress produced by going from one image to another along the continuum is approximately equivalent. In effect, hierarchy development allows for simultaneous development of what Wolpe calls "subjective units of disturbance" or "*suds*" (p. 120). Patients must develop a subjective scale of distress and then communicate to the therapist approximate levels of distress using the subjective scale. Wolpe (1973) stated;

> It is possible to use the scale to ask the patient to rate the items of the hierarchy according to the amount of anxiety he would have upon exposure to them. If the differences between items are similar, and, generally speaking, not more than 5 to 10 suds, the spacing can be regarded as satisfactory. On the other hand, if there were, for example, 40 suds for item number 8, and 10 suds for item number 9, there would be an obvious need for intervening items. (p. 120)

Once a hierarchy is developed and there is some consensus that the *suds* levels between items on the scale are nearly equivalent, then the therapist can move to the next step, which is the actual desensitization procedure.

**3.** *Counterposing relaxation and anxiety-evoking stimuli from the hierarchies.* Given a client who can relax upon command after having followed the Progressive Relaxation procedures, and given an adequate hierarchy on a reasonable scale of subjective distress, then the therapist can initiate the Systematic Desensitization process. Wolpe (1973) described the instructions to the patient during the first desensitization session as follows: "I am now going to get you to relax; and when you are relaxed I will ask you to imagine certain scenes. Each time a scene is clear in your mind indicate this by raising your index finger about one inch" (p. 121). The therapist asks the client to stop imagining the scenes after about seven or so seconds and continues to present relatively neutral images. This allows for practice with the client imagining scenes and communicating to the therapist the approximate level of *suds*. When the patient develops some proficiency during such exercises, then the therapist can move to the least anxiety-producing stimulus on the hierarchy. Usually, no more than one item from the hierarchy will be attempted in the first desensitization session. Subsequent sessions slowly move up the hierarchy until the patient can experience near complete relaxation even with what was previously a highly anxiety-producing image.

Refining one's approach when applying Systematic Desensitization is important, and experience teaches that one must be patient and flexible through the process of desensitizing patients. Wolpe (1973) spelled out some very detailed concerns related to administration of this procedure. For example, the duration of an image should usually last only about seven seconds, the spacing of sessions is usually once or twice a week, and the number of sessions needed varies depending on the patient and the patient's concern. To be effective as a behavioral therapist using Systematic Desensitization requires much practice under supervision of experienced practitioners and creativity in approaching the ''hitches'' that arise in such a standardized procedure. Nonetheless, Systematic Desensitization is a very effective method for remedying phobic responses and is useful armament for a counselor-generalist facing patients with such concerns.

### Kazdin's "Token Economy"

Alan E. Kazdin has been a leader in the behavior therapy movement. He has written extensively on the application of behavioral theory in clinical contexts (e.g., Agras, Kazdin, & Wilson, 1979; Kazdin, 1982; Kazdin & Wilson, 1978). His book, *Token Economy: A Review and Evaluation* (Kazdin, 1977) will be the focus of this section. In that book, Kazdin details the history, theory, and applications of token economies in applied settings. Kazdin (1977) described token economies as follows:

> *The token economy is a type of behavior modification program which relies heavily upon the principles of operant conditioning. There are relatively few major principles of operant conditioning, although there is extensive research bearing on the effective implementation of the techniques derived from the principles. An understanding of the principles and diverse basic research findings is fundamental to the success of token programs. (p. 1)*

Essentially, a token economy attempts to change the contingencies of behavior. Kazdin further stated that a *contingency:*

> *. . . refers to the relationship between a behavior (the response to be changed) and the events which follow the behavior. The notion of a contingency is important because reinforcement techniques such as the token economy alter behavior by altering the contingencies which control (or fail to control) a particular behavior. (p. 1)*

The focus of token economies, therefore, is the same as the focus of operant conditioning—what occurs after a behavior.

To reward behaviors, there are a number of options available to clinicians involved in behavior modification (Kazdin, 1977). Food and other primary reinforcers can be used. Social reinforcers such as praise, attention, and facial expressions are useful conditioned reinforcers (if they have been associated with primary reinforcers, such as healthy physical contact, in the past). Specific activities can be used to reward other activities. For example, the *Premack principle* (Premack, 1959) can be applied; the Premack principle is simply the giving of opportunities for the expression of a client's highly preferred activities, where such opportunities are made contingent upon performance of target behaviors. For example, if a child likes to play video games, making the child finish his vegetables at dinner in order to have time to play the games is application of the Premack principle (sometimes also called Grandma's law, since Grandmothers have used that tactic for many years). But specific to token economies is the use of tokens—''tangible conditioned reinforcers'' (Kazdin, 1977, p. 44), which are exchangeable for a variety of other reinforcers, including the ones previously described in this paragraph. Tokens are delivered immediately following the desired behavior, and they later can be traded for something the client desires. In this way, behavior patterns are not interrupted by eating, drinking, or activities that impede performance. Those activities are earned through the accumulation of tokens.

A token can be just about anything that is easily handled, such as a poker chip, tickets, stars, checkmarks, or toothpicks. But it is highly recommended that they should be something that clients cannot reproduce or purchase (or have purchased for them) on the outside. Some facilities choose to print their own currency as tokens, which can be easily controlled and handled. It is also wise to have the clinician place the client's initials on the currency when it is presented to prevent the transfer (voluntary or forced) of the tokens among clients. Regardless, Kazdin (1977) described several options in this regard, and his book should be consulted for the pros and cons of each option.

Once the tokens have been chosen, and once target behaviors have been identified, then it is necessary to associate the tokens with ''back-up reinforcers'' (Kazdin, 1977), which are items or events that are wanted by clients. These must be, to some degree, individualized for each client. They can be food, privileges, drinks, rest periods, or other rewards. But they should always be closely associated with the tokens. At first, only one or a few tokens may be required to obtain what is wanted. Later, more tokens may be necessary. The important initial issue is *repetition* and *contiguity* between the presentation of tokens and the presentation of what is wanted. The association of tokens with backup reinforcers, then, is accomplished through classical conditioning principles.

Once tokens have been clearly associated with the backup reinforcers specific to the client, then it is necessary to specify the contingencies for receipt of the token. Kazdin (1977) stated:

> *The introduction of the program includes precise specifications of the responses that are to be reinforced and punished and the specific token values associated with each response. In addition, the specific back-up events, the prices in terms of tokens, and the periods in which back-up events are made available are specified. To introduce the program, client manuals are sometimes written to*

*detail the contingencies. The contingencies may be described orally or displayed in a conspicuous place. The manner of introducing the program, verbal, written, or perhaps no formal introduction at all, in part depends upon the level of the clients. (p. 51)*

The contingencies essentially detail the consequences of certain behaviors.

Consequences may be applied to individuals (most usually) or groups. And there can be rewards (presentation of tokens) or punishments (which take several forms). Kazdin said: "Token economies are based primarily upon positive reinforcement, i.e., the delivery of tokens for specified target behaviors" (p. 69). But he also described commonly used punishments, including "time out from reinforcement" (a pause in rewards), reprimands, overcorrection (requiring the client to exaggerate in a positive way the target behavior), and response cost (the most common type of punishment, which usually involves the withdrawal of tokens or fines for unwanted behaviors). Response cost is one of the most used and useful methods in token economy programs (Kazdin, 1977). However, Kazdin (1977) noted that it is probably unwise to use response cost as the main method in a token economy system. Kazdin seemed to favor more positive approaches. Remembering that punishments have adverse side effects— including possible client confusion, aggression, or the negative reinforcement of unwanted behaviors when punishment is not consistent—the use of punishments should be limited and wisely administered.

Related to client progress, Kazdin (1977) has recommended levels of programs, where clients can progress up steps or stages. Level programs essentially require the planning of subprograms. Steps, stages, or subprograms are preferred to changing contingencies in the middle of one program. By including steps or stages, after a client has achieved a certain goal, a whole new subprogram is implemented, with different contingencies and different opportunities. It is the equivalent of allowing clients to graduate to new levels of accomplishment and reward. In this way, most clients do not stagnate, and they can continually progress to new levels of achievement. As long as the goals at each stage are realistic to the capability of clients in the program, success can be built into the program and expected of motivated and higher functioning clients. Levels are also useful in facilities where the ultimate goal is discharge of the client, such as psychiatric hospitals, vocational rehabilitation facilities (where job placement is the goal), or delinquency programs (where family reintegration is the goal). All in all, step programs are useful in many settings.

The three widest applications of token economy programs have been with school children, the psychiatrically institutionalized, and the intellectually impaired. Regarding the effectiveness of token economy programs in these settings, Kazdin (1977) noted: "Research with each of these populations has firmly established the efficacy of token reinforcement in altering a wide range of responses" (p. 110). Other applications, with supportive but less conclusive outcome research, include work with delinquents, offenders, and the chemically dependent. Over all, token economies can be adapted to a number of settings.

The success of a token economy program to a large degree depends on the involved professional personnel. The individuals administering the program, those individuals doling out the rewards or punishments, must be well trained. Training should include didactic instruction on basic operant conditioning principles. Trainees should be given feedback by professional supervisors about their effectiveness. Moreover, the professional staff should be rewarded for appropriate professional actions in the workplace. Coordinators or program managers should ensure that the front-line token economy personnel are well prepared, monitored, and rewarded for attending to and reinforcing wanted client behaviors.

The ideal outcomes of most programs are: (a) to have the client's behavior endure (response maintenance), especially when programs are terminated; and (b) to have the wanted behaviors generalize to situations outside of the treatment setting. It is noteworthy that response maintenance cannot be assumed to be an ordinary concomitant to the program. Research has shown that often, after the removal of token programs, client behaviors decline to a baseline (the level of behavior at the initiation of the program). In other words, although some research studies have demonstrated that wanted behaviors are maintained at a level above the baseline, this cannot be expected of all token economy programs with all client types. Therefore, when a program or client is expected to be terminated, it is wise to anticipate the end of the program, and to design the program so that rewards are *faded*. Essentially, *fading the contingencies* is a process of programmed and systematic withdrawal of rewards, usually moving from continuous to intermittent reinforcement schedules—to variable ratio or variable interval schedules where there are very few rewards. Also, contingencies can be transferred to the client himself or herself; in other words, the client can be reinforced for self-reinforcement. Regardless, a well-planned approach can minimize the effect of program termination and ensure a lasting effect of the token economy.

Related to generalization of wanted behaviors to other settings or situations (transfer or training), again, there are limitations. Kazdin stated: "In most token economies, altering behavior in one situation does not result in a transfer of those changes to other situations either while the program is in effect or after it has been withdrawn" (p. 177). One way to help ensure transfer of training is "to extend the program to settings in which transfer of training is desired" (p. 180). For example, where children have been involved in a token economy, parents or teachers can be trained to use token economy methods in the home or at school, respectively. Although it is difficult to design a smooth transition of a token economy program, it is incumbent upon the program manager to anticipate the need for transfer of training and to implement appropriate interventions in the targeted settings.

Readers interested in using token economy programs are encouraged to read Kazdin's (1977) book. He explains many of the subtleties of using this technique, and his book is both scholarly and practical. Another useful and related resource that actually predated Kazdin's book is *The Token Economy: A Motivational System for Therapy and Rehabilitation,* by Ayllon and Azrin (1968). It, too, is both scholarly and applied, and should be required reading for individuals who plan to implement, to manage, or to work with token economy programs.

Over all, the use of token economies is probably the clearest behavioral approach consistent with operant conditioning. It is the most closely aligned therapeutic method with the work of Skinner, whose research findings led to the inductive development of a theory of operant conditioning. As such, token economies represent a unique application of theory to professional practice.

## Recent Developments and Criticisms

There are several criticisms of Behavior Therapy. One of the most serious criticisms of Behavioral Therapy is that it can be inhumane. Behavior Therapy, consistent with behavioral theory, views the human being in a machinelike way, negating such internal concepts as free will and self-determination. The human is viewed as influenced primarily by external factors, and is almost exclusively modifiable by means of rewards, punishments, and associations. It is dehumanizing, especially from a humanistic psychology standpoint. Rogers, in a classic debate with Skinner in 1956, stated:

> *To the extent that a behaviorist point of view in psychology is leading us toward a disregard of the person, toward treating persons primarily as manipulable objects, toward control of the person by shaping his behavior without his participant choice, or toward minimizing the significance of the subjective—to that extent I question it very deeply. My experience leads me to say that such a point of view is going against one of the strongest undercurrents of modern life, and is taking us down a pathway with destructive consequences. (Kirschenbaum & Henderson, 1989, p. 86)*

Skinner responded by stating that the individual doesn't vanish according to behaviorism—that is, the individual is still viewed as a unique biological organism with a unique set of environmental influences—yet Skinner maintained that it is external objective experience that primarily directs behavior. In effect, free will and individual determinism vanish from the externalist framework. Where free will and self-determination are valued as human traits, behaviorism in fact dehumanizes.

A second related criticism of behaviorism is that it denies the internal, subjective psychological experiences of the individual. Subjectivity gives way to objectivity. Subjective experiences are not valued according to behavioral doctrines. Some say this is denying the obvious cognitive and self-reflective nature of human beings, that is, those human traits that differentiate the species from lower animals. However, the behaviorists maintain that human behavior is much like animal behavior—externally controlled—and even thinking and self-reflection are learned behaviors.

Finally, critics have attacked behaviorism by claiming that it is superficial. They claim that changing behavior is not enough, that, in fact, there are certain psychological processes that underly behavior. It is these underlying processes that must be addressed in therapy, not just the behaviors themselves. Research evidence has supported the behaviorist, however, by demonstrating its effectiveness on objective measures of success in treatment.

Behaviorism has advanced to the degree that behavioral principles have been applied in many settings. Even marital relationships, the domain of systemic-relational theory, have been shown to be modifiable by behavioral techniques (Bornstein &

Bornstein, 1986). And researchers continue to demonstrate the effectiveness of specialized behavioral techniques in specific settings (see Garfield & Bergin, 1986). In sum, behavioral theory leads to objectively effective techniques for changing targeted behaviors.

# Paradigm Fit

## Focus of Study

The focus of study is the behavior of the maladaptive or distressed individual. Clearly, the individual's behavior takes precedence over what the client feels or thinks. Internal psychological processes are downplayed or even, to the extreme, denied. The individual is viewed as primarily influenced by external factors, stimuli, which affect behavior directly and linearly. External stimuli are isolated and modified. In essence, the individual is the focus of study, but it is what occurs outside the individual that gets the attention of the behaviorally oriented therapist.

## View of Nature of Reality

Reality is composed of things that can be isolated and studied—people, objects, stimuli, responses. The nature of the universe is objectively knowable. It is assumed that all that is knowable is knowable through scientific principles. Just as with the positivistically oriented physicist, an attempt is made to define reality's basic components and laws. The behaviorist continually strives to reduce behavior to minute parts and to define the operational rules by which the parts operate. In this way it is very physical in its approach to human behavior, even though stimuli, responses, and contingencies are primarily non-physical entities.

## Consonance with Paradigm Propositions and Tenets

Behaviorism is a clear-cut example of a therapy consistent with the external model of the psychological paradigm. Regarding the general psychological propositions, the focus is on the individual (his or her behavior in a delimited environmental context). Individual behaviors can and must be assessed, and maladaptive or distressful behavior becomes the target of intervention. Causes of distress or maladaption are directly and linearly defined. Change occurs by means of an expert authority, a behaviorally oriented therapist, who defines the contingencies of behavior and attempts to modify them through a planned program. Professional expertise is best attained through professional training. Although responsibility and rationality are not viewed as internal psychological constructs, they are viewed within an environmental context. The therapist, however, is always viewed as responsible to develop reasonable, behaviorally sound, therapeutic means for influencing behavior. Therapeutic failure results from a misassessment of those factors influencing behavior or a misapplication of behavioral techniques.

Behavioral tenets of practice are practical, concrete, and directive. Counselors are expected to attend to basic operant and classical conditioning principles in defining what is important in assessment and treatment. Targets for intervention are to be operational (measurable) and amenable to observation by trained professionals. Outcomes and goals are attainable, realistic, yet significant to client functioning in specified contexts.

Behavioral approaches are straightforward and logical. They are targeted and results-oriented They are unique in their emphasis on external factors affecting human behavior.

## Chapter Conclusion

This chapter has presented, in some detail, two theories of learning—classical and operant conditioning—and two related specialized behavioral therapeutic techniques—Systematic Desensitization and Token Economy. The chapter diverged a bit from the organization of other chapters due to the unique nature of Behavior Therapy. Behavior Therapy is not a monolithic, consensually agreed-upon approach. Rather it is a conglomeration of many applications from basic theories and their extensions. There are many proponents and specialized techniques that can be considered behavioral therapies. Consequently, this chapter should not be viewed as a vehicle for perusing or overviewing the field of Behavior Therapy. Rather, it focused on two approaches deriving from two basic theories. Many influential behaviorists have not been identified in this chapter.

Regardless, by means of this chapter, students should have a good basic understanding of classical and operant conditioning principles and their applications to specific psychological problems. It is hoped that this chapter will pique the interest of behaviorally oriented students to the degree that they will independently seek additional information.

At this point in this text, the discussion of the psychological paradigm is complete. The next chapter will introduce the systemic-relational paradigm.

## References

Agras, W. S., Kazdin, A. E., & Wilson, G. T. (1979). *Behavior Therapy: Toward an applied clinical science.* San Francisco: W. H. Freeman.

Ayllon, T., & Azrin, N. (1968). *The token economy: A motivational system for therapy and rehabilitation.* New York: Appleton-Century-Crofts.

Bornstein, P. H., & Bornstein, M. T. (1986). *Marital therapy: A behavioral-communications approach.* Elmford, NY: Pergamon.

Eysenck, H. J. (1960). *Behavior therapy and the neuroses.* Oxford, England: Pergamon Press.

Ferster, C. B., & Skinner, B. F. (1957). *Schedules of reinforcement.* New York: Appleton-Century-Crofts.

Garfield, S., & Bergin, A. (Eds.) (1986). *Handbook of psychotherapy and behavior change.* New York: John Wiley & Sons.

Jacobson, E. (1938). *Progressive relaxation.* Chicago: University of Chicago Press.

Jones, M. C. (1924a). Elimination of childrens' fears. *Journal of Experimental Psychology, 7,* 382–390.

Jones, M. C. (1924b). A laboratory study of fear. The case of Peter. *Journal of Genetic Psychology, 31,* 308–315.

Kazdin, A. E. (1977). *The token economy: A review and evaluation.* New York: Plenum.

Kazdin, A. E. (1982). History of behavior modification. In A. S. Bellack, M. Hersen, & A. E. Kazdin (Eds.), *International handbook of behavior modification and therapy* (pp. 3–32). New York: Plenum.

Kazdin, A. E., & Wilson, G. T. (1978). *Evaluation of behavior therapy: Issues, evidence, and research strategies.* Cambridge, MA: Ballinger Publishing.

Kirschenbaum, H., & Henderson, V. (1989). *Carl Rogers: Dialogues.* Boston: Houghton Mifflin.

Marx, M. H., & Hillix, W. A. (1973). *Systems and theories in psychology.* New York: McGraw-Hill.

Pavlov, I. P. (1957). *Experimental psychology and other essays.* New York: Philosophical Library. (Original work published 1916.)

Premack, D. (1959). Toward empirical behavior laws: I. Positive reinforcement. *Psychological Review, 66,* 219–233.

Reynolds, G. S. (1968). *A primer of operant conditioning.* Glenview, IL: Scott, Foresman & Co.

Skinner, B. F. (1938). *The behavior of organisms.* New York: Appleton-Century-Crofts.

Skinner, B. F. (1948). *Walden Two.* New York: Macmillan.

Skinner, B. F. (1953). *Science and human behavior.* New York: Macmillan.

Skinner, B. F. (1989). *Recent issues in the analysis of behavior.* Columbus, OH: Merrill.

Thorndike, E. L. (1905). *The elements of psychology.* New York: A. G. Seiler.

Watson, J. B. (1930). *Behaviorism* (Rev. ed.). Chicago: University of Chicago Press. (Originally published in 1924.)

Watson, J. B., & Rayner, P. (1920). Conditioned emotional reactions. *Journal of Experimental Psychology, 3,* 1–16.

Wolpe, J. (1958). *Psychotherapy by reciprocal inhibition.* Stanford, CA: Stanford University Press.

Wolpe, J. (1973). *The practice of behavior therapy* (2nd ed.). New York: Pergamon Press.

Wolpe, J. (1990). *The practice of behavior therapy* (4th ed.). New York: Pergamon Press.

# PART FOUR
# The Systemic-Relational Paradigm

# 11

# The Systemic-Relational Paradigm:
## *External and Internal Models*

THE SYSTEMIC-RELATIONAL PARADIGM, which is founded on social systems theory, represents a revolution in thinking when compared to the organic-medical or psychological paradigms. Social systems theory, as it was briefly described in chapters 1 and 2, focuses on relationships as real and assessable processes. The focus changes, in a Gestalt-shift way, from the study of individuals to the study of interpersonal interaction within bounded systems of relationships. As such, the systemic-relational paradigm represents a unique way of viewing mental health concerns.

The systemic-relational paradigm is the second of two paradigms where specific models will be distinguished. As with the psychological paradigm, these separate models have clear-cut epistemological and causative differences. Yet the models do not meet all of the criteria for consideration as counseling paradigms. As with the psychological paradigm, the models will be titled the "internal" and "external" models. However, in the systemic-relational paradigm, the external model preceded the internal model chronologically, which is the exact opposite of what occurred in the development of the psychological paradigm.

The term *system* is used here to refer to a network of social relationships. Social relationships are the focus of study. Focusing on relationships is like focusing on the net of a web, where the strings are the main elements, and not the points where the strings connect. As it will be presented in this chapter, the systemic-relational paradigm is built on the assumption that relationships between people exist as observable processes. These processes result from the interactive properties of the component parts of the system (the individuals) and, importantly, the social context in which they occur. As processes, systems of relationships are amenable to study.

It is assumed that social systems have properties that are consistent across all systems of similar organization. For example, family systems, as social systems, are similarly organized within a cultural context, and certain properties of family social systems can be assumed to exist by nature of their similar relational organization.

The two models of the systemic paradigm can best be differentiated as follows. According to the external systemic model, influences on behavior of any component (person) of a social system, or on the system itself, derive from the effect of relational factors external to the system. The external position views social systems as "open" systems (i.e., open to outside relational influences), and therefore, factors outside of the boundaries of a system have a major influence on the system's behavior and on behavior of components in the system. For example, when you hit a baseball with a bat, the ball reacts in relationship to the bat, and the ball's internal changes produce a reaction to the external factor, causing the ball to "fly" and the bat to react. In this case, the ball and bat interacted, and if the ball is isolated as the system under study, it can be said that the ball was influenced by an outside relationship that affected its internal dynamics and consequently its relative position in a larger context. (The bat similarly was affected in relation to the ball.) Of course this example is a bit strained when thinking about social relations, because a ball is an inanimate object, whereas social relations may be viewed as an extension of living processes. Regardless, the idea of outside influence on a system is a major point of difference between the external and internal systemic positions, as will be demonstrated in the next paragraph.

The internal systemic model views social systems, and even biological systems, as primarily "closed" systems. From this viewpoint, outside influences do not affect a system in any way that is predictable by analyzing the properties of the relationships outside of the system. Almost all influences on behavior derive from the effect of relational influences *inside* of the system under study. This means that outside factors only "perturb" a system in a way that stimulates the system to do what it is internally structured to do. For example, when you hit a baseball with a bat it will fly; but when you hit a raw egg with a bat, the egg will splatter. The different reactions to external perturbation were not predictable based solely on a relationship of a spherelike object to a bat. Rather, the outcomes were determined by the internal "structures" of the systems that were perturbed. Baseballs and eggs are structured (internally) quite differently. And it was the structure of that which was perturbed that primarily determined the outcome of perturbation. Systemic internalists are more concerned with the way relationships are organized *within* the boundaries of a system, and they are less concerned with the nature of the external factors, which are viewed as only perturbing (triggering) rather than directly influencing systemic dynamics.

These two positions, the external and internal systemic perspectives, and the major proponents of each perspective, are discussed in two appendices in this text, entitled "The Dynamics of the External Systemic Model" (Appendix A), and "The Dynamics of the Internal Systemic Model" (Appendix B). The reason information on the systemic-relational paradigm has been separated from this chapter is because the material is very technical, and it may overwhelm readers unacquainted with such ideas. Interested readers, therefore, are referred to the appendices for thorough discussions of the two models. In fact, for a thorough understanding of the systemic-relational paradigm, it is recommended that Appendix A (on the external model) should be read before proceeding with chapters presenting theories aligned with the external model, and that Appendix B (on the internal model) should be read before reading the chapter presenting a theory aligned with the internal model.

For individuals trained in the organic-medical paradigm, or especially the psychological paradigm, systemic-relational thinking may appear quite alien. Because relationships are invisible (they can only be indirectly observed by studying the behaviors of people or things) they are less a part of our common everyday understanding of human behavior. In other other words, relationships may be viewed as abstractions which are a level higher than the *things* that are observed to reflect them.

## Historical Overview

General systems theory is a precursor and foundational theory to social systems theory. General systems theory is a set of propositions that provides a groundwork for scientific inquiry and interpretation. The basic premise of systems theory is that "relationship" is critical to the study of phenomena that occur within a larger contextual framework. The major proponent of systems theory was a biologist, Ludwig von Bertalanffy (1952, 1968). Bertalanffy (1952) attempted to go beyond classical theory in biology toward an "organismic conception" (p. 9), or a holistic view of organisms. He viewed organisms as "open systems" (Bertalanffy, 1952, p. 129) and, in an attempt to unify biological theory, he developed theoretical propositions related to "open systems," which he believed had implications beyond biology. In 1968, he presented the basic propositions of his general systems theory (GST). Ideally, he hoped that his theory would unite science, but in fact, it applies best to specialized (well-defined and well-bounded) systems (Sadovsky, 1974).

It was Bateson, (1972), Buckley (1967), and Parsons (1951, 1964) who aptly applied systemic concepts to sociobehavioral systems. And with the publication of "Toward a Theory of Schizophrenia" (Bateson, Jackson, Haley & Weakland, 1956; see also Bateson, 1972) a systemic-relational redefinition of the cause of emotional disturbance emerged. The Bateson et al. (1956) article hypothesized that interpersonal relationships and interpersonal communication have an effect on emotional adjustment. Bateson's work (as applied to individuals and families) and Buckley's and Parsons's work (from a sociological standpoint) set the stage for a theory of social systems. It is the special application of systems concepts to "social" systems that best applies to the mental health services.

## General Definitions of Systemic Terms

**1.** *A System.* A system is a complex of elements (components) standing in interaction (Bertalanffy, 1952). Each component is linked to each other component by relationship, and relationship is the focus of systems theory. A relationship is composed of all communication between two components. In two-dimensional form, a large

*Paul Watzlawick, systems theorist*

system of relationships looks like a web. Any movement in any component affects all other components through relationships, and subsequently, a component's movement affects itself (recursivity).

**2.** *Relationship*. Relationship is communication. Communication or information is the "energy" of social systems. According to Bateson (1972) and Watzlawick, Beavin, and Jackson (1967), human communication takes two basic forms: (a) digital (formal or technical communication), and (b) analogic (informal, nonverbal, or contextual). Digital communication is content-related, whereas analogic communication defines the nature of interpersonal relationships.

**3.** *Hierarchical Organization*. Social systems do not stand alone. They are linked to other systems in a hierarchical fashion. For example, a family therapy clinic may be linked to a state family services agency through a formal service contract. The state family services agency is linked to the legal and economic systems of the state, which are linked to the federal system through federal legislative mandate, etcetera. Each level represents a different step in the hierarchy of organization of a system.

**4.** *Homeostasis*. Systems seem to be self-preserving. Accordingly, they are homeostatic, which means they tend toward a steady state (Cannon, 1932). When outside influences affect the system, a homeostatic mechanism, typically in the form of a negative feedback loop, is activated (a process of returning the preset steady state). If the homeostat fails, it is usually because of overload, which will probably result in a new homeostatic setting. The homeostatic mechanism is described in detail in Appendix A, entitled "The Dynamics of the External Systemic Model."

**5.** *Causality*. As described in chapter 2, causality refers to the process of producing an effect. Generally, causality can be viewed as either linear (A causes B) or circular (where there is a reciprocal, recursive process). The issue of causality is important to the study of the systemic-relational paradigm, because systems theory is associated with a circular causal model, which is distinct against the linear causal models presented in the organic-medical paradigm and the psychological paradigm chapters.

**6.** *Rules and Roles.* Systems act in patterns that are characteristic of their rules and roles. The *rules* are the laws by which a system operates. The *roles* are the task orientations that components fulfill in carrying out the system's rules. Social rules may be explicit (formal or written) or implicit (understood), and "they provide directives for all eventualities" (Ruesch & Bateson, 1968, p. 28).

**7.** *Open or Closed Systems.* Systems are either open or closed. Open systems take in new information or material from outside their boundaries, and they export whatever is processed to outside systems. Closed systems are isolated from input (e.g., chemicals interacting in a closed test tube). According to the external systemic model, all social systems are open systems, but different social systems are open to different degrees. According to the internal systemic model, social systems must be viewed as "informationally closed." Humans, however, having an ability to communicate, and having a recursively organized, highly complex nervous system, operate within a language domain that extends their boundaries. Nonetheless, the extended language domain, whether communication occurs verbally, symbolically, or nonverbally, is still considered a closed domain, according to the internal model.

## The Systemic-Relational Paradigm

The propositions and tenets that follow represent something more than a collection of ideas about systems—they represent a distinct body of knowledge that is directly applied by mental health professionals. Since there may be less consensus about the nature of the systemic-relational paradigm when compared to the organic-medical or psychological paradigms, the propositions and tenets are offered as a starting point for critical debate. It is assumed that the systemic paradigm will be further developed and refined. Readers will recognize the theoretical contributions of authors such as Bateson (1972, 1979), Bertalanffy (1952, 1968), Dell (1982, 1985), Hoffman (1981), Maturana (1978), Varela (1979), Watzlawick and his associates (1967, 1974) and others as they read the following propositions.

### Propositions

**1.** The focus is always on relationships. According to systems theory, human beings are social animals and are best viewed in the social context of relationships. A relationship is the sum of communication between individuals at all levels of communication (formal, informal, nonverbal, and contextual). Relationships develop within rules and roles of larger (encompassing) systems of relationships.

**2.** Relationships can be isolated for study and defined, but only with an understanding that the acts of isolation and definition are relative to the observer and his or her system (relationships) of reference. Also, isolated relationships are viewed as relative to other relationships in a defined system of significance.

**3.** Cause is nonlinear and reciprocal (or circular) within the confines of the defined relationships of significance. Becvar and Becvar (1982) described cause as "a reciprocal concept to be found in the interface between individuals and between systems" (p. 7).

**4.** Change always occurs through social relationships (communication). Even biological differences are assumed to be affected by, and to affect, social relationships in a reciprocal manner. For example, genetics are as much affected by mating relationships (which are social events) as social relationships are affected by genetics (through communicational differences).

**5.** Professional expertise is best gained within the framework of relational training, where acceptable university educational programs are closely and formally linked to the rules and regulations of the professional marital and family therapy service delivery system. Assurance of competence is gained primarily through close supervision of developing professionals by supervisors who are trained in the rules of the professional marital and family therapy community.

**6.** Individual traits, such as motivation or responsibility, are redefined as reflecting the degree of engagement (fit) between interacting social systems, as viewed from the perspective of one of the systems.

**7.** Marital and family therapists are closely linked to the sociolegal system (as defined by laws and social service delivery programs).

**8.** Therapeutic failures are defined within a political context. Such failures represent the degree that client-systems are unable to link (formally or informally, nonverbally, and contextually) to relationships that "fit" within the rules and regulations of the sociolegal system. Neither a client nor a therapist can be held responsible for a failure; rather the failure is redefined as a "bad fit" therapeutically. However, the therapist may be politically and/or legally accountable for his or her actions in therapy.

**9.** Systemically oriented therapists are viewed as effective only to the degree that they affect, and are affected by, social relationships within the rules of the sociolegal system.

## Tenets of Practice

Given the propositions listed for the systemic-relational paradigm, the following tenets are offered as an extreme application of systemic principles to marital and family therapy. Briefly, they are:

**1.** Systemic-relational therapists focus on relationship issues. Preferably, clients are seen in the context of a defined system of significance, since relationships in context are the focus of study and treatment.

**2.** Systemic-relational therapists both affect and are affected by the relationships they counsel.

**3.** In families with an identified patient, concerns are redefined from the individual to a relational context. Identified patients are viewed as symptomatic of a problem within a larger relational network.

**4.** Using the systemic-relational framework, all discussions of individual concerns must be reframed to discussions of relationship issues.

**5.** A systemic-relational therapist must be well trained in defining relationships of significance from the perspective of the sociolegal system. A systemic-relational therapist also must be adept at connecting and severing relationships, in order to redirect relational influences in the system of significance. Although individual therapeutic directives may appear as linear interventions to an observer, systemic-relational therapists do not view therapy as a linear process. Instead, they view client-systems as simultaneously or recursively influencing and being influenced by the service delivery and sociolegal systems (of which the therapist is a part).

## Epistemological and Ontological Considerations

### General Considerations

Systems theory requires the study of relationships. Epistemologically, the things we see (people, objects, etc.) exist only in relationship, and when analyzed microscopically, they, too, are best viewed as relationships. It is no secret in physics (Capra, 1975, 1982) that the closer we analyze some "thing," the less it appears as a thing, and the more it appears as a dynamic process (things in relationships). Consequently, relationships become the primary source of our knowledge of the world. This can be taken to the ontological extreme by stating that things do not exist—that, in fact, things ultimately *are* relationships. This position, of course, challenges our perceptual sense, since humans at least act as if "things" exist.

The larger question, from an epistemological and ontological standpoint, becomes the nature of the human ability to observe the nature of what is observed. This is an issue that has plagued physicists (Heisenberg, 1958) and philosophers alike (Goldman, 1986). And it is a question that is receiving attention in the advanced systems theory literature (Dell, 1985).

### Defining Systems as "Things"

Probably the most difficult question for a tried-and-true systems theorist is, "If the nature of reality involves relationship, how is it that we see things before we can define relationships?" This question gets to the root of the human perceptual process, and it directly addresses the reciprocal relationship of that which is observed to that which observes. It is a question that is not easily answered.

From a systems perspective, as soon as a thing is defined, it must be analyzed into the relationships that constitute it as a perceptual unity. From a psychological perspective (globally speaking) the things we observe and our relationship to them are enough. An *assumption* is made that we and the things we observe exist. The focus

## BOX 11-1

### Example Family Evaluation Report

The following family evaluation is based on a real report. However the material has been extensively modified to protect the rights of the family members.

#### Family Evaluation

This report is a summary of an initial interview with the family of a 14-year-old male referred by the local juvenile authorities. The reason for the referral was to define the current level of family functioning as related to the legal problems of the 14-year-old identified problem, John Michaels.

The counselor met with John's natural mother, his stepfather, and with John in their home in an affluent suburb of a major metropolitan area on August 23, 1990.

*Background:*   John Michaels has been recently involved in vandalism of a home being built in a new housing development (near his home) and in other illegal activities in his neighborhood, including damage to a neighbor's property and possession of marijuana. The difficulties began around his thirteenth birthday and have continued for nearly one and one-half years.

John was cooperative during the interview. He relayed that he was to blame for the problems and he didn't want to live in his stepfather's house. He preferred to live with his natural father in a town nearly 150 miles away. He was no natural siblings, although he has one older stepsister who is emancipated from the home. In school, he has earned borderline grades in recent years, even though he was an excellent student in his early childhood, earning B's and A's. He currently has several friends who ''hang out'' together in the neighborhood. He claims they have a special meeting place in the ''woods'' near their homes. His friends were involved in the vandalism incident, which brought John to the attention of the juvenile authorities. John claims to be the leader of the group. He claims no hobbies and does not participate in sponsored teenage activities through his school or church. He likes to play video games in his spare time, and he has a video game attached to a television in his room. He denied having a girlfriend. He stated that drugs are available to children his age, but says drugs are not a big problem for him, even though he was caught possessing marijuana. His goals involve a desire to do undercover police work.

Jane, John's natural mother, described herself as a person of a meager background. She was a second child of a blue-collar worker and a homemaker. Her parents are both dead. She has limited contacts with her older brother, who lives across country. She says she had a failed first marriage, and described her ex-husband as ''on the fringe.'' She said he never supported her or John well, and after several incidents of abuse in the home, which John witnessed, she separated and later divorced. The divorce occurred four years ago. Two years after the divorce, she met Tom, her current husband, and they married in a public ceremony shortly after meeting. She said her life with Tom has been wonderful; they are doing well financially and socially, and she says she loves him very much. Currently Jane is a homemaker. She is also planning on taking some courses at a local community college.

**BOX 11-1** *Continued*

Tom, John's stepfather, is very involved in his construction business. He has been a contractor for seven years, starting in the construction business as a laborer right out of high school. He claims he has built a quality business, and he said he has been doing well financially for nearly four years, after three years of struggling. He met Jane just when things began to turn around for him, and he credits her with being his "good luck." He is divorced, and has one child, Tina, who is 22, married, and a mother of one child. He grew up in the suburbs in a middle-class family. His father was a factory worker, and his mother worked as a secretary. He has two younger brothers. He is in contact with his family on holidays, and sometimes socially on weekends. He enjoys being a grandfather. Otherwise, his life is focused on his business and on his home life with Jane and John.

*The Identified Problem:*   When asked to describe the problem in the family, John volunteered by stating his stepfather was the problem. He said, in so many words, that Tom was trying to run his life and had no business "butting into" his (John's) affairs.

Tom stated that John was out of control, and he needed discipline. He argued that John's biological father was trying to influence John and that the biological father should "mind his own business." Tom described in detail the problems John has caused in the neighborhood.

Jane agreed that John was the problem. She has tried to discipline him, but he rebels and does not obey her. She feels he is under the influence of a bad peer group. She described John as basically a "good boy," but claimed that he has begun to cause severe difficulties in the family.

*Interactions:*   Each pair of family members was asked to interact for observational purposes. They were directed to discuss their problems and attempted solutions.

John and Jane interacted first. They appeared to have difficulty discussing their concerns. As they began, their discussion quickly began to escalate into a heated argument over John's desire to live with his natural father. Their relationship can be described as "symmetrical" (competitive), escalating, and primarily negative. Jane said her relationship with John used to be very close, and she wants some sense of that closeness again. Attempted solutions have met with no success, and the solutions have been primarily placing restrictions on John.

John and Tom also began to argue quickly after they were given an opportunity to interact. Tom claimed that John's natural father would be a bad model for him, since he has had difficulty holding a job. He argued that the natural father would not be able to support John well, and that John should appreciate his current living situation, pointing to the physical environment. John responded that Tom wanted him (John) only as his slave to cut the lawn and do work around the house. This relationship can be described as symmetrical, escalating, and negative.

Tom and Jane's discussion was less heated, and Jane appeared to defer to her husband's judgment. She agreed with Tom that John should be put under restrictions

*Continued*

**BOX 11-1** *Continued*

by the authorities until he shows he can be trusted outside the home. Their relationship can be described as complementary and positive.

*Assessment:*   This appears to be a family that is split into two warring factions. John appears to be in a coalition with his natural father, while Jane and Tom also appear in a coalition. Each pair appear to be at odds with each other. The natural father, being absent from the situation and making only monthly weekend personal contacts with John, is geographically removed from the dynamics. Consequently, John appears scapegoated in a triadic relational configuration within the household. The problems seem to be getting worse over time, and solutions (discipline) have tended to exacerbate rather than to diffuse the situation. The parents have refused to let John live with his natural father. Regardless, John's natural father has not offered to take John, even though he has apparently hinted to John that he wants John to live with him.

*Recommendations:*   Family therapy is highly recommended. There appears to be an escalating family dynamic operating that, if left unchecked, could lead to further acting out on John's part or to severe problems in the family relationships. Jane relayed that it has almost gotten to the point of a fist fight between John and Tom, and she fears that things might get more physical. Contact will need to be made with the natural father, and it is recommended that the natural father should be involved in counseling with John, to clarify the nature of their relationship and the father's intentions related to care or custody of John. It is not recommended, however, that the natural father should attend sessions with Jane and Tom present, since such an arrangement might appear to be a re-engagement of the divorced pair, and could potentially cause further aggravation of difficulties. Strict communicational rules will need to be worked out with the natural parents regarding issues involving John. Exploration of the influence of the peer group also needs to be undertaken.

This concludes the assessment. Two hours were spent with the family. If further services are needed, please contact me.

Sincerely,

L. Harrison, M.A.
Family Therapist
Clinical Member—AAMFT

from an epistemological standpoint then becomes the act of assuming as well as what is assumed.

Ultimately, systems theorists must demonstrate and describe the relationship between what is assumed and the perceptual processes that lead to the assumption. It is in the areas of cognitive biology and cognitive psychology that such questions are addressed, and the works of Maturana (1970/1980, 1978) and Maturana and Varela (1973/1980) have paved the way by directly delimiting the nature of cognition in *relation* to social/consensual behavior. Maturana's ideas have the potential to extend systems theory beyond the stalemate defined by Sadovsky (1974) as the "paradox of wholeness" or, in other words, the problem of viewing systems of relationships as things. Maturana has demonstrated that an "absolute" reality is not consistent with the human perceptual process, and that reality is limited (bounded) not only by an organism's perceptual apparatuses but, in the case of organisms with highly complex, recursively organized, nervous systems, by the social context that simultaneously perturbs the nervous system during perception (primarily through language). Maturana claims his work has placed "objectivity in parentheses" (Simon, 1985), which is to say that he has given us a biological rationale for the limits of "reality," and he does this within a systems (relationship-focused) framework. What this means is that all "things" are relationships and that they only become whole through social interaction that defines something as objectively real through a spoken or unspoken consensus. For example, when two individuals look at a bowl of fruit on a table, they are simultaneously experiencing relationships with the bowl of fruit (perceptual relations) and each other (social relations). Though social interaction, they may act as if the bowl of fruit is in fact a bowl of real fruit, which is social consensual behavior and defines a reality. However, if one makes the statement that the fruit in the bowl is wax fruit, then the individuals will probably mutually interact over the redefinition of their reality, until there is agreement as to whether the fruit is real or wax. For example one may pick up a piece of fruit, squeeze it, taste it, etcetera, while the other watches, and they will probably come to some consensus as to whether the fruit is real or wax. In doing so they communicate both nonverbally and verbally. The verbal messages, of course, are culturally and linguistically linked, and the fact that the individuals know about wax fruit is representative of the cultural boundaries that place parentheses around reality. There are, after all, some societies where wax fruit does not exist, and consensus about whether a fruit is real or wax may be harder to attain in a society where a "new" reality (wax fruit) must be linguistically explored before a consensus can be achieved. In effect, all that is real is dependent upon all that has been socially, relationally defined as real. Every thought has been passed on relationally. People cannot think separately from relationship. And Maturana's work brings this point home by demonstrating that reality is not separate from a consensual/linguistic domain—the cultural and societal domain of which people are a part.

To summarize, Maturana's work has demonstrated that "things" exist not because they are whole in a physical sense, but rather because they appear whole. No matter how much it is believed some "thing" exists as a separate entity, Maturana would argue that it is through social relationships (past and present), a linguistic tradition (socially and culturally based), and perception (which is a relational process) that a reality is defined. This kind of thinking is a far cry from a world of things rather than relationships.

## Cause and Effect

The cause-and-effect perspective of social systems theory is one of its distinguishing features. As has been presented in the chapters on the organic-medical and psychological paradigms, cause and effect is basically defined as linear, that is, something effects something else in a fashion where a result is a direct, straightforward, and one-way outcome of what has caused it. The idea of a billiard ball striking another billiard ball is a classic example of linear causality; one ball causes the other to move. By the systemic-relational perspective, on the other hand, cause is not so simply defined. As mentioned earlier, cause is viewed as resulting from interaction (just as everything in systems theory is interactive). Accordingly, in human behavior, one person *cannot cause* someone else to do something within a social interactive context. One can only enter into interaction with another person. Interaction is not a one-way street. To say that a bully always gets his way only means that a bully has not confronted a bigger bully. You cannot have a bully without having someone to be bullied. Bullying is an interactive process.

When two people interact, a separate reality is defined within the confines of the relationship. As one person affects the other, he or she is simultaneously or recursively being influenced. Each individual acts and reacts not only to what other people say or do, but also to the very presence of the other people.

Additionally, relationships are not static entities. They change and develop over time, but they do not change in isolation. They reciprocally influence what occurs around them! In other words, a social network is a large all-encompassing network, where activity at one position may influence activity at another position, and subsequently (because of the recursive organization of a social system) activity of a component at one position ultimately affects itself. That is why statements such as "what goes around, comes around" appear to have validity.

## Professional Adherents

The professional field most associated with the systemic-relational paradigm is the field of marital and family therapy. The credential most valued in the field of marital and family therapy is "clinical membership" in the American Association for Marriage and Family Therapy (AAMFT). The AAMFT is a politically active voice of a group of practitioners who subscribe to the idea that relationships are identifiable and treatable processes, and that conjoint marital therapy (where both individuals in a couple are seen together) and family therapy (where all member of the family are present) are the preferred methods of treating emotional maladjustment.

The AAMFT in the 1970s changed its name from the American Association for Marriage and Family Counseling to the American Association for Marriage and Family

Therapy with the major intent to define marital and family therapy as a "treatment" method and alternative to standard psychotherapeutic approaches (which primarily involved one-to-one psychotherapy). The change in name also signified a break with the larger field of counseling, which was best represented by what was then the American Personnel and Guidance Association, and which is now the American Association for Counseling and Development (AACD). The American Personnel and Guidance Association (APGA) had close ties to education, vocational counseling, and the psychological model; the APGA better represented individuals trained in traditional schools or colleges of education. Regardless, the title of marriage and family "counseling" has been adopted by descendants of the APGA who have formed a family division of their own in the name of the International Association of Marriage and Family Counseling.

The AAMFT in its quest to distinguish marital and family therapists from other mental health service providers developed strict guidelines for its clinical membership class. In addition to clearly defined coursework requirements at the graduate level and the attainment of an acceptable graduate degree in the human services, the AAMFT requires the equivalent of two full-time years of supervised practice in marital and family therapy under the direction of an AAMFT-approved supervisor.

Coursework requirements (revised in 1983) include a minimum of: (a) three courses in human development; (b) three courses in marital and family studies (which include courses in social systems-related areas and family development); (c) three courses in marital and family therapy; (d) one course in research; (e) one course in professional studies; and (f) one *year* of supervised clinical practice of fifteen hours a week with eight to ten hours a week of direct contact with individuals, couples, and families.

At the time of this writing, eighteen states regulated the practice or title of marital and family therapy (sometimes called marriage and family counseling) for independent practice. A review of several of the statutes indicates that marital and family therapists are distinguished by law in their ability to treat relationship issues. For example, in the Georgia "Professional Counselors, Social Workers, and Marriage and Family Therapists Licensure Law" (Code 1981, Chapter 43-7A-1, enacted by the Georgia Legislature in 1984, p. 1406), marriage and family therapy is defined as follows:

> *"Marriage and family therapy"* means that specialty which centers primarily upon family relationships and the relationship between husband and wife and which includes, without being limited to, premarital, marital, sexual, family, predivorce, and postdivorce issues. This therapy also involves an applied understanding of the dynamics of marital and family systems, along with the application of psychotherapeutic and counseling techniques for the purpose of resolving intrapersonal and interpersonal conflict and changing perception, attitudes, and behavior in the area of marriage and family life.

As is evident, the terms *psychotherapeutic* and *counseling* are used in the law, which clearly identifies licensed marriage and family therapists as mental health professionals dealing with issues needing "therapy." However, the definition focuses on relationship issues, which helps to identify the field as a unique discipline in the mental health services.

## Therapies as Subcategories

Systemic-relational paradigm adherents have been prolific in developing specialized therapeutic approaches. In the next chapter a transitional therapy will be presented. Satir's (1967) Conjoint Family Therapy serves as a good example of a transitional (trans-paradigmatic) therapy, aligning closely with systemic-relational paradigm propositions, while holding over the concept of self-esteem from more purely psychological thinking. Satir's work, along with several other theorists of her time, must be considered ground breaking. Several other examples of paradigm-specific approaches will follow in the subsequent chapters. Haley's (1963, 1976) Strategic Problem-Solving Therapy and Minuchin's Structural Family Therapy (1974) are good examples of therapeutic approaches that are closely aligned with the external model of the systemic-relational paradigm. Structure-Determined Family Therapy, based on the theoretical works of Maturana (e.g., Maturana, 1978) is used as an example of an emerging therapeutic approach that can be aligned with the internal model of the systemic-relational paradigm. Over all, these example therapies should provide readers with a good idea of the nature and extent of systemic-relational thinking, especially as applied in the field of marital and family therapy.

## Chapter Conclusion

This chapter has introduced the systemic-relational paradigm. Two paradigm-specific models were defined—the external and internal models. An historical overview of the development of systemic-relational thinking was provided. Basic definitions of systemic-relational terms were provided. Propositions and tenets were outlined. Philosophical and causative issues were explored, and professional marital and family therapists, as represented by Clinical Membership in the AAMFT, were defined as adherents closely aligned with systemic-relational propositions and tenets of practice. The following chapters outline several paradigm-specific therapeutic approaches that can be used by individuals subscribing to systemic-relational paradigm propositions. Readers are referred to Appendix A for details about the external model of the systemic-relational paradigm, which should be read before proceeding with the next chapters. Also, before reading the chapter on "Structure-Determined Family Therapy" (chapter 15) readers would benefit by reading Appendix B, which is a description of internal systemic-relational model.

## References

Bateson, G. (1972). *Steps to an ecology of mind.* New York: Ballantine.
Bateson, G. (1979). *Mind and nature: A necessary unity.* New York: Bantam.

Bateson, G., Jackson, D., Haley, J., & Weakland, J. (1956). Toward a theory of schizophrenia. *Behavioral Science, 1,* 251–264.

Becvar, R. J., & Becvar, D. S. (1982). *Systems theory and family therapy: A primer.* Washington, DC: University Press of America.

Bertalanffy, L. von. (1952). *Problems of life.* London: C. A. Watts.

Bertalanffy, L. von. (1968). *General systems theory.* New York: George Braziller.

Buckley, W. (1967). *Sociology and modern systems theory.* Englewood Cliffs, NJ: Prentice-Hall.

Cannon, W. B. (1932). *The wisdom of the body.* New York: W. W. Norton.

Capra, F. (1975). *The tao of physics.* Toronto: Bantam.

Capra, F. (1982). *The turning point.* New York: Bantam Books.

Dell, P. F. (1982). Beyond homeostasis: Toward a concept of coherence. *Family Process, 21,* 21–41.

Dell, P. F. (1985). Understanding Bateson and Maturana: Toward a biological foundation for the social sciences. *Journal of Marital and Family Therapy, 11* (1), 1–20.

Goldman, A. I. (1986). *Epistemology and cognition.* Cambridge, MA: Harvard University Press.

Haley, J. (1963). *Strategies of psychotherapy.* New York: Grune & Stratton.

Haley, J. (1976). *Problem-solving therapy.* New York: Harper & Row.

Heisenberg, W. (1958). *Physics and philosophy.* New York: Harper and Brothers.

Hoffman, L. (1981). *Foundations of family therapy: A conceptual framework for systems change.* New York: Basic Books.

Maturana, H. R. (1978). Biology of language: The epistemology of reality. In G. A. Miller & E. Lenneberg (Eds.), *Psychology and biology of language and thought.* New York: Academic Press.

Maturana, H. R. (1980). Biology of cognition. In H. R. Maturana & F. J. Varela, *Autopoiesis and cognition: The realization of the living.* Boston: D. Reidel. (Original work published in 1970.)

Maturana, H. R., & Varela, F. J. (1980). Autopoiesis: The organization of the living. In H. R. Maturana & F. J. Varela, *Autopoiesis and cognition: The realization of the living.* Boston: D. Reidel. (Original work published in 1973.)

Minuchin, S. (1974). *Families and family therapy.* Cambridge, MA: Harvard University Press.

Parsons, T. (1951). *The social system.* New York: Free Press of Glencoe.

Parsons, T. (1964). *Social structure and personality.* New York: Free Press of Glencoe.

Ruesch, J., & Bateson, G. (1968). Communication: The social matrix of psychiatry. New York: Norton.

Sadovsky, V. N. (1974, June). Problems of a general systems theory as a metatheory. *Ratio,* 33–50.

Satir, V. (1967). *Conjoint family therapy.* Palo Alto, CA: Science and Behavior Books.

Simon, R. (1985, May-June). Structure is destiny: An interview with Humberto Maturana. *The Family Therapy Networker, 9*(3), 32–37; 41–43.

Varela, F. J. (1979). *Principles of biological autonomy.* New York: North Holland.

Watzlawick, P., Beavin, J. H., & Jackson, D. D. (1967). *Pragmatics of human communication: A study of interactional patterns, pathologies, and paradoxes.* New York: W. W. Norton.

Watzlawick, P., Weakland, J., & Finsch, R. (1974). *Change: Principles of problem formation and problem resolution.* New York: W. W. Norton.

# 12

# Conjoint Family Therapy:
## A Trans-paradigmatic Theory Bridging the Psychological and Systemic-Relational Paradigms

VIRGINIA SATIR'S CONJOINT Family Therapy (1967) holds an important place in the history of theories of counseling and psychotherapy. Along with therapies such as Bowen's Family Systems Therapy (Bowen, 1978), it breaks with the traditions of the psychological paradigm while seeding the fertile ground of the systemic-relational paradigm. Satir's work is seminal to the systemic-relational paradigm, as she reconceptualized the concept of deficient self-esteem within a relational framework. It is this reconceptualization of a psychological construct (self-esteem) within a relational framework that made her work unique and important to transitions between paradigms.

Actually, as Satir's ideas progressed, she began to deemphasize the idea of deficient self-esteem as a problem focus (Woods & Martin, 1984). She became more fully systemic-and process-oriented in her thinking in her later years. Yet, as late as 1982, in a chapter titled ''The Therapist and Family Therapy: Process Model,'' she still acknowledged the importance of self-esteem to her theory. She stated:

> The central core of my theory is self esteem. I now clearly see that without a direct link to the experience of the senses, there would be little change in feeling. Consequently, there would be little change in self esteem, and therefore little real, dependable change in behavior. (pp. 21–22)

Her early works can best be described as transitioning psychological and systemic-relational paradigm propositions, while focusing on feeling and sensing as a means of engaging clients. She is also best described as a humanist, as she has espoused an unyielding faith in the human potential to grow and to develop in positive ways.

Her therapy demeanor appeared at times to be a cross between those of Carl Rogers and Fritz Perls. Woods and Martin (1984) stated that she had "the warmth and acceptance of Carl Rogers" and the "strong experiential, here-and-now techniques reminiscent of Fritz Perls" (p. 8). Unlike these psychological theorists, however, she worked almost exclusively within a family context.

## Virginia Satir, MA, a Biographical Sketch

Virginia Satir was born in 1916 in Wisconsin, the eldest of five children. She was raised on a farm. Evidently, she was inquisitive from her earliest years, since she often spoke about her decision at age 5 to become a detective of parents. Satir (1982) stated:

> *When I was 5, I decided to become a children's detective on parents. There was so much that went on between my parents that made little or no sense to me. Making sense of things around me, feeling loved, and being competent were my paramount concerns. I did feel loved, and felt I was competent, but making sense of all the contradictions, deletions, and distortions I observed both in my parents' relationship and among people outside in the world was heart-rending and confusion-making to me. Sometimes this situation raised questions about my being loved, but mostly it affected my ability to predict, to see clearly, and to develop my total being. (p. 13)*

At an early age, Virginia was faced with adult responsibilities; her mother was ill, and she assisted in raising her siblings. Also, Virginia suffered from illnesses, including an ear problem that left her hearing impaired for several years.

Virginia attended the University of Wisconsin, where she earned a teaching degree, and later she taught and was the principal at a small school. She later attended the University of Chicago and earned an MA degree in psychiatric social work. After a failed marriage and a move to Texas, she returned to Chicago (in 1951), where she established an independent therapy practice. In 1955, she was employed by the Illinois State Psychiatric Institute to teach family therapy, which was her first formal experience theoretically conceptualizing her clinical applications. Soon after a second marriage, she left Chicago for California (in 1958). In 1959, she, Don Jackson, and Jules Riskin became the founding staff of the Mental Research Institute (MRI) in Palo Alto, California. Her ideas were refined at MRI, and she systematically communicated her ideas through the publication of her seminal *Conjoint Family Therapy* (Satir, 1967). MRI took an early lead and still maintains a favorable reputation as a pacesetter in the development of family therapy theory and practice. Satir later affiliated with the Esalen Institute in 1963 and finally returned permanently to independent practice.

During her lifetime, Satir earned many honors, including an honorary doctorate from her alma mater, the University of Wisconsin. She also received the American Association for Marriage and Family Therapy's "Distinguished Service to Families

Award.'' She is frequently identified as a major leader in the marital and family therapy literature.

Satir has authored or coauthored many books, including *Conjoint Family Therapy* (1967); *Peoplemaking* (1972); *Helping Families to Change* (Satir, Stachowiak, & Taschman, 1977); *Self-Esteem* (1975); *Making Contact* (1976); *Your Many Faces* (1978); and *Changing with Families* (Bandler, Grinder & Satir, 1976).

Satir is remembered by those who knew her best as a caring and feeling person. She was often referred to as ''the Columbus of Family Therapy'' (Banmen, 1988), since she traveled so many miles spreading the message of social systems theory and family therapy. She presented hundreds of workshops and over her lifetime saw thousands of families in therapy. She was energetic and productive to the end of her career.

Satir died September 10, 1988, of cancer.

## The Foundational Theory

### The Target of Counseling

In her book, *Conjoint Family Therapy,* Satir (1967) declared that family functioning was crucial to mental health and communication. Her ideas were greatly influenced by her work at the Mental Research Institute in Palo Alto, California, where she worked closely with Don Jackson, MD, who, at that time, was the director of the institute. Satir, consequently, was very much influenced by the works of Bateson, Jackson, and Haley, who were at one time or another affiliated with the Mental Research Institute group. These theorists have come to be associated with the ''communications'' school of family therapy.

Largely, then, Satir's (1967) focus is on the family, a point she makes clear in *Conjoint Family Therapy*, in which she described the homeostatic nature of family systems, the idea of ''family pain,'' the identified patient as a symptom of a dysfunctional family, and the need to be family-holistic in conceptualizing the problems of ''identified patients'' (pp. 1–2).

Moreover, Satir (1967) is very clear about her view of parental responsibility in the development of a child's self-esteem. Broadly speaking, her view of self-esteem aligns her with psychological thinking, as she implicitly speaks of low self-esteem as baggage that adults carry around from childhood. On the other hand, she defines self-esteem in relational terms. She stated:

> *A person with low self-esteem has a great sense of anxiety and uncertainty about himself.*
> *a. His self-esteem is based to an extreme extent on what he thinks others think of him.*
> *b. His dependence on others for his self-esteem cripples his autonomy and individuality.*
> *c. He disguises his low self-esteem from others, especially when he wants to impress others.*

*d. His low self-esteem comes from his growing-up experiences which never led him to feel that it is good to be a person of one sex in relation to a person of the other.*

*e. He has never really separated from his parents, that is, arrived at a relationship of equality with them. (p. 8)*

Obviously, her conception of self-esteem is highly systemic-relational. Level of self-esteem is conceptualized as critical to one's selection of a mate (low self-esteem begets mates with low self-esteem). Consequently, one's low self-esteem affects marital choice and is implicated in the transmission of low self-esteem across generations to one's children. Satir stated: "If the mates have low self-esteem and little trust in each other, they will expect their child to enhance their self-esteem, to be an extension of themselves, and to serve crucial pain-relieving functions in the marital relationship" (p. 45). Satir described those factors critical to the development of self-esteem in children, almost all of which involve parental direction. Satir, ultimately, links a child's self-esteem to parental self-esteem as follows:

*The close relationship between parental validation, self-esteem, independence, and uniqueness shows up when one observes how a dysfunctional person (an unvalidated child who is now an adult) still clings to his parents, or to substitute parent figures, or relates to his sexual partner as if that partner were, in fact, a parent. (p. 54)*

Since relationships are highly communicational, a person's poor self-esteem manifests itself in poor communication. It is through communication that the therapist attempts to undo the poor learning that has come primarily from dysfunctional parents—parents with poor self-esteem.

Poor self-esteem and poor interpersonal communication are correlative. In fact, Satir (1967) goes so far as to conclude that low self-esteem *leads* to dysfunctional communication. Further, she stated: "Dysfunction in communication will also follow when the individual is unable to handle different-ness" (p. 95). In effect, she believed that individuals should be accepting of others, no matter what the differences.

## The Process of Counseling

Counseling is a process of facilitating effective communication in a relational context. The therapist acts as an "official observer" of family interaction, and more important, as a teacher of clear communication. It is assumed that client-families are not able to see and to hear all that is communicated by family members, and the therapist can assist in making messages complete and clear at all levels of communication. Specifically, the therapist may intervene into interpersonal exchanges between members of a family, helping clients to clarify their messages. The therapist might also facilitate understanding among family members by having members enact roles either consistent or inconsistent with family functioning.

Actually, as Satir's ideas have evolved, she has moved away from a problem focus—that is, away from trying to correct deficient self-esteem—toward therapeutic process as a process unto itself (Woods & Martin, 1984). Where her ideas about process in her early works look remediative, in her later years, according to Woods and Martin (1984), she appeared to "invent process around an issue of relevance to the client; the process is the intervention" (p. 6). Regardless, even in her early works there is a process-oriented tone. She appeared to be primarily concerned with entering family interaction to produce changes in interaction. Fundamentally, then, the difference between her early and later ideas about family therapy process is that *her early work was deficiency corrective, whereas her later work appeared to be primarily growth enhancing*. In both cases, the therapeutic interactive process seemed to predominate over the content of therapy. In other words, she did not try to do therapy with words alone; instead, she actively entered into interaction sequences (verbally and nonverbally) between and among family members as a primary intervention.

## Counselor Role

In *Conjoint Family Therapy,* Satir (1967) made fifteen points about the role of the family therapist. Some of the most significant of those points are summarized in the following paragraphs.

First, Satir believed that a comfortable setting should be created in therapy. She felt that clients should, "perhaps for the first time, take the risk of looking clearly and objectively at themselves and their actions" (p. 160). One of the major tasks of the therapist is to facilitate a comfortable, threat-free, and sharing attitude.

Second, Satir stated that "the therapist decreases threat by setting the rules of interaction" (p. 165) and by the way the therapist "structures the interviews" (p. 167). Setting the rules of interaction is a critical issue to systemic-relational therapy. As experienced family therapists know, it is often difficult to control family interactions, especially in highly dysfunctional families. Consequently, a family's interactions may escalate within the therapeutic context to the degree it is deleterious to the family or to a member or members of the family. The therapist must structure sessions and must make it clear that certain rules apply in the therapeutic setting.

Third, the therapist attempts to allay family and individual defenses. Satir (1967) said:

> *In my opinion, the dysfunctional family operates within a reign of terror, with all members fearing they will be hurt and all members fearing they will hurt others. All comments are taken as attacks on self-esteem. Therefore, the therapist must reduce terror. So the therapist . . . exerts all his efforts to reducing terror, reducing the necessity for defenses. (p. 168)*

Two ways the therapist can deal with defenses are: (a) by interpreting anger as hurt; and (b) by explaining that pain is an acceptable and an expressible feeling in therapy. The therapist must, therefore, be an expert at "handling loaded material with care" (p. 169).

Fourth, the therapist "re-educates patients for adulthood, for accountability" (p. 171). The therapist assists the client in regaining a sense of self-accountability and self-control. By educating, the therapist is a teacher of what is expected of the patient. Accordingly, "the therapist delineates roles and functions" (p. 174) within the interpersonal context. Clients should be educated as to what their roles are within their family contexts.

Fifth, "the therapist completes gaps in communication and interprets messages" (p. 175). This is probably the most important therapist task, according to Satir. Any discrepancies in communication are interpreted: (a) about oneself—for example, saying one feels fine when one is acting distressed; and (b) between people—for example, focusing on nonverbal communication between members of a family. According to Satir, the therapist should separate the content of a message from its relationship message. Satir made the point that every communication has a content message *and* a relationship message. For example, when a teacher says to a student, "You are a good student," two messages are communicated. First, there is the content of the message related to the student's performance; and second, there is the relationship message—that the teacher is in a position to judge the student. In just about every communication between people, there is both a content and a relationship message. Satir believed that the therapist should separate and openly make these communications clear to the communicator and to the receiver. Further, Satir believed that the therapist "must also see himself as a *model of communication*" (p. 97).

Sixth, the therapist should avoid making judgments, and should be "congruent" in his or her responses. (Although she uses the term *congruence* in a way that is similar to Roger's, 1951, definition of the term, Satir never cited Rogers in her book. Instead she referred to Bateson, Jackson, Haley, & Weakland, 1956, in defining *incongruence*). Essentially, Satir believed that a therapist should be in touch with his or her feelings and should behave consistently with feelings. Also, she believed that the content and relationship messages in communications should be consistent.

In sum, the role of the therapist is that of an effective communicator, a model of interpersonal interaction, and a teacher of what is expected of patients in and outside of therapy.

## Goals of Counseling and Ideal Outcomes

Satir (1967) was very clear about what she felt was necessary as an outcome of treatment. She stated:

> *Treatment is completed:*
> — *When family members can complete transactions, check, ask.*
> — *When they can interpret hostility.*
> — *When they can see how others see them.*
> — *When one member can tell another how he manifests himself.*

— *When one member can tell another what he hopes, fears, and expects from him.*
— *When they can disagree.*
— *When they can make choices.*
— *When they can learn through practice.*
— *When they can free themselves from harmful effects of past models.*
— *When they can give a clear message, that is, be congruent in their behavior, with a minimum of difference between feelings and communication, and with a minimum of hidden messages. (p. 176)*

Although the list is long and appears overly ambitious by many standards, one can summarize Satir's goals of therapy by stating that she attempts to help family members to manifest individual self-esteem and effective interpersonal communication.

## General Procedures

### Assessment

Assessment and therapy occur at the same time, according to Satir. Her approach to assessment is much like Carl Rogers's (see chapter 8). Essentially, Satir believed *everyone* has the potential for growth and development. However, Satir (1982) believed that "any symptom signals a blockage in growth and has a survival connection to a system which requires blockage and distortion of growth in some form in all of its members to keep its balance" (p. 12). Accordingly Satir paid special attention to symptoms, while defining them within family contexts. Doing assessment consistent with a conjoint approach requires entering the process of the family, defining significant triadic relationships, assessing rules and roles (both overt and covert), and defining relationship messages observed in communications between family members.

The assessment of triadic relational concerns was critical to Satir (1967). In fact, in *Conjoint Family Therapy* she devoted a whole chapter to "The Family Triangle" (p. 55). Specifically, she addressed the idea of marital discord and its influence on children. She was very alert to the issue of the child "identified patient" (IP), and she concluded that symptomatic behavior of a child was representative of parental/marital dysfunction (deriving from low parental self-esteem). She stated:

> *I have been repeatedly struck by how readily the I.P. drops his role as intervener once family therapy is under way. Once he is assured that arguments do not bring destruction and that marital amicability lightens parental demands on him, the I.P. actively helps the therapist help his parents as mates, while at the same time he tries to get his parents to recognize him as a separate individual with needs of his own. As a matter of fact, the I.P. is often very helpful as "assistant marital counselor." (p. 56)*

In a sense, Satir communicated that the triangle (a triad with three relationships) is the building block of larger systems and is a unit requiring special assessment during the evaluation of symptomatic behavior. She believed that in a triangle, all three members could have "fears of being left out," and she felt it was critical, especially when dealing with children, to allay their fears.

Beyond assessing triadic structural concerns, Satir's (1967) ideas focused on assessing messages during communication, whether occurring within a triadic or dyadic framework. As mentioned earlier, both content and relationship messages must be assessed, since it is the relationship message that is critical to the ongoing interactions within a family context. Satir (1967) stated:

> *Communication is a complex business. The receiver must assess all the different ways in which the sender is sending messages, as well as being aware of his own receiving system, that is his own interpretation system.*
> *a. When A talks, B assesses the verbal meaning of A's message.*
> *b. He also listens to the tone of voice in which A speaks.*
> *c. He also watches what A does; he notes the "body language" and facial expressions which accompany A's message.*
> *d. He also assesses what A is saying within a social context. The context may be how B has seen A respond to him and to others in the past. It may also be B's expectations about what the requirements of the situation are.*
> *e. In other words, the receiver (B) is busy assessing both the verbal and the nonverbal content of A's message so that he can come to some judgment about what A meant by his communication. (p. 75)*

Through communication analysis, Satir was an expert at defining rules of family interaction (often unspoken rules). It was her contention that such rules should be brought into the open.

Although there is no clear-cut diagnostic phase to the conjoint approach, it is evident that Satir originally believed that assessment should be highly relational and focused on both the triadic structure of systems and on communication (messages and rules).

## Treatment/Remediation

Satir's (1967) treatment program is one of adhering to several basic principles. First, it is assumed that positive changes will result through the interpersonal process of therapy, which is a conclusion primarily based on her humanistic attitude that people have honorable motives and that everyone is healable (Woods & Martin, 1984).

Second, interventions are aimed at relationships and communication. Individuals and their social contexts are inseparable. However, she did not go so far in her early works as theoretically denying the existence of individuals. *Consequently, her efforts toward remediation were dualistic: they were aimed at the individual, but they were also aimed at relationships of significance.* Although this appeared to make practical sense to Satir, it also demonstrated her trans-paradigmatic thinking. In her conceptu-alization of problems and in her approach to treatment, she was both individual- *and* systems-acknowledging, but without a well-developed theory that allowed for acknowl-edgment of both in any systematic and comprehensive way.

Third, as will be more clear to readers when specialized techniques are outlined in a following section of this chapter, Satir was very active in therapy, physically and linguistically. She entered the family with a sincere, active, and commanding presence, while at the same time she exuded love and kindness. She was a person to be reckoned with in therapy. She made no apologies for her ''get in there and get your hands dirty'' attitude about therapy. She encouraged emotional expression, touching, and feeling. She wanted her clients to experience their relations fully in the present. In videotapes of her sessions, she at times appears very directive about how families ideally could be.

Her therapeutic interventions can best be described as bringing forth and reor-ganizing emotions in a social and linguistic context.

## Case Management

Satir (1967) was adamant about the need to have all family members, and especially marital partners, in therapy. Even during precounseling phone contacts, Satir strongly encouraged all family members to attend.

During the first interview, Satir started by asking questions. She often asked questions of all family members in order to get all perspectives on an issue. Often, her questions addressed symptomatic behaviors, in order to place them in a relational context.

Satir also recommended strongly the use of ''family life chronology'' in the early sessions of therapy. Essentially, a family life chronology is a social/relational history. It begins with marital partners. The therapist must go back into the marital relationship history, and explore issues from the very beginning of the relationship that might be significant to current concerns. Notes may be taken (or sessions recorded), but the important task of the therapist is to outline a kind of historical calendar on the marital relationship, with critical relational incidents recorded, including the first meeting, wedding plans, the marital ceremony, and so on. The therapist is alert to other past relational influences on the marriage as he or she explores the marital relationship. For example, if a parent-in-law was problematic early in the relationship, then it might be hypothesized that there might be continued strain in the parent-in-law relationship that might be influencing the marriage presently. Relationships with parents, siblings, in-laws, aunts, uncles, and any other individuals of significance are explored. Satir felt that ''different-ness'' between marital partners (which can be interpreted as differences between the respective social systems of significance) is a source of role strain. Conjoint therapy attempts to reconcile such different-ness.

The therapist continues therapy by asking children questions about their rela-tional history, paying special attention to the events of social significance in their lives.

Children are very important, and Satir (1967) believed that children should be active participants in therapy. Regarding the management of children in therapy, Satir stated: ''I found that a therapist has very few problems of control if he actively takes charge of the therapy process. If he knows how to do this, children respond as readily as their parents'' (p. 139). However, Satir did acknowledge that certain unique problems arise when children are present in therapy, and she did address some of the most common difficulties in her book, including the commonly encountered disruptive behavior of children. In effect, Satir placed the parents in charge of disciplining their children, even though Satir maintained control over the rules of therapy.

Conjoint family therapy sessions are process-oriented, and assessment and treatment appear to go hand in hand. Importantly, interventions are aimed at affecting family homeostasis. Case notes should reflect the therapist's ongoing assessment (of family relationships, communications, and structure) and ongoing interventions.

Over all, the conjoint family therapist builds a relational history of client-systems, and then intervenes into the present dynamics of the system.

## Specialized Techniques

Probably the most concise summary of techniques used by Satir was presented by Woods and Martin (1984). Readers are referred to their excellent article on Satir's works for a contemporary and straightforward presentation of Satir's ideas. Five techniques are presented.

**1.** *Verbalizing presuppositions.* The very presence of a family in therapy, unless the family is forced to attend by an outside party, can be interpreted as reflecting the hopes of family members that good outcomes will result from treatment. Satir was a master at expressing what she assumed was being communicated by the family by its attending the first sessions of therapy. She would express her feeling that the presence of family members meant they were hopeful, desiring change, and willing to take steps necessary to solve problems. In other words, the family's actions demonstrated a presupposition (an antecendent assumption) about what could occur in therapy, and Satir made it a practice of verbalizing such presuppositions.

**2.** *Denominalization.* Woods and Martin (1984) described denominalization as follows:

> *This involves obtaining specific behavioral descriptions for words such as love and respect. For instance, Satir wants to know exactly what must be done in order for the person to perceive that he or she is receiving respect. The clarified answer is often related to the individual's primary sensory-based representational system (i.e., visual, auditory, or kinesthetic). (p. 9)*

Denominalization, then, is a means of taking global terms and making them behavior specific.

**3.** *Family Sculpture.* Family sculpting is an artistic and therapeutic means of concretizing relational issues in a family. L'Abate, Ganahl, and Hansen (1986) described sculpting as follows:

> *Family sculpting is a method in which family members are asked to arrange one another as a living statue or tableau. Drawing upon their creative instincts and using such nonverbal dimensions as distance, posture, visage, and gesture, the family members give concrete representation to their impressions of the family. Such a process is not new to the family. It occurs every day in such activities as seating arrangement, but is infrequently recognized or consciously controlled for an expressive effect. Due to its form this method achieves several purposes in therapy. In brief, it may actively involve inactive or nonvocal members; increase the clarity of communication within the family; enhance the expression of emotions; promote awareness of the internal and interactional experiences of the participants; allow new insights into family functioning for both the therapist and family; intensify the family's experience in therapy; objectify and defuse some aspects of their experience; help family members differentiate; and bring them to a fuller awareness of their own interconnectedness in a way which linear verbal representations are incapable of achieving. (p. 166)*

Satir frequently used sculpting by having one family member take a physical stance in therapy, and then she assisted other family members to build a sculpture around the person's stance. She defined four basic stances that she felt could assist the sculptor in defining the operation of the system: blamer (an accuser), placater (an appeaser), superreasonable (a nonfeeler), and irrelevant (a seemingly uninvolved party). By sculpting, Satir hoped to integrate language with experience (Woods & Martin, 1984).

**4.** *Anchoring.* Dilts and Green (1982) defined *anchoring* as follows: "Anchoring is the learned association between a stimulus and a response or between one response and another. When the stimulus or initiating response is triggered, the associated response will be elicited" (p. 233). Essentially, a therapist's actions are used to connect client activities. Dilts and Green stated:

> *The anchor the therapist uses can be any external stimulus, a touch, a particular voice tone or gesture, or a snap of the fingers. We have learned that kinesthetic anchors (such as a specific touch on the client's knee, arm, shoulder) are the least difficult for the novice to learn. (p. 233)*

Woods and Martin (1984) described how Satir might have used anchoring with a marital couple:

> *Satir might ask her to look at her husband and "feel what she feels." When a positive response becomes evident in the individual (i.e., altered breathing, tears), Satir would touch her shoulder gently at the peak of positive emotion.*

> *Apparently, this helps connect the particular emotion with the touch which makes the feeling more concrete for the individual. (p. 10)*

Anchoring is a good example of how Satir brought feelings to the level of *interpersonal* physical experience.

**5.** *Reframing.* Reframing is a process of redefinition. Satir used reframing mostly to redefine behaviors from negative interpretations to positive interpretations. If a client is feeling sad when discussing a concern with another family member, a positive reframe of the sadness is, ''Your sadness is a way of expressing the depth of your concern.'' Satir used reframing to bring forth positive interpretations to individual actions. She felt that honorable motives were at the base of individual behaviors, and therefore, she always looked to express the positive viewpoint in therapy. In fact, Satir was a master of the positive reframe. It seemed to come quite naturally to her.

These five techniques are representative of Satir's way of doing therapy. However, specialized techniques were not the mainstay of her approach. Rather, as her approach matured, she began to focus more on the process of therapy as therapeutic in and of itself.

## Recent Developments or Criticisms

One of Satir's last works was titled ''The Therapist and Family Therapy: Process Model'' (Satir, 1982). In this work, Satir moved away from the deficiency model of self-esteem that appeared to be a driving force in *Conjoint Family Therapy.* Although she continued to acknowledge the importance of self-esteem in her theory, she focused more on facilitating the growth-enhancing aspects of the individuals (and the system) rather than attempting to remediate deficiencies of self-esteem. It is as if she began to view clients less as half-empty and more as half-full. Her efforts then became more focused on means of facilitating growth within a family context. Satir (1982) stated:

> *(a) therapy is a process which takes place between persons and is aimed at accomplishing positive change, and (b) the therapist can be expected to be the leader in initiating and teaching a health-promoting process in the family. The therapist is not, however, in charge of the persons involved. . . . The process I initiate is heavily weighted toward each member of the family becoming as whole as possible. (p. 13)*

Satir later stated: ''I have been trained as a human pathologist. I am now working as a 'health developer,' using the information of pathology to help me recognize trouble spots more or less. . . . It tells me that something needs attention'' (p. 22). Symptoms, rather than being indicators of maladaptive systems needing correction, became more fully signals of blocked process and signs of the need for growth enhancement. It is as if Satir's frame of reference had been reframed to the positive—therapy is not therapy at all; it is education and opportunity. She stated: ''I now see therapy as an educational process for becoming more fully human. I put my energies and attention on what can be added to what is present'' (p. 22).

Regardless of this switch in emphasis, Satir's approach can still be described as theoretically deficient. She still appeared, even in her latest works, to be straddling the psychological and systemic-relational philosophical fence. She was dualistic theoretically, as mentioned earlier. She attempted to make individuals more fully human, yet at the same time she defined personhood within a relational framework. She never fully identified whether individual psychological processes overshadowed relational dynamics, or vice versa. Instead, she tended to play a balancing act, using terms such as *self-esteem, self-worth,* and *congruence* almost flirtingly in a psychologically oriented way. At the same time, she always attempted to demonstrate the importance of relationships on the individual's concept of self. She never was able to fully cross over to more complete systemic-relational thinking, where there is no such thing as self-esteem—there are only relationships that affect human behavior. From a more fully systemic-relational framework, the term *self-esteem* is excess baggage. Since communication and relationship are critical factors systemically, they are the focus of study. No psychological construct is necessary to account for human behavior, since relationship and communication are quite adequate. As can be seen, Satir never fully made the break with the theories that preceded her.

## Paradigm Fit

### Focus of Study

The focus of Conjoint Family Therapy is dualistic. Satir's (1967, 1982) work always focused on the individual and the social system of significance. She was interested in an individual's functioning within a social context. She studied both the individual's developmental movement toward wholeness and the system's homeostatic functioning, especially as related to the symptomatic behavior of an identified patient. She was both system- and individual-enhancing in her approach to therapy.

### View of Nature of Reality

Reality appears to be simultaneously composed of individuals (as things) and relationships (which are processes that affect individuals). Satir, although learning a great deal from her contemporaries about systemic epistemology, such as Bateson, tended to place great value on the individual. In a sense, she was as much a humanistic psychologist as she was a systems theorist and therapist. She conceptually never was able to reconcile systemic epistemology with her observations of the self-determination and self-worth of individuals. Although she attempted to define self within a relational framework, a purist systems theorist might ask why such concepts needed defining at all. Psychological conceptualizations are not useful or relevant from a systemic-relational framework.

## Consonance with Paradigm Propositions and Tenets

Historically, Satir's work bridges paradigms. In fact, Satir's (1967) *Conjoint Family Therapy* must be viewed as a seminal work in the development of the systemic-relational paradigm. Although it appears easy by today's standards to criticize her work on systemic-relational grounds, at the time, her ideas were ground-breaking and trans-paradigmatic. She was one of the few mental health professionals able to recognize the validity of intuitions about the inadequacy of purely individual interventions, while at the same time she developed techniques and methods for intervening into relational dynamics assumed to be at the root of symptomatic behaviors. She bridged paradigms in a very positive way.

Looking back, one can see that she appeared dualistic in her thinking, focusing on individuals and relationships almost as if they were side by side. Although she defined relationships as significant to mental health and self-esteem, self-esteem was just as significant to relationships. Although self-esteem and relationships can be viewed as recursively interacting and mutually causative from a systemic-relational standpoint, Satir (1967) clearly defined self-esteem as causative of difficulties in a *linear* sense, appearing to side with psychological paradigm propositions. She also seemed highly bound by a physical view of biology, seeing the body as critical to emotion and learning. She did not appear to have a systemic-relational view of biological systems, as she attempted to intervene at the level of the individual as a bounded physical organism.

Over all, analyzing Satir's work from a counseling paradigm perspective reveals theoretical crossover, which is both laudatory historically but vulnerable theoretically.

# Chapter Conclusion

The works of Virginia Satir are best viewed as a transition between two paradigms of counseling and psychotherapy—the psychological and systemic-relational paradigms. Satir was very alert to the influence of relationships on personal psychological functioning, while she also recognized the impact of faulty self-esteem on relationships. She became more fully process-oriented in her later years, as she relegated the idea of deficient self-esteem to a less than primary role in her theoretical statements. She began to view herself as a health facilitator and growth initiator in therapy.

Satir's place in the history of paradigms of counseling and psychotherapy is secure, as she broke with the traditions of psychological thinking while entering the realm of systemic-relational epistemology and ontology.

# References

Bandler, R., Grinder, J., & Satir, V. (1976). *Changing with families*. Palo Alto, CA: Science and Behavior Books.

Banmen, J. (1988, September/October). Virginia Satir: The Columbus of Family Therapy. *Family Therapy News, 19* (5), 5; 23.

Bowen, M. (1978). *Family therapy in clinical practice*. New York: Jason Aronson.

Dilts, R., & Green, J. D. (1982). Application of neuro-linguistic programming in family therapy. In A. M. Horne & M. M. Ohlsen (Eds.), *Family counseling and therapy* (pp. 214–244). Itasca, IL: F. E. Peacock.

L'Abate, L., Ganahl, G., & Hansen, J. C. (1986). *Methods of family therapy*. Englewood Cliffs, NJ: Prentice-Hall.

Rogers, C. R. (1951). *Client-Centered Therapy*. Boston: Houghton Mifflin.

Satir, V. (1967). *Conjoint family therapy*. Palo Alto, CA: Science and Behavior Books.

Satir, V. (1972). *Peoplemaking*. Palo Alto, CA: Science and Behavior Books.

Satir, V. (1975). *Self-esteem*. Millbrae, CA: Celestial Arts.

Satir, V. (1976). *Making contact*. Millbrae, CA: Celestial Arts.

Satir, V. (1978). *Your many faces*. Millbrae, CA: Celestial Arts.

Satir, V. (1982). The therapist and family therapy: Process model. In A. M. Horne & M. M. Ohlsen (Eds.), *Family counseling and therapy* (pp. 12–42). Itasca, IL: F. E. Peacock.

Satir, V., Stachowiak, J., & Taschman, H. (1977). *Helping families to change*. New York: Aronson.

Woods, M. D., & Martin, D. (1984). The work of Virginia Satir: Understanding her theory and technique. *The American Journal of Family Therapy, 12,* 3–11.

# 13

# Strategic Problem Solving Therapy:
## *An External Model*
## *Systemic-Relational Therapy*
## *Focusing on Behavior*

JAY HALEY IS the founder of Strategic Problem Solving Therapy and a leader of the systemic-relational movement. Haley has been involved with the therapeutic application of social systems theory from his early days of research with Gregory Bateson (e.g., Bateson, Jackson, Haley, & Weakland, 1956). He has been a creative theoretician and an effective communicator of the systemic-relational viewpoint. His work is well respected and has thrived through the systemic "heyday," which appears to continue unabated. Haley has been prolific, and his several books and many articles help to chronicle his development as a systemic therapist over the years (Haley, 1963, 1973, 1984, 1987; Haley & Hoffman, 1967). His 1987 book, *Problem Solving Therapy* (published in its first edition in 1976), is probably his most concise and definitive work. In fact, it is considered by many to be a milestone publication of the "strategic approach" to family therapy. As an introduction to strategic therapy, it also serves as an easy reading guide on the "how to's" of family therapy.

   *Problem Solving Therapy* focuses on counseling families of triads or larger system structures. The issue of dyadic relational structures was dealt with in his earlier work, entitled *Strategies of Psychotherapy* (Haley, 1963). The summary of the work presented in this chapter is heavily based on *Problem Solving Therapy*.

## Jay Haley, MA, a Biographical Sketch

Jay Haley was born in 1923. He received his Bachelor of Arts degree from the University of California at Los Angeles in 1948 and pursued subsequent undergraduate training at the University of California at Berkeley, receiving a Bachelor of Library Science degree in 1951. He later worked as a librarian at Stanford University (1952–1953). In 1953 he earned an MA at Stanford University, where he studied communication, and, after graduation, worked on a "Project for the Study of Communication," which was directed by Gregory Bateson. During that project, Haley and others involved in the project studied hypnosis, animal behavior, films, schizophrenia, psychotherapy, families, and family therapy. About the same time, Haley entered into a private practice in hypnotherapy and marriage and family therapy.

Over his professional career, Haley has held several academic appointments, including professorships at the University of Pennsylvania, Howard University, and the University of Maryland. Most recently, he has served as the founder (in 1975) and codirector of the Haley/Madanes Institute of Washington, D.C.

Haley has published thirteen books as author, coauthor or editor. He has published numerous articles in professional journals on such diverse topics as film, hypnosis, schizophrenia, family therapy, religious power tactics, and communication. He is actively involved in presenting family and individual therapy workshops.

## The Foundational Theory

### The Target of Counseling

Haley (1987) clearly focuses on designing interventions that involve the relational context of a problem. His viewpoint is highly behavioral within the context of a systemic-

*Jay Haley*

relational therapy. He focuses on behavior and its relational context, and he focused on developing therapeutic "directives" to solve problems. Haley (1987) stated:

> *If therapy is to end properly, it must begin properly—by negotiating a solvable problem and discovering the social situation that makes the problem necessary. The act of therapy begins with the way the problem is examined. The act of intervening brings out problems and the relationship patterns that are to be changed. (p. 8)*

Thus, a relationally defined problem is the target of counseling. And interventions are aimed at solving the problem.

Haley (1987) goes on to describe the importance of what is defined as *analogic communication.* Analogic communication is opposed to *digital communication.* According to Haley, analogic communication is communication that "has multiple referents" (p. 92). There is no one response to an analogic communication. In human behavior, analogic communication is highly nonverbal, informal, and contextual. It takes into account many variables. On the other hand, digital communication "consists of that class of messages where each statement has a specific referent and only that referent. Something happens or it does not happen; there is *one* stimulus and *one* response. . . . If A, and only if A, then Z, and only Z' " (p. 91). Digital communication is technical and formal. So, when a girl says to a boyfriend, "I love you," while she looks seductively at another boy walking by, the digital message is contained in the words "I love you," whereas the analogic message is in her nonverbal behaviors in the context of her interaction with a passerby. Haley, and other theorists (e.g., Bateson, 1972; Watzlawick, Beavin & Jackson, 1967; Watzlawick, Weakland, & Fisch, 1974) believe that analogic communication is very important to human interpersonal communication, and it may be critical to the definition of a relationship. Consequently, the study of analogic communication is of major importance to understanding the relational context in which problems arise and maintain themselves.

Haley (1987) also viewed the family as a governed homeostatic system, in keeping with systemic-relational propositions. Accordingly, one of the tasks of the therapist is targeting the repeated sequences of behavior within which symptomatic behavior is embedded. Haley stated:

> *When dealing with a governed, homeostatic system that is maintained by repeating sequences of behavior, the therapist changes those sequences by shifting the ways people respond to each other because of the ways they must respond to the therapist. (p. 126)*

Consequently, the therapist attempts to affect the relationship dynamics that may be supportive of the unwanted or symptomatic behavior, even though the involved parties may be unaware of the relational context of the problem. The term *symptomatic,* in this sense, is family-dynamic symptomatic, not symptomatic in a classic organic-medical diagnostic sense. Haley believes that problems are relation-specific, and moreover, to change a symptom, one must change the operative relationships.

### The Process of Counseling

Haley (1987) believed that it was "sensible to interview the natural group where the problem is expressed and so to proceed immediately toward the solution" (p. 9). Usually, the natural group where a problem is expressed is the family. In fact, the initial interview in Strategic Problem Solving Therapy is a structured family interview that has distinct stages. The five stages are: (a) *a social stage,* which involves greeting the family and making the family members feel comfortable; (b) *the problem stage,* when each member is asked to define the problem; (c) *an interaction stage,* which places family members in dyadic or other interactions for observatory purposes; (d) *a goal-setting stage,* where the family members must operationalize their concerns and define what is to be changed through therapeutic interventions; and (e) the *ending the interview* or *"task-setting" stage,* which involves setting the next session and settling issues related to the logistics of the second session.

Through the stages of the first interview, the therapist gains needed information about the function of a symptom within a relational context, and the therapist then uses the symptom as leverage in changing the relational dynamics of the family. Importantly, *directives* will be used throughout the course of therapy to influence relational change. A directive is a recommended task, presented to the family as a means of studying or affecting a problem. However, directives are usually *not given* at the end of the first session, unless, of course, there is a highly experienced and skilled therapist involved. In fact the first directive may not occur until the end of the second session. One of the therapist's major tasks in the first session is to get the family back for the second session in order that a planned therapeutic directive may be given by the therapist.

It is through directives that the therapist maintains control of what occurs in therapy, since he or she can always anticipate what will result from the therapeutic directive. The therapist must always be one step ahead of his client-family. Although this sounds impossible, from a strategic standpoint it is quite plausible. Client-families only have several options when faced with a therapeutic directive: (a) to carry out the directive; (b) to fail totally to carry out the directive; and (c) to fail partially to carry out the directive.

Since initial therapeutic directives are usually aimed at solving a problem, if the directive is carried out, the family will be moving the "right" direction after the second session, and the therapist's subsequent activities are aimed at maintaining and building on the good changes that have occurred. On the other hand, if a client-system fails to carry out a directive, or fails even to give the directive a working chance, then the responsibility of failure is placed squarely on the shoulders of the family members. They are informed that they have missed an opportunity to begin to correct the problems that led to therapy. Follow-up directives may be formulated with the idea that resistance is a factor in the failure of the family to carry out the directive. Follow-up directives in subsequent sessions may be based on the assumption that resistance to therapeutic directives will persist. Resistance may be used strategically. In other words, the therapist may ask the family to do something the therapist does not want the family to do—to approach the family through the "back door," so to speak. Effectively, this makes full therapeutic use of the family's resistance. A classic example of a back-door directive is "prescription of the symptom." The client-family may be asked, in all seriousness, to demonstrate that it can produce the "symptom." The rationale for such a directive given by the therapist might be that, by producing the symptom, the family gives the therapist an opportunity to study the symptom within its context. Paradoxically, *resistant client-families may refuse to follow the directive, thereby changing in the wanted direction (removal of the symptom)*. Therefore, back-door directives (such as the paradoxical task just described) allow the therapist to strategically make use of client resistance. Haley (1987) has described methods to ensure the success of such directives.

The third possible outcome to a therapeutic directive is that the client-family makes only a half-hearted attempt to follow the directive, which results in a failure. Such attempts are viewed as fully failed attempts (reflecting resistance) and treated as in the previous example of the failed attempt.

Of course there is one other option: a failed faithfully carried out directive. In such a case, the therapist is accountable for a misapplied or mistargeted directive. The therapist has the responsibility to develop a more effective means of dealing with the presented problems. This is enough of a reason for a novice therapist to delay giving a therapeutic directive until at least the second session. By the second session, the therapist has the opportunity: (a) to study the audio/visual tape of the first interview; (b) to formulate effective directives; and (c) to develop strategies for addressing the outcome of the directive (as previously described). Second, the therapist can use the beginning of the second session to test some rough hypotheses about the usefulness of the directives before one is presented to the family at the end of the session.

Obviously, Strategic Problem Solving Therapy attempts to "cover all bases" in approaching problems in their relational contexts. It is designed to put the therapist in full control. The appropriateness of directives are based on the symptomatic behavior. Haley (1987) is very alert to how symptoms are operationalized, and therapeutic progress is viewed according to the effect of therapy on symptomatic behaviors. He stated, "Therapists who have the goal of removing symptoms or solving problems, and who do so, have done their job and earned their pay" (p. 219). But it is noteworthy that from the very beginning of his book, Haley makes it clear that it is the relational context and sequences of interactions that are the focus of Strategic Problem Solving Therapy. This point cannot be overemphasized. He stated:

> Even though this approach assumes that the therapist has failed if he or she does not solve the presenting problem, and even though the symptom is defined in operational terms that are as precise as possible, the therapy focus is on the social situation rather than on the person. It is possible to define a "problem" in different social units. In this book a problem is defined as a type of behavior that is part of a sequence of acts among several persons. The repeating sequence of behavior is the focus of therapy. A symptom is a label for, a crystallization of, a sequence in a social organization. (p. 2)

Haley's approach, even though it is behaviorally focused, is clearly systemic-relational in that all behavior is viewed in its interactional (communicational) context.

## Counselor Role

The counselor role is that of strategist. Haley believes that therapy is necessarily directive. His views on the directive and strategic nature of therapy derived from his study of the skillful Milton Erickson, a master hypnotherapist (Haley, 1973, Erickson, Rossi & Rossi, 1976). Erickson actively and spontaneously choreographed his therapy sessions, and he was strategic in targeting unwanted behaviors and ameliorating them through directive technique. His techniques were often straightforward in their intent, but he was especially skilled at what can be described as ''back-door'' technique, that is, directive techniques that place clients in therapeutic binds (see Erickson, Rossi, & Rossi, 1976). For example, Erickson might ask, ''Do you want to go into a trance quickly or slowly?'' Such a question appears to give a choice, but actually it gives no choice as to whether trance will be achieved. This essentially constitutes a *therapeutic* double bind. According to Haley (1987), the therapist, by the nature of the therapeutic context, cannot escape being directive, and this position is a direct offshoot of the position of Milton Erickson.

Haley also believes that the therapist should take a somewhat neutral role when dealing with relationships in therapy. Haley (1987) stated:

> *At the most general level, therapists should not side consistently with anyone in the family against anyone else. But that does not mean they should not temporarily side with one against another, because that is in fact the only way therapists can induce change. If they only place their ''weight'' in coalitions equally, they will continue the sequence as it was. In the same way, if they only join one person against another, they may maintain the system as it was by simply becoming part of the deadlocked struggle. That task is more complex: the therapist must temporarily join in different coalitions while ultimately not siding with anyone against anyone. (p. 126)*

The therapist, then, must play a balancing act in sessions, leaning one way when necessary, and another way at another time, but always maintaining the in-between position when the act is over.

The strategic therapist is also a negotiator in a sense. He or she must be able to negotiate a therapeutic contract with a problematic family, when in fact, the family members may see little connection between a symptomatic individual and their need to attend sessions. Haley, however does not negotiate about the presenting problem or the need to redefine problems in relational terms. He appears to believe that patients have difficulty thinking relationally, and he does the relational thinking for them. Consequently, he often takes the presenting problem at face value, even if it is individualized (related to an identified patient, IP). He then uses the presenting problem as leverage to get the individuals in the problematic system to return. He then attempts to influence change in the relational structure of the problematic relationships.

In summary, then, the strategic therapist must be directive, tactical, relationally neutral, and able to negotiate the terms of therapy so that problems become the evident focus of treatment.

## Goals of Counseling and Ideal Outcomes

The ideal outcome of Strategic Problem Solving Therapy is problem resolution. Haley (1987) stated:

> *The first obligation of a therapist is to change the presenting problem offered. If that is not accomplished, the therapy is a failure. Therapists should not let themselves be distracted into other matters so that they forget this primary goal. Moreover, by focusing on the symptoms the therapist gains the most leverage and has the most opportunity for bringing about change. It is the presenting problem that most interests the client; by working with that the therapist can gain great cooperation. If a person with symptoms is offered as a problem, the therapist may believe that changes must take place in that family system before that person can change. Yet he should not try to convince the family that the real problem lies in the family and not in the person. Such a distinction is artificial. The therapist who engages in pointless debate with the family about the cause of the problem, attempts to educate them about family communication, or tries to persuade them to accept "family therapy" may fail to achieve his or her ends. The goal is not to teach the family about their malfunctioning system but to change the family sequences so that the presenting problems are resolved. (p. 135)*

The actual mechanisms of change do not have to be understood. Only effective procedures and techniques for instigating and maintaining change need to be mastered by the therapist. The therapist, then, must be the consummate interpersonal technician.

# General Procedures

## Assessment

Assessment occurs throughout strategic therapy, as the therapist continually reassesses whether clients are responding to directives. However, in the first session, the therapist makes a concerted effort to define significant relationship dynamics, primarily through the five-stage process. For example, in the first session, the therapist observes children closely, since they are reflective of the family's status. For example, a symptomatic child is viewed as reflecting a symptomatic parental relationship. Haley (1987) stated: "If there is a child problem in a family, the adults are usually in disagreement about how to deal with the child. Sometimes they show this disagreement immediately and sometimes they present a united front in the beginning" (p. 16). Haley is very alert to triadic interactions, and recognizes their significance to social systems theory. Triangles allow for coalitions. They also involve hierarchy, the power structure of a family. Parents, for example, are hierarchically one level up from children in terms of the potential to wield power. Power is an issue that Haley addresses directly in his work. He believes at the practical level that power cannot be denied in therapy He disagreed with Bateson (see Bateson, 1979) on the issue of power. Bateson felt that power led to a false epistemology, that power was seductive, and that power was ultimately destructive when applied in interpersonal relations. Bateson viewed interpersonal relations within a fully circular epistemological framework, which is inconsistent with the linear influence implied by ''power.'' Haley, on the other hand, makes full use of power in his therapy, and he attempts to assess power hierarchy (primarily through triads) in the early stages of therapy. However, Haley's emphasis is more on communication than hierarchy. And if one were to define hierarchy according to Haley's perspective, one would ultimately be describing the digital and especially analogic communication patterns involved in cross-generational interactions.

As the therapist begins to get a sense of the relational dynamics of the family as organized around a symptom, he or she must maintain only tentative conclusions. Haley (1987) stated: ''The therapist may be misled and therefore ideas should not be too firm. Observation gives information that can be tested as the session continues'' (p. 17). And it is critical, from a strategic position, that the therapist not share his or her observations with family members. Haley stated:

> *It is also important that the therapist* should not share his observations with the family. *If the problem child is sitting between mother and father, the therapist may make a tentative hypothesis that the child's problem serves a function in their marriage. But that hypothesis should not be taken too seriously without further data, and the therapist should* never *comment to the family about the child's position. (p. 17)*

Being able to observe changes in family patterns at the analogic level means assigning digital explanations of problems to a secondary role. It is anticipated that family members will demonstrate their changes through observable relational dynamics. The therapist puts his or her effort into observing and affecting analogic (informal, nonverbal, contextual) family communication, rather than simply presenting information digitally to clients in therapy.

## Treatment/Remediation

Strategic Problem Solving Therapy involves giving directives. Treatment is a process of giving directives and assessing client responses. Haley (1987) stated: ''It is, of course, essential that a therapist know how to give directives so that they are carried out. It is a misfortune that most clinical training has not included this skill'' (p. 56). The purposes of directives include: (a) to get people to behave differently; (b) to make the therapist important in the lives of clients—because the therapist has taken action the family must react; and (c) to gather more information—the response of clients to directives is educational of family interaction and dynamics.

Directives are prescribed tasks. Haley (1987) believed they must be precisely and confidently given (not just suggested), targeted to involve everyone in the family, and reviewed before the family leaves the therapy session to ensure that everyone understands what is to happen. Directives may be straightforward (e.g., ''I want you and your spouse to go on a date alone''); or paradoxical. (e.g., prescribing the symptom and expecting resistance). The intent, however, is always the same, to change the relational dynamics around the symptom.

Some examples of directives used by Haley (1987) as described in *Problem Solving Therapy* include:

> *A father who is siding with his small daughter against the wife may be required to wash the sheets when the daughter wets the bed. This task will tend to disengage daughter and father or cure the bedwetting.*
>
> . . .
>
> *A mother and father who need an excuse to be affectionate with each other may be asked to show affection to each other in an obvious way at set times to "teach their child" how to show affection.*
>
> . . .
>
> *A husband and wife with sexual problems may be required to have sex relations only on the living room floor for a period of time. This task changes the context and so the struggle.*
>
> . . .
>
> *A man who is afraid to apply for a job may be asked to go for a job interview at a place where he would not take the job if he got it, thereby practicing in a safe way. (pp. 68–69)*

Assessment of family responses to directives always involves the three possible outcomes described by Haley: a faithfully carried out directive; failure to carry out a directive fully; or failure to carry out a directive partially. In every case, the therapist must be prepared to have an alternative action—another directive. In this sense, Strategic Problem Solving Therapy is a very structured treatment process.

## Case Management

Sessions are generally scheduled for about once a week, although if the family is demonstrating a great deal of emotion (a crisis), sessions may be scheduled more frequently. As problems begin to resolve, intervals between sessions may be lengthened, until there is termination. Usually, one goal of therapy is to have the client feel that he or she does not need the therapist anymore; it is wise to manage a case so that the client does not act dependently upon the therapist throughout the process of therapy.

Sessions may last an hour, or they may be shortened or lengthened strategically. If a family has failed to carry out a directive, the following therapy session may be made longer (and more expensive). If a family has carried out a directive, the session may be shorter (and less expensive). In this way, clients are rewarded for doing what needs to be done.

Case recording is recommended. Case notes should record the presenting problems, the relational problem formulation, the directives given, and the actions taken by the family.

## Specialized Techniques

**1.** *Straightforward, front-door directives*. Front-door directives simply direct the clients to do what is asymptomatic. Some clients will merely follow the directive of the therapist. However, a strategic therapist does not just give good advice. Rather, directives are always targeted at the sequences of interpersonal interactions at the foundation of problematic behaviors. Front-door directives, therefore, are directed tasks that attempt to straightforwardly affect relations of significance. To direct a husband to take his wife on a picnic at a time when otherwise she would be involved in problematic family interactions is a front-door directive. It affects a relationships among family members, and it does so by asking family members to do what the therapist really wants them to do.

**2.** *Back-door directives*. Back-door directives ask the family members to do something when the therapist does not expect them to do it. A back-door directive anticipates resistance among family members, or as Haley (1987) stated, the therapist, ''wants the [family] members to resist him so they will change'' (p. 76). Paradoxical directives are classically back-door. To tell an insomniac to set his alarm every hour on the hour all night long to monitor and to record his wakefulness is actually an opportunity for a resistant client to rebel by not setting the alarm and by sleeping. To instruct a mother who is overbabying her child to continue to do this because she is doing it incorrectly, and then to direct her to baby the child in a way that it is inconvenient, is a means of arousing resistance in the mother. In both of these cases, the therapist has anticipated that the client will rebel against the directive of the therapist, thereby demonstrating appropriate resolution of problem behavior.

**3.** *Front-door directives by metaphoric implication*. A front-door directive by analogy builds on the metaphoric nature of human interaction. Milton Erickson was a master of metaphoric directives (a metaphor is something that is not literally true). Sometimes, clients are unable to openly deal with their problems, and Erickson would use an analogous situation to direct clients as to what to do. Haley (1973) describe one of Erickson's directives as follows:

> As a typical example, if Erickson is dealing with a married couple who have a conflict over sexual relations and would rather not discuss it directly, he will approach the problem metaphorically. He will choose some aspect of their lives that is analogous to sexual relations and change that as a way of changing the sexual behavior. He might, for example, talk to them about having dinner together and draw them out on their preferences. He will discuss with them how the wife likes appetizers before dinner, while the husband prefers to dive right into the meat and potatoes. Or the wife might prefer a quiet and leisurely dinner, while the husband, who is quick and direct, just wants the meal over with. If the couple begin to connect what they are saying with sexual relations, Erickson will ''drift rapidly'' away to other topics, and then he will return to the analogy. He might end such a conversation with a directive that the couple arrange a pleasant dinner on a particular evening that is satisfactory to both of them. When

*successful, this approach shifts the couple from a more pleasant dinner to more pleasant sexual relations without their being aware that he has deliberately set this goal. (pp. 27–28)*

It is important to direct *actions and behaviors* (not just thoughts or feelings) through such metaphoric directives; in this way, actions will be affected by the accomplishment of analogous actions.

**4.** *Encouraging controlled relapses.* Encouraging controlled relapses is a special kind of paradoxical strategy. The question arises: What does the therapist do when a client's unwanted behavior appears to spontaneously remit after a paradoxical maneuver with resistant clients? Haley (1987) stated:

*The therapist must accept the change when it happens and let the family put her down by proving her wrong. If she wants to ensure that the change will continue, she might say to the members that probably the change is only temporary and they will relapse. Then the family will continue the change to prove to her that it is not temporary. Talking about the change being temporary serves to block off a relapse. (p. 78)*

The therapist might go so far as to plan a relapse, paradoxically asking the family members if they can find something valuable in their old ''miserable'' ways (Haley, 1973, 1987). A directed relapse also acts to make planned what previously occurred spontaneously (symptoms), and paradoxically, a directed relapse acts to put symptoms under control. In effect, the therapist cannot lose. If the symptom returns, it has reappeared under the therapist's direction and, therefore, it is under control; if the symptom does not return, then problems have been solved.

These four techniques represent some basic approaches to the directive counseling of the strategic problem solving therapist.

## Recent Developments or Criticisms

One of Haley's more recent works is a book by the title of *Ordeal Therapy: Unusual Ways to Change Behavior* (Haley, 1984). Again, as with Haley's book, *Uncommon Therapy* (Haley, 1973), he referred heavily to the work of Milton Erickson. Erickson used ''ordeals'' to produce change in clients. He would direct clients to do something so burdensome as part of the symptomatic behavior that being symptom free was a relief. Haley described one of Erickson's cases—an insomniac, whom Erickson directed to polish the floors into the late hours of night. Therefore, Erickson designed an ordeal that the patient would rather avoid by sleeping. Haley (1984) stated the ''rather simple premise'' of ordeal therapy as follows: ''If one makes it more difficult for a person to have a symptom than to give it up, the person will give up the symptom'' (p. 5).

Haley (1984) stated that ordeals should be ''appropriate to the problem of the person who wants to change'' (p. 6). It should be ''more severe than the problem''

(p. 6). Haley believed that it is best for an ordeal to be something that is good for the person. Just as polishing the floors is good for the insomniac (polished floors are always attractive), so too should other ordeals do something that is valuable in some way to the client. Ordeals should be something to which the person cannot easily object. Additionally, it should not violate a person's moral standards, and it should not harm the patient or other individuals. Haley stated: "Sometimes the person must go through it repeatedly to recover from the symptom. At other times the mere threat of an ordeal brings recovery" (p. 7). Regardless, Haley presents ordeals as effective strategies for facilitating behavior change.

At first glance, the idea of treating individuals through ordeals appears to indicate that Haley is abandoning the systemic-relational framework so characteristic of his earlier works. Although Haley is amenable to working with individuals when creating therapeutic ordeals, he still frames concerns within a relational context. Haley (1984) stated:

> The ordeal is a procedure that forces a change, and there are consequences to that. The therapist needs to be aware that symptoms are a reflection of a confusion in a social organization, usually a family. The existence of a symptom indicates that the hierarchy of an organization is incorrect. Therefore, when a therapist resolves a symptom in this way, he or she is forcing a change in a complex organization that was previously stabilized by the symptom. If, for example, a wife has a symptom that helps maintain her husband in a superior position as the one taking care of her, that changes rapidly when an ordeal requires the wife to abandon the symptom. She and her husband must negotiate a new relationship contract that does not include symptomatic behavior. . . . It is best for a therapist to understand the function of a symptom in the social organization of the client. If not able to understand it, the therapist must resolve the symptom warily while watching for repercussions and changes. (p. 16)

In fact, Haley has continued to take up the systemic-relational banner, arguing in support of systemic-relational interpretations even when dealing with otherwise assumed organic-medical concerns (see the discussion in chapter 1 and the debate between Haley, 1989, and Stein, 1989). Although Ordeal Therapy often targets the individual in therapy, it is still conceptualized within a systemic-relational problematic context.

There have been many criticisms of Haley's approach. His work has been portrayed as highly manipulative and even deceitful, especially as related to back-door or paradoxical techniques. Haley (1987) devoted a full chapter of *Problem Solving Therapy* to the topic of ethical issues, in which he argues for the validity and usefulness of his approach. He argued that concealment of certain information in certain relationships is basic to human relations, and that to think otherwise is to deny the nature of human interaction. He also argued that all therapy is directive, no matter how nondirective it may appear at face value. He argued that the therapist must assess the short-term effect of interventions, but also must assess long-term effects on the therapeutic relationship. He stated:

*The question in this situation is not so much a question of whether the therapist is telling a lie but whether she is behaving unethically. Even if he is deceiving the patient for his own good, is it ethical to deceive a patient? If it is essential for the cure that deceit be used, it might be justified on that basis. However, one must also be concerned about the long-term effect of a person experiencing an expert as an untrustworthy person, which may be more harmful than the continuation of the symptom. (p. 226)*

Haley essentially argued that a therapist must be ethically grounded in his approach, and client welfare (short- and long-term) must be a major determining factor of the appropriateness of therapeutic techniques. Effectively, then, it is considered ethical to "trick" a person out of a problem, "a method traditionally used by shamans" (Haley, 1987, p. 226), so long as it is in the short- and long-term interests of the client.

It can also be argued that Haley's approach, being highly behavioral, does not address underlying problems. For Haley, however, just solving the problem is not enough. He is alert to underlying social-relational factors that might begin or maintain a symptom. He, on the other hand, does not believe in individual psychological problems or traits per se. He frames underlying processes in systemic-relational terms (e.g., family organization), just as he frames presenting problems in systemic-relational terms. He would argue that the social context cannot be ignored when solving problems.

Although there has been some empirical support of the strategic approach with certain disorders (see Gurman, Kniskern, & Pinsof, 1986), the empirical jury is still out on Strategic Problem Solving Therapy.

Haley's approach has become very popular and is regarded as one of the leading therapies among systemic-relational paradigm adherents. However, his view and others like it have been criticized as being too warlike in their language and technique. It is as if the therapist is at odds with the client-system, attempting to outmaneuver and outwit the family. Haley's perspective places the therapist at odds with what might be considered the family's underlying relational dynamic, of which the family members might not even be aware. The therapist is continually attempting to stay one step ahead of the nonconscious relational process of the family, as if to prevent defeat by the family. Some theorists view this as a dichotomized and contrived view of therapeutic interaction; and this view is especially criticized by those theorists who have attempted to incorporate problem formulation within the therapeutic system (see Hoffman, 1988).

Criticisms aside, the strategic approach has become a popular and highly used family therapy approach.

## Paradigm Fit

### Focus of Study

Haley's Strategic Problem Solving Therapy is a systemic-relational therapy. Although problems are the focus of study, problems are distinctly and consistently defined within a relational context. Relationships, then, become the target of intervention. Relationship issues are viewed as underlying presenting problems.

Haley (1987) has defined a structured therapeutic process that facilitates the manifestation of relationship issues in problem formulation and problem resolution. Regardless, Haley does not explain his diagnostic findings to clients in a classic organic-medical sense. He deals with relationships while seemingly dealing with problems as things unto themselves. His approach must seem creative to clients who tend to think concretely about problems and linearly about solutions (if A is a problem, then the cause of A must be stopped). Haley's approach, however, engages reciprocal interpersonal interactions, attempting to alter the ways people act around each other in specified settings. He focuses on analogic (informal, nonverbal, and contextual) communication in both problem definition and in defining interventions, as opposed to focusing on digital (formal, technical) communication. In this way, Haley's approach is sharply consistent with systemic-relational paradigm propositions and tenets.

## View of Nature of Reality

Reality is viewed as composed of relationships. Relationships are viewed as communication *processes* between people. Relationships, however, can be structural to a degree, as reflected in concepts such as family organization and family structure. The act of viewing relationships, nonetheless, is always accomplished from a system of relationships, a viewing system, so to speak, which is implicit in Haley's continual reference to the individual relationships that affected his view of counseling. Haley views the therapeutic observing system as a system with power, in a linear sense, within a societal context. Although ideas about power in the therapeutic relationship break with pure Batesonian systemic epistemology, Haley has been clear about defining the context of therapy and the limits of power in this regard. In a sense, Haley's work has been influenced by two divergent systems of thought—cybernetic/systemic epistemology and hypnotherapy. His work is an integration of these two forces.

## Consonance with Paradigm Propositions and Tenets

There is clear consistency between Haley's Strategic Problem Solving Therapy and systemic-relational propositions and tenets. Relationships are the focus of study. Systems of relationships can be defined as significant and isolated for study and intervention. Cause is nonlinear within defined relationships (e.g., mom or dad is not the cause of a son's problems; rather their triadic relationship dynamics are out of sync). Change occurs through communication, as communication is relationship. And the focus is on analogic as opposed to digital communication. Individual disorders do not exist outside of relationships, as all psychological concepts are redefined within a relational explanatory framework. Finally, Strategic Problem Solving Therapists attempt primarily to influence relationships.

## Chapter Conclusion

Haley's Strategic Problem Solving Therapy is one of the most paradigm-aligned therapies presented in this book. It is an excellent example of how systemic-relational thinking translates to practice with problems that can be viewed by others as individual-specific. In the end, Haley's approach always turns to *external* relational factors as significant to the definition and solution of a problem. Haley is a master of techniques designed to produce changes. He is the consummate interpersonal technician. And he is strategic in his attempts to help people help themselves to change distressful situations.

# References

Bateson, G. (1972). *Steps to an ecology of mind*. New York: Ballantine.

Bateson, G. (1979). *Mind and nature: A necessary unity*. New York: Bantam.

Bateson, G., Jackson, D., Haley, J., & Weakland, J. (1956). Toward a theory of schizophrenia. *Behavioral Science, 1*, 251–264.

Erickson, M. H., Rossi, E. L., & Rossi, S. I. (1976). *Hypnotic realities*. New York: Irvington Publishers.

Gurman, A. S., Kniskern, D. P., & Pinsof, W. M. (1986). Research on the process and outcome of marital and family therapy. In S. L. Garfield & A. E. Bergin (Eds.), *Handbook of psychotherapy and behavior change* (3rd ed.). New York: John Wiley & Sons.

Haley, J. (1963). *Strategies of Psychotherapy*. New York: Grune & Stratton.

Haley, J. (1973). *Uncommon therapy*. New York: W. W. Norton.

Haley, J. (1976). *Problem solving therapy*. New York: Harper & Row.

Haley, J. (1987). *Problem solving therapy*. (2nd ed.). New York: Jossey-Bass.

Haley, J. (1984). *Ordeal therapy*. San Francisco: Jossey-Bass.

Haley, J. (1989). The effect of long-term outcome studies on the therapy of schizophrenia. *Journal of Marital and Family Therapy, 15*, 127–132.

Haley, J., & Hoffman, L. (1967). *Techniques of family therapy*. New York: Basic Books.

Hoffman, L. (1988). A constructivist position for family therapy. *The Irish Journal of Psychology, 9*, 110–129.

Stein, L. (1989). The effect of long-term outcome studies on the therapy of schizophrenia: A critique. *Journal of Marital and Family Therapy, 15*, 133–138.

Watzlawick, P., Beavin, J. H., & Jackson, D. D. (1967). *Pragmatics of human communication: A study of interactional patterns, pathologies, and paradoxes*. New York: W. W. Norton.

Watzlawick, P., Weakland, J., & Fisch, R. (1974). *Change: Principles of problem formation and problem resolution*. New York: W. W. Norton.

# _14_

# Structural Family Therapy:
## *An External Model Systemic-Relational Therapy Focusing on Family Structure*

STRUCTURAL FAMILY THERAPY is a systemic-relational therapy developed by Salvador Minuchin, MD, and his associates at the Philadelphia Child Guidance Clinic. Structural Family Therapy was developed in the late 1960s and early 1970s while Minuchin was the director (until 1975) of the Philadelphia Child Guidance Clinic. Minuchin refined his ideas in the years that followed as a trainer at the Family Therapy Training Center. In both positions, Minuchin would lead the development of a family counseling theory with an "emphasis on structural change as the main goal of therapy" (Colapinto, 1982, p. 112).

Structural family therapy is unique among the external model systemic-relational therapies because of its emphasis on the structure of families as a focus of study and as a target of intervention. Other externally oriented systemic-relational therapies tend to focus more on communication as a target of intervention. Minuchin, who had worked with severely disturbed and structurally different families from his earliest family practice (e.g., families of delinquents or anorexics), became acutely aware of the differences and significance of family organization and roles as they influence human behavior. In fact, the words *organization* and *roles* aptly and simply describe what is meant by Minuchin for the term *structure*. Structure refers to the patterns of interactions (which often become too rigid or stereotyped) that can be observed in families within a therapeutic context.

Minuchin's book entitled *Families and Family Therapy* (Minuchin, 1974) and his coauthored text entitled *Family Therapy Techniques* (Minuchin & Fishman, 1981) are used as primary resources in summarizing "Structural Family Therapy." Readers are directed to those books for a detailed discussion of theoretical tenets and techniques. For detailed case studies, Minuchin's (1984) *Family Kaleidoscope* is recommended.

## Salvador Minuchin, MD, a Biographical Sketch

Salvador Minuchin was born in Argentina on October 13, 1921. Little is known of his childhood, but in a book Minuchin wrote with Fishman (Minuchin & Fishman, 1981), there is a section that presents Minuchin's own family as an example of family theory. In that section, Minuchin described a difficult period of his life and the importance of a support system:

> *When I was eleven years old, I needed to go to school away from home, since my home town had only five grades, and I lived for a year with the family of my Aunt Sofia. (Although my aunt was married for over fifty years to my Uncle Bernard, until his death, in my nuclear family the head-of-the-house position was always given to the member of my parents' family and not to the in-law). The year I spent in her house was the worst of my entire life. Away from home, friends, and familiar context, I grew depressed, had nightmares, felt isolated, was bullied in school by a bunch of "city kids," did poorly in my studies, and failed two subjects. I probably needed psychological help, only nobody noticed how I felt. The next year was somewhat better. I moved to the house of a cousin who had young children, shared a room with another cousin my age, and developed a friendship with three other adolescents. We formed a four-muske-teers club that lasted throughout high school, so that by the time my family moved to the city, I had already developed a support system. (pp. 75–76)*

Given his support system, Minuchin must have done very well, since he went from failing subjects to earning an MD degree (in 1947 at the University of Cordoba, Argentina). In 1948 he served as a First Lieutenant in the Israeli Army after a residency in pediatrics and child psychiatry at the University of Argentina. He later moved to New York, where he obtained a fellowship in child psychiatry, and he followed the fellowship with an additional residency in psychiatry (in Valhalla, New York). He received training in Psycho-analysis, which he completed in 1967.

From 1952 through 1981 he held several positions that directly relate to his theoretical propositions. From 1952 to 1954 he was the "Psychiatric Director" of the Youth Aliyah Department of Disturbed Children in Israel. From 1960 to 1966 he was the "Director of Training in Family Therapy" at the Wiltwyck School for Boys in New York. At Wiltwyck, he also directed a research unit. From 1965 to 1975 he was the Director of the Philadelphia Child Guidance Clinic and a psychiatrist with the Children's Hospital of Philadelphia. From 1975 to 1981, remaining at the Philadelphia

*Salvador Munichin*

Child Guidance Clinic, he took a position there as the Director of the Family Therapy Training Center. During his time at the Philadelphia Child Guidance Clinic he was very productive: his most foundational theoretical works were published during his tenure there. While in Philadelphia, he also served as a professor at the University of Pennsylvania School of Medicine.

At the time of this writing, Minuchin is the Director of Family Studies, Inc., in New York City. He is also a Research Professor of Psychiatry at the New York University Medical Center.

Minuchin has received many awards and honors in his lifetime, including the "Distinguished Achievement in Family Therapy Award" in 1982 from the American Family Therapy Association. He received the "Family Therapy Award" in 1984 from the American Association for Marriage and Family Therapy.

Dr. Minuchin is married and has two children.

## The Foundational Theory

### The Target of Counseling

Minuchin (1974) described Structural Family Therapy as follows:

> *A body of theory and techniques that approaches the individual in his social context. Therapy based on this framework is directed toward changing the organization of the family. When the structure of the family group is transformed, the positions of members in that group are altered accordingly. As a result, each individual's experiences change. (p. 2)*

Minuchin works from the assumption that individuals are not bound by mentality into set ways of reacting; rather, he views the individual as an "acting and reacting member of social groups" (p. 2). He believes that to deal with a person's expressed problem individually is to build an artificial boundary between the person and his or her social context. His therapy further rests on three axioms: (a) "that context affects inner processes"; (b) "that changes in context produce changes in the individual"; and (c) "that the therapist's behavior is significant in change" (p. 9). As is evident, Minuchin's ideas are clearly consistent with basic systemic-relational tenets discussed in chapter 11. The target of counseling is the relational context of a problem, most usually the family's organization and structure.

What makes Minuchin's (1974) approach unique as a marital and family therapeutic approach is the focus on family structure, substructure, and boundary. Minuchin defines "family structure" as "the invisible set of functional demands that organizes the ways in which family members interact. . . . Repeated transactions establish patterns of how, when, and to whom to relate, and these patterns underpin the system" (p. 51). Essentially these transactional patterns are communication patterns that come to regulate the behaviors of family members. Because Minuchin believes a "power hierarchy" is a universal rule governing family functioning, transactional patterns take the form of *roles,* which are best understood as *task orientations within rule structures.* These roles also help to define subsystems—relational substructures within the family that are always composed of fewer relationships than the number of relationships in the larger family system. Minuchin believed that subsystems are "formed by generation, by sex, by interest, or by function" (p. 52). Subsystems are very important to families, because they are the means by which a family "differentiates and carries out its functions" (p. 52).

Any person can belong to a number of subsystems in a family. For example, in a family of four with one male child and one elder female child, the female child can be considered part of the "children/sibling" subsystem. She is also a part of the "female" subsystem. In the female subsystem, the female child might have less power compared to the mother (who is a member of the parental/executive subsystem). The female child, however, may have more power in the children/sibling subsystem than the younger brother. Certain roles are carried out within these subsystems, as within the larger family system.

Minuchin (1974) defined boundaries as "the rules defining who participates, and how" in family subsystems. Fundamentally, these boundaries define the "shoulds" and "should nots" of individual behavior within and between subsystems. For example, in a household with a grandmother, her overinvolvement in parentlike decision making might be greeted by verbal or nonverbal expressions by the parents of a rule that her responsibilities are limited in this regard. Again it is important to note that communication plays an important part in the determination of a boundary. Minuchin believes that boundaries, and thus rule communication, must be clear. He also strongly infers that they should be fair. In regard to the fairness of a boundary, judgment enters in from a therapeutic standpoint. A therapist must assess whether, in fact, individuals are fulfilling their roles appropriately. For example, parents are expected to have some authority (power) over their children. Minuchin stated:

*Parenting requires the capacity to nurture, guide, and control. The proportions of these elements depend on the children's developmental needs and the parents' capacity. But parenting always requires the use of authority. Parents cannot carry out their executive functions unless they have the power to do so. (p. 58)*

Certainly, Minuchin's ideas about structure, hierarchy, and boundaries must be viewed within a larger Western cultural context, where childrearing is primarily the responsibility of the parents and where children must reconcile their needs with the expressed needs of individuals in power positions in the family. At the same time, Minuchin believed that children should have some level of autonomy. This autonomy is manifest in the children/sibling subsystem, which should have rights to privacy, personal interests, and exploration. The fairness of boundaries, therefore, appears to be relative to societal context and the prevailing social mores.

Obviously, in certain situations, certain patterns or boundaries will be preferred; for example, with parents of young children, it is preferred that the parents, in coalition, fulfill the executive role in the family. In a one-working-parent family, an elder child may assume some of the executive function. There is role flexibility depending on the larger context of a family's functioning.

Although terms like *structure, subsystems,* and *boundaries* are useful in understanding how families operate, these terms relate to stabilizing factors within the family. In and of themselves, they are not useful in understanding how family systems change. In fact, Minuchin (1974) went into great detail about the need for families to be adaptable, and he described the process of change as an accommodation of inside and outside stresses on the family. He hypothesized that stress comes from four sources: (a) contact by one family member with extrafamilial forces (e.g., a stressful employer-employee relationship for a family breadwinner); (b) contact by the whole family with extrafamilial forces (e.g., an environmental catastrophe or economic depression); (c) transitions in the family evolution (e.g., when development of individuals affects role function—children becoming adults, as a case in point); and (d) idiosyncratic factors (related to individual biological differences in the family, such as physical or intellectual disability). Stressors, of course, can produce healthy changes, unhealthy changes, or no change at all in a family. Family therapy becomes an issue when the family, or at least one of its members, becomes maladaptive or symptomatic; then change becomes necessary.

## The Process of Counseling

Colapinto (1982) described the process of Structural Family Therapy as follows:

*Therapeutic change is then the process of helping the family to outgrow its stereotyped patterns, of which the presenting problem is a part. This process transpires within a special context, the* therapeutic system, *which offers a unique chance to challenge the rules of the family. The privileged position of the therapist allows him to request from the family members different behaviors and to invite different perceptions, thus altering their interaction and perspective. The family then has an opportunity to experience transactional patterns that have not been allowed under its prevailing homeostatic rules. The system's limits are probed and pushed, its narrow self-definitions are questioned; in the process, the family's capacity to tolerate and handle stress or conflict increases, and its perceived reality becomes richer, more complex. (p. 121)*

Essentially, the therapist attempts to "join" the family, to enter into its interactive process, and to affect its ways of operating.

Minuchin and Fishman (1981) described the "joining" process as follows:

*Joining a family is more an attitude than a technique, and it is the umbrella under which all therapeutic transactions occur. Joining is letting the family know that the therapist understands them and is working with and for them. Only under his protection can the family have the security to explore alternatives, try the unusual, and change. Joining is the glue that holds the therapeutic system together. (pp. 31–32)*

Joining is the equivalent of establishing a therapeutic relationship. But joining the family does not mean that the therapist must act congruently with the family process. In fact, the therapist, once accommodated by the family, is left free to "jar" the family members (Minuchin & Fishman, 1981, p. 32). Joining, therefore, means the therapist will be accepted to some degree even if he or she begins to challenge the structure and rules of the family. Joining, therefore, also means that the family has become somewhat invested in the actions of the therapist.

Beyond joining the family, the process of Minuchin's (1974) Structural Family Therapy can be broken down into four dimensions. Note the word *dimensions* is used, instead of the word *stages,* since the presented dimensions may actually overlap in time. These dimensions *should not* be considered sequential phases of therapy. The four dimensions are: (a) structural diagnosis; (b) probing within the therapeutic system; (c) sparking transformation; and (d) restructuring through a therapeutic contract. Essentially, Minuchin joins the family and analyzes its structure through exploring coalitions, subsystems, and the power hierarchy. He broadens the focus of the problem to include family interaction and structure, which in most cases will become the target of intervention. Importantly, he comes to an agreement with the family on the nature of the problem and on the goals for change (a therapeutic contract). And finally, he intervenes to create imbalance and to move the family toward a new, more adaptive structure.

### Counselor Role

Minuchin believed that the therapist must take a leadership role as he or she joins the family in therapy. Beyond developing a therapeutic alliance, the family therapist must *unbalance* the system to create change. This may be accomplished by forming a coalition with one or more family members against other family members. Although this may appear unfair, Minuchin believed that ''when the therapist unbalances a family system by joining with one member, the other members experience stress'' (p. 113). Further: ''Change, through therapy, like any other family change, is accompanied by stress, and the therapeutic system must be capable of dealing with it'' (p. 114). Stress, then, can be viewed as the family therapist's ally. In Minuchin's (1974) book, *Families and Family Therapy,* he gave the following example:

> *A family comes into therapy because the husband has migraines. He is ashamed of his humble origins, having been the first of his family to go to college. He married a woman whose family he admired for their intellectual accomplishments, and he has great respect for his wife's opinions. She is the rule setter, to whom he accommodates and defers. The therapeutic goal in this case is to change the relative power positions of the spouses, transforming the family structure so that the man will gain status, securing more respect from his wife and achieving self-respect. To that end, the therapist affiliates with the man in the initial sessions, supporting him, and sometimes joining him in a coalition that is critical of the wife. (p. 114)*

As is demonstrated in the previous quotation, taking sides through coalitions is done with the therapeutic goal clearly in mind.

Minuchin (1974) presented a number of varied therapeutic techniques to accomplish the therapeutic contract. In order to restructure the family, he believed that the therapist must accept the role of director as well as actor. In describing the role of the therapist, Minuchin stated:

> *He creates scenarios, choreographs, highlights themes, and leads family members to improvise within the constraints of the family drama. But he also uses himself, entering into alliances and coalitions, creating, strengthening, or weakening boundaries, and opposing or supporting transactional patterns. (pp. 138–139)*

In his text, Minuchin (1974) listed seven categories of ''restructuring operations.'' Many of those operations are further described in Minuchin and Fishman (1981). They are listed and briefly defined in the ''Specialized Techniques'' section of this chapter.

## Goals of Counseling and Ideal Outcomes

Minuchin (1974) defined a dysfunctional family as a system that has responded to ''internal or external demands for change by stereotyping its functioning'' (p. 110). He believed that structure in maladaptive families becomes so rigid that it blocks any possible alternative transactional pattern. Often, there is involvement of an identified patient, IP (an individual in the family), and, in fact, the IP may have been treated by a mental health professional individually for expressed concerns. Given an identified patient with the possibility or likelihood of family involvement, or given a dysfunctional family as a presented problem, the family therapist's function is to help the identified patient and/or the family by facilitating a transformation of the family.

Colapinto (1982) defined the goals of Structural Family Therapy as follows:

> *The basic goal of structural family therapy is the restructuralization of the family's system of transactional rules, such that the interactional reality of the family becomes more flexible, with an expanded availability of alternative ways of dealing with each other. By releasing family members from their stereotyped positions and functions, this restructuralization enables the system to mobilize its underutilized resources and to improve its ability to cope with stress and conflict. (p. 122)*

One of the main tasks of the therapist is to affect the structural homeostasis of the family that has supported the unwanted or symptomatic behaviors. Once the family organization and structure does not support unwanted behaviors, and once the family demonstrates its ability to sustain its changes in the face of family stressors, then therapy is no longer needed.

## General Procedures

### Assessment

Assessment and the "planning" process described by Minuchin and Fishman (1981) appear to go hand in hand. Planning, according to Minuchin and Fishman, is not a static process. They believed that the governing structure of the family only becomes known to the therapist as he or she "joins" the family, which takes time. Therefore, the therapist develops some preliminary hypotheses about the family, which he or she must be willing to discard as he or she becomes accommodated by the family. Minuchin and Fishman stated:

> *The therapist forms an idea of the family as a whole upon first examination of certain basic aspects of its structure. From the simplest information gathered on a phone call setting up the first appointment, or recorded on a clinic intake sheet, the therapist can develop some assumptions about the family. For instance, how many people are in the family and where do they live? What are the ages of the family members? Is one of the normal transitional points that stress every family a factor here? The presenting problem may be another clue that suggests areas of possible strength and weakness in each client family. From these simple elements, the therapist will develop some hunches about the family to guide her first probes into the family organization. (p. 51)*

Minuchin and Fishman (1981) described several "family shapes" that they felt were "commonly encountered" in therapy and helpful for beginning therapists to know, including "the pas de deux, three generation, shoe, accordion, fluctuating, and foster" (p. 51). The "pas de deux" structure is simply a dyadic family—husband and wife, parent and child, etcetera—where there is great reliance on each other. The "three generation" family involves grandparents. "Shoe" families, named by the parable of the "old woman who lived in a shoe," are large, many-children families, where often elder children carry some parental responsibility. "Accordion" families are families where the absence of one parent is common, for instance, military families, or families of a traveling salesperson. Accordion families must be able to change rules and structures around the presence or absence of the often-absent parent. "Fluctuating" families are characterized by shifting contexts (frequent geographic moves) or shifting composition (the serial love affairs of a parent). Fluctuating families must be able to adjust to almost continuous change and stress. "Foster" families are by definition temporary living arrangements for children. Minuchin and Fishman defined several other family structures, including stepparent families; families with a ghost (a death or desertion); out-of-control families (where the control of at least one family member is an issue); and psychosomatic families (where one member demonstrates nonorganic physical symptoms). Minuchin and his collaborators have explored and given detailed guidance on treating many of these family types. For instance, Minuchin, Rosman, and Baker (1978) presented the results of detailed studies of psychosomatic families and provided useful information about how such families should be approached in therapy.

## Treatment/Remediation

Treatment is a process of challenging "the dysfunctional aspects of family homeostasis" (Minuchin & Fishman, 1981, p. 64). There are three main treatment "strategies" according to Structural Family Therapy. They are: (a) challenging the symptom; (b) challenging the family structure; and (c) challenging the family reality (Minuchin & Fishman, 1981). Each is briefly described as follows.

**1.**   Challenging the symptom is a means of influencing the family interactional patterns that have emerged around symptomatic behaviors. In fact, Structural Family Therapy has been developed around identified patients, usually children, and it is best applied in circumstances where there is an identified child patient. Remembering that "the problem is not the identified patient, but certain family interactional patterns" (Minuchin & Fishman, 1981, p. 67), symptoms can be used as a means to affect family functioning. Symptoms are viewed as a *family's response* to stress, and it is necessary to assess the interactional patterns around the symptom, and then to challenge the meanings associated with those patterns and the patterns themselves. The focus around a symptom, then, is dualistic—the symptom is viewed as representative of family dysfunction under stress, while at the same time the family's roles and operational organization around the symptom must be viewed. The targets, however, are the organization and roles operating around the symptom, and the therapist must challenge those roles and the family organization. For example, with a misbehaving and symptomatic child, the father might have taken the authority role and the mother the protective role; the therapist might attempt to realign those roles so that the parents are in an egalitarian authoritative relationship over the child, where decisions are overtly expressed as shared parental decisions. In this way, the organization of the family is altered around the symptomatic behavior of the child.

**2.**    Challenging the family structure often involves the strengthening or weakening of subsystem boundaries. For example, an overinvolved father and teenage daughter might be distanced through therapy, as the mother-daughter subsystem is strengthened. Or a parent-eldest child coalition may be weakened as the sibling subsystem is strengthened. Weakening or strengthening such boundaries involves rule setting and communication. Minuchin and Fishman (1981) stated:

> By challenging the rules that constrain people's experience, the therapist actualizes submerged aspects of their repertory. As a result, the family members perceive themselves and one another as functioning in a different way. The modification of context produces a change in experience. (p. 71)

By changing the contexts of interactions, it is assumed that individual behavior will change.

**3.**    Challenging the family reality is essentially a means to construct a new meaning system, primarily by reframing current behaviors, interactions, or family organizational patterns. Minuchin and Fishman (1981) stated:

> The therapist takes the data that the family offers and reorganizes it. The conflictual and stereotyped reality of the family is given a new framing. As the family members experience themselves and one another differently, new possibilities appear. (p. 71)

For example, with an anorexic patient, refusal to eat when commanded by her parents may be redefined as a sign that she is "strong enough to defeat both parents" (Minuchin & Fishman, 1981, p. 72), which thereby demonstrates a structural reversal of parent-child authority. Reframes, such as these, can produce a "startled new look at reality," according to the authors.

### Case Management

During the initial sessions the therapist essentially does "interactional diagnosis" (Minuchin, 1974). Upon understanding the identified problem within its relational context, Minuchin believes a "therapeutic contract" must be entered. Minuchin believed that, like diagnosis, the therapeutic contract evolves over time in therapy; it need not be a formal written thing, although Minuchin felt that it was necessary for treatment. In that sense, the therapeutic contract is an expressed consensus among family members about the nature of the problems and the goals of treatment.

Sessions can be arranged weekly, or more or less frequently as needed. Minuchin believes that videotaping is useful to beginning students (Minuchin & Fishman, 1981). Case recording should reflect the therapist's early hypotheses about the family structure and ongoing reassessments of structural factors affecting behavior. Interventions should be recorded in case notes, and case notes should reflect the structural emphasis. Results of interventions should be assessed in terms of structural changes in the family and resolution of symptomatic/unwanted behaviors.

## Specialized Techniques

**1.**   *Actualizing Family Transactional Patterns*. There are basically two purposes to actualizing family transactional patterns. First, Minuchin and Fishman (1981) described "enactment" as a special means of actualizing a transactional pattern. Enactment is simply a therapist's request for the family to demonstrate a problem within the therapeutic context, for example, asking family members of an anorexic to demonstrate what happens at dinner. Minuchin and Fishman (1981) stated:

> *The therapist constructs an interpersonal scenario in the session in which dysfunctional transactions among family members are played out. This transaction occurs in the context of the session, in the present, and in relation to the therapist. While facilitating this transaction, the therapist is in a position to observe the family members' verbal and nonverbal ways of signaling to each other and monitoring the range of tolerable transactions. (p. 79)*

By facilitating enactments, the therapist provides an opportunity for the family's modes of operation to reveal themselves. Second, enactments essentially ensure that the family members are capable of performing the activities prescribed in the therapeutic contract. The therapist finds "considerable value in making the family enact instead of describe" (Minuchin, 1974, p. 141) functional behavior in the family context. The therapist may ask them to demonstrate what they can do "right" or to open communication channels by directing family members to address each other. The therapist may also move family members around physically, since space is a metaphor for closeness or distance in relationships. The important point here is to ensure that the family can do what it is supposed to do.

**2.**   *Marking Boundaries or Boundary Making*. Minuchin strives for a healthy balance between *enmeshment* (lack of subsystem differentiation that discourages individual autonomy) and *disengagement* (inappropriately rigid boundaries that prevent intersubsystem stress crossover) in families. From the standpoint of the individual in a family, enmeshment translates to interdependency, whereas disengagement translates to autonomy at the expense of family involvement. In enmeshed families, rules must be clearly defined so that inappropriate crossover of roles is avoided. In disengaged families, new rules must be defined that present opportunity for effective interaction across otherwise impervious bounds. Essentially, marking boundaries involves both:

(a) establishing an amount of "psychological distance" between people; and (b) affecting the duration of interactions between people (Minuchin & Fishman, 1981).

**3.** *Escalating Stress.* As was mentioned earlier, Minuchin (1974) believed that stress was a necessary concomitant to change. To create stress within the therapeutic context he uses techniques such as blocking transactional patterns (to "dam the flow" in certain communication channels), emphasizing differences or highlighting disagreements, bringing forth hidden conflicts, or forming therapeutic coalitions. "Unbalancing," a specialized way of forming a therapeutic coalition, is a classic stress-producing technique. Minuchin and Fishman (1981) described unbalancing (as compared to boundary making) as follows:

> *In boundary making techniques the therapist aims at changing family subsystem membership, or at changing the distance between subsystems. In unbalancing, by contrast, the therapist's goal is to change the hierarchical relationship of the members of a subsystem. (p. 161)*

By aligning with one member of the family, for example, the therapist may affect the power hierarchy, thereby unbalancing the family homeostasis, and consequently the structure of the family. Unbalancing has a stress-producing effect, but with a positive structural outcome.

**4.** *Assigning Tasks.* Tasks may be assigned as part of the session or as homework in order "to create a framework within which the family members must function" (p. 150). However, Minuchin prefers to have families perform tasks as part of therapy. He prefers not to assign homework tasks to be accomplished outside of the therapeutic session. From Minuchin's perspective, restructuring occurs best when it occurs within the context of the therapeutic system.

**5.** *Utilizing Symptoms.* When it is evident that the family members are unable to make a therapeutic contract that focuses on anything other than the symptoms (of the identified patient or family as a whole), utilizing symptoms becomes a reasonable therapeutic approach. Symptoms can be made to be burdens, exacerbated within the therapeutic context, deemphasized, relabeled within a relational context, used to help parents become educators, or downplayed while other more manageable symptoms become the focus.

**6.** *Manipulating Mood.* The therapist may choose to raise or lower the level and/or type of mood in the family in order to trigger deviation counteractive forces or to model appropriate mood.

**7.** *Support, Education, and Guidance.* The therapist takes on an executive function as a model or educator. This may work when parents are in need of direct guidance about what is behaviorally expected of them.

In *Family Therapy Techniques*, Minuchin and Fishman (1981) defined several other techniques that are useful in family therapy, including: focus (zeroing in on therapeutically relevant data); intensity (techniques for increasing the affective component of interpersonal interactions); complementarity (demonstrating the interdependency of family members); constructions (changing the mental schema from which the family operates); paradoxes (directives that place clients in therapeutic double binds); and reframing (redefining behavior according to the therapeutic as opposed to the problematic reality). All of these techniques derive from a philosophy where relational context is the primary focus of study and treatment.

## Recent Developments or Criticisms

Minuchin's Structural Family Therapy has emerged as a major player among the predominant family counseling theories. Minuchin, in addition to delineating his model in detail related to both therapy and technique, has followed a research agenda. His research results strongly support the effectiveness of Structural Family Therapy. His most comprehensive research project was reported in the book entitled, *Psychosomatic Families: Anorexia Nervosa in Context* (Minuchin, Rosman & Baker, 1978). In that book, Minuchin and his associates reported success rates with anorexics of 85.6 percent, which compares quite favorably to other studies of treatment of anorexics. Minuchin et al. cited the results of other research studies using other combined or individual therapies—success rates were in the 70 percent range. However, the Minuchin et al. study did not have a control group design, so the internal validity of the results is questionable. Regardless, the findings strongly support the use of family therapy along with medical methods in the treatment of anorexia. Minuchin published other works involving psychosomatic disorders, also showing the effectiveness of family therapy; but, unfortunately as of the mid-1980s, there were no known independent studies replicating the results (Gurman, Kniskern, & Pinsof, 1986).

*Salvador Minuchin signing autographs at the 1990 "Evolution of Psychotherapy" conference.*

Related to concerns about Structural Family Therapy, one of the major criticisms of Minuchin's approach is that it is not significantly different from the approaches of the communication family theories, specifically Haley's (1963, 1973, 1976) Strategic Problem Solving Therapy. It can be argued that Minuchin's "structure" ultimately reduces to communication (e.g., rules), which is more directly what the communication family theorists target in therapy. Minuchin has countered that structure is the operating dynamic in symptom manifestation, and he has argued against any approach that simply targets the symptom as the problem.

On the issue of taking sides or forming coalitions to unbalance the family system, Minuchin's (1974) Structural Family Therapy is clearly different than other systemically oriented family therapies. Notably, Minuchin's position is different from Haley's (1976) position about maintaining balance by avoiding extended coalitions. Minuchin's position is also inconsistent with the ideas of Satir (1967), another seminal systemic therapist. Minuchin's therapeutic coalition may be viewed as a hidden agenda by some theorists. It assumes that the therapist knows what is best for the family. It does not appear to be mutual counselor-client activity. Regardless, the use of therapeutic coalitions demonstrates Minuchin's emphasis on structure as a primary focus in therapy.

Minuchin's Structural Family Therapy can also be viewed as sexist, if it supports patriarchal attitudes about the power hierarchy in families. In a sense, his approach assumes that the therapist knows best what should occur structurally within a cultural context. This position is antithetical to the more egalitarian feminist stand, where power is viewed as ideally shared between men and women, regardless of cultural context.

Therefore, although Structural Family Therapy is a well-recognized and respected family counseling theory, it is not unaffected by criticism by theorists in the mental health field.

## Paradigm Fit

### Focus of Study

The focus of study of Structural Family Therapy is "structure," which is clearly defined by Minuchin as repeated patterns of interaction. Interpersonal interaction, within a family context, is the focus of study. In fact, Minuchin appears profoundly systemic-relational in his thinking. Even though *structure* is a term that is associated with "thingness" in common usage, his definition of structure is clearly relational.

Minuchin's approach unquestionably assesses the individual in his or her relational context. Symptoms are not viewed as inherent to individuals; rather, they are viewed within the family matrix. His therapeutic method makes full use of the therapeutic relationship within the family context. Unlike the views of other theorists, the therapist is not looked at as outside the family looking in and attempting to create change. Rather, Minuchin's view is much more like the therapist engulfing himself or herself in the family patterns to affect change simultaneously from the inside and outside; that is, the therapist is viewed as an outside expert, yet the intent of Structural

Family Therapy is for the therapist to enter the structure of the family and to join the family members, while holding an important place *within* the family.

## View of Nature of Reality

Minuchin views things as "holons" (Minuchin & Fishman, 1981). A holon is simultaneously the whole of something and its parts. The individual self, therefore, is everything inherent in the individual, yet it is simultaneously and continuously affected by the social context, of which it is a part. It is a "self-in-context" position. This is quite different, for instance, from Satir's (1967) view of self-esteem, which is a prerequisite to healthy communication. Minuchin's concept of self-in-context does not separate self in any way from the social tapestry. Of self-in-context, Minuchin and Fishman (1981) stated: "There is a circular, continuous process of mutual affecting and reinforcing, which tends to maintain a fixed pattern" (p. 14). Minuchin (1974) stated: "The individual's psychic life is not entirely an internal process. The individual influences his context and is influenced by it in constantly recurring sequences of interaction" (p. 9). Minuchin's view of reality is very much relational, and he reframes otherwise concrete concepts into relational terms.

## Consonance with Paradigm Propositions and Tenets

Structural Family Therapy is a good example of theory consistent with the external model of the systemic-relational paradigm. In fact, it is one of the purist examples of a systemic-relational therapy. Working primarily from a practitioner's stance, Minuchin has developed a holisitic, family-focused therapeutic approach that incorporates state-of-the-art systemic concepts and theory. He uses such terms as *homeostasis, balance, roles,* and *rules.* He conceptualizes problems within their relational correlates. He targets patterns of interaction in therapy. And he assesses success by assessing the relational dynamics operating in the family rather than simply symptom removal. In this way, Structural Family Therapy is highly systemic-relational.

Regarding systemic-relational propositions and tenets, it is quite clear that relationships are the focus. Minuchin believes that patterns of interaction can be isolated for study, but he is mindful of the therapeutic system, always viewing the therapist as affected not only by the professional therapeutic community, but by the family itself. Therapy becomes much like a recursive dance, where the family enacts its "sickness" and the therapist probes and pushes, challenges and reconstructs. The family is viewed as an organism, as alive, but composed of interacting parts. Causation is within the recursive interactive patterns that emerge in families. It is through the therapeutic relationship that change occurs, as the therapist enters into the recursive cycle of the repetitive interactive patterns that make up a family's structure. Professionals are viewed as experts, and diagnosis is not an act of a professional defining an individual's illness; rather it is an ongoing interactive process where the therapist hypothesizes recurrent family patterns and continually reassesses the transformational process during therapy. Consequently, therapy, although seemingly imposed from outside, is a two-way street—the therapist and the client-system become one, as each must accommodate the other.

## Chapter Conclusion

Over all, Minuchin's (1974) approach is a clear example of a systemic-relational therapy. Structural Family Therapy focuses on relationships and relational networks. Its emphasis on recurrent patterns of interaction (structure) makes it distinct even among other systemic-relational therapies. Change is primarily instigated from outside the family, but the therapist has the unique opportunity to enter the family and to interact in a way that what he or she has learned outside can significantly influence the internal workings of the family. The therapist, an expert of relationships, imposes a systemic-relational agenda on the family, which has been shown to be effective in diminishing symptoms.

## References

Colapinto, J. (1982). Structural family therapy. In A Horne & M. M. Ohlsen (Eds.), *Family counseling and therapy* (pp. 112–140). Itasca, IL: F. E. Peacock.

Gurman, A. S., Kniskern, D. P., & Pinsof, W. M. (1986). Research on the process and outcome of marital and family therapy. In S. L. Garfield & A. E. Bergin (Eds.), *Handbook of psychotherapy and behavior change* (pp. 565–624). New York: John Wiley & Sons.

Haley, J. (1963). *Strategies of psychotherapy*. New York: Grune & Stratton.

Haley, J. (1973). *Uncommon therapy*. New York: W. W. Norton.

Haley, J. (1976). *Problem solving therapy*. New York: Harper & Row.

Minuchin, S. (1974). *Families and family therapy*. Cambridge, MA: Harvard University Press.

Minuchin, S. (1984). *Family kaleidoscope*. Cambridge, MA: Harvard University Press.

Minuchin, S., & Fishman, H. C. (1981). *Family therapy techniques*. Cambridge, MA: Harvard University Press.

Minuchin, S., Rosman, B. L., & Baker, L. (1978). *Psychosomatic families: Anorexia nervosa in context*. Cambridge, MA: Harvard University Press.

Satir, V. (1967). *Conjoint family therapy*. Palo Alto, CA: Science and Behavior Books.

# 15

# Structure-Determined Family Therapy:

## An Internal Model Systemic-Relational Therapy Focusing on Family Structure

THIS CHAPTER WILL be purposefully organized a bit differently than the other counseling theory chapters. It is an attempt to translate the latest developments of social systems theory into practice. As such, the ideas presented here must be viewed as tentative, at best, since the major proponents of an internal model of family social systems theory have come from the ranks of biologists rather than therapists. Consequently, publications that apply internalistic systemic-relational ideas to mental health practice are just beginning to make their way to the counseling literature. Additionally, no one proponent of a therapeutic approach has emerged, although the biologist, Humberto Maturana, is pointing the way for mental health practitioners, as he has extended his biological theories into the social and philosophical realms.

This chapter is an application of Maturana's (1978) ideas about structure determinism to family therapy. As described in Appendix B, Maturana's ideas have provided a competitive viewpoint to the traditional systemic-relational idea that biological and social systems are open systems (cf. Bertalanffy, 1952, 1968). Maturana views biological systems as informationally "closed" systems; and, since he believes that social systems are essentially higher order biological systems (Maturana, 1980; Maturana & Varela, 1987), social systems, too, are viewed as informationally closed. What this means is that living systems are changed and influenced primarily from within themselves, internally, through relations with their sensory/effector mechanisms and a closed, recursively organized nervous system. Consequently, the outside world is not reflected by the nervous system, but is literally constructed by the interactions of the nervous system. Accordingly, everything ultimately boils down to the internal workings of the living system's nervous system. For example, when one presses one's finger hard against a desk top, one does not feel the desk top; instead, one feels the pressure between one's finger bone and the sensory nerve cells in the finger. The outside world is not knowable, except as perturbation to the internal structure of the sensing nervous system.

Related to therapy, the issue becomes how a therapist can enter into the internal dynamics of the living social system called a "family." Based on several articles that have begun to explain this position (e.g., Dell, 1982, 1985; Efran & Lukens, 1985; Mendez, Coddou, & Maturana, 1988), an internalist social systems therapeutic perspective is emerging. Readers should be aware, however, that these ideas have not been tested in any empirical sense. So far, in this text, care has been taken to report primarily on philosophically grounded and empirically (or anecdotally) well-supported theories. However, in keeping with a basic theme of this text that philosophy (epistemology/ontology) is critical to the definition of theories in the mental health field, Structure-Determined Family Therapy (SDFT) is being presented. SDFT represents a change in perspective, a philosophically unique position, which cannot be ignored in any presentation such as this. Therefore, it is presented as a unique and potentially viable position within the systemic-relational paradigm.

# The Foundational Theory

## Families as Living Biological Systems

### *Autopoietic Systems.*
In an intriguing work, Maturana and Varela (1973/1980) attempted to bridge the gap between theoretical biology and the social and behavioral sciences. Maturana and Varela defined the criteria for living systems, which they described as "autopoietic machines." Autopoietic machines (systems) are essentially composed of relationships that are autonomous and self-creative. In fact, the word *autopoiesis* means self (auto-) production (-poiesis).

The focus is systemic in that the organization of relationships, rather than the properties of components of a system, is the central concern. Essentially, the criteria given by Maturana and Varela (1973/1980) for "autopoietic machines" are as follows (see also Varela, 1979):

**1.** "Autopoietic machines are homeostatic machines" (p. 78), that is, they tend toward a steady operating state (dynamic equilibrium [Cannon, 1932]);

**2.** Autopoietic machines are processes, such as interactions or transformations. These processes continuously regenerate themselves through components which are process-generated; and

*Humberto Maturana at the 1990 "Systemic Constructions" conference.*

**3.** Autopoietic machines continually specify their own boundaries by the organization of relationships and through their operations, and not by static organization of components.

To simplify, autopoiesis defines the dynamics of living autonomy. Generally, what is viewed as alive can be considered autopoietic. For example, living systems "transform matter into themselves in a manner such that the product of their operation is their own organization" (Maturana & Varela, 1973/1980, p. 82). For example as living human bodies, humans eat (they are organized to take things within their boundaries) to maintain an equilibrium, and, in the process, they regenerate themselves and the organized processes that led to their eating. Essentially, what Maturana and Varela have done is to focus on the organization of relationships in defining "living" things rather than to focus on individual traits or individual processes of such things. To say that one eats and breathes does not define one as living; but to say that one eats and breathes and, in the process, regenerates one's own organization for eating and breathing is to say that one is alive.

But the controversial part of Maturana and Varela's (1973/1980) work from a social systems theory standpoint is not in defining living systems as autopoietic, but in stating that all autopoietic systems are living systems. This means that any system, if it has autopoietic properties, is essentially alive. They stated:

> *If living systems are machines, that they are physical autopoietic machines is trivially obvious. . . . However, we deem the converse to be true: a physical system if autopoietic, is living. In other words, we claim that the notion of autopoiesis is necessary and sufficient to characterize the organization of living systems. (p. 82)*

The question then becomes: Does the system have to be "physical" to meet the criteria? Can it be social? Can family systems be alive? If so, what are the implications for the social and behavioral sciences?

### Beer's Application to Social Systems

Maturana and Varela (1973/1980), as biologists addressing biological issues, did not directly address whether social systems are living system. However, Beer (1980), in an introduction to Maturana and Varela's essay, concluded without qualification that "human societies are biological systems," and Beer claimed that Maturana and Varela's work "conclusively proves the point" (p. 70). Maturana (1980) himself, in a separate introduction to his work, acknowledged the social significance of his biological theory. Maturana stated, "To the extent that human beings are autopoietic systems, all their activities as social organisms must satisfy their autopoiesis" (p. xxvi). Likewise, a social system cannot operate if its components cease to be autopoietic. Maturana stated, "The realization of the autopoiesis of the components of a social system is constitutive to the realization of the social system itself. This cannot be ignored in any consideration about the operation of a social system without negating it" (p. xxv). Therefore, the relationship between a living human being and a living social system (in which he or she exists) is one of mutuality through interaction, or what Maturana and Varela (1973/1980) called "coupling" (p. 107). In coupling, neither of the coupled entities is more important, because each derives from each other. As Maturana and Varela stated, "Biological phenomena depend upon the autopoiesis of the individuals involved; thus, there are biological systems that arise from the coupling of autopoietic unities, some of which may even constitute autopoietic systems of a higher order" (p. 118).

Given this conclusion, Maturana and Varela's (1973/1980) work has provided a biological rationale for the formation of a social system—the social system is a biological system in itself. It is a biological system of a higher order. Essentially, human beings fulfill roles in a social system that keep the social system alive and, in so doing, they maintain relationships necessary for their own existence.

Families are living systems; they are alive.

## The Target of Counseling

One of the few publications appearing in the family therapy literature that directly applies Maturana's biological theory to family therapy is an article by Mendez, Coddou and Maturana (1988) entitled "The Bringing Forth of Pathology." In that article, the authors define a means for affecting the internal workings of a closed family system "orthogonally" (literally meaning at a right angle). What this means is that the social system is perturbed in some way consistent with its living structure, and then the system reacts to the perturbation as it is structured to react. If you poke a frog with a stick it will likely hop away; if you poke a rattlesnake with a stick, it will likely strike. The difference between these two responses is due to the structure of the organism as it is perturbed. As in this example, Maturana and his associates indicate that it is the structure of the system that *determines* the outcomes of therapy, not the external perturbation. The stick only "triggered" the internally determined reactions. Applied to the social realm, threatening a known violent family is likely to bring about a different response than threatening a known peaceloving family. The structure of that which is perturbed (in these cases, living family systems) is predictive of the response after perturbation.

Maturana and his associates do not believe that autopoietic systems (including social systems) can be instructed in any linear fashion. What Maturana calls "instructive interaction" (linear educational effect) is defined as a myth. Accordingly, Maturana believes that a therapist can never instruct an individual or a family in a straightforward way. If the therapist could directly instruct, the individual or the family would mimic the therapist's behavior identically, which most would agree doesn't often happen in therapy. The best a therapist can do is to perturb a family orthogonally (not straightforwardly). Maturana believes that the therapist actually perturbs the individual or family, primarily through language in a structurally bounded domain of interaction, and the perturbation then affects the organism as it is structured to react. Trying to do family therapy with a French-speaking family using the German language is less likely to affect the family than is therapy spoken in French. Because the family is structured in a way that it is perturbed within a domain of interaction where the French language has been neurologically and interactively linked to its behavior, it is somewhat structurally immune to perturbations in other languages. Maturana's work effectively communicates that therapists must be able to *enter into* the interactive domain of clients and families in a way that is consistent with past structural transformations. Yet at the same time the interactions cannot be too consistent with what has occurred in the past, or the therapist's interactions will not effectively perturb the system. Mendez, Coddou, and Maturana (1988) stated:

> *Languaging is not a means of transmitting knowledge or information. Languaging is a manner of coexistence, a manner of living together in recursive co-ordinations of consensual actions such that the structure of the participants changes in a manner contingent upon their participation in it. (p. 154)*

Therefore, through language a family has formed, and through language, its structure can change; but the therapist must know how to enter effectively into the operative linguistic domain in order to perturb the family in a way that changes can occur.

Family relations constitute the "operational domain" of living biological organisms (people); the family members and their relations constitute a living family structure (an autopoietic system).

The target of intervention, therefore, is the operative interactive domains of the individuals in a family and the operative domain of the family itself. Language is the key to the door of this operative interactive domain. The intent is to perturb the system in order to produce "structural changes" in the family and its members.

## The Process of Counseling and the Counselor's Role

Because each individual is viewed as a closed biological organism, and because social systems such as the family are also viewed as closed biological systems, each develops a reality from its internal structural workings as influenced within its operative linguistic domain. The operative linguistic domain effectively extends the boundaries of the system, but it does not do away with the boundaries. The operative linguistic domain of a living system is the boundary of its reality. Therefore, there is no objectivity. There is also no pure subjectivity. The social linguistic domain constitutes a boundary for reality that puts reality in parentheses, so to speak. Maturana (1978) has defined this as "objectivity in parentheses." There is no absolute reality. Reality is always relative to the social linguistic domain through which people interact. Consequently, there may be, at any one time, a number of legitimate realities operating—not a universe, but a multiverse (Mendez, Coddou, & Maturana, 1988). Consequently the initial process of counseling entails putting aside conclusions that are absolutist. As Mendez, Coddou, and Maturana (1988) stated:

> *Inadequate behavior in a particular social domain is not inadequate in a different one . . . neither social domain is perverse. Thus, for example, an adolescent who smokes marijuana is seen as normal by his or her peers, and as a drug addict by his or her family relatives, but both peers and family relatives may be claiming that their views are right to the exclusion of the other because they know how things really are. When one domain of existence, when one versum in the multiversa, is claimed to be the real, objective one, all the others become unreal, false or illusion; or, conversely, when objectivity is put in parentheses all domains of existence, all versa, become different, equally legitimate domains of reality. In these circumstances, when a therapist, a patient or any person changes his or her views about objectivity, he or she changes his or her views about him- or herself and others as well as his or her domains of obedience and concessions of power in the social domain. For this reason, putting objectivity in parenthesis entails abandoning the objectivist view that a system and its components have a constancy and a stability that is independent of the observer that brings them forth, and entails accepting that the only constancy and stability that they (system and components) have depends on the coherences proper to their constitution in the domain of reality where they exist as they are distinguished, and that they, therefore appear and disappear with realizations and not realization of their distinction. (p. 154)*

The therapist must accept each person's reality as reflecting his or her biological existence in a social linguistic domain, and the therapist must communicate the legitimacy of each person's reality through the process of counseling. In effect, conflicts among family members are conflicts of realities, and the differences will need to be resolved, or the family will disintegrate.

Related to the therapist's role beyond identifying the multiversa that constitute a family, Mendez, Coddou, and Maturana (1988) stated:

> *If the purpose of the therapist is to help the members of the consulting family out*
> *of their existential emotional contradiction, he or she must help the disintegra-*
> *tion of the present kind of family, and help its former members in bringing forth*
> *something else which may or may not be another family, but which is not a*
> *network of sufferings. In order to do so, the therapist must choose an action*
> *(statement, intervention or interaction) that is not confirmative of the present*
> *family. Such action has to be an interaction outside the domain of conversations*
> *that defines the particular consulting family, but which takes place in the domain*
> *of existence of at least one of its members. In other words, the action taken by*
> *the therapist will have to be an adequate orthogonal interaction. If the interac-*
> *tion of the therapist is indeed an adequate orthogonal interaction, it will trigger*
> *in one or more members of the family structural changes such that they will no*
> *longer be able to participate in the network of conversations of characterizations,*
> *accusations and recriminations that constitute the family in which they or others*
> *suffer in emotional contradiction. (p. 159)*

In other words, the therapist must perturb the family, or at least one of its members, through language or action.

To summarize the process of counseling and the role of the therapist, Mendez, Coddou, and Maturana (1988) defined three activities that must occur: (a) the therapist while initially interacting with the family members "must listen to their behavior and abstract from it the recurrent conversations that constitute its organizaiton and define it as a family of a particular kind" (p. 168). It is assumed there will be some conflict of realities that involves accusations or recriminations; (b) the therapist must interact "orthogonally" with the members of the family, meaning that "he or she must interact with them through dimensions of their individual identity that do not involve them in the conversations for characterizations and accusations through which they constitute the family in which they exist in emotional contradiction" (p. 169). In other words the therapist must connect linguistically or behaviorally with individual family members without so connecting with the larger contradictions that constitute the system needing change; and (c) the orthogonal interactions of the therapist must "trigger" change at the structural level in at least one individual or the family as a whole, as long as there is continued distinction that the family should continue to exist. However, unless the therapist fully understands the nature of the multiversa and the operative domains of the individuals and the family, predictions about the outcome of triggering through perturbation cannot be made.

## Goals of Counseling and Ideal Outcomes

The goal of Structure-Determined Family Therapy is recognition of multiversa—muliple and equally valid realities within a family context—so that the family members and the family may constitute a pattern of recurrent interactions that do not deny the operative domains of individual family members or the family itself. Mendez, Coddou, and Maturana (1988) stated:

*If the members of a family are united by the passion for living together, and act with objectivity-without-parenthesis in the possession of truth, they cannot but struggle to impose upon each other what is correct and what is the truth, and they cannot but do so as an ethical and moral obligation of proper coexistence, falling necessarily into a recurrent network of conversation for characterizations and accusations which unavoidably leads to suffering. This situation changes when we put objectivity in parenthesis, and change both for the family and for the therapist. Yet, this change is not a mere shift of emphasis, it is a change that involves a fundamental change in our responsibilities. Indeed, the question of pathology disappears as a central question for us therapists, and the suffering and unhappiness of the individuals appear instead as the fundamental experiences of the members of the family that command our attention in the consultation. . . . In these circumstances, our therapeutic task is to contribute to the disintegration of that system (the family in our case) so that something else appears in its stead. If, when this happens, the passion for living together is conserved, then the consulting people will integrate another family in which that suffering of its members will not be a constitutive feature because these, de facto or through awareness, will operate with objectivity-in-parenthesis. (pp. 170–171)*

In a phrase, the goal of therapy is an operative domain where differing realities can be accepted and behaviorally and linguistically incorporated into the continued operation of a structurally changed family system.

## General Procedures

### Assessment

Assessment according to Structure-Determined Family Therapy (SDFT) is a matter of sociolinguistic analysis and the marking of boundaries of operative interactive domains. The operative interactive domains are defined as social structures, and they can be identified by the individuals who make up what can be distinguished as a social system of significance. Once social structures have been defined and associated with sociolinguistic correlates, a reality has been defined. The task of the therapist, then, is to enter into the reality and to perturb it, primarily by means of perturbing at least one individual in a way that he or she cannot continue to act as if a problem exists within that context.

### Treatment/Remediation

Treatment is linguistic and behavioral. Ideally, individual family members will be educated about objectivity in parentheses; that is, they will come to understand that multiple realities exist for members of a family, and that each is legitimate. The therapist's task is to facilitate such an understanding both behaviorally and linguistically. Accordingly, a new family framework for action and understanding will result that allows the acknowledgment of differences without accusations and recriminations. Symptoms, which result from accusations, recriminations, or distinctions from the perspective of an observing system, are therefore placed in a context in which they are viewed as logically legitimate from another perspective.

### Case Management

Although mental health professionals who have applied Maturana's ideas have begun to define what constitutes SDFT, very little has been said about the mechanics of therapy. It can only be assumed that therapy occurs within a therapeutic context, probably with a frequency consistent with other systemic-relational approaches. It can also be assumed that therapy would end with the acceptance, amelioration, or diminution of symptoms, or with the disintegration or transformation of the problematic family system. Specialized techniques have not been developed.

## Recent Developments or Criticisms

Structure-Determined Family Therapy is new to the systemic-relational paradigm. In fact, its name has been invented for this text around the works of Maturana and his associates, and, as such, does not constitute a well-accepted therapeutic approach within the systemic-relational paradigm. However, there is no question that Maturana's theoretical works are significant to the family therapy field. He has given a biological rationale for the existence of social systems, and he has shown how language plays a role in the definition of a social system and its maintenance. His work also represents a break with the work of the external systemic theorists. SDFT is significant as the *first* internal model systemic-relational theory. On the other hand, it can be argued that SDFT is not operationally significantly different from Minuchin's (1974) Structural Family Therapy. In fact, when one assesses Minuchin's specific techniques for entering (joining) a family structurally, there is similarity at face value with SDFT. However, Minuchin and Fishman (1981) unquestionably define social systems as open to information; they stated:

> *Living systems with these characteristics are by definition open systems, in contrast with the closed "equilibrium structures" described in classical thermodynamics. . . . The family, a living system, exchanges information and energy with the outside. Fluctuation, either internal or external, is normally followed by a response that returns the system to its steady state. But when the fluctuation amplifies, the family may enter a crisis in which transformation results in a different level of functioning that makes coping possible. (pp. 21–22)*

Comparatively, Maturana's theory leads to the conclusion that not all types of external stimulation will influence a structure—only certain types of stimulation, primarily constrained by the organic structure of the organism, can and will perturb a system. A fly on a bull-elephant's back may not affect the animal's behavior, but the sounds of approaching human hunters may produce quite a drastic response. Although this example is extreme, the point is that some systems must be viewed as closed to certain types of stimulation. Perturbation primarily derives from the makeup of the organism (or in the case of family therapy, from the organization of relations and their social histories). Although practically speaking there is similarity between Minuchin's approach and SDFT, Maturana's ideas continually remind the therapist that his or her actions must be tailored to the social and linguistic domains of at least one individual in the family, and predictions about outcomes cannot be directionally determined without a keen sense of the interactive process within a family structure.

# Paradigm Fit

### Focus of Study

Structure-Determined Family Therapy focuses on the study of internal relational dynamics occurring within the boundaries (biological and social) of living systems. There is continuous *interaction* between receptor and effector mechanisms within the organism. There is internal structural modification arising from simultaneous biological and social *interactions*. There is continuous change and process resulting from interaction. The theory is clearly interactional, and accordingly closely aligned with systemic-relational ideals.

### View of Nature of Reality

According to Dell (1985), Maturana's ontology is highly relational. Dell stated that *"Structure-determined living systems automatically become organized into interactional systems.* Whenever two or more structurally plastic living systems interact they will begin to co-evolve a closed pattern of interaction. They will form a system'' (p. 13). Autopoietic systems, therefore, always exist in interaction, and they are only knowable through interaction with an observer. From an observer's perspective, two or more autopoietic systems in interaction may be viewed as constituting another system. The relational-observational nature of Maturana's ontology is highly systemic.

### Consonance with Paradigm Propositions and Tenets

There is consistency between Structure-Determined Family Therapy (SDFT) and the propositions and tenets of the systemic-relational paradigm. The focus of SDFT is on relationships, primarily internal to the operation of biological systems, *but* as affected within a social and linguistic domain. Relationships can be isolated for study. In fact, through Maturana's work the idea of isolation of relationships as a process derived from distinctions made by an observer (who also operates from a social and linguistic tradition) completes the systemic circle—everything is viewed in relationship, even the act of viewing. Causality within the boundaries of a social system is reciprocal, just as is the organization of the internal workings of living systems. Change occurs through perturbation, where the internal workings of the organism are "triggered" by relations within a social and linguistic domain (which is ultimately limited by the biological relations of the perceiving organism). Professionals act as triggers, while at the same time they operate with knowledge of the social and linguistic domains of the individuals within a family and the family itself. What might be viewed as individual traits of family members or of the family itself are actually observations from the perspective of an observing system of relationships. Individuals do not exist outside of their systems of support.

Therapy is highly context-relevant, and it is aimed at perturbing relationships within the family seeking treatment. "Disorders" are viewed as distinctions made by a community of individuals, not as inherent to individuals. Therapists must be educated as to the linguistic operative domains in which clients may be operating. The therapist must be an expert at entering linguistically and behaviorally into the domains of individual family members and the family itself.

## Chapter Conclusion

This chapter has served to introduce Structure-Determined Family Therapy. As a counseling theory, SDFT is unrefined. Nevertheless, it represents a break with the traditions of externally-oriented systemic-relational therapies and, consequently, it is of historical significance. It also is of significance in bridging the gap between systemic-relational thinking and the contextual paradigm, which is the next topic of study.

## References

Beer, S. (1980). Preface to "Autopoiesis: The organization of the living." In H. R. Maturana & F. J. Varela, *Autopoiesis and cognition: The realization of the living*. Boston: D. Reidel.

Bertalanffy, L. von. (1952). *Problems of life*. London: C. A. Watts.

Bertalanffy, L. von. (1968). *General systems theory*. New York: George Braziller.

Cannon, W. B. (1932). *The wisdom of the body*. New York: W. W. Norton.

Dell, P. F. (1982). Beyond homeostasis: Toward a concept of coherence. *Family Process, 21*, 21–41.

Dell, P. F. (1985). Understanding Bateson and Maturana: Toward a biological foundation for the social sciences. *Journal of Marital and Family Therapy, 11* (1), 1–20.

Efran, J., & Lukens, M. D. (1985, May-June). The world according to Humberto Maturana. *The Family Therapy Networker*, 23–28; 72–75.

Maturana, H. R. (1978). Biology of language: The epistemology of reality. In G. A. Miller & E. Lenneberg (Eds.), *Psychology and biology of language and thought*. New York: Academic Press.

Maturana, H. R. (1980). Biology of cognition. In H. R. Maturana & F. J. Varela, *Autopoiesis and cognition: The realization of the living.* Boston: Reidel. (Original work published in 1970.)

Maturana, H. R., & Varela, F. J. (1980). Autopoiesis: The organization of the living. In H. R. Maturana & F. J. Varela, *Autopoiesis and cognition: The realization of the living.* Boston: Reidel. (Original work published in 1973.)

Maturana, H. R., & Varela, F. J. (1987). *The tree of knowledge: The biological roots of human understanding.* Boston: Shambhala.

Mendez, C. L., Coddou, F., & Maturana, H. R. (1988). The bringing forth of pathology. *The Irish Journal of Psychology, 9,* 144–172.

Minuchin. S. (1974). *Families and family therapy.* Cambridge, MA: Harvard University Press.

Minuchin, S., & Fishman, H. C. (1981). *Family therapy techniques.* Cambridge, MA: Harvard University Press.

Varela, F. J. (1979). *Principles of biological autonomy.* New York: North Holland.

# PART FIVE

# The Contextual Paradigm

# _16_

# The Contextual Paradigm:
## *An Emerging Paradigm*

IN A PARTICULARLY cogent work, Colapinto (1979) described how the epistemological foundations underlying psychologically based and systemically oriented psychotherapies were incompatible. He argued that empirical evidence, in and of itself, could not resolve which one of these two positions should predominate in mental health services. He argued instead that sociocultural values were the bases for decisions as to the effectiveness of one approach over the other. But in a revealing and prophetic section of his article, Colapinto stated:

> *A real integration between models—the simultaneous acceptance of the complete models, epistemological assumptions included—is impossible if the models are epistemologically conflicting,* unless a third, new epistemology is developed in order to decide when each one of the now subordinated models is to be applied. *Short of this, what usually goes under the name of "integration" is that one model—or more specifically some isolated concepts or techniques—is subsumed under a second prevailing one. (p. 438) [emphasis added]*

In effect, this chapter, a presentation of a contextual epistemology and a new philosophy for mental health services, acts to rise above what has gone before in a way consistent with Colapinto's affirmation. It is based primarily upon "The Third Epistemology" (Cottone, 1989). The third epistemology is a means to integrate the organic-medical, psychological, and systemic-relational paradigms of counseling and psychotherapy through a high-level theoretical framework.

The contextual paradigm, unlike the others presented in this text, is prospective. In other words, it is viewed as the most likely candidate for paradigm status emerging from current developments in the mental health field. As an emerging paradigm, it is based less on empirical evidence and more on the intuitions of therapists and theoreticians who, in the future, may be viewed as transitional theorists. In this case, the transitional theoretical works appear to be emerging primarily from theorists aligned with the systemic and psychological paradigms. (e.g., Dell, 1982, 1985; Gergen, 1985; Goolishian & Winderman, 1988; Hoffman, 1988, 1990).

Operationally, there are clear differences between the proposed contextual paradigm and the other paradigms presented in this text. First, the propositions of the contextual paradigm, outlined in this chapter, are completely conditional, whereas with the other paradigms the propositions were presented as accepted assumptions, or in some cases as axioms. Second, there is no one established profession that has a history of theoretical linkage to the contextual position, although it will be proposed that the professional field of counseling, by nature of its broad theoretical base (historically), and by nature of its youth as a profession, has the potential to fill the theoretical void originating from anomalies unsolved by the other paradigms. In this way, counseling, which has been a mental health profession without an epistemology, may establish itself in a paradigm-specific role. Given such a role, counseling may emerge as a soundly grounded, theoretically-based competitor among the mental health professions. Third, the paradigm-specific therapy, Cognitive-Consensual Therapy, presented as an example of a contextual therapy, is propositional. It is a best attempt to build a theory of counseling and psychotherapy around an emergent, prospective paradigm. However, a transitional (trans-paradigmatic) therapy, the Milan Systemic Family Therapy (Boscolo, Cecchin, Hoffman, & Penn, 1987), is offered as an approach that breaks new ground and that strongly hints to the emergence of the contextual paradigm. Therefore, the reader is asked to be understanding and open-minded, as the prospect for the development of a new paradigm in the mental health services is explored.

## Historical Overview

### Foundations

The term *contextualism* is probably best originally associated with the works of S. C. Pepper. In what is now viewed by many as a classic work in philosophy, Pepper's (1942) *World Hypotheses: A Study in Evidence* described four world views, one of which he defined as the contextual position. The contextual position is based on process and change as a primary ontology.

In the mental health field, the term *contextualism* has been adopted and modified by several theorists and therapists who have openly or tacitly recognized the limits of existing mental health paradigms (Cottone, 1989; Cottone & Greenwell, 1991; Rosnow & Georgoudi, 1986; Efran, Germer, & Lukens, 1986). Generally, although not to the level of full consensus, these theorists can be associated with a position based on a belief that change and process should be assumed to be basic to reality—that absolutes should not be viewed as absolutes—that mental health professionals should not be locked into believing in people as entities or in believing in systems of relationships as deterministic, although morally neutral, structured patterns. Through their actions, these theorists are asking the mental health field to recognize the wealth of anecdotal evidence pointing to the limitations of purely organic-medical, psychological, or systemic-relational thinking. They are directing the field to look forward philosophically to a new method of addressing the anomalies evident in current professional practice. Like Colapinto (1979), they eschew the seductions of an artless merging of existing paradigms into hybrid positions as a means to address such anomalies. They are also asking mental health professionals not to attempt to base their theories solely on scientific constructions singularly derived from the physical sciences. Rather they seek evidence based on a combination of empiricism and therapy-specific intuitions. As critical theorists, they are attempting to build a new way of thinking in the mental health services.

As a philosophical foundation, this chapter will be built on two of my own works. Although this may appear to be self-serving, actually the motivations are primarily defensive. The ideas presented in this part of the text came after much study and deliberation, and they are not easy to grasp; therefore, I feel it is best to communicate by means of ideas with which I am best acquainted. But readers should understand that I am not the only proponent of these idea; readers are referred to the excellent works of the authors listed in the previous paragraph (especially Rosnow & Georgoudi, 1986) to supplement the ideas presented here and to ground them historically.

The first of my works is an article entitled, ''The Third Epistemology: Extending Maturana's Structure Determinism'' (Cottone, 1989). In that work, an argument was made that reality involves change and process. By using the empirical and theoretical works of Maturana and his associates (1960, 1968), arguments were presented that the visual and other perceptual processes are ''transformational'' rather than simple transmissions of that which is observed (perceived). The argument was made that an objective reality does not exit separately from a living cognizing being. The human cognitive process (where cognition is defined as a combination of language and perception) was defined as a simultaneous *process* between physical but everchanging living systems (people) and an evolving social system with a linguistic tradition (a group of communicating people). According to the third epistemology, reality is defined as *involving change, in relation to change, as defined in an everchanging social/consensual domain.* In effect, that article delineated the primary contextual position. Change is both the focus of study (epistemology) and the foundation of the view of nature (ontology). *Whereas the organic-medical, psychological, and systemic-relational paradigms all focus on how structures or patterns change, the contextual paradigm focuses on how change is structured or patterned.* This is a primary difference.

The second of my works, coauthored with one of my students, Robert Greenwell, is entitled, ''The Contextual Paradigm of Marital and Family Therapy'' (Cottone & Greenwell, 1991). An earlier work (Cottone & Greenwell, in press) summarized the weaknesses in the systemic-relational paradigm revealed by the credible challenge from feminist theorists (e.g., Bograd, 1984, 1986; Taggart, 1985; Walters, Carter, Papp, & Silverstein, 1988). Feminist theorists have effectively defined systems theory as weak and unacceptable in accounting for violence in a relational context. They have argued that the victim should not be viewed as part of the cause, and since the victim can be implicated from a circular-systemic cause-and-effect perspective, the feminist theorists have argued against the validity of the systemic-relational position. Because the third epistemology is both individual and system-acknowledging, it rectifies the problem of individual blame, while fully avowing recursive sequences in human interactions (Cottone & Greenwell, 1991). Therefore, a solution to the anomaly arising from the intuitions of feminist theorists emerges through the "third epistemology."

The feminist criticism of the systemic paradigm is of critical importance on two counts and, therefore, it deserves further discussion. First the feminist critique is a contemporary example of how anomaly arises from the professional and political realm while acting to challenge a predominant theory. In this way, the feminist critique helps to demonstrate one of the basic criteria of a counseling paradigm—competitive viewpoints and the presence of anomalous anecdotal, observational, or empirical evidence. Second, it demonstrates the power of therapeutic intuition in the molding of a new paradigm. The feminist critique of social systems theory is a classic example of professional and political developments acting to motivate and to guide paradigm shift in the mental health services.

## The Feminist Critique of Social Systems Theory

The feminist critique of family social systems theory and family therapy has been one of the most credible attacks on systemic-relational thinking to date. The feminist critique can be summarized by two interrelated positions. One position relates to violent acts within family contexts—focusing on the issue of power and how power realizes itself in abusive incidents in a linear cause-and-effect way. The second position relates to the influence of a patriarchal society on the roles women play in culture, in society, and in the home/family context.

Regarding abuse itself, Bograd (1984, 1986) has made a powerful statement in her publications, and because she stated her position so clearly and effectively, her works will be cited at length to present a representative picture of the feminist stand. Essentially, Bograd (1984) argued that family systems approaches to wife battering or incest may introduce "subtle biases against women" (p. 566). Further, she stated: "These biases can reside in the very language of family systems theory, in formulations of transactional sequences leading to domestic violence, and in certain kinds of interventions—most notably conjoint therapy" (p. 566). Bograd (1986) summarized the systemic perspective as follows:

> *Common to all family systems approaches to incest or wife battering are the assumptions that:*
>
> *1) the sexual or physical abuse serves a functional role in maintenance of the family system;*
>
> *2) with equal influence, each family member actively participates in perpetuating the dysfunctional system;*

*3) violence against women occurs in family systems characterized by certain relationship structures;*

*4) incest or battering is the product of an interactional context character-ized by repetitive sequences of transactional behavior. (p. 38)*

Bograd went on to state that "two biases" are evident in family systems accounts of battering and incest in a family context: "(1) minimization of incest and battering as acts of violence and (2) "woman blaming" (p. 38).

Related to the feminist position on such matters, Bograd (1984) stated:

> *Feminist values are clear regarding the allocation of responsibility for wife battering incidents: 1) no woman deserves to be beaten; 2) men are solely responsible for their actions. . . . Feminist values emphasize: 1) the distinction between the verbal expression of anger and physical retaliation; 2) the belief that men and women can control their behavior; 3) the rights of men and women to physical safety; and 4) the ways in which blaming the victim shifts attention from the patriarchal context of battering. From a feminist perspective, a systemic formulation is biased if it can be employed to implicate the battered woman or to excuse the abusive man. (pp. 560–561)*

In effect, the feminist perspective requires a return to linear thinking. Abusive males, in certain contexts, are to be blamed for abusive incidents; women should not be implicated.

The second feminist position that challenges systems theory is the issue of patriarchal cultural context and its effects on the options of women. Walters, Carter, Papp, and Silverstein (1988) believed that patriarchal dictates limit the choices women can make related to roles. They stated:

> *Systems therapy discriminates against women by seeking balance and equilib-rium for the family system as a unit, without addressing the unequal access of each individual to choice of role. The pretense that men and women are genderless cogs in the system prevents us from noticing that women are held more responsible than men for making it work, in the family and in family therapy, and that the "complementary" roles, tasks, and rewards of the stable system are allocated by gender, unequally, to its male and female members. (p. 23)*

Roles are not randomly assigned. Rather, the imbalance in the societal context constrains the options of both men and women. In a patriarchal society, that leaves women with the one-down position.

Power, control, and linearity are even more blatant in cases of sexual abuse of young children. Few in our culture would argue that a two- or three-year-old child should be in some way theoretically implicated in sex abuse by an adult (especially to the degree of sodomy or intercourse). The explanatory power of systemic circular causality breaks down in such cases.

In order for social systems theory to accommodate the feminist critique (that is, to answer it in a way that is responsive to feminist insights and consistent with basic systemic-relational propositions) systems theory must be able to account for the linearity that is obvious to observers of certain abusive events. At the same time, systems theorists must not negate circular epistemology, which is at systems theory's foundation. To date, systemic responses to the feminist critique have been inadequate.

## The Contextual Solution

To accommodate the feminist critique of social systems theory, a contextual position must be both individual-acknowledging and system-acknowledging. It must delimit and account for linear causalities while not denying that, within certain constraints, circular causal processes are at work (Cottone & Greenwell, in press). The "third epistemology" (Cottone, 1989, Cottone & Greenwell, 1991) does this.

The third epistemology is a fully contextual philosophy. It is based on an assumption that reality involves "change." What this means is that everything is assumed to be in a state of flux. But, if everything involves change, how is it that humans observe structures? The third epistemology also attempts to answer this question.

Maturana's (1978; 1970/1980; Maturana & Varela, 1973/1980) work is critical to understanding how it is that people, as changing processes, see structures. Other philosophers going back to the likes of Heraclitus (who believed you could never step into the same river twice) have recognized the inevitability of change. But other philosophers have never been able to fully provide a picture of how it is that humans can perceive "things" (in an objectified sense) while being in a process of change themselves. The works of Maturana demonstrated that the human perceptual process is a *transformational* process, not one of just transmission of images. The eye, for example, does not operate like a camera, which makes an impression of some external absolute reality. Rather, the eye sees what it is organized to see, and it sees through a process of transformation of perceptual perturbation into nervous system activity (as opposed to receiving information from outside of its boundaries). If a human is not organized to hear or see something, it can't. The dog whistle is a classic example. If someone blows a dog whistle, unless a person sees a dog respond to it (or has some mechanical means of registering the sound), then he or she cannot make a decision as to whether the whistle sounded in an absolute sense. Dog whistles may be blown all around all the time, but because human perceptual organs are not organized to perceive them, they do not perturb the human nervous system. Essentially there are limits to what humans can perceive, and the nervous system, including the perceptual organs, defines those limits.

But the perceptual organs and the nervous system, according to Maturana (1978) are not static things unto themselves. Maturana has shown through his work that the nervous system is a process of continuous change—transformation. It is "plastic" (Maturana, 1970/1980). And the process of perception, rather than being a process where a static organ reacts to a static outside world, is from Maturana's point of view a process of change. So the picture of reality that results from Maturana's thinking is as follows: reality emerges in an ever-changing nonstructured medium within which changing organisms live and perceive, primarily through a process of perception that is transformation (change).

Although this may sound confusing to the newcomer to such ideas, actually these ideas make a great deal of common sense. Humans as biological organisms have evolved (changed) over a period of time. Human genetic histories are not static histories, as each person represents the transformation of gene pools through the parental *relationship* from which he or she was an offspring. Every individual then represents a *transformation* of genetic material. And from the time of birth, the human being is in a process of development and change—aging—which is hard to deny (although many have tried). In addition to this everchanging biological tradition, humans are socially dependent and raised in a social context with very few certainties. In effect, coming to the paradoxical conclusion that change is the one thing humans can depend upon is a highly defensible position.

So what Maturana has provided to the contextual position is an understanding that not only can the external world be viewed as changing, but the individual can be viewed as changing, and, importantly, *perception can also be viewed as a change (transformation) process.*

Additionally, Maturana has demonstrated theoretically that thinking is not a process that derives absolutely out of human organic makeup; rather it is a process that emerges simultaneously as the human nervous system is perturbed both perceptually *and socially.* ''Perceptual perturbation alone is not enough to define a reality. But perceptual perturbation in a social context allows consensual behavior about what is real or unreal within the boundaries (parentheses) of social interaction'' (Cottone, 1989, p. 361). For example, what makes an egg ''food'' to cooks in a kitchen is not perception of the egg, but perception of the egg as acted upon by cooks in their social and linguistic traditions. When we see a mother hen interacting with an egg, we see quite a different reality. Of course, a hungry cook in need of a hen's egg and a mother hen cannot come to a consensus (either behaviorally or linguistically) about the egg, because their nervous systems are not structured in ways that such a consensus can be reached. So their realities remain quite different.

When it is recognized that even social and linguistic traditions are not static, then a complete picture of a changing reality is possible. In a complex society, what is ''good'' or ''bad'' and ''right'' or ''wrong'' are not absolutes. There is a constant process of negotiation of these issues verbally and behaviorally, openly and tacitly among members of a society and culture. Moreover, language is an ever-changing process. Any conclusion, therefore, must be viewed as temporary (even the conclusion that is being presented in these pages). All is fleeting in an ever-changing social and linguistic context, as what is perceived is transformation, which is assumed to be relative to other changes in a perceived world.

This relates to the discussion of social systems theory and the feminist critique as follows. Once one fully assumes that reality involves ever-changing process, then structure must be viewed as fleeting. Structure arises as a perceptual phenomenon out of interpersonal interactions (consensualities). According to the third epistemology, what is observed, the observer, and objectification in a social/consensual domain are *all* linked conceptually through change. If people act as if something is true, then it is true within the social context, at least for the moment. Consequently, issues of cause and effect, and circularity versus linearity, translate to the issue of consensus over the perceived social structures that are implied in any discussion of causality. For example, if something is *viewed* as influencing something else, and there is *consensus* (verbal or nonverbal, implied or explicit) about the existence of one structure affecting another in a straightforward way, then linearity is a reasonable conclusion. On the other hand, if two "things" are viewed as mutually and reciprocally affecting each other without substantial influence by outside factors, then a structural boundary is established, and causality can be defined as circular within that boundary. In other words, *the definition of causality is contingent upon the definition of structure.*

What this means for family therapy is that it no longer matters whether therapists work with individuals, families, or larger social structures, because all are viewed as change in an ever-changing world. They only exist as structure when there is consensual agreement by involved parties that an individual's, a family's, or a larger social structure's boundaries have *an impact upon* some other perceived structure. For example, when a victim, an examining physician, and a family therapist are in agreement that a husband physically harmed his wife beyond the extent of provocation, then, structurally the husband exists as an abuser—that is, he has boundaries which define him as a "problem" which is real within the context of the therapeutic system involving both the professionals and the victim. Should the husband agree that he was at fault (in a linear sense), then a clear consensus is attained. To proceed only with systemically oriented marital counseling in such a case would be an injustice to the victim and an act in direct contradiction to the reality defined by the actions of all involved individuals.

Conversely, if the involved parties (the husband, wife, or other professionals) individually communicate to a therapist that both the husband and the wife appeared equally involved, that the relationship dynamics were the principal factors involved in a progressively deteriorating situation, and that there is hope for the relationship, then a conjoint approach to therapy seems more reasonable. In this case, a consensus around the relationship as a causative factor in the abuse has been attained, and, if the relationship is viewed as structurally bounded, then a therapist's intervention into the relationship makes good sense. Cause may be linear or circular, individual or relational, depending on the "structures" defined as causative through consensus.

Essentially, the contextualist position allows the therapist to build around consensus. It requires the therapist to recognize not only the positions of the involved parties (e.g., the abuser and the abused) but also the positions of other involved professionals. And it fully accounts for the consensually established societal standards (e.g., laws or professional ethical codes) that cannot be ignored when a person's safety is at issue. In effect, those standards constrain consensualities. A family therapist, for instance, could not (in our contemporary cultural context) come to a consensus with a step-father that the 16-year-old step-child he raped was not sexually abused. While the perpetrator may argue that the act was simply 'instruction,' the law forbids consensus around such a position.

This is not to deny that some consensual positions may be forged by fear of violence, or derived from the deception of one or more parties to an agreement. Epistemologically, awareness is maintained that explanations of reality are consensual creations (neither simply objective or subjective). Legitimacy is only a matter of consensus through time. It always takes at least two people to define a consensus and, likewise, to challenge one. In cases where two consensual positions clash, solution is a matter of resolution of the differences. Otherwise a means of judgment, usually a consensually agreed-upon means (such as the courts), must be engaged to resolve disputes. In any case, realities are social constructions, and what appears to be true is what is believable through at least one relationship (current or historical).

## Propositions

The basic propositions of the contextual paradigm are as follows:

**1.**   The focus of study is on human consensus (both linguistic and behavioral) as a process within social groups.

**2.**   Change is viewed as fundamental and inevitable. Reality, from an ontological perspective, is viewed as intrinsically involving change and process. It is *assumed* that structure, as a fundamental reality, will prove to be fleeting as scientists continually change from relative agreement to relative disagreement about the nature of reality.

**3.**   Individuals or groups are inherently viewed as process and change, but they are enstructured through the perceptual process by observers operating within a consensual domain. Essentially, individuals or groups are not "things," although they may be viewed and acted upon as "things" by others. For example, individuals are not static entities, but rather they are processes in constant change (e.g., aging).

**4.**   Cause may be viewed as either linear (proportional, unilateral, or temporal) or circular (recursive or holistic) with the understanding that the process of definition of cause is intimately associated with the enstructuring process of those "things" viewed as causative (cf. Cottone & Greenwell, in press). For example, if a child hits another child and makes the second child cry, and observers agree that the hitting was unprovoked, then a conclusion that the first child misbehaved and *linearly caused* the child to cry, is a reasonable conclusion. The first child is defined structurally as causative. Conversely, if it is observed that two children over the course of their interaction begin to behaviorally escalate into an argument and a fight, then a conclusion of circular cause and effect is reasonable; it was the relationship, observed as real by observers, that was at fault. In either case, cause followed a definition of a causative structure. (See Cottone & Greenwell, in press, for a thorough discussion on the differing types of linearity and circularity.)

**5.**   Professional expertise is never attained in the sense of attaining a trait or characteristic. Professional expertise is perceived by others who view a therapist-counselor as socially and consensually linked to a system of thought and action that may be viewed as "expert" within certain contexts. In Western societies, such expertise is founded on "science," which itself is activity defined as acceptable within a scientific community (i.e., a social context with a behavioral and linguistic tradition). Science is not absolute; it is agreed upon (cf., Maturana, 1978). And science itself changes (Kuhn, 1970).

**6.** Professional therapists-counselors are sanctioned, within a sociolegal context, to practice within certain constraints. A professional therapist or counselor is viewed as a means for transmission and understanding of consensual activity within his or her "science." Professional activity is often legally limited by a consensus (expressed or understood) about the limits of the science at its foundation. A viable profession, therefore, continually communicates changes in its "science" to those in decisional contexts related to the definitions of professional practice (most usually state and federal legislators).

**7.** Individual clients may be viewed as either responsible or irresponsible to the degree they act reasonably within larger consensual domains, collectively called "society." Some professional counselors may be called upon to assess whether a client can change for the better (responsibly) or for the worse (irresponsibly) according to the values implicit in sociolegal or other dictates, with the understanding that such dictates are themselves changeable. In a sense, a counselor links the changes of perceived individuals or groups (clients) with the changes within a larger domain. The behavior or ideals of individuals or groups may change: (a) more quickly; (b) concomitantly (concurrently and harmoniously); or (c) more slowly than those of the larger (encompassing) social context. To the degree that the changes of an individual or group are not harmonious with those in the larger enstructured social context, there is "poor contextual fit." In other words, counselors identify mismatch or social incongruence between the changes in a person or group and the changes in a larger context.

**8.** Where social mismatch or incongruence is observed, a counselor is responsible to redirect changes in the individual or group defined consensually as "the problem." The counselor may act to slow down or accelerate behavioral and linguistic changes in an identified client or system. Since change is inevitable, entry into the linguistic and behavior process of the identified entity under study constitutes therapy. *The intent of therapy is coevolution between therapist and the individual client or group.* Successful therapy is coevolution.

**9.** Failure results from mistransformation of either the client (individual or group) or of the counselor. Mistransformation means the client *remains* out-of-sync, or the counselor *becomes* out-of-sync, with the changes in the larger social context.

## Tenets of Practice

**1.** The therapeutic act is aimed at contextualizing (enstructuring, destructuring, or restructuring) those "things" perceived by clients as having an impact upon them. Contextualizing ultimately is accomplished through activity between a counselor and clients toward linguistic and behavioral consensus.

**2.** Contextual therapist most often begin therapy with a defined social system of significance (e.g., a family) and work from a systemic stance in defining the "problem." However, if the therapist is relinquished to a role of disputing a consensus of individual "blame," then the therapist effectively can switch to defining an individual as "problem causative" to assist in building a consensus as to the definition of the problem. Initially, if there is no clearly attainable systemic consensus, it is recommended to move from an attempt at a systemic definition of a problem to an attempt at individual definition of a problem. In fact, to do the opposite (reframe the problem from the individual to the family) may be very difficult, requiring adept counselors and well-tested techniques. The ease of reframing the problem from the family to the individual probably stems from the predominance of psychological thinking in the Western cultural context; it may not apply in all cultures. In any case, the definition of a problem is embedded in the counseling relationship—it is mutual activity.

**3.** Where there is difference of opinion—a conflict of consensualities—reconciliation occurs by means that are themselves agreed upon. This agreement about the means of reconciliation may be made by the involved parties or it may be dictated by a larger sociolegal consensus (e.g., the courts).

**4.** It is perfectly acceptable for a contextual therapist to act as a systemic therapist in some contexts, and as a psychological or organic-medical therapist in others, depending on the nature of the consensus that is operating. The therapist's flexibility in this regard also depends on the degree of practice-related flexibility allowed legally by a professional license.

**5.** Contextual therapists will be expert at producing experiences for clients that help clients to define or redefine concerns within certain frameworks for understanding and action. Contextual therapists make full use of relational factors at play in the process of building consensus (since consensus is simultaneously a cognitive and social activity). *Cognition* is defined as the combined result of the processes of perception and language. *Social activity* is defined as any activity involving interpersonal communication at the formal, informal, nonverbal, or environmental-contextual levels.

## Epistemological and Ontological Definitions

The epistemology of the contextual paradigm is that of studying the process of consensus in human interaction. Since it is assumed that humans operate in consensual domains with linguistic traditions, the study of language is a principal concern, especially when the processes of language development and language evolution are focuses of attention. But the idea of consensus must not be viewed solely as a formal language-based activity. In fact, consensus is probably best understood by the actions of individuals as they relate mutually, verbally and non-verbally, within certain interpersonal contexts. When, for instance, two people walking together on a sidewalk simultaneously act to avoid a small mud puddle in the middle of the sidewalk, their actions define the mud puddle as real in an objectified sense, even though no word may have been spoken. Their *mutual activity represents consensus,* and the reality derived from the consensus occurs within the biological boundaries of their social interaction—

their interpersonal context. This is similar to what Maturana (1978) meant by "objectivity in parentheses." Objectivity is always limited within social contexts.

The term *co-operation* has special meaning in this sense. The term is hyphenated to emphasize joint action. Humans are acting consensually when they *co*-operate. Co-operation means that the activities of at least two individuals are integrated. Lack of co-operation is an indication of differing consensualities.

Ontologically, what is real cannot be simply defined as either objective or subjective. Contextualism carves an otological niche between objectivity and subjectivity. It assumes that what is real involves "change" in an absolute sense, but it also assumes that reality proves to be fleeting in an absolute sense! It is assumed, as stated earlier, that scientists will continually move from one relative consensus to other relative consensual positions about the nature of reality, never firmly reaching an absolute consensus (although the prospect of an absolute consensus cannot be absolutely doubted). Until an absolute consensus arises, unchanging and unchallenged, *then reality is assumed to involve process and change,* where the act of assumption, itself, derives from activity in an ever-changing social consensual domain.

It must also be kept in mind, since the human observational ability is a process (remembering that perception is transformation and not transmission), what one observes is as much a result of transformation within an observing system as it is inherent in that which is observed. In other words, humans operate in a world of flux. At times "things" appear more concrete, at other times they appear more fluid, but always at the level of consensus through interaction. By saying that reality involves "change, in relation to change, as defined in an ever-changing social consensual domain," a contextualist recognizes fully that what is perceived, the perceiver, and the act of perceiving are all understood as involving change and process. Therefore, the observer, the act of observation, and that which is observed are conceptually linked through "change."

It is also noteworthy that simultaneity is a basic condition of a contextual ontology. Without simultaneous social and perceptual activity, the ontological position becomes one of assuming that a thing, for example, "mind," integrates or mediates social and perceptual stimulation in a sequential way. If some "thing," such as a "mind," has to act sequentially to integrate social and perceptual stimulation, then there is a structure necessary to enstructure, and the argument for process as a primary ontology is contradicted.* From a contextual position, there is no such *thing* as "mind." Mind is a simultaneous relationship between biological and social processes.

## Cause and Effect

Contextually, cause and effect is relative to the observer operating in his or her social/consensual domain. Cause is not inherent in that which is observed. Nor is it

---

*In fact the idea of simultaneity versus mediation contrasts the contextual position to the widely understood "constructivist" movement. Some constructivists believe that "mind" mediates experience, socially or otherwise, whereas for the contextualist there is no such thing as "mind as entity."

immanent to the observer. Instead, cause is best understood as embedded in the perceptual and interpersonal process of consensus.

In the classical physical sense, cause is structural. By Newtonian laws, some "thing" affects another "thing," thereby causing some reaction. From a mental health standpoint, "cause" has been translated to be either: (a) linear and impactful; or (b) reciprocal and mutual. The linear position is best exemplified by the causative perspective emerging from organic-medical propositions, where mental illness is viewed as caused by "germs," or "brain damage," or "genetics." Comparatively, psychological propositions lead to a conclusion that individual maladaptive responses are caused by such things as weak egos, irrational thoughts, retroflections, or external stimuli that produce responses. From a systemic standpoint, on the other hand, cause is viewed as circularly holistic or recursive, where interaction within a system's structural boundaries is implicated as causative of maladaptive behavior. Therefore, systemically, the reciprocal interaction of family members, and not an individual, is viewed as the culprit.

But from a contextual perspective, one does not simply look at "things" as causative. Neither does one look at interpersonal interactions as causative. Rather, one looks to the process whereby structures exists, the process of enstructuring, which occurs in the human social/consensual domain *simultaneously* along with perceptual perturbation. For example, picture a father and a 3-year-old daughter watching the movie *Superman II*. In the movie there is a scene where Superman walks across the street and is hit by a car. Superman walks away unscathed, but the automobile is destroyed. The 3-year-old, unknowledgeable about cars in an absolute sense, gets the impression that cars can be injured when experiencing impact by a human leg. The father then takes the daughter out to the garage and has her hit the fender to see that the car is "hard" and causes "hurt," whereas the human body is soft, fragile, and is easily hurt by cars. He then convinces his daughter that the reason why Superman was uninjured by the car was because Superman is "pretend," a movie character—not real. Other family members agree; the movie scene was not real, because real people get hurt when hit by real cars. In this case, reality was "structured" around social-consensual and perceptual activity. If the child would have acted consensually in relation to Superman, then she would have walked in front of moving cars without concern, only coming to another consensus about the reality of cars upon surviving an accident and subsequently being educated as to what "hit" her. On the other hand, the father, having been earlier educated about cars, communicated to his daughter that Superman was pretend, which was supported by subsequent family agreement (social-consensual activity).

What is understood is understood through social relationship. All thoughts derive from social activity. Thoughts cannot be separated from social activity, because one's earliest language is socially developed and transmitted. Reality emerges through consensus, as does cause and effect. Most agree that cars, in fact, can hurt human beings.

Once a structure is defined, then cause and effect can be defined. Otherwise, there is no cause and effect in a classical sense. What caused Superman to be able to walk away from an accident unscathed was "pretend," which became real to a little girl within a social/consensual domain with a linguistic tradition. What caused hurt for the little girl hitting a fender with her father was the "thing" called a "car." From a contextual perspective, both "pretend" and a "car" were real within the confines of the father-daughter and family relations.

## Professional Adherents

Since the contextual paradigm is prospective, defining a group of professional adherents poses quite a problem. In order to meet the criteria for a counseling paradigm, it is necessary to surmise about what professional developments could lead a professional group to associate with such a metatheoretical position. What is needed is a youthful profession that is asserting its political muscle, while not demonstrating an allegiance to an epistemological position. Also, the training of professionals has to be founded on a broad knowledge and skill base, which would allow for intervention at the level of the individual (even diagnostically, if necessary) or at the level of an identified social system of significance. The field of counseling is one such profession.

At first glance, professional counseling appears to be a hybrid of psychology, education, and mental health services. Training in counseling has emerged historically through professional schools of education at major universities, although counseling programs at some universities are affiliated with other academic units. Such programs base their coursework strongly on psychological theory, yet the field has not grown primarily from a scientific tradition, as is the case with psychology. Rather, counselors have continuously had an identity primarily as practitioners, and there is no scientist-versus-practitioner split in the professional groups representing counselors, as has occurred in professional groups of psychologists. At the same time, counseling, as a youthful profession, has defined its mission broadly, and appears open and flexible in terms of incorporating diverse interests into its fold. This broad mission is appealing but also has drawbacks. One drawback is the failure of counseling theorists to define an agreed-upon unifying framework that would allow counseling's tacit eclecticism (drawing on concepts from many counseling theories) to become philosophically grounded (see the attempt to build a philosophical eclecticism by Patterson, 1985, and Thorne, 1967). Regardless, professional counseling is growing and emerging as a major player in the mental health field. As such, it has the potential to mature into a philosophically based mental health profession.

At present, the major professional group representing professional counselors is the American Association for Counseling and Development (AACD). The AACD, formerly the American Personnel and Guidance Association, has begun to spread its wings politically. Due to its large and motivated membership, professional and political concerns have received recent and concentrated attention. This attention, although late in coming, has led to an effective lobbying effort at both the federal and state levels. At the time of this writing, thirty-two states have passed professional counseling regulatory statutes (licensure, registration, and certification laws), and momentum has been building as more and more state AACD-affiliates appear on the verge of successful lobbying efforts. Concurrently, counseling is expanding its affiliations through associations with groups that have the potential to extend counseling's professional role—for instance, through the affiliation with the International Association for Marriage and Family Counseling (IAMFC). Within approximately one year of affiliation, the IAMFC was awarded full division status in the AACD, growing as an affiliate at nearly 200 members per month. The IAMFC has become a viable political entity representing marriage and family counselors wishing to affiliate primarily with the AACD as opposed to the American Association for Marriage and Family Therapy (AAMFT). The IAMFC is now having some influence on accreditation standards for the general field of professional counseling, and will further infuse the field with ethical and professional standards recognizing systemic-relational theory.

At present, the major certifying board for the generic field of professional counseling is the National Board of Certified Counselors (NBCC). As conceived and implemented, the NBCC is not a specialty certification board. Rather, it is a national board for identifying generally qualified practitioners in counseling. Although there are other specialty certifying boards in professional counseling that have a closer practical linkage to health services (e.g., the Board for Rehabilitation Certification or the American Academy of Certified Clinical Mental Health Counselors), the NBCC standards are the most generally recognized and broad-based standards for identifying the academic content areas and degree requirements for professional counseling. Therefore, the standards of the NBCC will be presented as representative of professional standards across the field.

In order to be certified by NBCC, a person must hold a valid graduate degree with a major in counseling or a related professional field. If the graduate degree program is accredited by the Council for the Accreditation of Counseling and Related Educational Programs (CACREP), the degree automatically meets NBCC educational requirements. Otherwise, candidates for certification must show they have specific coursework in counseling theory and supervised practice in counseling, plus coursework in six of the following eight areas: (a) human growth and development; (b) social and cultural foundations; (c) the helping relationship; (d) group dynamics, processing, and counseling; (e) life-style and career development; (f) appraisal of individuals; (g) research and evaluation; and (h) professional orientation. It is in these coursework requirements that the clear practitioner bent is evident, as is the knowledge base of training.

In addition to attainment of an acceptable graduate degree, those candidates for NBCC certification without CACREP accredited degrees must also have two years of acceptable post-master's-degree supervised experience. Supervision must be accomplished by a qualified licensed or certified counselor, or another qualified mental health professional acceptable to the board. Given acceptable graduate academic training and the required supervised experience, applicants must pass a national counselor certification examination, which is administered by NBCC. The examination consists of multiple-choice items covering the areas listed previously under coursework requirements.

As can be seen, the standards for NBCC certification are strict and broadly based. In this way, the NBCC standards help to define the field of counseling differentially from other mental health professions.

## Therapies as Subcategories

Given that the contextual paradigm is prospective or propositional, there is no fully developed and researched counseling theory aligned with the paradigm. However, the Milan Systemic Family Therapy (Boscolo et al., 1987) is proposed as an example of a trans-paradigmatic theory. The Milan approach leaves behind the structural underpinnings of many of the more purely systemic-relational therapies and emphasizes linguistic and social interaction in problem definition and treatment. The Milan approach is breaking new ground, and appears to be leading the way to a new way of conceptualizing problems.

In addition to the Milan approach, and in keeping with the design and format of this text, a pure example of a paradigm-specific therapy is offered. Cognitive-Consensual Therapy is developed and presented as a philosophical offspring of contextual thinking and as a new theory of counseling and psychotherapy. (See Chapter 18.)

## Chapter Conclusion

This chapter has grounded an emergent paradigm philosophically and operationally. The propositions and tenets of the contextual paradigm have been defined. Epistemological and ontological issues have been addressed. Causality has been defined as secondary to the enstructuring process. The profession of counseling has been defined as a reasonable prospect for professional adherence to contextual precepts. And two counseling theories have been introduced, which will serve to elucidate how contextual ideas translate to therapeutic practices. The next chapter outlines Milan Systemic Family Therapy, a trans-paradigmatic (historically transitional) therapy between the systemic-relational and contextual paradigms.

## References

Bograd, M. (1984). Family systems approaches to wife battering: A feminist critique. *American Journal of Orthopsychiatry, 54,* 558–568.

Bograd, M. (1986). A feminist examination of family systems models of violence against women in the family. In J. C. Hansen and M. Ault-Riche (Eds.), *Women and family therapy* (pp. 34–50). Rockville, MD: Aspen Systems.

Boscolo, L., Cecchin, G., Hoffman, L., & Penn, P. (1987). *Milan systemic family therapy.* New York: Basic Books.

Colapinto, J. (1979). The relative value of empirical evidence. *Family Process, 18,* 427–441.

Cottone, R. R. (1988). Epistemological and ontological issues in counseling: Implications of social systems theory. *Counselling Psychology Quarterly, 1,* 357–365.

Cottone, R. R. (1989). The third epistemology: Extending Maturana's structure determinism. *The American Journal of Family Therapy, 17,* 99–109.

Cottone, R. R. & Greenwell, R. (1991). *The contextual paradigm of marital and family therapy.* Manuscript submitted for publication.

Cottone, R. R., & Greenwell, R. (in press). Beyond linearity and circularity: Deconstructing social systems theory. *Journal of Marital and Family Therapy.*

Dell, P. F. (1982). Beyond homeostasis: Toward a concept of coherence. *Family Process, 21,* 21–41.

Dell, P. F. (1985). Understanding Bateson and Maturana: Toward a biological foundation for the social sciences. *Journal of Marital and Family Therapy, 11*(1), 1–20.

Efran, J. S., Germer, C. K., & Lukens, D. (1986). Contextualism and psychotherapy. In R. L. Rosnow & M. Georgoudi (Eds.), *Contextualism and understanding in behavioral science: Implications for research and theory,* (pp. 169–186). New York: Praeger.

Gergen, K. J. (1985). The social constructionist movement in modern psychology. *American Psychologist, 40,* 266-275.

Goolishian, H. A., & Winderman, L. (1988). Constructivism, autopoiesis and problem determined systems. *The Irish Journal of Psychology, 9,* 130–143.

Hoffman, L. (1988). A constructivist position for family therapy. *The Irish Journal of Psychology, 9,* 110–129.

Hoffman, L. (1990). Constructing realities: An art of lenses. *Family Process, 29,* 1–12.

Kuhn, T. S. (1970). *The structure of scientific revolutions* (2nd ed.). Chicago: University of Chicago Press.

Maturana, H. R. (1978). Biology of language: The epistemology of reality. In G. A. Miller & E. Lenneberg (Eds.), *Psychology and biology of language and thought.* New York: Academic Press.

Maturana, H. R. (1980). Biology of cognition. In H. R. Maturana & F. J. Varela, *Autopoiesis and cognition: The realization of the living.* Boston: D. Reidel. (Original work published in 1970.)

Maturana, H. R., Lettvin, J. Y., McCulloch, W. S., & Pitts, W. H. (1960). Anatomy and physiology of vision in the frog (*Rana pipiens*). *Journal of General Physiology, 43*(6), 129–175.

Maturana, H. R., Uribe, G., & Frenk, S. (1968). A biological theory of relativistic colour coding in the primate retina. *Arch. Biologia y Med. Exp.,* Supplemento No. *1,* 1–30.

Maturana, H. R., & Varela, F. J. (1980). Autopoiesis: The organization of the living. In H. R. Maturana & F. J. Varela, *Autopoiesis and cognition: The realization of the living.* Boston: D. Reidel. (Original work published in 1973.)

Patterson, C. H. (1985). *The therapeutic relationship: Foundations for an eclectic psychotherapy.* Belmont, CA: Wadsworth.

Pepper, S. C. (1942). *World hypotheses: A study in evidence.* Berkeley, CA: University of California Press.

Rosnow, R. L., & Georgoudi, M. (1986). The spirit of contextualism. In R. L. Rosnow & M. Georgoudi (Eds.), *Contextualism and understanding in behavioral science: Implications for research and theory,* (pp. 3–22). New York: Praeger.

Taggart, M. (1985). The feminist critique in epistemological perspective: Questions of context in family therapy. *Journal of Marital and Family Therapy, 11,* 113–126.

Thorne, F. C. (1967). *Integrative psychology.* Brandon, VT: Clinical Psychology Publishing.

Walters, M., Carter, E., Papp, P., & Silverstein, O. (1988). *The invisible web.* New York: Guilford.

# 17

# Milan Systemic Family Therapy:

## *A Trans-paradigmatic Theory Bridging the Systemic-Relational and Contextual Paradigms*

"MILAN SYSTEMIC FAMILY THERAPY" (Boscolo, Cecchin, Hoffman & Penn, 1987) is probably best understood as a trans-paradigmatic therapy. In this case the boundary between the systemic-relational and contextual paradigms appears to be crossed. Since the contextual paradigm is only prospective and propositional, there are no clear-cut existing therapies that best exemplify the paradigmatic propositions listed earlier in chapter 16. However, Milan Systemic Family Therapy certainly, and perhaps inadvertently, has characteristics that appear more contextual than systemic in nature. For this reason it is presented as more aligned to the contextual paradigm than to the systemic-relational paradigm, and the reader should not be confused by the term *systemic* in the title of Milan Systemic Family Therapy.

Probably no other type of therapy exemplifies a shift in practice away from the influence of the cybernetic model of early social systems theory as does the Milan Systemic Family Therapy (Boscolo, Cecchin, Hoffman & Penn, 1987). The Milan approach is probably the first therapeutic model to fully include the therapist (or the therapeutic team) as part of the "problem" formulation. Hoffman (1988) stated:

*My acquaintance with the Milan team went by stages. In 1978, the team came to Ackerman [referring to the Ackerman Institute] to demonstrate their work. More than anything else, I was astounded by the way they attended to the team/family interface. This was the first time, to my knowledge, that the therapist had been routinely included as part of the problem. For instance, in cases where a therapist came for an "impasse" consultation [where an outside therapist brings a client-family from his or her caseload to a Milan therapy center to perform therapy in front of a Milan team in order to get advice], an intervention might consist of commending the therapist for protecting the family from change. Both family and therapist might then co-operate in changing very fast. Or a family might be praised by the team for missing a session as a way to indicate that they wanted to slow down the therapy. This practice called into question the frame between family and therapist much as Escher's two hands drawing each other break the artist-subject frame. (p. 121)*

Beyond inclusion of the therapist as part of the larger "system" within which problems are defined and treated, the Milan approach also moves away from a strict directive or instructive mentality in therapy, which is characteristic of more purely systemic-relational therapies.

Actually, there are two Milan teams. They were once united under the leadership of Mara Palazzoli Selvini, MD, a researcher and therapist who was instrumental in the foundation of the the Centro per lo Studio della Famiglia de Milano (the Center for the Study of the Family of Milan). There, she and her team members, including Luigi Boscolo, Gianfranco Cecchin, and Giuliana Prata, developed a unique method for treating mental disorder, deriving ultimately from the ideas of Bateson (1972, 1979) and his successors at the Mental Research Institute in California. Over the years, the Milan team developed three guiding principles for family therapy: hypothesizing, circularity, and neutrality (see Selvini, Boscolo, Cecchin, & Prata, 1980). However, due to differences in interest between research (primarily Selvini and Prata) and teaching (Boscolo and Cecchin) the original team split into two Milan groups, with Boscolo and Cecchin primarily focusing on education and the training of therapists. The break also allowed for the emergence of some fundamental differences in the way the two Milan groups practiced therapy. Cecchin and Boscolo began to move away from a strategic approach to therapy, which was characteristic of the original Milan group. Instead, they began to experiment with the process of questioning as an intervention itself, thereby downplaying the directive therapeutic intervention that began to become commonplace among systemically oriented therapists, and which Selvini and Prata maintained. In effect, Boscolo and Cecchin began to view therapy more as conversation or dialogue and less as directive intervention. Hoffman (1988) stated:

*However, Boscolo and Cecchin had moved away from the emphasis on strategy associated with the early Milan method. This was demonstrated by their increasing tendency to treat the questioning as an intervention all by itself. The portentous message at the end of the interview was less and less emphasised and the adversarial language from game theory was falling away.*

*The [sic] was also a stronger emphasis on ideas. Instead of seeing everything in a family in terms of manoeuvres, coalitions and games, the focus was on beliefs, premises and myths. This shift was in part influenced by Bateson's own constructivist belief that, in living organisms, the kind of abstract premises that have to do with survival are laid down at a deep-structure level. Thus, rather than attempting to change family structures, interaction patterns and the like, Boscolo and Cecchin aimed at the governing ideas that held many lesser attitudes or behaviors in place.*

*This development had an interesting philosophic impact. We were at last beginning to see a ''conversation'' or ''discourse'' model for therapy replacing that of the ''game,'' which had for so long been such a fertile metaphor for the field. We were also beginning to see the effect of constructivism and second-order cybernetics on the practice of family therapy. (pp. 121–122)*

In effect, the Milan team of Boscolo and Cecchin has provided new insights as to how therapy should proceed. In fact, it is the Boscolo and Cecchin emphasis on meanings and social relations in defining problems, and their emphasis on dialogue and conversation as interventional methods, that makes their approach unique. They have broken new ground, verging from more purely systemic-relational propositions and tenets into the realm of what has been defined as the contextual paradigm. In this text, the ''Milan'' approach, from this point forward, will mean the approach that has emerged from the Cecchin and Boscolo collaboration.

## The Foundational Theory

### The Target of Counseling

Instead of the team of therapists acting to produce a ''result,'' the act of therapy has been redefined by the Milan group as ''conversation.'' Essentially, the therapeutic team attempts to enter into the developmental process of the family, infusing information, which then is assumed to facilitate changes in the way the family operates. In this way, the target of therapy becomes *the process* at the core of a family's existence. With therapy viewed as conversation, a change in emphasis occurs where directive interventions are downplayed.

As applied by Milan-style therapists, the information-infusing process resulting from viewing therapy as conversation is a relatively new development in counseling theory. Tomm (1984a) described the theoretical significance of the Milan team's approach as follows:

*Their earlier view tended to regard systems essentially as stable or homeostatic and secondarily as changeable. Their more recent view emphasizes that systems are essentially always changing or evolving and only appear to be stable. The implications of these differing views are significant. If a therapist regards systems primarily as stable and structured, and secondarily as flexible and changing, then he or she tends to be directive. The therapeutic task becomes one of determining the nature of the current maladaptive family structure, hypothesizing a more adaptive structure and "pushing" the system from the former to the latter. The therapist can be directive because he "knows" what the maladaptive structure is and, having the goal of another structure in mind, "knows" what the end point should be. He can tell family members how they should behave. If, in contrast, the therapist regards systems primarily as evolving and only "appearing" to be stable, then his or her approach tends to be facilitative. The therapist does not know what the future course or evolution for any particular system will or should be. He or she tries to identify points of apparent "stuckness" at which new "connections" are introduced to liberate the family to continue to evolve without the need for symptoms. Since there is no fixed image of how the family is or should be, an approach based on an evolutionary perspective cannot be directive in the sense of telling the family members how to behave. (p. 120)*

Given the basic propositions of the systemic-relational and contextual paradigms in this text, it can be seen that the Milan group has begun to push the limits of the systemic-relational paradigm. Its ontology is one of change and process, and by focusing on meanings instead of family structures or patterns, the Milan perspective more clearly represents contextual ideals. For example, Tomm (1984a) stated: "Consensual 'meanings' are assigned to specific behaviors and events, and to the patterns that connect them. Once created, this reality becomes the map which channels family members' actions along redundant patterns" (p. 120). Consequently, the Milan approach more fully contextualizes problems. The focus of study and the target of behavior becomes the change process and the consensual meanings associated with that process.

But conversation is often not used alone as a therapeutic method. For example, Milan-style therapists still maintain the use of specific interventions to facilitate change. Yet Milan-style interventions are primarily process-facilitative rather than result-directive. Probably the best example of a Milan-style intervention is the *prescribed family ritual*. A ritual is actually a task which is recommended to the family. Tomm (1984b) stated:

*The ritual is offered in the sense of an experiment, a trial, a symbolic gesture or a transitory rite. There is no implication that "this is the way things should be done" in the course of regular family living. Nor is there any insistence that the ritual actually be carried out, only the claim that to do so may be very useful. Indeed, the ritual need not even be carried out to have a therapeutic effect. And when it is carried out there is certainly no expectation that the activity should become a permanent part of the family's daily life. (p. 266)*

Systemically, all family members are viewed as somehow involved in problems within a family context, and prescribed family rituals are interventions often targeted to challenging basic family *premises*. According to Boscolo et al. (1987), premises are "reference values or guiding principles that are programmed in at the level of deep structure and out of the reach of conscious mind" (p. 19). Premises are similar to deep-seated rules. For example, instead of an identified patient (IP) always attending therapy, the family members of the IP's four-person noncommunicative family might be asked by the therapist to decide which two of the four family members will come to the next session. The therapist might further prescribe that subsequent sessions are to be attended by other pairs of family members to ensure that all are involved in therapy over the course of several sessions, but only two family members should attend each session. Also, each session must be attended by a different pair. This intervention sets up a family ritual that challenges the *premise* that there is one sick individual in the family. Before each therapy session, the family must get together and decide which two individuals in the family are to attend the session. This requires communication between family members across otherwise bounded relations. The intervention, therefore, challenges both a family premise and the family's means of communication (see Boscolo et al., 1987, for a more detailed discussion of the actual case where this ritual was prescribed).

Broadly stated, then, the target of therapy according to the Milan approach is the process of family functioning. The Milan therapist attempts to facilitate already progressing family development and change by infusing new information into the family and by challenging family premises.

## The Process of Counseling

In keeping with Maturana's "Structure Determinism" (Maturana, 1978, 1970/1980; Maturana & Varela, 1973/1980, 1987), The Milan team views its task as "perturbation" through interaction. What this means is that specific results are not expected from specific interventions. Instead, the team acts to create new meanings through nondirective but meaning-confrontive techniques. By challenging the language context of a defined problem, the Milan approach infuses a system with new meaning opportunities. The family is sent away from therapy after being questioned in a way that queries its basic premises, and an intervention is implemented to further perturb the system.

There is an optimistic attitude among Milan-type therapists. It is basically assumed that the family will use the new information to change constructively and that it will reorganize around meanings that will help it survive in a way that is less destructive of individual members of the family and of the family itself. That optimism, in part appears to stem from the use of "therapeutic teams."

The Milan approach makes use of therapeutic teams to facilitate the process of counseling (Boscolo & Cecchin, 1982). In fact, the therapist, as a general rule, is not alone when doing therapy. While doing therapy, the therapist (usually one acting therapist, but no more than two acting therapists) is observed through one-way mirrors by other therapists who call-in messages (sometimes by specially designed telephones) to the treating therapist. The behind-the-mirror team members (called the "treatment team'' or ''T-group'') may also call the therapist out of the treatment room for conferences about what is occurring during therapy. The basic purpose of the treatment team is to allow development of effective hypotheses about family functioning, and consequently to develop effective interventions. The team approach also provides feedback to the acting therapist about his or her role in problem definition.

The Milan associates (Boscolo & Cecchin, 1982) have also experimented with ''observing teams'' (O-groups). Observing teams are teams that watch the treatment teams and then comment about the behaviors of T-group members (usually only at the end of sessions). The feedback of the observing team is useful to the treatment team, because it helps to define the therapeutic context. Differing hypotheses between the T-group and the O-group can then be discussed. Boscolo and Cecchin stated: ''From the differences between the two sets of hypotheses and interventions, new ideas are developed with new solutions which may be useful in the next session with the family'' (p. 157). In this way, the therapeutic context is recognized and accommodated in problem formulation, as consensus is developed around hypotheses which direct the actions of the therapeutic team. In this way the *context* of therapy is accounted for and assessed, just as the process of the family in therapy is assessed.

## Counselor Role

To summarize the therapeutic role according to Milan Systemic Family Therapy, only three terms are required: hypothesizing, circular questioning, and neutrality (Selvini-Palazzoli, Boscolo, Cecchin & Prata, 1980). Boscolo et al. (1987) defined neutrality in the following way:

> *Neutrality, the traveling companion of circular questioning and hypothesizing, is pervasive throughout the Milan team's theory and methodology. It is best described by its results. If anyone in the treatment family were asked ''Whose side is the therapist on?'' everyone would agree he or she is on no one's side. (p. 97)*

Further, the authors described how neutrality means a rejection of the psychiatric labeling of individuals in the family. In effect, no one in the family is viewed as ''good'' or ''bad.'' The therapist plays the role of family advocate, and the therapist is careful to establish a therapeutic and fair relationship with all members of the family.

Circular questioning (defined more thoroughly in the ''Specialized Techniques'' section of this chapter) is a nonjudgmental technique that helps to prevent the therapist from ''taking sides.'' In effect, the therapist asks questions, circulating around the family in the process of questioning, and probes the consensus among family members without siding with one or another member of the family. Judgments are not made. Questions are not conclusive. It is only during the process of hypothesizing about the premises in the family that judgments are made, and, then, they appear linearly judgmental only in the first stages of hypothesis formulation.

Boscolo and Cecchin (1982) defined hypotheses as '' 'maps' which introduce a pattern in the territory, without ever being the 'territory' '' (p. 164). Hypothesis formulations often begin with linear causal explanations related to a member of the family. For instance, the mother may be *blamed* for the problems in a family. However, through the process of discussing the family dynamics, the treatment team members often take positions that support or dispute the roles of individual family members in problem development and maintenance. In this way, the therapeutic team mirrors the circular questioning technique in its process of hypothesizing. Mother may be viewed as causative of the problems, then father, then a child, etcetera, until a matrix begins to appear that allows for a more systemwide hypothesis about the "family problem." It is the systemwide hypothesis that most often is addressed by an intervention in therapy.

Boscolo et al. (1987) described three types of hypotheses:

*One class of hypotheses refers to who is with whom in the family: alliances, coalitions, or "marriages."*

*A second class of hypotheses refers to individual and family premises or myths.*

*A third class of hypotheses is based on the analysis of the communications in the family and between the family and other systems, including, of course, the therapist. For instance, in this case we try to describe double-bind messages which make the psychotic member's behavior intelligible. . . . But we are not looking for an individual double bind, created by one person toward another one. The context created by all the family members results in numerous double binds. (p. 322)*

Hypotheses range from structural assessments of the family to more global contextual concerns that influence the process of the family and therapy. The idea of process is important in hypothesis formulation, and it pervades the Milan approach. Accordingly, one can view the actions and procedures of the Milan team members as process-oriented, while at the same time they probe for consensual "realities" in the family. Those consensual realities are then addressed through interventions that are primarily process-relevant. The intent of interventions is to facilitate change, although, as mentioned earlier, the direction of change is basically unpredictable. The "premise," so-to-speak, of the Milan approach is that the family, as a surviving living system, will change in a way that better suits its survival needs.

## Goals of Counseling and Ideal Outcomes

The goal of Milan Systemic Family Therapy is transformation of the family through engagement of the family's evolutionary process. Essentially, therapy should undo what is stuck.

# General Procedures

## Assessment and Treatment/Remediation

Assessment and treatment go hand in hand according to the Milan approach. In fact, the Milan team has ritualized what has been called the "five-part session" (Tomm,

1984b). Tomm (1984b) has given an excellent summary of the five-part session, and readers are referred to his excellent work for a more thorough understanding of the basic assessment and treatment process. According to Tomm, the five-part session involves: (a) a presession; (b) the family interview; (c) an intersession; (d) an end-of-session intervention; and (e) a postsession.

Assessment actually begins in the *presession*. The presession is a period of treatment-team interaction that occurs before the family is actually interviewed and after some basic referral issues have been communicated (from the referral call). Tomm (1984b) said:

> *The team discusses whatever is known about these issues and then generates some hypotheses about what might be happening in the family that resulted in the referral. They draw on their general knowledge about families and their specific experience with similar problems to develop these hypotheses. They also discuss the types of questions that could be asked to elicit data to validate or refute the hypotheses they have generated. Thus, before the therapist actually meets the family he or she has some ideas about how or where to proceed. (p. 254)*

The generation of hypotheses is essentially the beginning of assessment.

The *family interview,* which follows the presession, involves a therapist or therapists (usually one, but no more than two) meeting with the family to discuss concerns. Tomm (1984b) stated: ''The actual interview is devoted almost entirely to asking questions'' (p. 254). The interview may begin very generally, but the therapist may become very specific in inquiring about the family's operation. Since the Milan-style therapist believes that, ultimately, change will occur outside of therapy as the family processes the information presented in therapeutic sessions, no directives or opinions are necessarily given in this stage. Rather, questions are used to pique the interests of the family members. In fact, as the Milan approach has been refined, it has been hypothesized that questions, in and of themselves, can introduce information into the family, without providing outcomes or answers! This view places great confidence in the family's own resource for self-direction.

The *intersession* is a discussion by members of the treatment team. The family is excused, or left in a sound-secured treatment room, while the interviewing therapist meets with the treatment-team members. Tomm (1984b) described the task of the intersession as follows:

> *The task is to elaborate a systemic hypothesis and to generate an intervention. Essentially, this is a period of intense brainstorming. Team members are encouraged to articulate any intuitive impressions, even to ''discharge'' their lineal hypotheses (e.g., ''He's a real bastard!''), and then move on to build a more circular and systemic understanding (''Why is he showing us this annoying behavior?'', ''What effect is it having on whom?'', etc.). The mental work entailed in synthesizing the data into holistic patterns to generate a systemic*

*hypothesis and in creating an intervention that fits is both taxing and exhilarating. (p. 255)*

The intersession may be brief or extended, depending on the interaction of the team. The main task is to come to some consensus about what intervention will occur in the next part of the session.

The fourth part of a session is the *end-of-session intervention*. Tomm (1984b) described it as follows:

> *This [intervention] may take many forms: a systemic opinion (with or without a prescription for no change), a reframing of family beliefs, a prescription to carry out a detailed ritual, a declaration of therapeutic impotence, an analogic enactment, etc. In the early stages of therapy, it usually consists of an explanation for why the family is experiencing its current dilemma. The delivery of the team's opinion is usually succinct and often brief. The specific wording and phraseology is carefully chosen and sometimes repeated in a hypnotic fashion. The content of the intervention tends to be unexpected. Thus there is an element of surprise which leaves the family with some degree of confusion and perplexity. There is usually minimal further interaction or discussion even if the family raises questions. (p. 256)*

In effect, the therapy group attempts to leave the family to its own resources.

The final part of the Milan-style session is the *postsession*. This involves a discussion by treatment-team members (the T-group) about the family members' immediate reactions, and it involves an attempt to assess the usefulness of the hypothesis that led to the intervention and to generate other potential hypotheses for future sessions. If an observing group (O-group) is involved, a postsession dialogue between members of the T-group and the O-group may ensue, which allows for communication about differences or similarities in the different group hypotheses. Essentially, the postsession provides the treatment team with an invitation to curiosity, which is so necessary in the ongoing process of therapy (Cecchin, 1987).

The Milan-style five-part session, which is the framework for each session in therapy, fundamentally is an ongoing process of assessment and treatment. Assessment never ends, as therapists are continually asked to generate hypotheses, new maps for directing actions, which themselves may change as new ideas come to the fore. Treatment begins with the presession, where possibilities for action follow early hypothesizing. In this sense, the client and the therapist are in continual interaction from the time of referral and the first presession to the time of termination and the last postsession.

## Case Management

Milan-style sessions are generally spread out over the course of several months. In fact, the family may be seen for an initial session, and the following session may not occur for another month. Additional sessions may occur on a monthly basis, but they are usually quickly spread out so that the intervals between sessions become six months or even a year. The rationale for infrequent sessions is what is described as a family's need for time to process the information in the sessions, and to prevent overinvolvement of a therapeutic team. In other words, the changes that occur should not be directed, but instead should derive from the new information provided in sessions through the therapeutic questioning and prescribed rituals. The family, then, through its actions, assimilates or accommodates this information in its own style and in a way that best fits its social context. Milan therapists are optimistic. However, they are not blinded to the potentially powerful effect of therapy. Therefore, they do formal follow-ups with the families, in order to assess the direction of change and to amend interventions, if necessary.

## Specialized Techniques

**1.** *Circular Questions.* A classic example of technique deriving from the Milan approach is "circular questioning." Boscolo et al. (1987) described circular questioning as follows:

> *Circularity is based on the idea that people are connected to each other in particular patterns through time, and it is these patterns that we identify as families. Family members demonstrate their connection through the communication of information in the form of verbal and nonverbal language. This language describes the exchange of messages that, in problem systems, are often confused or unacceptable to the family. The circular questions define and clarify these confused ideas and questionable behaviors as well as introduce information back to the family in the form of new questions. In this manner the therapeutic system and the family system co-create multiple meanings through language which allow the consideration of more rather than fewer alternatives. (p. 96)*

For example, the therapist might start the first session with the question: "What is the problem in the family now?" After someone states the problem (for instance, that a son is too independent), then the therapist might pursue questions that circulate around the family as the problem is placed in its interpersonal context. The therapist might ask: "Who first noticed that the son was too independent?" Other questions might follow, such as: "Who agrees most that the son is the problem?" "Who agrees least that the son is the problem?" Boscolo et al. (1987) said:

> *This type of questioning becomes another attempt to clarify coalition patterns in the system. It is important to note that the questions only ask for structural alignments, comparisons, and classifications from the family. They are in no way declarative in themselves. (p. 96)*

Very simply, questioning becomes a therapeutic intervention, as the therapist probes the relational dynamics underlying the ''premise'' of a system. Again, premises are defined as ''reference values or guiding principles that are programmed in at the level of deep structure and out of the reach of conscious mind'' (p. 19). In effect, a premise is a nonconscious but shared belief that guides the behavior of family members. Through questioning, the Milan team attempts to ferret out premises, and the team's task is to ''hypothesize'' as to what premises underlie the behavior in the family.

(For additional information on circular questioning, see the excellent articles by Penn, 1982, and Fleuridas, Nelson, & Rosenthal, 1986).

**2.** *Future Questions.* In ferreting out premises, the Milan approach makes full use of questions that not only probe the alignment of relations in the family, but also test hypotheses. ''Future questions'' are used to:

> . . . *challenge a family premise or advance a new one. Future questions evoke a different map for the family and are usually employed at a later point in the interview, after information is collected that describes the present sequences around the problem and the coalitions in the family. (p. 34)*

For example, the therapist might ask: ''If someone else was to have the symptoms [of the identified patient] who would it be?'' Or, ''If mother and father were to get along perfectly, what would happen?'' Or, ''If the problem were solved, how would the family interact?'' The Milan associates believe that a family's activity is often organized around a premise, and, therefore, future questions have the effect of ''upsetting'' or perturbing the family, thereby challenging the premise by introducing new information into the system. At the same time future questions clarify hypotheses, future questions also set the stage for change. Importantly, the questioning is carried out in a neutral fashion, and the family, in effect, defines what possibilities there are for change.

**3.** *Prescribed Family Rituals.* A ritual is described by Boscolo et al. (1987) as ''an ordering of behavior in the family either on certain days [odd days, even days] or at certain times [after dinner, in the morning]'' (p. 4). A prescribed family ritual is a *recommendation* by the treatment team, presented by the therapist who is interviewing the family, to behave a certain way. It is accomplished by the therapist at the ''end-of-session intervention'' part of a session. Tomm (1984b) stated: ''In general, rituals have the effect of introducing more clarity where there appears to be too much confusion'' (p. 266). As stated earlier, the outcome of the ritual is less important in ritual formulation than its potential to produce a change through information infusion in the family. Rituals should target premises, the deep rules of the family that may operate at less than a conscious level. By targeting premises, a family ritual challenges the basic process of the family and infuses the family with new operative information.

**4.** *Positive Connotation.* A positive connotation is a special kind of reframe. A reframe is a redefinition of behaviors, thoughts, or feelings. A positive connotation is more pervasive than a simple redefinition of a problem. It is also less strategic than the types of reframes used by more classic systemic-relational paradigm therapists. A positive connotation is a new definition of the relational factors that maintain a symptom. Positive connotation operates at the level of the family; it describes a relational rationale for the unwanted behavior. In this sense, it provides a believable context for symptomatic behavior. Any relational reason given by a therapist for maintaining a symptomatic behavior can be considered a positive connotation. For example, if a child is misbehaving in a way that redirects parental activity away from marital strife to attention of the misbehaving child, then the child might be congratulated for his actions and his ability to keep his parents from fighting. The intent of positive connotations is not just to influence the family, but to actually allow for the therapist to enter into a framework for understanding the operation of the family. It is not a trick, as a paradoxical directive may be viewed. Rather, it is means of placing a symptom in a systemic light.

These four techniques are examples of how the Milan group puts theory into practice.

## Recent Developments or Criticisms

There have been few independent outcome studies of the Milan approach to family therapy. However, one recent study performed by researchers independent of the Milan team was published in 1989. Mashal, Feldman, and Sigal (1989), after reviewing the literature on outcome reports of Milan-style therapists, summarized the results of a two-year independent follow-up project of Milan-style therapy. Although the Mashal et al. study has some design limitations that may threaten both the internal and external validity of the study, the findings shed some independent and preliminary light on the effectiveness of Milan-style therapy. It is noteworthy that the Mashal et al. study dealt with clients who were ''refractory'' to other treatments (meaning other treatments had failed). Mashal et al. reported:

> The rate of positive family change reported by fathers and mothers in our study was 55% and 58%, respectively. These rates are marginally lower than the usual improvement rates of two-thirds (65–73%) reported for family systems therapy. About half our families reported disliking the therapy, and about two-thirds reported that at least one family member went on for further treatment. Thus, our findings do not offer support for the superiority of the Milan approach for families that were refractory to other treatments.
> The reports of the 9 identified child-patients differed markedly from those of parents; 89% reported better family functioning and 78% better self-functioning at follow-up. We have no adequate explanation for the discrepancy between the outcome reports of parents and their children. (p. 465)

Although the results are not overwhelming, the authors of the study reasoned that there were several possible factors that might have negatively affected the success rates, including the small sample size, the refractory nature of the clientele, the older ages of the identified patients, the length of the follow-up (an average of two years), and the cultural differences between Italy and the United States that could have affected different outcome rates across cultures. In this light, the results are not overly discouraging.

One of the most interesting aspects of the Mashal et al. study was the assessment of therapy delivery issues as well as outcomes. The researchers asked the family members to respond to issues such as the length of treatment, the length of time between sessions, the team approach (behind a one-way mirror), and the need for additional therapy. Findings suggested: (a) if parents reported liking the group behind the one-way mirror, they also tended to report liking the therapy; (b) fathers who liked the time interval between sessions tended to like the therapy; (c) there was no statistically significant relationship between reactions to videotaping and enjoyment of the therapy; (d) fathers who were satisfied with the length of treatment tended to be satisfied with treatment; (e) mothers who reported liking the treatment also reported positive outcomes (as did fathers, but the finding related to fathers was not statistically significant); (f) there was a greater likelihood of a family member seeking other treatment if mothers did not report enjoying the therapy; and (g) the families of client-patients rated as more severe on a measure of psychopathology were more likely to seek additional treatments.

The Mashal et al. study, although preliminary at best, suggests that therapists should proceed with caution when implementing Milan-style therapy; the need for additional outcome studies and studies of treatment delivery issues is acknowledged.

## Paradigm Fit

### Focus of Study

The focus of study of Milan Systemic Family Therapy has shifted a bit from family dynamics and structures to meanings and process in a family context. From a paradigm perspective, there is no question that the Milan approach has broken new ground. Along with other family therapy theorists (e.g., Hoffman, 1988; Goolishian & Winderman, 1988), the Milan team has moved to a more problem-centered focus, *as opposed to viewing the family as the problem*. In this way, meaning systems, or systems of thought, have become the focus of study and treatment. But the ideas have not become fully contextualized. In other words, the Milan approach is similar to a one-way street—it sees "mind as social" (Tomm, 1984a), but it fails to see fully the social as cognitive (thereby overlooking the cognitive role in problem definition and causation). In this sense, it focuses primarily on treating problems as family-relevant rather than treating families or individuals as problem-relevant. That the individual can be implicated (perceived and socially accepted) as the problem, and treated effectively as such, is not addressed adequately in theoretical writings of the Milan team. The individual is not treated on-par with the system, which is rectified in a fully contextualized philosophy (Cottone & Greenwell, 1991). Consequently, while there are Milan-style methods for redefining problems within relational frameworks, there are no well-developed methods for redefining relational concerns to individual causation. Where linearity is eschewed by Milan theorists, it is revalidated along with circular epistemology in a fully contextualized philosophy (Cottone & Greenwell, 1991, in press).

## View of Nature of Reality

Reality is viewed primarily as social and changing. This is more clearly a contextual position than what is proposed by systemic-relational theorists. The idea that family process in some way needs to be facilitated by therapy, although not new to therapy (see chapter 12, on Satir's ideas), is very clearly embodied in the ideas and techniques of the Milan team. The Milan-style therapist attempts to enter into the family process, to perturb it, and to send it on its way. Other process-oriented therapies (for example Satir's conjoint approach) ultimately attempt to affect some structure or psychological construct (the body or the self-concept) through an interactive process. The Milan team attempts only to affect the meaning process through interaction. The results of therapy and the means of change are not articulated or even theorized by the Milan group, since change is assumed *to be* at a very basic level.

## Consonance with Paradigm Propositions and Tenets

Related to paradigm propositions and tenets, Milan Systemic Family Therapy shows crossover between the systemic-relational paradigm and the contextual paradigm. Although there is a distinct focus on relationships, even to the degree there is no true accounting of the individual cognitive process, there is also the beginning of a focus on the consensual process in human interaction. This places the Milan-style therapist somewhere between systemic-relational and contextual epistemology.

　　Whereas a systemic theorist would say that change in relationships is influenced by other social relationship, the Milan team would say that change in relationships is inevitable, but stifled by other social relations. The Milan therapist acts to unstifle the relational process, rather than attempting to define a relational problem and to solve it.

　　The definition of a problem from the Milan perspective is much like a discovery process. There is no delimited diagnostic process. Rather, definitions and therapy intertwine as hypotheses are generated and tested through the process of therapy. No one hypothesis is viewed as correct. An hypothesis is viewed as a temporary means for entering the family meaning context. On the other hand, a more purely systemic-relational therapist attempts to assess relationships, almost as if they are things, and then tries to change them. As Hoffman (1988) stated: "Family therapy has contributed its own unofficial diagnoses implicit in the idea that dysfunctional family structures are to blame for many of the problems of individuals. . . . The therapist was sort of a repairman—a social engineer" (p. 111). The act of defining a relationship, then, was almost equivalent to the act of defining something to be fixed, even if that "thing" to be fixed was *dysfunctional family interaction*. The Milan approach appears to have moved away from the idea that there is something to be fixed.

Consequently, the Milan group's idea of a family premise looks similar to what a contextualist would call an unspoken but operational family consensus. However, where a contextualist would assume that the consensus is continually changing and evolving, the Milan-team appears to concretize the idea of a premise, which is more purely systemic-relational than contextual theorizing. Boscolo et al. (1987) stated:

> If you talk in terms of Bateson's ideas about premises, you talk about structures laid down in childhood. They are "hard-programmed"; they explain how a person tends to repeat the same kind of relationship his parents had. If a person has had parents who separated or divorced, there's more of a probability that this marriage will divorce or separate. If a person had two parents who were overclose, he or she will tend to repeat this. . . . Most interaction doesn't touch the premise. It's very hard to change a premise. (pp. 206–207)

From a more purely contextual position, consensualities are always evolving within a larger social-consensual domain. The reason why children of parents who divorce are likely to divorce is the fact that divorce has become almost matter of fact in a cultural and societal context. Any ideas about divorce are affected by the fact that divorce occurs in a social context as a means of attempting to resolve differences. It cannot be concluded that a divorce mentality has become simply *inherent* to a family or an individual, which the idea of premise implies. A contextualist would argue that since individuals are viewed as cognitive, their ideas and consensualities are continually evolving through perceptions and social interactions. (Where cognition is also an evolving process.) A premise, as defined by Boscolo et al., does not appear to be consonant with contextual ideas. It is a theoretical holdover from systemic-relational ideas.

Cause is defined as circular by the Milan group, which is in keeping with systemic-relational propositions. It is the idea of circularity, so basic to the Milan approach, that demonstrates its inconsistency with contextual propositions. The transitional nature of Milan Systemic Family Therapy is obvious when analyzing the issue of circularity and causality. Although the Milan team has defined mind as social, it has failed to theoretically account for a social consensus about linear causality. Instead, the Milan approach holds true to the preeminence of circular epistemology at the expense of a fully contextualized epistemology, where causality is implicit to the enstructuring process, and where in certain situations linearity is as reasonable a conclusion as circularity.

Where the Milan-style therapist attempts to facilitate family change, the contextual therapist attempts to produce fit between evolving consensualities. In this sense, the contextualist must be more trans-systemic in his or her conceptualizations, whereas the Milan-style therapist focuses more on the system of defined significance.

And finally, therapists aligning with the Milan approach appear somewhat bound to a family type of therapy. A contextual-style therapist, on the other hand, can be more flexible in the use of technique, switching to individual means of intervention or to group or family approaches, always mindful of the consensualities operating and the structures that emerge through the social-consensual process. In this way, the practical allegiance of the Milan team is more clearly systemic-relational.

In summary, just as Milan Systemic Family Therapy has broken new ground theoretically, appearing at times to be a contextual therapy, it still maintains theoretical and practice-relevant linkage to systemic-relational propositions and tenets. Regardless, it fills a theoretical role as a trans-paradigmatic (transitional) therapy between the systemic-relational and contextual paradigms, a role that is unique among current theories of counseling and psychotherapy.

## Chapter Conclusion

All in all, Milan Systemic Family Therapy has entered the realm of contextual theory. In fact, the Milan team is leading the way to a new way of thinking about counseling and psychotherapy. Boscolo et al. (1987) have adopted process-oriented techniques and procedures. Milan Systemic Family Therapy fully recognizes that therapy is a process and that change is inevitable in families, especially when they are infused with information. The Milan approach is an excellent example of a trans-paradigmatic therapy and, depending on the acceptance of contextual propositions and tenets among members of therapeutic communities, the Milan approach may be securing itself a place in the history of counseling and psychotherapy.

The following chapter presents a more purely contextualized therapy—Cognitive-Consensual Therapy.

## References

Bateson, G. (1972). *Steps to an ecology of mind.* New York: Ballantine.

Bateson, G. (1979). *Mind and nature: A necessary unity.* New York: Bantam.

Boscolo, L., & Cecchin, G. (1982). Training in systemic therapy at the Milan centre. In R. Whiffen & J. Byng-Hall (Eds.), *Family therapy supervision: Recent developments in practice* (pp. 153–164). London: Academic Press.

Boscolo, L., Cecchin, G., Hoffman, L., & Penn, P. (1987). *Milan systemic family therapy.* New York: Basic Books.

Cecchin, G. (1987). Hypothesizing, circularity, and neutrality revisited: An invitation to curiosity. *Family Process, 26,* 405–413.

Cottone, R. R., & Greenwell, R. (1991). *The contextual paradigm of marital and family therapy.* Manuscript submitted for publication.

Cottone, R. R., & Greenwell, R. (in press). Beyond linearity and circularity: Deconstructing social systems theory. *Journal of Marital and Family Therapy.*

Fleuridas, C., Nelson, T. S., & Rosenthal, D. M. (1986). The evolution of circular questions: Training family therapists. *Journal of Marital and Family Therapy, 12,* 113–127.

Goolishian, H. A., & Winderman, L. (1988). Constructivism, autopoiesis and problem determined systems. *The Irish Journal of Psychology, 9,* 130–143.

Hoffman, L. (1988). A constructivist position for family therapy. *The Irish Journal of Psychology, 9,* 110–129.

Mashal, M., Feldman, R. B., & Sigal, J. J. (1989). The unraveling of a treatment paradigm: A followup study of the Milan approach to family therapy. *Family Process, 28,* 457–470.

Maturana, H. R. (1978). Biology of language: The epistemology of reality. In G. A. Miller & E. Lenneberg (Eds.), *Psychology and biology of language and thought.* New York: Academic Press.

Maturana, H. R. (1980). Biology of cognition. In H. R. Maturana & F. J. Varela, *Autopoiesis and cognition: The realization of the living.* Boston: D. Reidel. (Original work published in 1970.)

Maturana, H. R., & Varela, F. J. (1980). Autopoiesis: The organization of the living. In H. R. Maturana & F. J. Varela, *Autopoiesis and cognition: The realization of the living.* Boston: D. Reidel. (Original work published in 1973.)

Maturana, H. R. & Varela, F. J. (1987). *The tree of knowledge: The biological roots of human understanding.* Boston: Shambhala.

Penn, P. (1982). Circular questioning. *Family Process, 21,* 267–280.

Selvini-Palazzoli, M., Boscolo, L., Cecchin, G., & Prata, G. (1980). Hypothesizing—circularity—neutrality: Three guidelines for the conductor of the session. *Family Process, 19,* 3–12.

Tomm, K. (1984a). One perspective on the Milan systemic approach: Part I. Overview of development, theory and practice. *Journal of Marital and Family Therapy, 10,* 113–125.

Tomm, K. (1984b). One perspective on the Milan systemic approach: Part II. Description of session format, interviewing style and interventions. *Journal of Marital and Family Therapy, 10,* 253–271.

# 18

## Cognitive-Consensual Therapy:

### *A Contextual Theory Focusing on Cognition and Consensus*

THIS CHAPTER IS a best attempt to develop a therapeutic approach that is consistent with contextual paradigm propositions and tenets, which were defined in chapter 16. As such, the focus will be on the processes of cognition and consensus as involved in "enstructuring" the world. The purpose of this chapter, beyond the obvious intent of presenting a new theory of counseling and psychotherapy, is to demonstrate how philosophy (epistemology/ontology) and a paradigm framework allow for the logical development of theories of counseling and psychotherapy. A basic premise of this text is that philosophy is predominant as an organizational framework within which theories of counseling emerge. Accordingly, deduction, rather than induction, is the primary process and the root of significant developments in the field. It is hoped that by demonstrating that theories can be purely deductively developed, according to a proposed paradigmatic framework, readers will recognize the potential significance of paradigmatic thinking for the future of counseling theory.

It is also noteworthy that Cognitive-Consensual Therapy focuses on cognition, as opposed to "affect" or "behavior," two other accepted spheres of human functioning (see the related discussion in chapter 19). It logically follows that other contextual therapies may be developed, emphasizing the affective or behavioral aspects of interpersonal consensus, or any combination of the affective, cognitive, or behavioral spheres. As such, the contextual paradigm is fertile ground for future within-paradigm variation.

Cognitive-Consensual Therapy (CCT) is founded on a contextual philosophy. Reality is assumed to be ever-changing. This is not a new viewpoint. In fact, as mentioned in chapter 16, the ancient philosopher Heraclitus made statements to the effect that the same person could never step in the same river twice. The idea that reality can be viewed as involving change and process has intrigued philosophers for thousands of years. But until recently, the equation for a contextual philosophy has been less than complete. Certainly, individuals can be viewed as changing. And certainly the world can be viewed as changing. But how is it that people see structures? If *static structures* (such as perceptual organs or the nervous system) are needed to perceive other structures, then the philosophy fails.

Through Maturana's work (Maturana, 1978, 1970/1980; Maturana & Varela, 1972/1980; 1987) concerns about the static nature of perception and the static nature of what is perceived have been addressed (see the more complete discussion on this issue in chapters 15 and 16). Maturana has shown that the perceptual process can be viewed as a process of transformation and change, and not simply the transmission of images of existing structures. Maturana has demonstrated that the nervous system is continuously changing through experience, and that reality cannot be viewed as absolute. Maturana's conclusion, when applied within a larger philosophy of change, completes the contextual equation. Everything can be viewed as involving change and process. What is perceived, the perceiver, and the process of perception are all philosophically linked through the concept of ''change.'' This is an epistemologically and ontologically consistent perspective. Further, what is viewed as concrete or real in an objective sense occurs not through objectified properties of the perceived entity, but through a simultaneous process of perception and interpersonal consensus, where ''things'' are enstructured. Furthermore, it must be understood that the process of enstructuring, itself, is an ever-changing process.

Although some people might argue that this type of philosophy conflicts with the commonly perceived concrete world, the fact remains that in the therapeutic realm, such a criticism is not so serious. The therapeutic enterprise is not a concrete enterprise. It is not the equivalent of constructing buildings. It is a social and linguistic enterprise (Szasz, 1974), where realities are constructed. In this sense, the contextual philosophy at the foundation of Cognitive-Consensual Therapy does not make claims of application beyond the social realm. Although CCT is based on an ontological position, it is applied in a therapeutic context solely. It is not meant to be a pervasive philosophy, although certainly some individuals may choose to apply it as one. Further, it is expected that the contextual philosophy will change and develop through time, so it cannot be said to be finally determined. In this way, Cognitive-Consensual Therapy is fully contextualized. It is not the final word, even on itself as a counseling theory. It becomes real only in a community of professionals who believe it has some merit and who will work to develop, modify, and refine it.

Unlike other counseling theories, CCT is primarily concerned with how change is structured. Other counseling theorists, almost across the board, have defined some structure (self-concept, psyche, family, etc.) related to human functioning, and then they have described how such a structure can be changed. CCT requires a complete reordering of framework. It is a fully process-oriented therapeutic approach. Instead of focusing on structures, it focuses on the process of enstructuring, attempting to modify the ways people concretize their social worlds.


# The Foundational Theory

## The Target of Counseling

The target of counseling is the process of human interaction. It is understood that humans live in a continually evolving medium of cognition (perceiving and languaging) and social interaction. What is real is only temporarily real; what is known is only temporarily known. Counseling, therefore, must focus on those realities constructed by individuals within specific social contexts. For example, a wife may argue that her husband is "not understanding." She might take the position that being a homemaker, a mother, an employee, and a spouse is too demanding, and that her husband, who works one job, must share the household responsibilities. The husband, on the other hand, may argue that although he only works one job, he is the primary breadwinner, and all his efforts must be concentrated on the one job. In this scenario, there is a conflict of consensualities. Two different realities have been constructed.

In addressing a conflict of consensualities, the therapist must first identify social systems of significance, remembering the realities result from both cognitive and social activity in an ever-changing social-consensual domain. The husband may be operating from a system of relationships that define the male breadwinner as dominant (a patriarchy), and he may be interacting in social contexts where perceptions and views on this topic are languaged or acted upon from a patriarchal point of view. For instance, he may work in a setting where there are few self-supporting or family-supporting female co-workers. The wife, on the other hand, may be operating from a context where there are professional and familial expectations placed upon *both* husbands and wives. She may be socially interacting with others who demonstrate and communicate a point of view quite different from her husband's. Neither of these two perspectives is wrong, but the fact that there has been lack of co-operation, at least from the perspective of one of the marital partners, means that there is a conflict in consensualities. The target of counseling becomes the interaction surrounding the conflict of consensualities.

It is noteworthy that the term *consensualities* is used in the plural sense. Practically speaking, it would be very unusual for a lack of co-operation to result from simply one conflict of one consensuality. (Again, the term *co-operation* is hyphenated to emphasize joint coordination of activities.) There may be many consensualities operating at any one time, each evolving in its own way, and each within its own process of communication. Remembering that human interaction may be viewed as complex (involving verbal, nonverbal, informal, and contextual messages), several consensual positions may be communicated at one time. There may be an open verbal disagreement between spouses regarding the assignment of familial responsibilities. There may also be a nonverbal disagreement regarding the activities of one spouse's role in the home. And, there may be a larger social message that operates to prevent one or both spouses from operating in ways that would allow for a purely egalitarian marriage. All of these factors must be accounted for by the Cognitive-Consensual Therapist.

It is also important to understand that a consensus is not a structural thing. Importantly, "it is assumed that consensus is not structure, even though structure derives, ultimately, from consensual behavior. Consensus is viewed as an ongoing interactive process" (Cottone, 1989, p. 108). Consequently, understanding the following is basic to understanding CCT: (a) that perception is a transformational process; (b) that language is continually evolving; and (c) that social agreements are fleeting. Nothing about a social consensus is static. A contextual reality, then, is not concrete; it is fluid.

Where there is language, social interaction, and co-operation, there is an evolving consensuality. Where there is lack of co-operation, there is a differing consensuality. The question arises as to whether people, as in the marital example, can come to consensus about differences in consensualities, and whether they can come to *agreement* as to how to reconcile them. The task of the Cognitive-Consensual Therapist is to facilitate such an agreement linguistically and interactively.

## The Process of Counseling

The counseling process is fully interactive. From the moment clients enter a counselor's office, an interpersonal framework is defined. For example, counseling will invariably first involve the client's social system of significance (e.g., the family system). If a social system of significance has not been identified before therapy has been initiated, then the therapist attempts to define significant social systems and later to engage active social relationships in therapy. It is important to involve as many individuals implicated in "problems" as is practically possible from the very beginning of therapy, since the basic philosophy of CCT is that reality (and therefore the defined problem) derives from simultaneous cognitive and *social* processes.

In therapy, the counselor interacts with the clients to probe their concerns and to define agreements and disagreements. The language used to express an agreement and/or disagreement is important; the use of specialized language by clients must be understood and analyzed, since it is reflective of a social system of significance. Social systems of significance often have unique social and linguistic traditions. Teenagers, for example, often speak differently from their parents (e.g., slang or jargon), reflecting different linguistic groundings. A specialized linguistic grounding is a clear message of involvement of other individuals. Determining which individuals external to those convened for therapy may be influencing the language and actions of individuals in therapy is critical. In this sense, linguistic dialects, jargon, and vernacular are very important to defining the interpersonal limits of a consensuality.

Once consensualities or disagreements become openly expressed in therapy, then the therapist begins to assess whether a new consensus can be facilitated. If a new consensus is not feasible, then the therapist must determine whether one of the positions taken by opponents in the group is more closely reflective of the larger sociolegal consensus by which the therapist is constrained. In fact, the therapist may be confronted with consensualities that are contradictory to the evolving sociolegal consensus. For example, in a patriarchal and incestuous family, forced to attend therapy by a legal authority, the father may take the stand that incest is acceptable and that doing otherwise is against the family's wishes. In this case, the therapist is up against a consensus inconsistent with his or her role in a larger sociolegal setting. The therapist in such a situation must attempt to facilitate the societal consensus, clearly communicating the illegality of incest to the family, and, where necessary, the therapist must act in accordance with the sociolegal consensus to help to ensure that the incest does not recur and that family members are not harmed.

It is also possible that the therapist will be confronted with a family or group that defines the problem as immanent to one individual. Even the implicated (blamed) individual may agree that he or she is the problem Such an agreement may go so far as to define the implicated individual as ''ill'' or ''sick.'' (Often this kind of agreement occurs after there has been some contact with an organic-medical therapist.) Although a Cognitive-Consensual Therapist prefers to define and to treat problems within their social context, fully aware of the social and cognitive underpinnings of reality, he or she does not necessarily argue against a consensus of individual blame, if such a consensus can lead to therapeutic resolution of problems. In such a case, a psychiatric diagnosis is defined as a temporary means of identifying and solving problems, and it can be used to restructure social relations in a way that a new process of interaction is facilitated. (The Psychoeducational Approach described in chapter 20 may be used, consistent with the organic-medical and systemic-relational paradigms, for example.) In other words, any consensus that helps to resolve disagreements among involved individuals in therapy is useful, so long as it is considered ethical by standards consensually agreed upon by members of the professional and sociolegal communities, to which the therapist belongs.

This is not to say that Cognitive-Consensual Therapy is an eclectic therapy. It is, instead, a firmly philosophically grounded theory that allows for flexibility of response, with the understanding that the limits of professional activity are legally defined. Like eclecticism, any acceptable means of therapy can be used if a consensus is developed consistent with the approach. Unlike eclecticism, CCT is founded epistemologically and has specialized techniques all its own. As Keeney (1983) noted:

> One way of incorporating a diversity of views is to become an eclectic. For instance, a therapist may use ''gestalt work'' at one time and ''strategic family therapy'' at another. This therapist's theories and techniques are like an eclectic concert program—different music is played at different times.
>
> Another approach to incorporating diverse perspectives involves combination. Here the clinician takes bits and pieces from various approaches and ''integrates'' them into his own unified model. It is an illusion to view this as an eclectic approach. More accurately, any combination of views is itself a new theory. Combining Beethoven and Bach gives you neither, but something else. An ''integrated theory'' simply becomes another theory which an eclectic may add to his files. . . . However, as we mentioned, another jump in learning is possible. Third-order change . . . emerges when different epistemologies are

*discerned. Entering the labyrinth of epistemological comparison means going beyond theory and becoming aware of a difference that may make the most profound difference in one's orientation to clinical understanding and action. (p. 160)*

It is exactly this third-order type of change that the contextual epistemology represents, which is embodied theoretically in Cognitive-Consensual Therapy.

Practically speaking, the process of CCT is a process of negotiation. It attempts to resolve differences of opinion and action. It ideally provides for new definitions of concerns that will allow agreement about what activities should be undertaken by the therapist and clients to diminish or to ameliorate problems and to maintain client behavior within standards defined as acceptable within sociolegal boundaries. But the Cognitive-Consensual Therapist is always mindful that he or she is not trying to change "something." Rather, the Cognitive-Consensual Therapist proceeds from the assumption that change is inevitable, and that he or she is simply facilitating already progressing change. As long as the counselor represents a social and linguistic tradition different in some way from the social and linguistic background of the client, and so long as the counselor maintains interpersonal contacts with the client, change is inevitable. Change of clients or change in their social systems of significance may be slower or quicker than what is occurring in a larger social context (out of sync with other changes), but it is change nonetheless, which is always the therapist's ally.

## Counselor Role

The counselor role as a Cognitive-Consensual Therapist is that of facilitating interactions (both behaviorally and linguistically) so that clients come to view and to understand different ways of acting and thinking. Basically, the counselor attempts to enter into co-evolution with clients. The counselor recognizes that he or she will be educated in contact with the client's social system, and that the client, likewise, is influenced by the service delivery system of which the therapist is a part. Through behavioral and linguistic interaction, there can be an integration, and, hopefully, co-operation of the systems. Through therapeutic integration of ideas and actions, a newly evolving consensus may emerge, consistent with constraints imposed by relations with the larger service delivery system and the societal context.

The counselor also plays the role of the professional authority. This role derives from his or her linkage to the larger professional community and the sociolegal system. The counseling relationship is viewed as a complementary relationship, where the therapist plays the one-up role. Regardless, this is not to say that the client does not influence what occurs in therapy. Whereas the counselor role is that of an authority, the therapeutic process is one of give-and-take. The therapist is alert to client needs and desires. The therapist is ethically obligated to serve the client primarily—to solve expressed problems. However, problems are never defined in isolation by the therapist alone. They are defined through the process of therapy as a mutual activity. And once defined, they are contextually interpreted as temporary means for moving the individual or the family along a developmental course.

*The counselor role, therefore, is largely trans-systemic*. The counselor is continually cognizant of how things can be viewed from a metaperspective. This means that the therapist must be continually alert to social and biological influences on himself or herself, on the client, on the larger sociolegal system, and across professional mental health communities. It requires high-level intellectual work, since being trans-systemic requires educated abilities to understand, to analyze, and to synthesize *beyond individual boundaries or organizational constraints*. It requires extensive knowledge of the cultural and subcultural factors operating in a community. The counselor is not simply viewed as an interpersonal technician. Neither is the counselor role that of the expert authority who imposes diagnoses and treatment approaches as if they were absolute realities. The role of the counselor is always relative to the professional community, the client system, and the larger social context. For example, broadly speaking, it is consistent with the professional role of the Cognitive-Consensual Therapist to define whether a client aspires to behaviors within the range of accepted social and legal standards. Such assessment is not absolutist, since it is recognized that social and legal standards *change*.

## Goals of Counseling and Ideal Outcomes

The ideal outcome of therapy is client co-operation in a desirable social context. This means there is client behavior consistent with social and legal standards in the contexts to which the client-system has aspired, or to which the client is obligated (by law or otherwise).

Beyond client co-operation in desirable social contexts, it is also important that the client becomes integrated at a nonverbal and informal level in contexts consistent with his or her socially defined needs and desires. This means, at some basic level, there is communication from a group that the client is welcomed.

Ideally, clients will demonstrate ''acceptance of'' and ''acceptance in'' a desirable social context. This is best assessed by means of observing whether the client is capable of appropriate two-way communication in the desirable social context. It is easily observed by assessing whether a client is viewed as attractive by other members of a new or acceptable social group.

# General Procedures

## Assessment

Assessment occurs in *stages* in Cognitive-Consensual Therapy. The *first stage* can be defined as the ''trans-systemic stage.'' During the trans-systemic stage, the client is assessed in his or her present social, cultural, and subcultural contexts. Interpersonal relations of significance are defined. Language is assessed and matched with observed or described social group affiliations, past or present. In other words, the Cognitive-Consensual Therapist attempts to place the client in his or her social matrix, presently and historically. The therapist, accordingly, attempts to define which social groups the client or client-group describes as meaningful, as structures to be reckoned. It is always kept in mind that these social groups of significance are not "things," rather they are evolving social phenomena made real through social interactions.

Once significant groups have been defined, they are analyzed at the level of linguistic traditions. The *second stage* of assessment, then, is linguistic. Since cognition involves both perception and language, language specification is critical to understanding the consensualities that emerge, or potentially can emerge, within social groupings. If at some point it becomes obvious that there are linguistic limitations, perhaps through the intellectual or biological limits of clients or treatment groups, then a subphase of stage two is recommended. This subphase involves the taking of a client or treatment group history to assess whether there are potential genetic correlates to observed behaviors (e.g., a family history of schizophrenia, depression, or intellectual deficiency). Cognitive-Consensual Therapy does not deny that professionals and clients may agree that a biological system is of critical importance to either the definition of a problem or to treatment options.

The *third stage* of assessment involves defining agreement and disagreement among members of the therapeutic group. It is at this point that consensualities and conflicts of consensualities are defined. Any lack of co-operation is a hint of a failed attempt at consensus. Any challenge to the therapist is also a message of a different consensuality. Additionally, when clients *blame* an individual or a group for a problem, in all likelihood a conflict of consensualities has been defined between the blaming individuals and the blamed party.

The *fourth stage* of assessment is not necessarily accomplished in all cases. The fourth stage is individual assessment of an identified patient or patients. It is used when a consensus about group involvement in the problem is not attained and when one person is clearly implicated as "the problem." It is a means of linking traditional diagnostic approaches, valued in Western culture, with the definition of the problem and the method of solution. It is viewed as a last-resort means of assessment. Accordingly, diagnoses are viewed as conventions, agreed-upon criteria, deriving from the interactions of a group of experts acting to develop a professional consensus, which itself is changeable (e.g., the *Diagnostic and Statistical Manual of Mental Disorders,* American Psychiatric Association, 1987).

## Treatment/Remediation

Treatment begins with the establishment of a professional relationship. The therapist should come across as a well-educated, experienced, confident, credentialed, and well-established professional. Beginning therapists should affiliate with therapists who can meet more mature qualifications.

The therapist's social skills are critical. The therapist must be able to interact with clients in a way that demonstrates that he or she understands (and if possible, speaks) the language of his or her clients at the cultural and subcultural levels. The therapist must also demonstrate that he or she understands *and* speaks the language of the larger service delivery and sociolegal systems.

Once clients or treatment groups have been assessed, it is necessary to determine the target of intervention. As stated earlier, the target will always be the process of human interaction. This means, at some level, the therapist will interject information into the therapeutic process that will affect the direction or speed of change occurring in the identified patient and/or the group of significance. Since all behavior is cognitive and social, the therapist will attempt to engage the perceptual process, providing ample stimuli to clients as he or she defines the problems and solutions to be undertaken. For example, the therapist may make use of family assessment measures or individual diagnostic instruments and may make the assessment results generally known. Or the therapist may assist clients getting involved with outside groups or individuals who can be supportive through the process of change.

The therapist must always be cognizant of disagreements among members of a treatment group. It is not necessary to have an unquestioned consensus about the issues at hand in therapy among members of the treatment group, but it helps. It may be likely, however, that there will be an individual or individuals who are unable to perceive, to understand, or to behave consistently with the treatment goals as defined primarily by others. In such a case, the individual or individuals may be defined as socially out of sync with their group affiliation and unable to reconcile to group demands; such clients may be separated for individual, or, preferably, other group treatment. If that individual is defined as the ''identified patient,'' then either psychological or organic-medical means of treatment may be undertaken.

Essentially, the Cognitive-Consensual Therapist defines a problem in a way that it is reasonable to clients, and then he or she treats the problem according to methods that would logically follow from the definition of the problem. For instance, if the problem of a child's misbehavior is defined by the therapist as resulting from parental conflicts, and the parents and the child openly or tacitly agree, then marital and family counseling would be a reasonable means of treatment. On the other hand, if the parents are resistant to a relational interpretation of the problem, and the child is diagnosed as hyperactive by school and other ''authorities,'' then either organic-medical treatments may be coordinated or a behavior modification program may be implemented. The therapist always yields to consensus, unless yielding means giving into illegality or immorality according to professional, legal, and local standards. However, if it appears that no consensus is possible, then the therapist defines the inability of the treatment group members to come to consensus as the problem, which cannot be disputed without verifying the therapist's diagnosis. (If one or more individuals disagree, then their actions verify the counselor's position). In such cases, the goal of counseling would be the development of a means for assisting the family members to develop acceptable consensual positions (e.g., group communications training).

## Case Management

Therapy is not necessarily a long-term process, although it can be long term if it is agreeable to both the client and the therapist and consistent with the goals of therapy. For instance, if both the client and the therapist agree that the goal of therapy is self-awareness, then more sessions may be necessary than with therapy aimed at solving a perceived situational problem. As a general rule, however, due primarily to socio-economic constraints, shorter term problem-solving therapy is preferred.

Cases begin with the defined social group of affiliation. Essentially, every one of the group members is viewed as a client, just as the group itself can be viewed as a client. But the Cognitive-Consensual Therapist must focus on each individual in understanding the cognitive-consensual framework from which that individual is operating. Individuals do not exist in isolation. It is assumed that they are the sum of their ever-changing biological and social relations. In this way CCT is deterministic. The parts and the whole are equally important, if such are enstructured and there is consensual agreement in the social context of Cognitive-Consensual Therapists. The whole is not necessarily greater than the sum of its parts, as it is with social systems theory or Gestalt therapy; any conclusion about the predominance of the whole over parts occurs only within a social context. It can be just as easily concluded that the reason why a whole looks or acts greater than the sum of parts (especially in the social world) is that some of the parts are unknown or yet to be perceived. So, the Cognitive-Consensual Therapist must be alert to parts and wholes, and to the definition and significance of both for progress in therapy.

Relatedly, co-therapy, or the use of treatment or observing teams, is highly recommended (as with Milan-style therapy). In this way, treatment decisions occur in a consensual framework, which is fully consistent with the contextual philosophy.

Therapy may proceed as systemic, dealing primarily with a family system, for example. But individuals may be separated in counseling for several purposes, including the building of a consensus between the therapist and one client, or the building of consensus between several individuals. In fact, the therapeutic boundary of CCT is not the therapist's office. Instead, CCT may occur, through therapist coordination, in outside settings with outside individuals, or any place where an appropriate consensus among clients or involved individuals may be facilitated.

Individual counseling, consequently, always involves another or other individuals in addition to "the client" and "the counselor." Therapy is not simply dialogue between the therapist and the client. It is social, just as reality is viewed as highly social. Therapeutic understanding and therapeutic change are social activities, and, almost across the board, the Cognitive-Consensual Therapist will engage other relationships in therapy.

The Cognitive-Consensual Therapist, then, may work with individuals or groups, switching between the two even while counseling one family or dealing with one problem. The Cognitive-Consensual Therapist defines the importance of his or her actions and conclusions consistent with the professional community of Cognitive-Consensual Therapists with which he or she associates (physically, geographically, socially, or theoretically).

Typically, individuals or families will be seen in therapy approximately one session per week, as is mutually agreeable to the client and the therapist with the therapist's guidance. Sessions are designed to be pleasant and, to some degree, entertaining. Clients should feel good about coming to therapy. Counselors, therefore, are encouraged to use their social skills and a sense of humor when dealing with clients.

This is not to say that the therapist should belittle the client, but it is to say that the client should feel positive about coming for therapy and confident about the counselor's ability to deal with concerns. Sessions may be scheduled at any frequency depending upon the nature of the concern, the degree of consensus among treatment group members, or other factors that are discerned as important by the therapist (e.g., client financial concerns).

Case notes should describe individual cognitive and consensual frameworks, actions (including perceived nonverbal communications), and the interpersonal contacts that may constitute a social group of significance (in or outside of the therapy group). The therapist should also identify the conflicts in consensualities that he or she perceives and the actions he or she believes must be taken to facilitate changes. Recording of sessions (audiotaping and especially videotaping) is highly encouraged.

## Specialized Techniques

**1.** *Probing for Consensualities.* This is a specialized assessment technique. The therapist essentially interviews the members of a system of significance, attempting to define agreements and disagreements among the clients (or outside individuals identified as significant) on issues of relevance. For example, the therapist might ask: "Who agrees with mother that father is not home enough?" Or, "Who takes up sides for Johnny when he argues with his sister?" Or, "What does Marie do when Jimmy and Tommy argue?" In these ways, agreements and disagreements on topics of concern can be identified, thereby revealing any conflicting consensualities potentially operating in the disagreements.

**2.** *Building Consensus.* Building consensus is the process whereby the therapist attempts to design experiences supportive of a definition of the problem and, consequently, an appropriate way of behaving.

The appropriateness of a behavior is defined within a social context by the therapist as a certified/licensed authority. A preferred behavior can never be illegal, should never be immoral according to reasonable societal and moral standards, and should never influence individuals by creating socially or physically painful experiences. As long as the wanted behaviors: (a) are not harmful to others; (b) are reasonable within an accepted social and professional (ethical) context; and (c) are consistent with the social context to which the client-system aspires (by choice or legal mandate); then they are "appropriate."

Cognitive-Consensual Therapists build consensus around their diagnosis of a problem and around their proposed solution to the problem. For example, assume that a teenage girl appears socially uncomfortable in the presence of boys her age. Assume further that her parents have brought her to therapy because they believe her "shyness" is to the extreme and is influencing her social relations in a negative fashion. The girl, however, seems a bit confused over her situation, and she is unsure what it all means. The Cognitive-Consensual Therapist, in this situation, might proceed by assessing the girl psychologically, or by observing her in social contexts, fully recognizing the power of the therapist's professional opinion (see Handelsman, Basgall & Cottone, 1986;

Snyder, 1974; Snyder, Shenkel, & Lowery, 1977). (Whenever possible, the therapist should incorporate professional information from outside sources to strengthen his or her position.) While the therapist is assessing the girl, he or she is developing a relationship with her, and during this process, assuming that she is involved with therapy and communicates cooperatively, the therapist might communicate to her (verbally, nonverbally, and contextually) that she is interacting well, and that her condition is an adjustment concern that can be overcome by some behavioral exercises. The therapist then communicates the same message to the parents, who agree. The therapist then demonstrates a simple communication technique to assist the girl when meeting new people, and practices with her in the counseling setting. The therapist gives her a homework assignment and describes himself or herself as a teacher. The therapist then develops a therapeutic contract detailing approximately how long it will take to address the concern and outlining some of the other activities that will be involved. The parents are to be involved to some degree throughout the process. Through these actions, the Cognitive-Consensual Therapist has built a consensus around the definition of the problem as ''shyness'' and the solution as behavioral. According to CCT tenets, it would be predicted that the likelihood of success on this case would be enhanced through the development of a firm agreement among the parents, the child, and the counselor about the nature of the problem and the solutions to be undertaken.

On the other hand, if the parents were convinced that their daughter's behavior was because of an earlier diagnosed ''schizophrenia,'' and the daughter disagrees and maintains a position that her problem is shyness, then the therapist's approach may have to be quite different. The therapist might have to support or challenge the previous definition of the problem, or he or she might have to attempt to develop a totally different consensus that is inconsistent either with a diagnosis of ''schizophrenia'' or ''shyness.'' To do this, the therapist might have to develop a creative redefinition of her problem through a combination of techniques known as ''challenging consensus'' and ''reframing'' (defined as follows).

**3.**    *Challenging Consensus.* The process of challenging a consensus is necessary when there are conflicts of consensualities. As stated earlier, lack of co-operation is a signal to a conflict of consensualities. In such a case, disputation of a consensually grounded position becomes necessary. Challenging a consensus *always* involves the presentation of an alternative position. Challenging a consensus may involve helping clients to come into contact with other individuals with different opinions and actions. It may involve activities that help the client to espouse a different position. But it *must* involve presentation of material that can be *perceived* as nonsupportive of the unwanted position. The client must come *to perceive* and *to understand* (linguistically) a different standpoint. Since consensus involves both cognitive (perception and language) and social activities, it is important that stimuli are involved that can perturb a client's nervous system while there is simultaneous definition of what is perceived within a social context (where at least one other person supports the wanted viewpoint).

**4.**    *Reframing.* Reframing is probably the most universal therapeutic technique (L'Abate, Ganahl, & Hansen, 1986). Reframing is the process of redefining a concern. Reframing may involve redefining a perceived individual problem as a relational

problem (''Your problem is your marriage''), or it may involve the opposite approach—
redefining a relational concern as an individual one (''Your marital problem is really a
problem of your spouse's alcoholism''). It may also involve a creative redefinition of
concerns from one context to another (''Your problem is not in your marriage, it's in
your relationship with your father''). Reframing can downplay problems (''Your
depressions are your body's means of telling you something must change''), or
reframing can emphasize a certain aspect of a problem (''It is not your feelings that are
a concern, it's the way you think that needs to be changed''). L'Abate et al. provide
a thorough discussion on the different types of reframing, and readers are referred
to their book for additional information on the technique. In any case, reframing
will always restate a concern in new ways so that a different consensus may be
achieved.

   **5.**   *Spreading Individual Blame to Relationships.* Spreading blame is the process
of contextualizing a problem from an individual or an isolated group to a larger social
context. It involves defining all of the individuals who may be perceived as implicated
in a problem. It involves taking statements of an individual's fault in a problem, offered
by one or several members of a group, and spreading the blame to several members of
the group or to a larger social context. For example, a daughter who becomes
involved in drug abuse, whose behavior begins to negatively affect family relations,
may be defined by family members as the ''cause'' of the family problems. The
Cognitive-Consensual Therapist, however, might choose to define her social group
of affiliation (the peer group or drug culture) as the problem needing a remedy. If,
in fact, a consensus around the new definition of causation is agreeable, then
spreading of blame has occurred. Spreading the blame is actually a special kind of
reframing where cause is redefined, usually from one individual to one or more
relationships.

   **6.**   *Individual Diagnostic Techniques.* Individual diagnostic techniques include
individual psychological assessment (of personality, interests, aptitudes, skills, values,
psychopathology, intelligence, etc.). Individual diagnosis may involve the use of
mental status examinations to assess the degree of ''symptomotology.'' It may involve
any interpersonal means of defining a problem within an acceptable counseling-theory
framework. *In all cases, the use of individual diagnoses or assessment techniques is
temporary, and the fleeting nature of the usefulness of evaluation is clearly communicated to the client by the Cognitive-Consensual Therapist.* The primary purpose of
using such techniques is consensus-building. The data provided by assessment devices
may be very credible to clients during the therapeutic process.

   **7.**   *Relational Assessment Techniques.* Any technique used to define a relationship, such as structured interaction, may be use by the Cognitive-Consensual Therapist.
For example, a therapist might ask a marital couple to engage in a discussion about
perceived problems so that the therapist may observe the nature of the relationships
(e.g., whether it can be viewed as symmetrical or complementary). As with individual
assessment methods, the purpose of such techniques is to assist in the building of
consensus, remembering that cognition (perception and language) are involved. Assessment methods, therefore, are an easy way for counselors to facilitate relationship
self-observation.

## Recent Developments or Criticisms

Obviously the major new development related to Cognitive-Consensual Therapy is its emergence as a counseling theory. This is a new theory of counseling and psychotherapy. Consequently, there have been no criticisms by other theoreticians or theorists.

CCT has been presented for two purposes. First, it helps to operationalize the proposed contextual paradigm. It shows how paradigmatic thinking can facilitate theory development, just a theory development aids in the definitions of counseling paradigms. Second, it demonstrates how closely theories of counseling and psychotherapy are linked to philosophy. CCT as a theory of counseling has been *purely deductively conceived*. At the time of this writing it has not been implemented in any comprehensive form (although plans for implementation and refinement of the theory are under way, and a second text, entitled "Cognitive Consensual Therapy," is planned). Consequently, the development of CCT helps to validate the usefulness of paradigmatic thinking in the counseling field. This is not to say that paradigmatic thinking is the be-all and end-all of theory development in counseling and psychotherapy. Rather, it can be viewed as an opportunity.

Due to the newness of CCT, at this point it might be wise to address some potential criticisms of the theory. Some potential theoretical criticisms of CCT follow.

First, it can be argued that CCT can never truly exist, since once a practitioner senses he or she grasps CCT, then it must have changed, or, as an application of contextual philosophy, it has failed. This is true. CCT is not static. It is ever-changing. It is changed in every communication about it, because individuals who learn of CCT and attempt to communicate its basic premises cannot help but modify it through their own experiences and sociolinguistic biases. It is fully anticipated that CCT will develop, if it survives, as a continually changing therapeutic approach, shaped within the context of a professional mental health community.

Second, some might argue that CCT is not unlike some psychological or systemic-relational therapies that are process oriented—for example, Rogers's Person-Centered Therapy (cf. Rogers, 1951). However, there is much that is different between Cognitive-Consensual Therapy and the other therapies associated with the other paradigms presented in this book. Cognitive-Consensual Therapy has no absolute conception of mental health. It also does not value the individual alone over the social system, or vice versa. There is no therapeutic ideal, such as Rogers's fully functioning person. Mental health, according to Cognitive-Consensual Therapy, can never be a crystallized concept. Any conception of mental health is cognitively *and* socially founded. Mental health may vary according to local dictates and individual perceptions. Cognitive-Consensual Therapy, therefore, provides a fully contextualized definition of mental health. But there may be limits to this position. The Cognitive-Consensual Therapy position that the definition of mental health is fully contextualized may lead to a conclusion that Cognitive-Consensual Therapy is a relativistic theory, where right and wrong depend only on the demands of the moment. Consequently, it appears, according to Cognitive-Consensual Therapy, that there is no one way to define what is valued in human interaction. However, any conclusion that Cognitive-Consensual

Therapy is relativistic is a naive conclusion. This is so because Cognitive-Consensual Therapy does not negate the possibility of multiple consensualities or of a singular consensus, deriving primarily from universal or near universal human cognitive and social experiences. Cottone and Greenwell (1991) stated:

> The contextualist would have to consider at least the implications of varying levels of consensus. That is, there may be a consensus at the level of sociopolitical structuring of relations between men and women, and yet a different level of consensus that serves as a criterion (fuzzy and unsteady perhaps, but persistent) for judging the validity of that sociopolitical consensus. Once the possibility of levels of consensus is seriously entertained, then one must begin to entertain the possibility of a fundamental level of consensus, where the consensus is universal and highly undifferentiated—though not undifferentiable—a consensus that is universal because it is somehow grounded in an experience that is universal. At this level, then, reality would be no longer derived from consensus but consensus from reality. . . .
>
> It should be evident, then, that contextualism is not viewed as a metaphysical relativism or nihilism. (pp. 24–25).

CCT is relativistic only to a degree. It assumes that mental health may differ according to perceptions in different social contexts, but it does not deny the possibility of a grounded universal or nearly universal conception of mental health (based on a pervasive underlying consensus). However, according to contextual propositions, even a universal conception of mental health must be viewed as changing or developing, since to believe otherwise is to contradict a basic assumption of contextual thinking. Nothing is an eternal verity.

A third criticism of CCT is that it is simply a highly refined eclectic philosophy. This argument was addressed briefly in a previous section of this chapter through a citation by Keeney (1983), which distinguished therapies based on epistemological positions as higher level approaches, going beyond either: (a) purely eclectic approaches that allow multiple therapeutic applications; or (b) approaches based on merged or combined theories. Patterson (1986) in discussing eclectic therapists, stated:

> It is difficult to know just what eclecticism means. While most eclectics may not be antitheoretical, they appear to be atheoretical. They seem to have little in common; they do not subscribe to any common principles or system. Thus there seem to be as many eclectic approaches as there are eclectic therapists. Each operates out of his or her unique bag of techniques; on the basis of his or her particular background of training, experience, and biases; and case by case, with no general theory or set of principles for guidance. Essentially, it amounts to flying by the seat of one's pants. (p. 460)

Patterson's statement demonstrates a theoretically conservative stance about the nature of eclecticism. However, Patterson presented an optional, more liberal interpretation of eclecticism as well, saying that eclecticism could be a theoretical, comprehensive, and synthesizing approach. He stated: "Eclecticism is simply a more comprehensive, loosely organized theory than a formal theory and attempts to be all-inclusive" (p. 461). Nevertheless, whether one interprets eclecticism conservatively or liberally, eclecticism is quite different from Cognitive-Consensual Therapy. CCT is formally and theoretically based. CCT is not loosely organized; rather, it is organized around specific, well-formulated theoretical and paradigmatic propositions and tenets. Although CCT and eclectic approaches are both integrative, CCT is integrative primarily at the levels of epistemology and ontology, whereas eclectic approaches appear to be integrative primarily at a practice-relevant level. Where some eclectic approaches are able to integrate theories within one or even two paradigms (e.g., Thorne's 1961, 1967, "Integrative Psychology"), they fail to incorporate (or to be able to integrate) all four paradigms, most usually excluding systemic-relational or contextual propositions. Because CCT is *fully contextual,* at the practical level it is able to draw on any methods or techniques consistent with operating consensualities, while maintaining theoretical and philosophical underpinnings.

CCT can be criticized as too demanding for the therapist, requiring knowledge of many therapeutic methods and techniques. It is true that the Cognitive-Consensual Therapist must be thoroughly grounded in technique, but it is not necessary for the Cognitive-Consensual Therapist to be an expert in every therapeutic approach. Rather, it is recommended that the Cognitive-Consensual Therapist should have a firm understanding of paradigm propositions and tenets across the four paradigms. Additionally, the therapist should be skilled in at least one, but preferably two approaches associated with each paradigm. This is, indeed, asking much of therapists, but it also reflects a faith in the capability and the level of professionalism of professional counselors. It requires in-depth training, social skill, intelligence, a professional attitude, and an intellectual spirit.

Readers are referred to the Cottone and Greenwell (1991) manuscript for a listing of additional qualifications or limitations of contextual thinking, and, consequently, limitations of CCT.

All in all, Cognitive-Consensual Therapy, because of its close linkage to the contextual paradigm, is able to counter most attacks that would portray it as theoretically flawed, incomplete, or a hybrid. However, the test of time will be the critical test of CCT.

## Paradigm Fit

### Focus of Study

The focus of study of Cognitive-Consensual Therapy is clearly human consensus as a simultaneous cognitive and social-linguistic activity. All problems are defined within a social context. Even the therapist's definition of a problem derives from the therapist's social context (i.e., the professional therapeutic community, out of which CCT has emerged). Thinking is viewed as both cognitive and social. From the time humans are born, their biological systems and social systems shape their interactions, where the biological and social systems, too, are interactive. Nothing is structural according to CCT. Even the process of enstructuring is nonstatic. So, clearly, the focus of CCT is consistent with the propositions and tenets of the contextual paradigm.

### View of Nature of Reality

As with the contextual paradigm, change and process is fundamental to reality. Structures are viewed as fleeting perceptual phenomona observed within a social-linguistic context. There is nothing immanent in structure. It derives from the interaction of humans, biologically, in a social consensual domain. And even biology is ever-changing; genetics, for example, are influenced through a social process, as each person represents the biological *relationship* of his or her parents, passing changes down the reproductive line. Each individual, too, is viewed as a changing biological process (e.g., the aging process). There is clear consistency with CCT and contextual thinking as presented in chapter 16.

### Consonance with Paradigm Propositions and Tenets

There is a clear-cut match between the propositions and tenets of the contextual paradigm and the basic tenets of Cognitive-Consensual Therapy. The focus is on consensus as a cognitive and social activity. Change is viewed as fundamental and inevitable. Individuals or groups are viewed as ever-changing. Cause may be linear or circular, depending on the fleeting structures that are defined through consensual activity as cause-relevant. The professional counselor is viewed as an authority as is consistent with Western society's sanction. Responsibility (as with cause) is defined within larger social-consensual restraints—those of the sociolegal system. And therapy is considered a coevolution process. As can be observed, CCT was clearly designed to be a specialized therapeutic approach consistent with the defined propositions and tenets of the contextual paradigm. In this regard, it may be one of the most purely paradigm-specific counseling theories in this text.

## Chapter Conclusion

This chapter has presented a new theory of counseling and psychotherapy. Cognitive-Consensual Therapy (CCT) is a counseling theory designed around contextual paradigm propositions and tenets of practice. Some basic operational principles of CCT were presented according to the same organizational framework used in this text to describe other theories of counseling and psychotherapy. Potential criticisms of CCT were also addressed. It is hoped that through this chapter, CCT has been operationalized to the degree that students will have a sense of its implementation and that more experienced counselors may begin to experiment with its application as a therapy of choice.

# References

American Psychiatric Association. (1987). *The diagnostic and statistical manual of mental disorders* (3rd ed., rev.). Washington, DC: Author.

Cottone, R. R. (1989). The third epistemology: Extending Maturana's structure determinism. *The American Journal of Family Therapy, 17,* 99–109.

Cottone, R. R., & Greenwell, R. (1991). *The contextual paradigm of marital and family therapy.* Manuscript submitted for publication.

Handelsman, M. M., Basgall, J. A., & Cottone, R. R. (1986). The Barnum effect: Implications for testing in family therapy. *American Mental Health Counselors Association Journal, 8,* 80–86.

Keeney, B. P. (1983). *Aesthetics of change.* New York: Guilford.

L'Abate, L., Ganahl, G., & Hansen, J. C. (1986). *Methods of family therapy.* Engelwood Cliffs, NJ: Prentice-Hall.

Maturana, H. R. (1978). Biology of language: The epistemology of reality. In G. A. Miller & E. Lenneberg (Eds.), *Psychology and biology of language and thought.* New York: Academic Press.

Maturana, H. R. (1980). Biology of cognition. In H. R. Maturana & F. J. Varela, *Autopoiesis and cognition: The realization of the living.* Boston: D. Reidel. (Original work published in 1970.)

Maturana, H. R., & Varela, F. J. (1980). Autopoiesis: The organization of the living. In H. R. Maturana & F. J. Varela, *Autopoiesis and cognition: The realization of the living.* Boston: D. Reidel. (Original work published in 1973.)

Maturana, H. R., & Varela, F. J. (1987). *The tree of knowledge: The biological roots of human understanding.* Boston: Shambhala.

Patterson, C. H. (1986). *Theories of counseling and psychotherapy* (4th ed.). Cambridge, MA: Harper & Row.

Rogers, C. R. (1951). *Client-centered therapy.* Boston: Houghton Mifflin.

Snyder, C. R. (1974). Acceptance of personality interpretations as a function of assessment procedures. *Journal of Consulting and Clinical Psychology, 42* 150.

Snyder, C. R., Shenkel, R. J., & Lowery, C. R. (1977). Acceptance of personality interpretations: The "Barnum effect" and beyond. *Journal of Consulting and Clinical Psychology, 45,* 104–114.

Szasz, T. S. (1974). *The myth of mental illness.* New York: Harper & Row.

Thorne, F. C. (1961). *Personality: A clinical eclectic viewpoint.* Brandon, VT: Clinical Psychology Publishing.

Thorne, F. C. (1967). *Integrative Psychology.* Brandon, VT: Clinical Psychology Publishing.

# Cross-paradigmatic Issues

# 19

# Cross-paradigm Approaches and Other Related Issues

THIS BRIEF CHAPTER introduces the issue of cross-paradigm therapies. As discussed earlier in chapter 1, there are four basic types of therapies that derive from paradigmatic thinking. The first type was described as *paradigm-specific*. Paradigm-specific theories closely align with a paradigm's propositions and tenets of practice. "Psychiatric Case Management," for example, was presented as a paradigm-specific theory associated with the organic-medical paradigm. "Rational-Emotive Therapy" was presented as an example of a paradigm-specific theory in the psychological paradigm. And "Strategic Problem Solving Therapy" was described as a good example of a paradigm-specific theory associated with the systemic-relational paradigm. These therapeutic approaches are examples of theories that fit nicely within the metatheoretical frameworks that paradigms represent.

A second type of theory presented in this text has been titled *trans-paradigmatic*. Trans-paradigmatic theories *historically* have acted as bridges between an established way of thinking and an emerging metatheoretical framework. Trans-paradigmatic theories have been *ground-breaking and transitional* in some way. They have pointed a new direction, primarily by straddling the philosophical fence between established theory and a developing epistemology (a new focus of study). Classic examples presented in this text are: "Psycho-analysis," which bridged the organic-medical and psychological paradigms; "Conjoint Family Therapy," which bridged the psychological and systemic-relational paradigms; and "Milan Systemic Family Therapy," which appears to be bridging the systemic-relational paradigm and the emerging contextual paradigm. In each of these cases, the theories are less purely paradigm-specific than what preceded them. They are also less purely paradigm-specific than what followed.

Regardless, they are vulnerable theoretically and philosophically when taken out of their historical context, because they are often an uncomfortable mix of mutually exclusive philosophical foundations. For example, Freud's (1940/1949) Psycho-analysis teeters between a disease-focused organic-medical theory and a learning theory more consistent with psychological propositions. There is a constant tension between biological drives (e.g., libidinal impulses) and social learning (the development of the super-ego). Freud opted for a balance between these two forces as mediated by the ego, but his approach was more clearly psychological than biological. Psycho-analysis could have just as easily become a set of techniques for altering the physical drives through surgical, pharmacological, or other physical treatment means. Yet Freud moved away from physical treatments to the realm of the "talking cure." Therefore, physically based disorders are remedied primarily by nonbiological, psychological intervention strategies. Likewise, Satir's (1967) Conjoint Family Therapy straddles the philosophical fence, as she moved toward a relational focus in treatment, always defining "self-esteem" as relationally based, when in fact it is best understood as a psychological construct. Satir did a good job or redefining self-esteem as a relational concept, but self-esteem is excess historical baggage when one considers that a more purely systemic-relational interpretation conceptualizes how one feels about oneself as abiding in the external relational matrix within which the person lives (as opposed to abiding within the person). Again, trans-paradigmatic thinking led the way historically, but such thinking often is vulnerable to criticism when assessed by paradigm-specific criteria.

The third type of theory is called *cross-paradigmatic*. A cross-paradigmatic theory is a *contemporary* attempt to link paradigms. The theory is developed *after* the paradigms have become established theoretically and professionally. The theory then endeavors to link divergent philosophical approaches through a mix of techniques that derive from the two paradigms. The best example of a cross-paradigmatic theory to date is Carol Anderson's "Psychoeducational Approach" to treatment of families with

*Thomas Szasz, Salvador Minuchin, Jay Haley, and Mary Goulding (left to right) at the 1990 "Evolution of Psychotherapy" conference.*

a schizophrenic member (Anderson, Hogarty, & Reiss, 1980; Anderson, Reiss, & Hogarty, 1986). Anderson is a good example of a theoretician who is knowledgeable about theories that derive from different philosophical and professional orientations (paradigms), and she has actively developed a theory and a method that crosses paradigms. In this case she crossed the organic-medical paradigm with the systemic-relational paradigm. Beyond development of a theory-based approach, she has sought to support her ideas with empirical evidence of the effectiveness of the cross-paradigmatic method. Anderson's theory will be presented in the next chapter.

There are other examples of emergent cross-paradigmatic theories. Bandura (1986) is actively developing a theory that crosses psychological paradigm ideas with systemic-relational ideas. Best known originally as a proponent of the behavioral approach to therapy (see Bandura, 1969), his recent theoretical work is beginning to recognize the social aspects of thought and action (Bandura, 1986). The concept of "triadic reciprocal causation" (Bandura, 1989; Wood & Bandura, 1989) is a good example of a theoretical construct that crosses paradigms. Triadic reciprocal causation explains psychosocial functioning in terms of behavior, cognition, and environmental factors/events that all interact bidirectionally. Triadic factors, reciprocity, and bidirectional influence are concepts that all point to a theory that is crossing into the systemic-relational realm, although Bandura has not described his ideas within an historically grounded systemic-relational framework. It will be interesting to see whether Bandura begins to recognize the practical and political consequences of crossing paradigms, as he further develops his theory into intervention strategies deriving from the concept of triadic reciprocal causation.

By way of contrast to Bandura, Anderson fully recognizes the larger paradigmatic influences on her theory, and she conceptualizes her method clearly as an approach that crosses ideas of biological influence and social-relational influence. For this reason, her approach will be presented as a classic cross-paradigmatic theory. This is not to say that it is the only such approach. In fact there have been numerous attempts at cross-paradigmatic theory development (e.g., Bornstein & Bornstein, 1986), and there are unending cross-paradigmatic possibilities. However, at this time, Anderson's approach is one of the best known and respected theories in the cross-paradigmatic mode.

The fourth type of theory is classified as a *within-paradigm variation*. Within a paradigm, theories may be developed that cross spheres of human activity. There are three spheres of human activity that are often addressed by theories of counseling and psychotherapy. The three basic spheres of human functioning are: affect (feeling), cognition (language and perception), and behavior (action). Readers should not confuse or misinterpret theories that cross spheres of human functioning (as a way to conceptualize problems or to develop intervention strategies) as cross-paradigmatic; they are not cross-paradigmatic. Rather they represent variations within paradigms. An example of a theory that is a within-paradigm variation is Meichenbaum's (1977) "Cognitive Behavior Modification." Meichenbaum (1990) described his approach as "an integrative approach in the field of psychotherapy." In fact, it does integrate cognitive and behavioral theory. It is also unquestionably aligned with the psychological paradigm. But is is noteworthy that Meichenbaum appears to be having difficulty *integrating* some anomalous data that points to the influence of relationships on the relapse rates of people treated with cognitive behavioral approaches. It appears that the best predictors of relapse are factors related to the marital relationships of treated individuals. Meichenbaum addressed this issue at the "Evolution of Psychotherapy" conference in 1990 in Anaheim, California. He appeared to be seeking a data-based means of determining when treatment should move to the relational realm. He posed the question in a panel discussion, and he was answered by Watzlawick (a systemic theorist) who stated that he (Watzlawick) approached *all* his cases from a relational framework; this answer appeared unacceptable to Meichenbaum, who later relayed personally that he was perturbed by the relational theorists' lack of a database to make such decisions. Contrasted with cross-paradigm theories, within-paradigm variations allow for ease of application of techniques among the spheres of human activity but, when applied across paradigms, there are theoretical difficulties with integration. It appears that Meichenbaum's theory will require major modification to account for systemic-relational factors influencing client outcome. Yet, his approach is one of the most highly developed, researched, and accepted theories that can be considered a within-paradigm variation.

## Chapter Conclusion

This chapter has clarified the different types of theories of counseling and psychotherapy that derive from a paradigmatic analysis of the mental health enterprise. The four types of theories were briefly defined as: (a) *paradigm-specific;* (b) historically *trans-paradigmatic;* (c) contemporarily *cross-paradigmatic;* and (d) a *within-paradigm variation.* Examples were given within each category. The next chapter presents Anderson's "Psychoeducational Approach," which is a lucid example of a cross-paradigmatic theory.

## References

Anderson, C. M., Hogarty, G. E., & Reiss, D. J. (1980). Family treatment of adult schizophrenic patients: A psycho-educational approach. *Schizophrenia Bulletin, 6,* 690–505.

Anderson, C. M., Reiss, D. J., & Hogarty, G. E. (1986). *Schizophrenia and the family: A practitioner's guide to psychoeducation and management.* New York: Guilford Press.

Bandura, A. (1969). *Principles of behavior modification.* New York: Holt, Rinehart & Winston.

Bandura, A. (1986). *Social foundations of thought and action: A social cognitive theory.* Engelwood Cliffs, NJ: Prentice-Hall.

Bandura, A. (1989). Human agency in social cognitive theory. *American Psychologist, 44,* 1175–1184.

Bornstein, P. H., & Bornstein, M. T. (1986). *Marital therapy: A behavioral-communications approach.* Elmford, NY: Pergamon.

Freud, S. (1949). *An outline of psycho-analysis.* New York: W. W. Norton. (Original work published in 1940.)

Meichenbaum, D. (1977). *Cognitive behavior modification.* New York: Plenum.

Meichenbaum, D. (1990). *Cognitive-behavior modification: An integrative approach in the field of psychotherapy.* Paper presented at the "Evolution of Psychotherapy" conference, December 13, 1990, in Anaheim, California.

Satir, V. (1967). *Conjoint family therapy.* Palo Alto, CA: Science and Behavior Books.

Wood, R., & Bandura, A. (1989). Social cognitive theory of organizational management. *Academy of Management Review, 14,* 361–384.

# 20

# Psychoeducational Treatment of Patients With Schizophrenia:

## A Cross-Paradigmatic Therapy Linking the Organic-Medical and Systemic-Relational Paradigms

THIS CHAPTER DESCRIBES a relatively new approach to treating adult individuals with schizophrenia and their families. As a therapeutic model, it clearly is consistent with organic-medical propositions. However, with its emphasis on families, it crosses into the realm of the systemic-relational paradigm, which emphasizes relationships as both a focus of study and a target of intervention. Therefore, it is an excellent example of a contemporary attempt to develop a theory and techniques that integrate divergent paradigms.

The basic proponent of the Psychoeducational Approach is Carol Anderson, who worked closely with two associates, Hogarty and Reiss, in the development of psychoeducational theory and intervention strategies. These authors have published two seminal works in this area. The first major work was an article entitled, "Family Treatment of Adult Schizophrenic Patients: A Psycho-Educational Approach," which appeared in the *Schizophrenia Bulletin* (Anderson, Hogarty & Reiss, 1980). The second work was a book, entitled *Schizophrenia and the Family: A Practitioner's*

*Guide to Psychoeducation and Management* (Anderson, Reiss & Hogarty, 1986). In these two publications, the authors laid out, in detail, the process of psychoeducational counseling of families with an individual member with schizophrenia (an identified patient, IP). The Anderson, Reiss, and Hogarty (1986) approach is highly medical in its orientation, and highly educational. It has been found to be one of the most effective treatment approaches for schizophrenia in terms of relapse prevention (Gurman, Kniskern, & Pinsof, 1986). It is one of the few therapies that holds strictly to one paradigm's propositions (the organic-medical paradigm) while also drawing from another paradigm's propositions (the systemic-relational paradigm). Therefore, it is offered as a unique approach to treating severely disturbed mental patients.

## Carol Anderson, PhD, a Biographical Sketch

Carol M. Anderson was born in 1939 in Minneapolis, Minnesota. Her father was a plastering contractor, her mother a homemaker. Carol was the youngest of four girls in the family. She attended the University of Minnesota and received a BA degree in Child Development and Psychology in 1961, followed by a Master's in Social Work in 1964. Her interest in psychiatry began when, as a student, she worked on an inpatient child psychiatry unit at the University of Minnesota. Later positions include: (a) work in a residential treatment center for emotionally disturbed children; (b) treating street gang members and school referrals in the inner city of Detroit; and (c) work in the inpatient and outpatient divisions of the Yale–New Haven Hospital in New Haven, Connecticut.

Her specific training and interests in family work began when she worked with the families of patients hospitalized at the Yale–New Haven acute care therapeutic community in 1967. In this system, families were strongly encouraged to be involved in the patient's treatment, and sessions were held three times a week. While these

*Carol Anderson*

sessions seemed useful to most patients and families, schizophrenic patients did not seem to benefit to any marked degree from the relatively unstructured form of family therapy employed at that time. Furthermore, the families seemed unduly burdened by the implicit messages of blame for the patient's problems. These experiences initially caused her to concentrate her family work on a less disturbed population and later to develop a new model of family intervention.

In 1973, she moved to Pittsburgh where she was given the opportunity to set up an outpatient family therapy program and a Family Therapy Institute as part of the Department of Psychiatry. For several years she worked primarily with outpatients, still focusing on families and marriages and, simultaneously, focusing on the development of a training clinic. In the 1970s she became aware of the British studies on expressed emotion and other research demonstrating the vulnerability of schizophrenic patients to the impact of their environments. The documentation that patients with schizophrenia had problems negotiating the intensity of "expressed emotion" provided an explanation of why they did not respond well to the model of family therapy used in the 1960s, which primarily helped family members to express and communicate their feelings to one another. Anderson felt a more structured model of intervention was in order. In 1978, as part of a larger research project on aftercare, she developed a model for schizophrenic patients and their families that included support, an educational workshop, and ongoing help in managing the impact of the disorder. She coined the term "family psychoeducation" to describe this combination of interventions. The Psychoeducational Approach has become a model for the development of many similar programs and has been used in varying ways throughout the United States and in several countries around the world.

During this time, Carol also returned to graduate school and received her PhD in Interpersonal Communication, in 1981, from the University of Pittsburgh. In 1982, she published her first book, *Mastering Resistance,* with Susan Stewart (Anderson & Stewart, 1983). In 1986, the manual for the psychoeducational project, *Families and Schizophrenia,* was published with Douglas Reiss and Jerry Hogarty (Anderson, Reiss, & Hogarty, 1986). For ten years she traveled widely and conducted workshops on these concepts in the United States, Europe, and Asia. She was given the "Distinguished Contribution to Family Therapy" award by the American Family Therapy Association (AFTA) in 1985 and the "Distinguished Professional Contribution to Family Therapy" award by the American Association for Marriage and Family Therapy in 1987. She served on the board of directors of the AFTA for many years, moving from member to secretary to vice-president, and finally served as president for the 1988–1989 year.

She continues to publish articles and books on a variety of subjects. In 1988, she co-edited a journal special issue, entitled "Chronic Disorders and the Family" with Froma Walsh, and in 1989, she co-edited *Women in Families* with Monica McGoldrick and Froma Walsh. Most recently, she has become the administrator of the Western Psychiatric Institute and Clinic, a 279-bed hospital that houses the Department of Psychiatry for the University of Pittsburgh School of Medicine. While clinical and academic pursuits have been curtailed, she continues to attempt to apply systemic principles to administration.

# The Foundational Theory

## The Target of Counseling

The basic premise of the Anderson et al. (1980, 1986) approach is that schizophrenia, as a disorder, has inherent associated deficits, which the authors call a "psychophysiological deficit" (Anderson et al., 1980, p. 492). The authors are painstaking in describing, through a thorough and relevant review of the literature, their hypothesis about the psychophysiological deficit. They stated:

> *In general, then, it could be argued that overstimulating environments contain the pathogens sufficient to exploit the hypothesized psychophysiologic deficit in many schizophrenic patients, precipitating, in turn, the vicious cycle of hyperarousal, distraction, disattention, and disease for the patient, and increasing frustration and hopelessness for families. The nature of the offensive stimuli seems, in our view, to be traced to the conditions of social environments that necessitate adaptive responses to complex and/or vague, excessive, and emotionally charged stimuli. (p. 492)*

This basic hypothetical position on the physiological concomitants to schizophrenia provides direction for the approach of the authors, which essentially involves medication management of the patient, combined with: (a) workshop education of the identified patient's family; and (b) family therapy. The component of family intervention, using both didactic and family counseling techniques, is viewed as conjunctive to medical treatment. The dual emphasis of the psychoeducational approach on biophysiological concomitants to schizophrenia *and* family-relational factors is evident in the authors' intervention strategy, as they stated: "The highly structured model of family intervention . . . is designed to be used in conjunction with a program of maintenance chemotherapy to simultaneously decrease environmental stimulation and the patient's hypothesized vulnerability to it" (p. 492). Family involvement is an essential part of the Anderson et al. approach.

## The Process of Counseling

The process of counseling according to the Psychoeducational Approach occurs in stages. The first stage occurs during patient assessment in an inpatient (hospitalized) setting. The first stage is defined as "Connecting with Families" (Anderson et al., 1986). Anderson and her associates stated:

> *The family clinician's initial contacts with both the patient and members of the family are crucial in that these contacts help to decide whether or not treatment will occur, and help to establish the ongoing treatment relationship. Since the needs of family members are so often neglected, it is important to pay explicit attention to beginning the process of "connecting" with the family immediately,*

*and to continue this effort over several sessions. Optimally, the family should be seen while the patient is being initially evaluated, not just to gain information about the patient, but also to assess their stresses and resources, and to provide them with support. This connecting phase has five primary goals that lay the foundation for the entire process of treatment:*

1. A relationship should be established between clinician and family in which there is a genuine working alliance, a partnership that aims to help the patient. . . .
2. Clinicians should understand family issues and problems which might contribute to the stress level of the patient or family members . . . .
3. Clinicians should gain an understanding of the family's resources and their past and current attempts to cope with the illness. . . .
4. Family strengths should be emphasized and maximized. . . .
5. Rules and expectations of treatment should be established through the creation of a contract with mutual, attainable, and specific goals. *(pp. 29–32)*

The initial stage of treatment, therefore, has some very specific objectives.

The second stage of treatment is educational. A "Survival Skills Workshop" is presented. The workshop is a group-type workshop, where several families of schizophrenics will be taught about the nature and course of the disorder (see the section on "Treatment/Remediation" that follows, for details of the workshop contents). Patients are excluded from the workshops for two reasons: (a) the workshop occurs soon after medical treatment begins, and the patient may not be medically stabilized; and (b) family members appear "more comfortable in discussing their concerns without patients present" (Anderson et al., 1986, p. 75).

The third stage of treatment is called "Reentry." Anderson et al. (1986) described reentry as follows:

*This phase of treatment begins immediately following the patient's discharge from the hospital and lasts until the patient is ready to focus on work and social functioning. For some patients and families, this phase may last only a month or two, but more likely it will last as long as a year or more. The length of time is determined by the patient's ability to resume responsibility with the family. This ability is measured by the performance of small tasks agreed upon by the clinician, the patient, and the family. The patient's ability to do these tasks consistently, without increases in symptoms, is a prerequisite for moving on to the next phase of treatment. (p. 132)*

Three types of contacts are made with the family during this stage of treatment. First, there are *regularly scheduled family sessions* to address concerns (see the "Treatment/Remediation" section that follows for details). The family sessions usually occur about every two weeks. The second type of contact with the family is through *phone consultation.* Phone consultations allow the clinician to diffuse any difficulties that occur in the home and also provide extra contacts that can be used to monitor the family and to assess the patient's progress. Third, *crisis contacts* are made when an emergency arises—for example, when acute symptoms emerge, or when there is irreconcilable family conflict. One of the basic ideas behind the contact approach in the reentry phase is that the clinician should be available and ready to assess and to intervene into any situation so that the progress made during the first two stages of treatment is not lost.

The fourth stage of treatment is social and vocational rehabilitation. Anderson et al. (1986) stated:

> *If and when patients are able to demonstrate that they can maintain themselves outside a hospital without major crises, and after they are able to gradually resume some responsibility within their families, it is possible to begin to focus on their reintegration into a larger social and work world. The time it takes to reach this stage differs from patient to patient. Some are able to return to work relatively quickly and/or are able to establish meaningful social contacts. Others, however, go through a prolonged period of amotivation, apathy, and depression. Such patients frequently complain of loneliness and hopelessness while their families complain of the patient's lack of interest in life and the frustration of trying to find ways to help. Over time, these patients and families become increasingly aware that the patient's quality of life is poor. Thus, it is imperative to help them to improve their social relationships and to increase their positive involvement with social, community, and vocational activities. (p. 194)*

Success in this stage of treatment is a good sign, and the likelihood of continued success is increased with successful personal, social, and vocational rehabilitation.

A fifth stage of treatment may or may not be necessary. It can be called the maintenance or termination stage. Depending on the patient's social and vocational adjustments, a decision needs to be made as to the nature and extent of needed continued treatment. Anderson et al. (1986) stated:

> *At this point, the clinician, patient, and family are faced with four choices: (1) Treatment sessions can continue to focus on goals related to the original contract, (2) treatment sessions can move to a focus on the more traditional topics of family or marital psychotherapy using more traditional methods, (3) treatment sessions can become less frequent and focus on maintaining the present level of functioning, preventing the development of other crises, and giving an ongoing sense of "lifeline," or (4) treatment can be terminated. (p. 245)*

As these stages reveal, the "overall basic theme" that guides what psychoeducational counselors do is: "Only one change should be made at a time" (Anderson et al., 1986, p. 194). Social and vocational rehabilitation allows for a full reintegration into the social realm and provides for self-sufficiency and independence. And maintenance, if necessary, may continue until a smooth, relapse-free termination may occur.

### Counselor Role

The counselor role is similar to the role of counselors in Psychiatric Case Management. Counselors act as monitors, educators, and problem solvers. They monitor the patient's progress towards goals. They also must be alert to signs or symptoms of recurrence of active disorder. Additionally, they must be well-educated about side and main effects of medical treatments. As educators, they attempt to communicate medical and social "facts" to the families and the identified patients, through didactic means and through structured family interventions. As problem solvers, they make their best efforts to prevent problems or to solve problems once they arise, especially in the latter stages of therapy. They attempt to restate "problems" into reasonable goals of treatment—goals that ideally are agreed to by all members of the family. In other words, counselors must be continually alert to the interpersonal stressors that arise through the IP's reintegration in society, and they must be able to translate these difficulties into operational tasks with attainable goals. The tripartite counselor role (as monitor, educator, and problem solver), gives counselors a direct sense of what they are to accomplish, especially during different stages of treatment.

### Goals of Counseling and Ideal Outcomes

Goals vary at different stages of treatment, but there are two primary goals: symptom remission and functional independence. Because there is no known "cure" for schizophrenia, the best that can be expected is a full remission of problematic symptoms, even to the degree that medications can be discontinued with minimal risk of relapse.

## General Procedures

### Assessment

Assessment during the hospital phase of treatment is very medical. Neurological or other physical disorders as a root cause of behavioral difficulties must be discounted. Histories must be taken. The patient must be interviewed, assessed through a mental status assessment, and diagnosed according to standard psychiatric procedures. Once diagnosed, it must be determined whether the patient has a family or system of significance that may be approached for treatment. Willing families of identified patients then can be engaged in the treatment process according to standard psychoeducational procedures. Once the family has expressed a willingness to cooperate, a basic decision must be made about the family's potential to consummate a therapeutic contract. Family assessment may also occur, using such standard procedures as developing a family genogram (a three-generational map of the family's history). If a positive decision is made about treating a patient and his or her family, then the psychoeducational components to treatment may begin.

## Treatment/Remediation

The medical aspect of treatment, of course, usually involves medication prescription and medication management. A physician, accordingly, must be involved throughout treatment, either as a primary care professional, or at least as a monitor and consultant on the medication issue. If the physician is not the primary care professional, that responsibility should be assigned to one individual, preferably a member of a team of psychoeducational practitioners. Anderson et al. (1986) believed it was less important to choose team members based on type of college training than to choose on the basis of past successful experience working with schizophrenics. The primary care professional has responsibility to have ongoing contacts with the IP and the family through the stages of treatment.

In connecting with the family during initial family contacts, the primary care professional (clinician) essentially attempts to form a working alliance with the family members. The clinician should also be able to fully understand how family factors can affect the stress level in the family context and subsequently the adjustment of the identified patient. Family resources and strengths are emphasized. And importantly, "rules and expectations of treatment" must be established so there is agreement about attainable goals and outcomes (Anderson et al., 1986).

The educational component occurs in a structured workshop setting with professionals presenting material to the families of individuals with schizophrenia. The authors call their workshop the "survival skills workshop." Anderson et al. (1986) described the contents of the one-day psychoeducational workshop in outline form, as follows:

| | |
|---|---|
| *9:00–9:15* | *Coffee and informal interaction* |
| *9:15–9:30* | *Formal introductions and explanation of the format for the day* |
| *9:30–10:30* | *Schizophrenia: What is it?* |
| | *History and epidemiology* |
| | *The personal experience* |
| | *The public experience* |
| | *Psychobiology* |
| *10:30–10:45* | *Coffee break and informal discussion* |
| *10:45–12:00* | *Treatment of schizophrenia* |
| | *The use of antipsychotic medication* |
| | *How it works* |
| | *Why it is needed* |
| | *Impact on outcome* |
| | *Side-effects* |
| | *Psychosocial treatments* |
| | *Effects on course* |
| | *Other treatments and management* |
| *12:00–1:00* | *Lunch and informal discussion* |
| *1:00–3:30* | *The family and schizophrenia* |
| | *The needs of the patient* |

> *The needs of the family*
> *Family reactions to the illness*
> *Common problems that patients and families face*
> *What the family can do to help*
>> *Revise expectations*
>> *Create barriers to overstimulation*
>> *Set limits*
>> *Selectively ignore certain behaviors*
>> *Keep communication simple*
>> *Support medication regime*
>> *Normalize the family routine*
>> *Recognize signals for help*
>> *Use professionals*
> 3:30–4:00   *Questions regarding specific problems*
>> *Wrap-up*
>> *Informal interaction (p. 76)*

The content of the workshop is fully consonant with organic-medical propositions. Families and IPs are presented with concise but in-depth information on schizophrenia and its consequences. But the intent is also to influence the social environment of the IP.

The third component of the approach is family therapy. Importantly, the family therapy component of the approach is consistent with both organic-medical propositions and systemic-relational propositions. According to Anderson et al. (1986), the basic goals of family treatment are to "connect" with families and to help the family enter "into a cooperative relationship with the treatment team *to help the patient*" (p. 33). In this sense, however, the family is not viewed as the patient, as some systemic-relational paradigm adherents might argue. The focus remains on the identified patient—the individual with schizophrenia.

Family sessions are structured in four phases: (a) the social phase; (b) the discussion phase, which involves a discussion of previously assigned tasks and any problems that have arisen since the previous session; (c) the problem-solving phase; and (d) the task assignment phase. All family sessions follow this basic format. The predictable structure of the sessions helps to keep the sessions "low-key" and nonstressful.

The content of the sessions often deals with medical concerns. The family members are made aware of the "*prodromal signs* of the illness (subtle symptoms preceding an acute psychotic episode)" (Anderson et al., 1986, p. 155). The issue of medication compliance also is raised. And effective methods for family members to live with each other under extraordinary circumstances are explored. Ultimately, the patient must resume responsibility.

## Case Management

A therapeutic contract with the family is established formally. Related to the nature and extent of the contract, Anderson et al. (1986) stated:

*The contract specifies a step-by-step move from crisis intervention to the limited goal of patient survival in the outside world, to the long-term goal of encouraging genuine reintegration into social and work functioning. Such a contract involves a mutual agreement about the goals, content, length, and methods of therapy. The family's main complaints and concerns are translated by the clinician into clear, specific, and attainable goals. If a complaint is unreasonable or a goal is unattainable, the clinician negotiates with the family toward "the possible." If there are crucial goals the family has not mentioned spontaneously, the clinician can suggest they be placed on the treatment agenda, but should never do so unilaterally. (p. 57)*

The treatment contract differentiates the process of inpatient treatment and outpatient treatment. Inpatient treatment goals are much more short-term, whereas the outpatient treatment goals must deal with leaving the hospital, reintegrating the IP into the home, and assisting the patient to the degree there can be extended social and vocational rehabilitation.

After inpatient treatment, there are regularly scheduled family therapy sessions, phone contacts, and if necessary, crisis interventions. However, Anderson et al. (1986) are careful in their approach to avoid overstimulation of the patient by too frequent or too intense family therapy contacts. The authors believed that therapy contacts approximately every two weeks are optimal. They stated, "The patient's vulnerability to intensity and overstimulation, requires a slow treatment pace" (p. 133).

Through social and vocational rehabilitation, the patient begins to make outside social contacts. This is a slow process in which the family is first actively involved. Later, more vocational-relevant activity may occur. In addition to the very detailed chapter on social and vocational rehabilitation in the Anderson et al. (1986) text, readers are referred to a thorough explication of principles of psychiatric rehabilitation by Anthony (1980), which focuses more on the case management aspects of vocational rehabilitation of individuals with psychiatric disabilities.

## Recent Developments or Criticisms

The Psychoeducational Approach has received much attention in the literature, especially related to innovative family therapy techniques. As a therapeutic approach, it is highly empirically founded, both at the level of conceptualizing the problem (a psychophysiological deficit vulnerable to relational stressors) and at the level of outcomes (assessment of relapse rates). It has been found to be highly effective, as reported by Anderson et al. (1986):

*Results of our outcome study using this model during the first year of posthospital treatment have been encouraging in terms of the usefulness of family interventions. Among treatment takers (n = 90), 19% of those receiving family therapy alone experienced a psychotic relapse in the year following hospital discharge. Of those receiving the individual behavioral therapy, 20% relapsed, but no patient in the treatment cell that received both family therapy and social skills training experienced a relapse. These relapse rates constitute significant effects for both treatments when contrasted to a 41% relapse rate for those receiving only chemotherapy and support. Further, the combination of treatments yields an (additive) effect not possible with either treatment alone. When patients who were entirely faithful in adhering to their maintenance chemotherapy were included, a clear and significant effect for family therapy was also observed. (p. 24)*

At this time, the Psychoeducational Approach is being studied with other disorders by independent researchers. The establishment of a supportive literature by independent researchers will be critical to the survival of the Psychoeducational Approach. It will also be interesting to see how this approach compares to other approaches when treating different types of emotional disorder, especially in different contexts.

To date, there have been no major criticisms of the theory published in the literature. It can be anticipated, however, that as the approach is applied to different problems in different settings, limitations will be manifested.

## Paradigm Fit

### Focus of Study

The focus of study of the Psychoeducational Approach is clearly the individual with the disability in his or her relational context (family). The family is viewed as critical to treatment. Since the identified patient is viewed as having a "psychophysiological deficit," there is clear consistency between the Psychoeducational Approach and organic-medical propositions. Since family and relational stressors are potential triggers to exacerbation of the disorder, the family context is also important. This recognition of relational influences on behavior is consistent with systemic-relational paradigm propositions.

Psychoeducational practitioners thoroughly study the disorder of schizophrenia in order to know what can be known about its etiology, progression, and probable outcomes. Schizophrenia, as a disorder immanent to the afflicted individual, is also a "thing" under study. Therefore, the psychoeducational counselor must be knowledgeable about the disorder of schizophrenia, and he or she must be knowledgeable about his or her client as a person afflicted with the disorder. But the psychoeducational clinician must also understand family-relational dynamics and how they affect individuals. At best, psychoeducational clinicians should have training in both organic-medical and systemic-relational treatment approaches.

### View of Nature of Reality

Reality is viewed as "things." People, as things, are largely viewed as biological organisms, and the environment is seen as a potential stressor or trigger of predisposed outcomes. Nature is viewed as understandable, and it is assumed that causes can be defined in a deterministic way. "Cause and effect" is linear, as certain factors are presumed to be causative of schizophrenic behavior in an "A causes B" way. For example, it is assumed that the psychophysiological deficit directly *makes* the individual vulnerable to environmental overstimulation. But within a family context, family processes may be viewed as circular phenomena, meaning that small bits of information may have disproportional effects. Although the individual is viewed as a biological entity, he or she is a biological entity bound to survival in a socially laden environment.

## Consonance with Paradigm Propositions and Tenets

To a large degree there is consonance between the Psychoeducational Approach and the propositions of the organic-medical paradigm. Individuals are the focus of study. They are assessed, and it is assumed that the root of their behavior is biological. Extreme personality predispositions are classified and diagnosed according to the frequency, intensity, and duration of symptoms (in this case, symptoms of schizophrenia). Causes are directly defined and, if unknown, it is assumed that scientific inquiry will determine them in the future. The condition of schizophrenia is isolated for treatment, although the Psychoeducational Approach diverges from organic-medical tenets of practice in its simultaneous involvement of the family in the IP's treatment. There is, according to the Psychoeducational Approach, an assumption that environmental stressors are primarily socially and relationally based. This crosses to the realm of the systemic-relational paradigm operationally, since relational factors are addressed when dealing with family concerns in the latter stages of psychoeducational intervention. Therefore, the Psychoeducational Approach can be described as drawing from basic ideals of both the organic-medical and systemic-relational paradigms.

# Chapter Conclusion

Over all, the Psychoeducational Approach to treatment of families with an identified patient disabled by schizophrenia is a promising method deriving from both the organic-medical and systemic-relational paradigms. As mentioned earlier, the approach crosses into the systemic-relational paradigm by its accentuation of relationship concerns (and family stressors) within a medical context. As such, it is distinct among other treatment approaches for psychiatric patients (see the discussion of other approaches in Luber & Anderson, 1983). In fact, Anderson et al. (1986) make a very forceful statement on the limits of family therapy alone. They stated:

> *Traditional family treatment strategies are often unsuccessful and at times even stimulate noncompliance, crises, and relapse. There are probably several reasons for the failure of more additional [sic] family approaches. Perhaps the most significant is the number of potentially negative metacommunications inherent in the practice of traditional family therapy that needlessly erect obstacles and*

*resistances to change, and that exact an unnecessary price from families in terms of pain, guilt, and anxiety. For instance, many family therapists suggest that schizophrenia is best treated through family sessions without medication or other treatments. For families of schizophrenic patients this communication implicitly suggests that we know what schizophrenia is (a family disease), what causes it (families), and what cures it (family therapy). This message can have a number of undesirable effects. . . . To suggest cavalierly that family therapy is the method of treatment is evidence of unwarranted arrogance when there is so much evidence that medication programs are a vital part of patient care. (pp. 330–331)*

As can be seen, by attempting to cross paradigms at the level of theory building and at the level of intervention, the psychoeducational theorists have built on the strengths of both paradigms, while avoiding the pitfalls of dogmatic within-paradigm thinking.

# References

Anderson, C. M., Hogarty, G. E., & Reiss, D. J. (1980). Family treatment of adult schizophrenic patients: A psycho-educational approach. *Schizophrenia Bulletin, 6,* 490–505.

Anderson, C. M., Reiss, D. J., & Hogarty, G. E. (1986). *Schizophrenia and the family: A practitioner's guide to psychoeducation and management.* New York: Guilford Press.

Anderson, C. M., & Stewart, S. (1983). *Mastering resistance: A practical guide to family therapy.* New York: Guilford.

Anthony, W. A. (1980). *The principles of psychiatric rehabilitation.* Baltimore, MD: University Park Press.

Gurman, A. S., Kniskern, D. P., & Pinsof, W. M. (1986). Research on the process and outcome of marital and family therapy. In S. L. Garfield & A. E. Bergin (Eds.), *Handbook of psychotherapy and behavior change* (3rd ed.). New York: John Wiley & Sons.

Luber, R. F., & Anderson, C. M. (1983). *Family intervention with psychiatric patients.* New York: Human Sciences Press.

McGoldrick, M., Anderson, C. M., & Walshe, F. (Eds.). (1989). *Women in families: A framework for family therapy.* New York: W. W. Norton.

Walsh, F. & Anderson, C. (Eds.) (1987). Severe and chronic disorders and the family (Special Issue), *The Journal of Psychotherapy and the Family, 3*(3).

# PART SEVEN
# Conclusion

# 21

# Experimental Issues And Conclusion

THE REDEFINITION OF Kuhn's (1970) "scientific paradigm" in a way that the term *paradigm* may be applied to the mental health services may be viewed as an opportunity for a new understanding of counseling theory. Paradigm crisis in the mental health services was described as resulting primarily from practical-theoretical, professional, and political concerns rather than scientific anomaly. Subsequently, four counseling paradigms were defined: the organic-medical, psychological, systemic-relational, and contextual paradigms. Each paradigm was defined according to basic operational propositions and tenets of practice. Deductively defined, but empirically testable, counseling paradigms represent competitive scientific theories. It is now possible for counseling researchers to begin to test one paradigm against another in competitive tests of strength at predicting outcomes within specific therapeutic contexts.

The following questions are examples of questions that may be addressed through paradigmatic research: Will the organic-medical paradigm be supported as superior to other paradigms in medical settings? Will systemic-relational approaches supersede psychological ones when marital or family problems are addressed? Will the results be better for the contextual paradigm compared to any other paradigm in diverse settings? These kinds of questions may now be addressed in the literature. In this way, counseling has attained the status of an experimental paradigmatic science.

But the conclusion that paradigmatic thinking is "good" for counseling is a value judgment that reflects contextual leanings. In fact, as was mentioned in chapter 1, there is a contextual bias to this text. By this time it should be clear to readers that paradigms represent separate and bounded consensualities. Each is real as preferred and acted upon by a group of professionals who, through a spoken or unspoken consensus, act according to paradigmatic ideals. In other words, paradigms of counseling and psychotherapy are good examples of socially constructed realities. This text, accordingly, makes the obvious more than obvious, primarily by means of a contextual philosophy that places the social realities of paradigms in context. To the degree that one accepts the validity of the paradigm framework in counseling and psychotherapy, one accepts the contextual philosophy at its foundation.

To argue in favor of contextual ideals, however, is not to argue that the contextualist position (and the idea of equally valid and competitive counseling paradigms) must be accepted. Readers may choose to take the position that counseling theories are not so easily professionally, politically, or practically classified. A differing distinction about the similarities or differences among theories may be made and valued. Or the position may be taken that there is only one right or acceptable theory or paradigm, and that other positions will be proven "wrong" or "not valid." For example, theoretical absolutists might argue that time will prove only one theory or paradigm to be valid, and they will seek evidence to support such a position. Further, theoretical absolutists subscribing strictly to organic-medical, psychological, or systemic-relational propositions will find fault with a conclusion that context plays a role in the definition of what is acceptable or unacceptable as a treatment method. They will be prone to take the position that their theory or paradigm is the "right" one, and that others are not and cannot be as effective, no matter what the context. For them, the definition of a theory or a paradigm is a definition of more than a province, and research will be designed to prove their ideas correct when compared to contextual research that tries to define appropriate contexts for applying theory-derived techniques.

It should also be understood that the contextual position adopted in this text *is not absolutist*. Rather, it is anticipated that some readers will agree and, through further study and discussion on such ideas, a consensus will be attained as to the validity or usefulness of these ideas. It is further anticipated that there will be a process of modifying and clarifying these ideas through professional interaction. Therefore, these ideas become "real" only as acted upon by individuals within a professional/academic community. Competitive viewpoints propounded by individuals linked (or linking) to other networks of professionals are equally as valid. Or, it may be that the ideas presented in this text will die a slow death, if no one agrees with them. Regardless, if paradigms of counseling and psychotherapy are viewed as real within a professional and academic community, the question arises, "How can paradigms be empirically tested?" The need for and the design of contextually motivated *critical paradigmatic experiments* (experiments that test one paradigm against another in a critical test of effectiveness), therefore, must be addressed.

## Paradigmatic Research and Contextualism

Given a clearer definition of paradigms as applied to mental health services, devising critical paradigmatic experiments becomes an easier task. As Deese (1972) stated:

> *At its best, a critical test can only tell us that one theory—for the moment—is to be preferred. It cannot tell us that one particular theory is true for all eternity.*

*We are deprived of the comfort of an absolute truth in science, for the strongest test of a scientific theory is only a comparative one. (p. 32)*

Accordingly, any one counseling paradigm can be matched against any other of the four paradigms in competitive tests of strength at predicting therapeutic outcomes within specified contexts. For example, the psychological and systemic-relational paradigms might be compared as applied to solving marital problems. Such an empirical test could take the form of a random assignment of individuals in couples to either of two paradigm treatment possibilities, psychological or systemic-relational, or to a control group receiving no treatment. Those receiving psychological treatment would be provided services as described previously in the chapter on the psychological paradigm. Marital partners would be separated, individually assessed, and then counseled on how to adjust to the personalities or traits of the other. All relationship problems would be redefined as an individual's problem in adjusting to the personality or behaviors of the spouse. Those receiving systemic-relational treatment, on the other hand, would be provided conjoint therapy involving reframing of all individual problems to relationship difficulties. Systemic therapy would always occur in therapeutic relationship with a marital therapist subscribing to the philosophy that relationships exist as treatable processes. Under no circumstances would individual diagnosis or individual counseling occur without jeopardizing the integrity of systemic-relational treatment as compared to psychological treatment. Marital outcome measures could be: (a) length of marriage (post therapy) across groups; (b) number of divorces per group; or (c) marital satisfaction across groups as measured by appropriate instruments.

Family therapy, medical treatments, or contextual approaches could be tested similarly. Identified patients, or their families, could be randomly assigned to treatments representing organic-medical, psychological, systemic-relational, or contextual therapy, as in the marital therapy example; the recidivism rates of identified patients could serve as possible outcome measures.

Accordingly, true tests of one paradigm against the other within a specified context could be accomplished. Directional theoretical predictions would derive from the context under study as much as they would derive from the paradigms under study. For instance, in the marital counseling example described previously, predictions would support systemic-relational intervention over psychological interventions or control group activity, since systemic-relational ideas have been specifically developed to address problems of a marital (relational) sort.

This experimental design is similar to other outcome studies in the mental health services with three significant differences:

**1.** Because paradigms are superordinate theoretical structures with political and professional as well as practical-theoretical implications, the design is not just therapy or model comparative.

**2.** The design provides for a test of epistemological or ontological distinctions, as well as a test of professional orientations. Some example questions answered by paradigmatic design are as follows: Should clients be treated individually for problems defined in a marital or family context? Should clients be treated systemically for problems defined within a psychological or medical context? Which one (the psychological or organic-medical paradigms) produces the best result in none-medical settings? Does the flexibility of the contextual paradigm translate to higher success rates when compared to treatments aligned with the other paradigms?

**3.**    The design is more closely aligned to the theoretical comparisons that occur in the well developed, paradigmatic sciences. As redefined for the mental health services, paradigms may mirror true theories in the established sciences.

The design is also similar to the design used in another mental health field, vocational rehabilitation, where the "psychomedical" paradigm was preliminarily compared to the "systemic" paradigm in a test of strength at predicting rehabilitation decisions, and systems theory predominated (Cottone, 1987; Cottone, Grelle, & Wilson, 1988). [At the time of the Cottone et al. study, it was believed that the "psychomedical" paradigm constituted a unique approach; today, however, the psychomedical paradigm appears more as a mix of two purer paradigm orientations, the organic-medical and psychological paradigms. Regardless, the Cottone et al. study still stands as an early example of paradigm-relevant research.] The vocational rehabilitation system has traditionally been a psychological service delivery system. Clients with disabilities are evaluated in order to define their vocational strengths and weaknesses, where strengths and weaknesses have been primarily defined by means of standard psychometric and work sampling techniques. The Cottone et al. study pitted psychological test data (from intelligence, aptitude, and other vocational ability measures) against systemic data (social and interpersonal data) in a competitive test of accuracy at predicting the actual recommendations of service delivery professionals. Psychological and systemic data were excised from actual vocational evaluation reports, and vocational evaluator subjects were unaware of the actual recommendations of the report-writing professionals. The results showed that subjects were consistently able to assess more accurately the recommendations of report-writing professionals on the basis of systemic versus psychological data. Accordingly, vocational evaluators, rather than simply assessing vocational strengths and weaknesses on the basis of psychological test data, appeared to base their opinions on social and interpersonal data. In this way, they were probably screening clients on sociosystemic factors, while allegedly collecting psychological data to make "objective" decisions about a person's potential work skill or ability. The results supported a "systemic theory of vocational rehabilitation" (Cottone, 1987). The Cottone et al. study is an example of how clear definitions of a competitive paradigm must be generated before a theory-comparative test at the paradigm level can be accomplished.

By defining the four basic counseling paradigms through basic propositions and tenets of practice, critical paradigm experiments may be more easily defined within mental health contexts.

## Paradigm Research in Context

One of the criticisms that can be raised about what is proposed in this chapter is that it does not address the issue of organic-medical, psychological, or systemic-relational epistemology. It assumes a contextualist epistemology at the level of metatheoretical questioning and research design. It is also not purely positivistic. Generally, according to positivistic tenets: (a) all ideas are reduced to the operational level, (b) theory is *built* on inductive reasoning; and (c) cause is directly (often singularly) defined. These may appear to be valid criticisms to those individuals who are not able to eschew the trappings of singular paradigmatic thinking. Such criticisms reveal a failure to view mental health services from a metaperspective. On the other hand, it is possible that such critics have taken the metaperspective, but rejected the multiparadigm view in favor of singular paradigmatic thinking and a more purely positivistic science. In that case, the critic has legitimately taken a stand that only one paradigm can be supported. The singular paradigmatic position is one that can be understood and respected, although from the multiparadigm perspective, it appears to be very limited in its scope.

It has been argued by Colapinto (1979, p. 427) that the search for meaningful evidence in the mental health services derives from the "epistemological context" directing investigation. Conversely, Colapinto argued that "epistemologies cannot be tested through empirical evidence" (p. 430). By way of contrast, the position taken in this chapter is that therapeutic approaches based on differing epistemological notions can be competitively tested. Further, it is proposed that a competitive test at the paradigm level (as a paradigm is defined in this text) is an alternative approach that can move mental health research beyond the shackles of a strict positivism to the freedom of a postpositivist empiricism. In postpositivistic empiricism, general theory and scientific fact are viewed as interacting, whereas in a strict positivistic perspective it is assumed that experimentation within certain scientific rules produces objective or absolute evidence. In keeping with a postpositivistic perspective, critical paradigmatic experiments are tests of *relative* strength of theoretical ideas at predicting empirical outcome. Absolute truth is not at issue. Critical paradigmatic experiments, therefore, are in keeping with a *postpositivistic empiricism.*

Some may argue that comparative tests, where one approach is assessed as being better than another, even if such a conclusion is constrained to specific contexts, is linear in its approach, favoring linear as opposed to circular epistemological frameworks. It does not logically follow, however, that acceptance of circular epistemology is a rejection of a competitive empirical framework at the paradigm level. To reject critical paradigmatic experimentation due to social system theory's rejection of linearity, for example, is wrong from a contextual position; it is the equivalent of rejecting the competitive societal context within which mental health services have emerged and continue to develop. It would be like saying that something that spins around cannot move forward in a larger context.

Likewise, there is nothing in the list of propositions of the organic-medical or psychological paradigms (two linear causal paradigms defined in this text) that favor them in tests of competitive strength at producing therapeutic outcomes. A postpositivistic empiricism plays no favorites, as it is recognized that context plays an important role in the definitions of problems to be studied. Postpositivistic empiricism, as proposed in this chapter, is consistent with a contextualist view of knowledge, where context is critical and conclusions are tentative in a dynamic system of thought and ideas (see McGuire's, 1986, discussion on this topic under the rubric of perspectivism).

In this sense, empirical confrontation takes on the role of a discovery process rather than an assessment of absolute outcome; hypothesis testing, theory, and context all play an important part in outcome and subsequent hypothesis generation (McGuire, 1986).

Mental health researchers should assess the effectiveness of different therapeutic approaches associated with different paradigms, and they should do so within specific and well-defined contexts. In this way, Gurman's (1983, p. 229) "ethical imperative" is quite appropriate; the efficacy of treatment is a political and ethical concern. The proposed "critical paradigmatic experiment," therefore, is derived from the perspective that any therapeutic approach cannot be viewed out of the context of a mental health service delivery system in a competitive society. By redefining paradigm crisis in mental health services to include practical-theoretical, professional, and political factors, the professional service context of counseling theory is recognized. In this light, postpositivistic empiricism is quite appropriate, because counseling researchers must demonstrate, *within certain contexts and for the moment,* which specific paradigm-aligned counseling theories are better within specified contexts.

## Questions and Answers on Paradigmatic Research

The following questions and answers were developed around a debate between Taggart (1989) and Cottone (1989a, 1989b) that appeared in the *Journal of Marital and Family Therapy* in the summer of 1989. Readers are referred to those original articles for an historical understanding of these issues. The questions which follow have been derived from Taggart's criticism of critical paradigmatic experiments.

**1.**    Isn't paradigmatic research more motivated by market share than ethics? In other words, isn't the critical paradigmatic experiment the equivalent of accepting capitalistic competitiveness at the expense of theories where process is viewed as more significant than outcome?

*Answer:* One major intent of developing a contextualist view of research and of defining "critical paradigmatic experiments" was to place Gurman's (1983) "ethical imperative" in a different theoretical light. As stated earlier, the efficacy of treatment is a political and ethical concern. The ethical issues are not secondary. On the other hand, to leave important questions unexplored, to rely solely on subjective and anecdotal evidence in making claims about mental health professions (as has been done by some theorists), and to fail to reach relative consensus as to how to advance counseling theory beyond dialectic or stalemate, is a serious ethical concern.

Alternatives to critical paradigmatic experiments may be less supportive of front-line therapists legally constrained to practice within disciplinary boundaries (by licensure laws, for example). On the other hand, certain research agendas, and certain research reviews (such as those by Gurman & Kniskern, 1978, and Gurman, Kniskern, & Pinsof, 1986, which give some basic conclusions about the effectiveness of marital and family therapy) are important to the mental health services because they give hints to effectiveness of certain therapeutic orientations. Such research agendas/reviews are very *useful* to practitioners in the field, especially when making claims about the effectiveness of their treatments. Mental health practitioners are ethically obligated to facilitate the informed consent of clients seeking treatment. Clients have the right to know the risks versus the benefits involved in certain treatments when compared to alternative treatment methods. Mental health professionals have a legal and ethical obligation to ensure that clients are informed about and treated with effective methods. Critical paradigmatic experiments can help in this regard by comparatively testing specialized approaches (based on epistemological notions) within specified contexts.

**2.**   How can an experiment be considered "critical" when it is designed? Critical paradigmatic experiments cannot be designed in advance; they are only retrospectively definable, based on the results of the study.

*Answer:* If the word *critical* is meant to mean a "final arbitrator of" a theoretical position, then it is true that "critical paradigmatic experiments" cannot be designed in advance. However, the use of the term *critical* in "critical paradigmatic experiment" is intended to mean "fault finding." Critical paradigmatic experiments will find fault with one theoretical position in comparison to another within a specified context. In this sense, any experiment that is designed to test the theoretical assertions of one position against another is critical, and if the design incorporates theory at the level of paradigm (however paradigm is defined in the larger field of study), then it is legitimately able to claim the title "critical paradigmatic experiment."

Nowhere is it claimed that one critical paradigmatic experiment is enough. Rather, contextual empirical investigation is "a discovery process rather than an assessment of absolute outcome." This process involves years of various kinds of critical paradigmatic experiments posing questions within clearly specified contexts. This process does not divorce itself from other investigations that continue to be conducted in the field. It is the combination of critical paradigmatic experiments and other research procedures that can provide a clearer view of the effectiveness of the mental health enterprise. And communication with individuals outside the profession will be best enhanced if there is a research agenda that challenges and supports foundational theory in the mental health services.

Critical paradigmatic experiments can be designed in advance. Although researchers might not use the term *paradigm* in their design as it is meant here, such experiments are done frequently, and an example will be cited and described under question four, which follows.

**3.**   Are critical paradigmatic experiments "absolutist" in any sense?

*Answer:* Some might argue that if one accepts the idea of a critical paradigmatic experiment, then one has absolutely accepted the contextual paradigm. It is true that one must accept change and process as a primary philosophy in developing a contextual view of research. However, the contextual paradigm cannot be absolutely accepted—it is constantly changing—even the idea that change is fundamental will at times be more acceptable than at other times. The contextual paradigm, as presently conceived, is not the final word. However, paradoxically, it may be the final paradigm. This is so, because the contextual paradigm, as an evolving paradigm, may continually be at the forefront of changes in the mental health field. No other paradigm of epistemological and ontological significance may emerge without linkage, in some way, to contextual ideas (since, if a new paradigm does emerge, then its emergence is at least partial verification of the contextual position of change and process).

Some individuals may be unable to accept that contextual thinking can lead to meaningful empirical investigation. In this regard, a critique of critical paradigmatic experiments is to some degree a critique of Kuhn (1970), since his position is an explication of the postpositivistic position of science. This text has only redefined "paradigm" for the mental health services (see chapters 1 and 2) and placed paradigmatic struggles within a contextual view of knowledge. The multiparadigm view, then, is postpositivistic and contextualistic.

**4.**   Have there ever been any "critical paradigmatic experiments" in mental health research previous to the definition of such?

*Answer:* Yes, there have been paradigmatic struggles addressed in the mental health services, but they cannot be found within the boundaries of singular paradigmatic questioning. Paradigmatic struggles have occurred at the border of psychology and medicine and at the border of psychology and systems theory. Related to medicine, questions about the degree of heritability (versus environmental maleability) involved in mental illness, intelligence, and personality traits are paradigmatic.

One good example of a well-designed study that addresses issues at the boundary of psychological and organic-medical thinking is the recent work of Tellegen and associates (1988). Tellegen et al. administered a highly reliable and valid personality measure to monozygotic and dizygotic twins with one group of each reared apart and one group of each reared together. By design and advanced statistical analyses, they were able to focus on the relative merits of genetics versus environmental factors on personality traits. Their findings supported earlier studies on this issue—"that, on average, about 50% of measured personality diversity can be attributed to genetic diversity." Their results also produced a surprising finding: of the fourteen traits studied, the median variance component for shared familial environment was less than 10 percent. They stated:

> *Our findings suggest more saliently, nonetheless, that the common environment generally plays a very modest role in the determination of many personality traits. This conclusion . . . runs counter, however, to the belief, influential among psychologists, that personality similarity is profoundly enhanced by a shared family environment. (p. 1037)*

Beyond the obvious implications of their work, it is noteworthy that Dr. Tellegen is a professor of *psychology* producing findings that are critical of the psychological model.

In the case of my own work used as an example earlier in this chapter (Cottone et al., 1988) the psychological (psychomedical) and the systemic-relational paradigms were competitively tested. The systemic evidence used in the study was social and interpersonal data reduced only to the level of a triadic relational configuration. The results supported systems theory in a setting that has been treated primarily as a psychological service delivery system. Again, a group of psychologists produced research disputing the psychological model.

In both these cases, researchers were assessing the application of theory within specified contexts. These results are not absolute proof. They may not even be recognized as crucial to a paradigm shift. But they add to a critical (fault-finding) literature about common beliefs related to current practices.

**5.**    Isn't it true that no matter how postpositivistic an empiricism, it is still positivistic?

*Answer:* Some might argue that unless outcome measures are different in some way from what has been used in the past, they cannot be paradigmatic. From a contextual perspective, if the question is posed appropriately, the outcome measure will follow naturally. Some counseling researchers appear to be searching for complex outcome measures where simple ones suffice. The need for complex measures to answer paradigmatic questions is not clearly borne out in the history of science. A classic example is the study done by a British expedition to assess Einstein's idea that space is curved by mass. The expedition team simply took photographic impressions during a total eclipse of the sun. If the images of stars appeared in the photographs in the area supposedly eclipsed by the moon, then the light from the stars would have to have traveled in curved space. Einstein's ideas were supported. The outcome measure was nothing complicated for the science of the day—measures taken off of a photographic image.

Contextually speaking, effort must be put into defining significant contexts for assessing theoretical questions. Outcome issues should not be addressed before design issues.

**6.**    Isn't it true that certain mental health professions will benefit more by critical paradigmatic experimentation than others, since some mental health professions have large, established research communities, and others do not? For example, with the research resources available to psychology and psychiatry, won't family therapy researchers have difficulty disputing their findings?

*Answer:* Well-designed critical paradigmatic experiments should begin to answer important practical questions in the mental health field. Optimism, in this regard, stems from a firm belief that certain paradigms will predominate within certain contexts and that researchers will design experiments that are clearly context-specific and design-fair. However, from an ethical standpoint, there may be concern. It is true that unethical researchers may push aside evidence that contradicts the theory of their disciplinary affiliation. It can also be argued, even from a contextualist position, that no research is truly objective—that, for instance, it is "subject dependent" (Maturana, 1978). But the contextualist concern is really not a negative issue related to the proposals in this chapter, because the claim is not absolutist, and it is recognized that all findings will prove to be fleeting in the larger ever-changing context of our world. This position, then, attempts to define a foundation for a *research consensus* wherein context-specific assessments of mental health services may be made. This is certainly consistent with contextual thinking.

**7.**    Doesn't the idea of a critical paradigmatic experiment between the systemic-relational paradigm and the psychological paradigm place relationship on the same logical level as the individual, which is inconsistent with the systemic-relational ideal that relationships are complex interpersonal processes? In other words, doesn't this type of research treat relationships as "things?"

*Answer:* No. To study the effectiveness of a process-orientation compared to an orientation that views people as individualized entities is not to view processes as things. To compare the speed of a bowling ball rolling down a grassy hill to the speed of a surfboard sliding down the same grassy hill is not to say that a ball and a surfboard are logically equivalent. It is instead to recognize that there are differences that are significant differences within specified contexts. In this case it can be generally assumed that the ball would reach the bottom of the hill more quickly. On the other hand, when comparing a bowling ball to a surfboard as a means of traversing a deep lake, then the surfboard may be more efficient. Context is as much a critical issue in critical paradigmatic experiments as is the nature of the mental health treatments. *Contextual research is a measure of difference at the point where treatments and contexts come together; it is not a process of equalization of theoretical premises.*

Also, the image of critical paradigmatic experiments should be like a footrace, where two worthy competitors aim the same direction, as opposed to a tug of war, where two opponents are going opposite directions. Critical paradigm experiments do not place paradigms in an either/or opposition. Instead they place paradigms in a "which one in which setting" framework. Several paradigms may be validly descriptive of the same phenomena, although each paradigm may predominate in one or more therapeutic or problematic settings.

## Conclusion

This book has attempted to demonstrate the need for a clear definition of competitive paradigms in the mental health services. Kuhn's (1970) term *paradigm* was critically reviewed and modified to account for the practical-theoretical, professional, and political nature of crisis in the mental health field. Four counseling paradigms were defined: the organic-medical, psychological, systemic-relational, and contextual paradigms. Propositions and methodological tenets of the four paradigms were delineated. A model experimental design was offered for paradigmatic research in the mental health services. A postpositivistic empiricism, consistent with a contextual view of knowledge, was defined as an alternate framework for assessing the effectiveness of counseling theories. Paradigmatic thinking, therefore, offers the mental health professions an opportunity to test their theoretical foundations critically against competitive viewpoints of professional and philosophical significance.

## References

Colapinto, J. (1979). The relative value of empirical evidence. *Family Process, 18,* 427–441.
Cottone, R. R. (1987). A systemic theory of vocational rehabilitation. *Rehabilitation Counseling Bulletin, 30,* 167-176.

Cottone, R. R. (1989a). Defining the psychomedical and systemic paradigms in marital and family therapy. *Journal of Marital and Family Therapy, 15,* 225–235.

Cottone, R. R. (1989b). On ethical and contextual research in marital and family therapy: A reply to Taggart. *Journal of Marital and Family Therapy, 15,* 243–248.

Cottone, R. R., Grelle, M., & Wilson, W. C. (1988). The accuracy of systemic versus psychological evidence in judging vocational evaluator recommendations: A preliminary test of a systemic theory of vocational rehabilitation. *Journal of Rehabilitation, 54* (1), 45–52.

Deese, J. (1972). *Psychology as science and art.* New York: Harcourt Brace Jovanovich.

Gurman, A. S. (1983). Family therapy research and the ''new epistemology.'' *Journal of Marital and Family Therapy, 9,* 227–234.

Gurman, A. S., & Kniskern, D. P. (1978). Deterioration in marital and family therapy: Empirical, clinical and conceptual issues. *Family Process, 17,* 3–20.

Gurman, A. S., Kniskern, D. P., & Pinsof, W. M. (1986). Research on the process and outcome of marital and family therapy. In S. L. Garfield & A. E. Bergin (Eds.), *Handbook of psychotherapy and behavior change* (3rd ed.) (pp. 565–624). New York: John Wiley & Sons.

Kuhn, T. S. (1970). *The structure of scientific revolutions* (2nd ed.). Chicago: University of Chicago Press.

Maturana, H. R. (1978). Biology of language: The epistemology of reality. In G. A. Miller & E. Lenneberg (Eds.), *Psychology and biology of language and thought.* New York: Academic Press.

McGuire, W. J. (1986). A perspectivist looks at contextualism and the future of behavioral science. In R. Rosnow & M. Georgoudi (Eds.), *Contextualism and understanding in behavioral science,* (pp. 271–301). New York: Praeger.

Taggart, M. (1989). Paradigmatic play-offs and the search for market share. *Journal of Marital and Family Therapy, 15,* 237–242.

Tellegen, A., Lykken, D., Bouchard, T., Wilcox, D., Segal, N., & Rich, S. (1988). Personality similarity in twins reared apart and together. *Journal of Personality and Social Psychology, 54,* 1031–1039.

# Appendix A

# Systemic-Relational Paradigm:

## *The Dynamics Of The External Systemic-Relational Model*

The section goes into greater detail on the dynamics of the external model of social systems theory. Appendix B, by comparison, details the dynamics of the internal model of the systemic-relational paradigm. Through these appendices readers should be able to get details of how social systems operate, and readers also should be able to compare the external and internal models. As separate models within the systemic-relational paradigm, they are quite distinct operationally.

## The External Model

To understand the external model of social systems theory, it is important to understand that systems are structured processes. As systems theory has developed over the years it has become more complex. Systems cannot be simply viewed as homeostatic machines—they must be understood as surviving living processes that change within an environmental context. Systems theory's original propositions have been defined as the "first cybernetics," and the study of how systems change has been defined as the "second cybernetics" (Maruyama, 1968). This section will expound upon systemic concepts as related to the dynamic operation of social systems and how systems operate and change within their social contexts. It is an external systemic position.

## The Importance of Triads

Triads (three-person and three-relationship systems) can be viewed as the building blocks of larger social systems. Triads have properties that have great relevance to social systems. In fact, a triad may be "homeostatic" in families and larger systems.

### Triads and Dyadic Conflict Diffusion

Triads are notorious for their coalitional capabilities. For example, when two individuals disagree publicly, and neither appears to be "winning the argument," a third party is often "looked to" as a means to offset the fragile balance in the relationship. Many individuals have been caught in the uncomfortable position of being asked to take sides while viewing a disagreement between friends. Agreeing with one party immediately places the onlooker in opposition to the other party in the dyadic disagreement. A true coalition, therefore, offsets the balance and places the loner in a position of being "odd man out." This demonstrates a basic principle of triadic relationships: when two disagree in the presence of a third, there is a tendency toward triangulation. As Becvar and Becvar (1982) have described triangulation, "Thus while a dyad may be relatively stable during calm times, as soon as difficulties arise, a third person is often drawn in to form a triangle, or a two against one situation, in order to solve a problem" (p. 25). Once a triangle is formed, triadic rules apply, and one of the basic rules of triads is their tendency to be balanced.

### Triadic Balance

Hoffman's (1981) application of Heider's (1958) theory clearly defined the basic rules of triadic balance in social systems. Essentially, triads are balanced when: (a) the three relationships are positive; or (b) one relationship is positive, while the other two are negative, which is a "two-against-one" coalition or a "scapegoating" situation (see also Cartwright & Harary, 1956). Since any two of three components in a triad can form a positive coalitional relationship, there are three possible balanced options using a "two-against-one" configuration. For example, in a triad composed of a husband, wife, and child, balance can be achieved by forming a two-against-one arrangement against the husband, wife, or child. Ideally, however, balance would be achieved through a thoroughly positively balanced triad, where every member of the triad would be in a positive relationship with every other member in the triad.

As an offshoot of Heider's (1958) work, it also can be hypothesized that in a triad with two positive relationships and one negative relationship there is imbalance (e.g., my friend can't be a friend to my enemy). Heider (1958) said that in unbalanced situations, "tension will arise and forces will appear to annul the tension" (p. 207). This is so, according to his theory, because "where balance does not exist, the situation will tend to change in the direction of balance" (p. 207).

The tendency toward triadic balance is significant to understanding the homeostatic process in social systems.

## The Homeostatic Process

Cannon (1932), a biologist, is credited with developing the term *homeostasis*. He applied the term to biological organisms. As Cannon (1932) described it, homeostasis "does not imply something set and immobile, a stagnation. It means a condition—a condition which may vary, but which is relatively constant" (p. 24). Cannon's use of the term *homeostasis* was embraced by Bertalanffy (1968), who is considered the major proponent of general systems theory. Bertalanffy used Cannon's definition in conceptualizing the *dynamic equilibrium* observed in biological and other "open" systems. However, the term *homeostasis* was inadequate for describing the actual process of maintaining a steady operational state. Bertalanffy sought other concepts to explain the process. He found an explanation in the concept of "feedback," as that term is used in information theory and cybernetics. Feedback is a system's internal method of control, which is based on "*actual* performance rather than its *expected* performance . . . and involves sensory members which are actuated by motor members and perform the function of tell-tales or monitors—that is, of elements which indicate a performance" (Wiener, 1950, p. 12). Feedback, therefore, helps to maintain a system's steady operational state by providing performance information to the monitoring mechanisms of the system.

## Feedback Mechanisms

In very simple or closed systems, feedback mechanisms structurally allow a linear process to correct itself by way of an informational feedback loop, thereby making the process circular (Bertalanffy, 1968). An example of a simple feedback mechanism is the thermostat in a home heating system. The thermostat is a homeostatic sensor that feeds back performance information to the furnace activating mechanism. However, in complex open systems, feedback mechanisms may not be so simple (Buckley, 1967). Complex open systems constantly interchange material with other systems in their environments. Buckley (1967) defined the basic features of a feedback mechanism in complex social systems as involving: (a) characteristic criterion variables which must remain within certain limits; (b) a basic feedback mechanism activated by a sensory apparatus that is able to distinguish deviations from a criterion; and (c) behavior directing centers which deal with deviations by producing either a reduction or increase in the deviation. A decrease in deviation means acceptance by the system; an increase in deviation probably means expulsion from the system. Therefore, in a complex social system, when behavior deviates from some expected norm, the homeostatic mechanism engages, and the result depends on the nature of the feedback within the structure of the existing system. Should the system become overloaded and unable to deal with deviations, then the system would probably have to change.

### Types of Feedback

According to Rosenblueth, Wiener, and Bigelow (1968) and Watzlawick, Beavin, and Jackson (1967), there are two basic kinds of feedback: negative and positive. "Negative feedback'' is homeostatic, which means it essentially brings things back into the acceptable limits of the system's structure. Positive feedback, on the other hand, is radical; it is ''a message that change has taken place'' (Becvar & Becvar, 1982, p. 19). (Positive and negative feedback should not be confused with positive and negative reinforcement from the operant conditioning model; they are totally different concepts from totally different theoretical orientations.)

The effect of positive or negative feedback can easily be observed in isolated dyads (two-person systems) when a third person begins to affect the dyadic relationship, thereby engaging typical triadic balance concerns. Feedback directs dyadic relationships, just as it directs all systems. Negative feedback, if not adversely affected by outside systemic influences, keeps the relationship intact. Positive feedback, on the other hand, is a message that the relationship's rules and/or roles have significantly changed or that the relationship is no longer functional. For example, in a rehabilitation workshop, if a counselor sets a rule for a client (client A) to stay away from another client (client B), and client A obeys, then there has been negative feedback. Information of client A's obedience is fed back, through counselor observation, that any deviation from the rule has been dealt with effectively. Conversely, if client A persists in attempting to interact with client B, the rule may be pushed to the limit, thereby requiring constant intervention by the counselor when client A approaches client B. Client A's persistence, as observed by the counselor, is positive feedback that the dyadic system (the counselor-client relationship) and its rule are not operating effectively, which would require real change in the system. The real change could take one of several forms from the perspective of the rehabilitation counselor, including punishment of client A for each overture to client B, moving client B out of client A's reach, removing client A from the system, or allowing client A to make contact with client B. In this case, by isolating the counselor-client dyad for study, the feedback process can be observed, as a third relationship influences the dyad in one direction.

## Types of Relationships and Deviation Amplification

Watzlawick et al. (1967), based on Bateson's (1972) work, described two basic types of relationships within which rules develop. First, there is the ''symmetrical'' relationship, which ''is characterized by equality and the minimization of difference.'' (p. 69). Since analogic (informal, nonverbal, contextual) communication as opposed to digital (formal, technical) communication is the focus of interpersonal relationship, in a symmetrical relationship two individuals essentially mimic each other's nonverbal communication in an ongoing sequence. For example, if a client raises his or her voice to a counselor, the counselor would respond in kind by raising his or her voice. Second, there is the ''complementary'' relationship, which ''is based on the maximization of difference'' (Watzlawick et al., 1967, p. 69). Using the same example, if a client raises his or her voice to an counselor, the counselor would then respond by lowering his or her voice. Neither the symmetrical nor the complementary relationship is necessarily ''good'' or ''bad.'' In fact, many ''healthy'' examples can be given for both types. For instance, in a marital relationship, symmetry may be healthy for some couples, whereas complementary may be healthy for others. However, when a relationship goes to the extreme, the individuals in the relationship, and the relationship itself, are endangered. A married couple in an extreme symmetrical relationship would appear to be verbally fighting or competitive all the time, and if the relationship should escalate, there would be concern that the two individuals would do physical battle. On the other hand, a complementary relationship that has slowly deviated from its norms would appear to be severely ''one-up and one-down,'' or even pathologically sado-masochistic.

Relationships may start as reasonably symmetrical or complementary, but they may become more extreme as time goes by. The process of change in such cases is *deviation amplification*. This means that each person's response in a relationship exchange becomes a bit more extreme than his or her previous response. Therefore, in a sequence of mutual interaction, deviations from the functional relationship amplify until the relationship becomes dysfunctional.

## Deviation Amplification and Outside Systemic Influences

The symmetrical or complementary nature of a relationship tends to be somewhat fixed when negative feedback keeps the relationship ''on course.'' Therefore, negative feedback helps to maintain the homeostasis of the symmetrical or complementary relationship. But what happens when negative feedback fails?

Social theorists (e.g., Buckley, 1967; Maruyama, 1968) have recognized that slight, almost imperceptible deviations in feedback occur, and when those deviations continue in one direction (become more extreme on repetition), then they push the homeostasis of the system to its limits. Random, outside, systemic influences on a relationship constantly draw a relationship one way and then another. But when outside influences are limited, deviations may become so extreme in one direction that they are no longer manageable within the structure of the homeosatic mechanism, and, in effect, positive feedback occurs. Returning to the example of the married couple in a symmetrical relationship can help to demonstrate the effect of undirectional outside influences. Given severe, outside, systemic pressures on the symmetrical marital relationship, such as recession and extended unemployment of the breadwinner, fighting may get worse and worse in the relationship (deviating from ''fair fighting'' in one direction), and at some point the individuals may find that their symmetry has led to unacceptable physical abuse. This relationship's old rule, that the members ''will stay in the relationship no matter what,'' must change. At some point, one individual in an abusive symmetrical relationship would say, ''I'm getting out; the relationship is over.'' Therefore, deviation amplification, as in this symmetrical relationship, is actually a process of escalation through feedback. Without the influence of outside counteracting forces, a critical point may be reached, therefore leading to a message of change (positive feedback), which then requires a new homeostasis.

Another example of deviation amplification and positive feedback is that of a father and daughter whose relationship has gone from the complementary configuration (when the child is too young to act independently) to symmetry (during the early teen years when the teenager begins to challenge the father's authority). Assuming that the teenage girl is linked to outside relational influences, such as a boyfriend-girlfriend relationship, and that this relationship is engaging the daughter while disengaging her from the family unit, it can be predicted that the homeostatic means of the family will activate, which may typically take the form of more severe restriction of the teenager by the parents. Given the outside systemic influence (the boyfriend-girlfriend relationship) and the fact that the family can no longer meet all of the teenage girl's personal needs, it can be predicted that there will be escalation in the father-daughter relationship. Thus a father-daughter symmetrical escalatory cycle may proceed, with more frequent and more intense arguing about dating rules and family activities. Arguments may center around times for dates, limits on freedom (paradoxically), and other dependence/independence issues. It may even escalate to physical confrontation or physical intervention by the father to prevent contact with the outside systemic influence (the relationship with the boyfriend). If taken to the extreme, the father-daughter relationship may escalate to the point where the daughter and father argue constantly. True disengagement of the daughter might occur only when a message of real change in their relationship occurs—positive feedback. For instance, a positive feedback message would occur if in the middle of an argument the daughter asserted, "I'm pregnant!" This message is a true indicator that the father-daughter relationship has changed. A positive feedback message has been communicated (about pregnancy) that clearly communicates that change has occurred in the system. The daughter no longer is a child; she is to be a mother.

In effect, the external model of social systems theory fully accounts for external influences on a system. While the system attempts to maintain itself homeostatically, it also changes under outside relational influences. Note that the influence on a singular relationship (a dyad) is always conceptualized as *external* to the dyad, as a third factor enters into interaction, thereby engaging triadic relational dynamics. Influence is *external* to relationships.

# References

Bateson, G. (1972). *Steps to an ecology of mind.* New York: Ballatine.

Becvar, R. J., & Becvar, D. S. (1982). *Systems theory and family therapy: A primer.* Washington, DC: University Press of America.

Bertalanffy, L. von. (1968). *General systems theory.* New York: George Braziller.

Buckley, W. (1967). *Sociology and modern systems theory.* Englewood Cliffs, NJ: Prentice-Hall.

Cannon, W. B. (1932). *The wisdom of the body.* New York: W. W. Norton.

Cartwright, D., & Harary, F. (1956). Structural balance: A generalization of Heider's theory. *The Psychological Review, 63,* 277–293.

Heider, F. (1958). *The psychology of interpersonal relations.* New York: John Wiley & Sons.

Hoffman, L. (1981). *Foundations of family therapy: A conceptual framework for systems change.* New York: Basic Books.

Maruyama, M. (1968). The second cybernetics: Deviation-amplifying mutual causal processes. In W. Buckley (Ed.), *Modern systems research for the behavioral scientist* (pp. 304–313). Chicago: Aldine. (Original work published in 1963.)

Rosenblueth, A., Wiener, N., & Bigelow, J. (1968). Behavior, purpose, and teleology. In W. Buckley (Ed.), *Modern systems research for the behavioral scientist* (pp. 221–225). Chicago: Aldine. (Reprinted from *Philosophy of Science,* 1943, *10* 18–24).

Watzlawick, P., Beavin, J. H., & Jackson, D. D. (1967). *Pragmatics of human communication: A study of interactional patterns, pathologies, and paradoxes.* New York: W. W. Norton.

Wiener, N. (1950). *The human use of human beings: Cybernetics and society.* Boston: Houghton Mifflin.

# Appendix B
# Systemic-Relational Paradigm
## The Dynamics Of The Internal Systemic-Relational Model

This appendix goes into greater detail on the dynamics of the internal model of social systems. By comparison, Appendix A provides details on the dynamics of the external model of the systemic-relational paradigm. Through these appendices, readers should be able to get details of how social systems operate, and readers should also be able to compare the external and internal models. As separate models within the systemic-relational paradigm, they are quite distinct operationally.

## The Internal Model

Ultimately, the external systemic model had to account for how systems change under the influence of external factors. Cybernetics, the study of living and nonliving self-control processes, developed to the degree that it accounted for how systems change under the influence of factors external to a system's structure. But in the recent social systems theory literature, a different perspective has emerged. Primarily as the result of publications by Paul Dell (1982, 1985), in journals in the field of marital and family therapy, social systems theorists have been introduced to the work of Humberto Maturana. Maturana is a biologist who has studied the nature of perception (Maturana, Lettvin, McCullock, & Pitts, 1960; Maturana, Uribe, & Frenk, 1968). His work in the area of perception is well respected and serves as a foundation for a philosophy that is challenging the external systemic point of view (Maturana, 1970/1980, 1978;

Maturana & Varela, 1973/1980). His ideas demonstrate how social systems are predictable based on viewing them as "closed" systems, where the internal structure of the system under study is the best determinant of behavior when external perturbation occurs. This position has been called "structure determinism" (Maturana, 1978).

## Maturana's Basic Ideas and the Internalist Perspective

This section provides a summary of some of Maturana's most significant ideas. As a direct resource, the reader is referred to Maturana's 1978 publication, which is a concise presentation of his views on matters of relevance to the internal systemic-relational model.

### Empirical Basis

The empirical foundation for Maturana's theoretical work is a publication by Maturana et al. (1960) that identified the structural mechanism for perception in frogs. Maturana et al. (1960) concluded: "We have shown that the function of the retina in the frog is not to transmit information about the point-to-point pattern of distribution of light and dark in the image formed on it" (p. 170). Further, they stated that "transformation of the image" [not transmission of the image] "constitutes the fundamental function of the retina" (p. 170). Essentially, this means that an image is transformed according to the structure of the sense organ, and the message the organism receives is a result of the transformation and, subsequently, the "integrative ability" of the cells in the nervous system "to combine the information . . . into an operation" (p. 170). In other words, a frog perceives visually that which has been transformed by the retina in a way that is specific to the organization of the frog's nervous system. If a frog is not organized to perceive something, it can't.

In a later work, which detailed a biological theory of color coding in the primate retina, Maturana et al. (1968) concluded that the activities of a nervous system do not reflect an independent environment and, therefore, do not reflect an absolute external world. They further concluded that an animals' interactions with an environment were best represented by the animal's own organization and not by an independent external reality. Through the Maturana et al. (1968) publication, Maturana extended his earlier ideas related to the visual perception of frogs to the perceptual process of primates, a class of animals that includes the human being. The 1968 work led to refinement of his position and to the conclusion that "the external world would only have a triggering role in the release of the internally-determined activity of the nervous system" (Maturana, 1980, p. xv). This insight was a foundation for his epistemological position that a transcendental absolute reality is not knowable, and he described reality as "subject dependent" (Maturana, 1978, p. 60). Hence: "We literally create the world in which we live by living it" (Maturana, 1978, p. 61), or, equivalently, our world is transformation, which we simultaneously live and create.

## Biological Structure

Understanding the structure and organization of an organism is absolutely necessary to understanding the organism. According to Maturana (1978): "Behavior . . . is necessarily determined by the structure of the nervous system at the moment at which the behavior is enacted" (p. 42). Maturana's analysis of the nervous systems of living organisms is quite detailed in his work, especially as related to the operation of nerve cells, or neurons. Maturana and Varela (1973/1980) concluded that neurons "are not static entities whose properties remain invariant. On the contrary, they change" (p. 126). Although Maturana has described a learning nervous system as a structurally closed system, changes in the nervous system may occur from external (outside the structure) or internal (inside the structure) perturbations. Perturbations are simply interactions that trigger internal changes. Regardless, perception by the organism does not, in and of itself, allow identification of the external of internal source of perturbation. In the operation of the nervous system, hallucination and external perception are indistinguishable (Maturana, 1980). What is perceived is always a result of transformation within the structure of the organism. Furthermore, the continuous transformation within the organism during the perceptual process promotes recursive interactions within the organism's structure and actually produces changes of the state or structure of the nervous system of the organism. According to Maturana (1970/1980), "The nervous system is continuously changing through experience" (p. 18). Further, he stated, "The learning nervous system . . . must be able to undergo a continuous transformation," which he described as "structural dynamism" (p. 36). Essentially, he views a structure-determined, learning nervous system as having "plastic structure" and "plastic interaction" since there are "changes in state which involve structural changes in its components" (Maturana, 1978, p. 35). Structure, therefore, is foundational to his theoretical position, even though it can best be described as "plastic."

## Plastic Structure and the Emergence of Language in a Consensual Domain

Maturana's position is that the learning nervous system is essentially a closed structural system, one that changes, and then reacts not only to its own changes, but to changes perturbed in a social/consensual domain, which, in the case of humans, involves language. Maturana's (1970/1980) picture of a structure-determined nervous system "interacting with some of its own internal states as if they were independent entities" (p. 29) biologically links organic function and cognitive product. That is to say, within the nervous system, our thoughts have a mind of their own, and they can interact with the structures that produce them.

In essence, Maturana has given a biological rationale for the emergence of language. Language arises simultaneously through: (a) a complex, structurally closed nervous system that allows recursive interactions; (b) internal or external nervous system perturbation; and (c) a social/consensual domain that simultaneously perturbs the nervous system. And, ultimately, it is through the relationship between the nervous system and the social/consensual domain that language emerges and reality is defined. If two people view an apple, and they can't agree that they see, in fact, a real apple, then what is it that they see? The people in this situation will probably continue to mutually interact until there is consensual behavior about the "apple," and, hence, a reality will be defined. The activities of the nervous system, in this example, are simultaneously perturbed by retinal transformational of the image of the apple and by mutual interactions in a social domain with a linguistic tradition.

## Objectivity in Parentheses

Maturana believes his findings have placed "objectivity in parentheses" (see Simon, 1985, p. 37). Accordingly, for a human being, what is real results from simultaneous relationships among what is observed (which results from perturbation that may or may not be externally triggered), the observer's neuronal network (which is defined as structurally closed, but is constantly changing through experience), and consensus (in a social/interactive domain that involves language). Therefore, hallucination and external perception are only distinguishable by means of simultaneous nervous system perturbation in a social/consensual domain. Maturana (1978) stated: "Although every internal or external interaction of an organism is mapped in the relations of relative neuronal activities of its nervous system, where they cannot be distinguished as individual experiences, they can be distinguished socially in terms of behavior within a consensual domain" (pp. 56–57). Consensual behavior serves as a context for perceptual interpretation. Therefore, the operative consensual domain of interacting organisms, their context, is the parenthetical boundary of objectivity.

## Structure Determinism

The importance of structure as related to Maturana's ideas is clearly demonstrated in his concept, "structure determinism." The term *structure determinism* derives from Maturana's ideas about cause and effect. Maturana does not view cause and effect as linear (A causes B). This is so whether the objects of study are interacting components or systems affecting each other. He believes that systems "couple," and, during coupling, they are mutually perturbed, changing each other in a recursive link. Changes, therefore, always occur through perturbation. However, since learning nervous systems are closed structures, a system's changes through perturbation are primarily a result of the system's structure and not the properties of the perturbing entities. This means that "cause and effect" is primarily within the boundaries of the system. As Efran and Lukens (1985) have described this point of view, "Toasters 'toast' and washing machines 'wash' because of how each is built or structured" (p. 25), even though both a toaster and a washing machine can be plugged into and stimulated by the same electrical outlet. Since organisms react differently to what appear to be similar stimuli, a simple linear cause-and-effect perspective is precluded. Behavior, then, is structure-determined, and it is the structure of that which is perturbed that primarily defines the outcome of perturbation.

Maturana's work clearly represents the internal systemic perspective. It is the structured internal workings of a system that primarily determines behavior. Humans can be perturbed both physically and through language (within a linguistic domain), but the outcome is best viewed as a result of the structure of the organism (or person) perturbed. And, Maturana's view is clearly systemic in that it focuses on *relationships* between processes within the structure of living things. Further, his work has been applied to the operation of *social* systems, by Dell (1982, 1985) and others.

# References

Dell, P. F. (1982). Beyond homeostasis: Toward a concept of coherence. *Family Process, 21,* 21–41.

Dell, P. F. (1985). Understanding Bateson and Maturana: Toward a biological foundation for the social sciences. *Journal of Marital and Family Therapy, 11,* 1–20.

Efran, J., & Lukens, M. D. (1985, May-June). The world according to Humberto Maturana. *The Family Therapy Networker,* 23–28; 72–75.

Maturana, H. R. (1978). Biology of language: The epistemology of reality. In G. A. Miller & E. Lenneberg (Eds.), *Psychology and biology of language and thought.* New York: Academic Press.

Maturana, H. R. (1980). Introduction. In H. R. Maturana & F. J. Varela, *Autopoiesis and cognition: The realization of the living.* Boston: D. Reidel.

Maturana, H. R. (1980). Biology of cognition. In H. R. Maturana & F. J. Varela, *Autopoiesis and cognition: The realization of the living.* Boston: D. Reidel. (Original work published in 1970.)

Maturana, H. R., Lettvin, J. Y., McCulloch, W. S., & Pitts, W. H. (1960). Anatomy and physiology of vision in the frog (*Rana pipiens* ). *Journal of General Physiology, 43* (6), 129–175.

Maturana, H. R., Uribe, G., & Frenk, S. (1968). A biological theory of relativistic colour coding in the primate retina. *Arch. Biologia y Med. Exp.,* Supplemento No. *1,* 1–30.

Maturana, H. R., & Varela, F. J. (1980). Autopoiesis: The organization of the living. In H. R. Maturana & F. J. Varela, *Autopoiesis and cognition: The realization of the living.* Boston: D. Reidel. (Original work published in 1973.)

Simon, R. (1985, May-June). Structure is destiny: An interview with Humberto Maturana. *The Family Therapy Networker, 9* (3), 32–37; 41–43.

# Index

# Biographical Sketch

R. Rocco Cottone, Ph.D., is an Associate Professor and Coordinator of the Marital and Family Counseling Sequence in the Department of Behavioral Studies at the University of Missouri–St. Louis. Dr. Cottone earned his Ph.D. degree at St. Louis University. He earned his bachelor's and master's degrees at the University of Missouri–Columbia. He holds professional licenses in counseling, rehabilitation psychology, and marital and family therapy. He is a member of the American Psychological Association and the American Association for Counseling and Development. He is a clinical member of the American Association for Marriage and Family Therapy. Comments related to this text are welcomed and should be addressed to Dr. Cottone at the University of Missouri–St. Louis, Department of Behavioral Studies, 8001 Natural Bridge Road, St. Louis, MO 63121-4499.